Date Due

~~MAY 14 1976~~		
~~MAR 8 1978~~		

DEMCO NO. 38-298

SYSTEM
AND
UNSYSTEM

An Ethnic View of Organization and Society

JOSEPH ANTONIO RAFFAELE

A Halsted Press Book

Schenkman Publishing Company
JOHN WILEY AND SONS
New York - London - Sydney - Toronto

Copyright © 1974
Schenkman Publishing Company, Inc.
Cambridge, Massachusetts 02138

Distributed solely by Halsted Press, a Division
of John Wiley & Sons, Inc. New York.

Library of Congress Cataloging in Publication Data

Raffaele, Joseph A.
  System and unsystem; an ethnic view of organization
and society.

    "A Schenkman publication."
    1. Industry—Social aspects—United States.
2. Industry and state—United States. 3. United
States—Civilization—1945–   4. United States—
Social conditions—1960–   I. Title.
HD60.5.U5R32   309.1'73'092   74-5214
ISBN 0-470-70484-5 cloth
ISBN 0-470-70483-7 paper

Printed in the United States of America

To my father: Member in his lifetime of a vanishing
tribe of honorable gentlemen.

CONTENTS

Preface

System and Unsystem is an ethnic view of management and manipulation in American society. Actually, its perspective goes back to my days as the son of a Sicilian who moved his family to Anastasio turf on the Brooklyn waterfront. In that early experience, the managers were Irishmen and the manipulated, Italians. Although my hostility to the Irish was later tempered by a pretty colleen from an adjoining ethnic neighborhood, I still remember vividly the supreme humiliation of having to prove our eligibility for welfare to an enemy Celt.

Obsession for power drove us "Wops," a thrust that for some in the clan brought highly successful criminal careers. In addition to this thirst for power, my hangup was an inability to express myself in Wasp language. So I enrolled in liberal arts at City College of New York at night, working as a factory hand during the day and a numbers runner in the swing shift. After Gianni, my father, grasped what a Bachelor of Arts would get me in a job, he threatened malediction.

When my boss got shot, I switched hastily to the full-time program. Then war broke out and experience with system and unsystem continued in the United States Army. What with my knowledge of French, Sicilian, and Italian, I was poised to save democracy in Europe; the Army shipped me instead to the combat zone of the China-Burma-India-Theater of War where they speak Chinese, Burmese, and Hindustani. Promotions came fast, from Private to Major; each command used a classical management precept of upgrading as a means of dumping a problem elsewhere. My military career was catapulted from a reception line of inquisitive medical personnel. I do not remember anymore who triggered the greater indignation, the medic who charged me to push back my Sicilian foreskin or the last one who asked me who was buried in General Grant's tomb.

My army career fell into crisis through a communication from the Department of Defense advising me of a lack of educational qualifications, including failure to take a correspondence course in basic economics. The finding, if it stuck, would have swindled me out of lush pension rights. I wrote a denunciatory letter to the United States Secretary of Defense.

My army career, and pension rights thus terminated, I became an arbitrator and mediator of labor disputes. The experience as labor boss at the waterfront was especially illuminating. After instructing and encouraging the stevedores and longshoremen to make their deals over instead of under the table, the mayor, to mend his political fortunes, pulled the rug from under me by intervening in a dispute. One day, after listening for hours to longshoremen threatening to knock off the ship and to stevedores hinting they would then knock off *me,* I resigned after telling them to take up bird watching.

Less hectic days followed as a part-time arbitrator in industry and instructor of economics in an institution of higher learning. The goings-one there evoked memories of my boyhood, for the university provided quarters for many flourishing mafia-like rackets. The premises were being used by professors as a base of operations for lucrative deals with government and industry and by researchers for rewriting pieces to persuade editors of learned journals to print the same technical ideas over and over again. The university as a community of scholars turned out to be instead a cacaphony of soloists adept in the politics of self-promotion, whose orchestration was arranged by administrators behaving more like politicians than educators. Accordingly, the experience gained at the university reinforced that acquired in Brooklyn. The distinction between system and unsystem blurred. A mafia theory of economics began to take shape in my mind.

During these days of reflection, I wrote a book inadvertently disrespectful of sacred jurisdictional lines in the academic world. The work interpreted economic events as a political process in a cultural setting. Without realizing it, I had pulled off an intellectual coup. Was I surprised when the work was hailed as a scholarly inter-disciplinary contribution.

Weary of the tranquil life, I organized a prep school for urban blacks. They taught me that teaching is a communicative art, requiring in addition to scholarship an outpouring of compassion and irreverence. We came to terms quickly. But sadly, the association terminated after a year because of the political needs of the university management to cater to a black hoodlum. I was shorn of epaulettes, sword, and gold buttons. The prep program was given another name. My mafia theory of society burst into bloom and *System and Unsystem* is the result of its nurture.

A famous letter written by Niccolò Machiavelli asking Lorenzo de Medici for a job suggests how a college professor with practical experience can make his contribution to the nation. Like Niccolò, he can offer princes of power neither horses, cloth of gold, weapons, precious stones, nor similar ornaments. However, from his more detached position, he can analyze the operation of the system in which he lives. A professor who works part-time in the power structure brings additional credentials to this task. His involvement reflects an understanding of power; he has to learn how it works if he wishes to survive. A further deposition accrues to him if he was born outside the values of American society; he can observe with greater detachment, and therefore with more comprehension. To put the matter in risky terminology, he can bring to his task a cold-bloodedness about the American way of life. Charles Reich's *The Greening of America* confirmed the need for such a contribution.

Various avenues exist to fulfill this assignment. One can, for example, describe the characteristics of those who make major economic and political decisions. One soon finds that these managers are upper class Wasps or facsimile Wasps moving freely between organizations of government and industry. This finding is no big deal. One can be lured into thinking that the United States is run by a few wicked Wasps. Like that tenacious perennial, the mafia conspiracy, this approach makes for good book sales. Another tactic is to describe the rank and file chorus of ethnics in addition to the star players. A third is to focus the narrative on institutions. A fourth is to analyze decision making processes. A fifth, a favorite of intellectuals, is to focus attention on loving grass sitters among undergraduate students. All these means have some use. Their danger lies in the way they provide generalizations unrelated to the real world. Each falls short of explaining the system's dynamics.

Accordingly, social analysis should issue from a study of life in suburb-cities where the population is clustering. To be relevant, urban literature must generalize from particular life experiences. Much of modern social analysis is made up of elites insulting each other in elegant prose, and much of the communication in the system is propaganda from top to bottom. The view of ethnics surfaces in distorted fashion. Decisions issue from abstractions which the educated delight in making but which contain considerable error. If intellectuals who make generalizations about entire populations were required to share or even understand the life of those specific individuals who comprise them, their failure in judgment would decline. As is, however, social analysis is too important to be left to intellectuals.

The ethnic turbulence in the United States today reflects the obsolescence of this elite thinking. In the cities, a hostility rises against decisions made by a clash of conservative-liberal elite opinion in the recesses of large organizations. Ethnics hold in contempt the intelligentsia who call the shots. Their abstractions have the same qualities of opaqueness as do those of intellectuals; but the latter's observations monopolize communication lines. Disdain for intellectualism and readiness for exploiting this contempt suggest the initial stages of fascism. American society reels like a drunken Titan; its disposition to anarchy is contained by sheer force of habit.

The naiveté and hatred that exists in the ranks of liberals further inhibits reform of the system. Liberals flit from one vision of perfection to another, one often diametrically opposed to the other, and take a hard stance at each interlude of insight. They are desperate for new causes. Their high I.Q.'s and academic achievement seem inversely related to their ability to contain their ego needs and improve their powers of observation. Their authoritarian minds are indisposed to indulging in consensual politics with ethnics. Those who hate the system in its entirety generate through their teaching and prose a decline in consensual politics. Theirs is an all or nothing philosophy; whatever the system does is no good.

Liberals assign to the alienated young a sublime mission to improve the society and thus play into the hands of conservatives resisting social change. Their counter culture fantasy suggests a latter day version of the revival movement in religion. Just feel right and everything will be all right. You don't need politics. Although critics of this concoction are disarmed by their professional and personal loyalties to youth, the idea has neither analytical nor strategic value and should not be allowed to go unchallenged.

Accordingly, it is not conservatives who raise the greater obstacle to change. Conservatives can be nailed on the traditional values they profess. It is the self-flagellation and holier-than-thou stance of liberals that raises the greater problem. Weaknesses in democracy can be ameliorated by more democracy. The system changes by eyeball to eyeball politics. Liberal naiveté, hatefulness, and humorlessness produce little stomach for such experience. It's time to take power away from liberals and give it to the people.

The clash of elite liberal and conservative opinion constitutes a process in which a few decide what is best for the many. Operating from centers remote from the people, managers manipulate human and economic resources. Their choices reflect their estimates of power, and the burden of these choices rarely falls on those who make them. The technology of manipulatory decision making has produced a legacy of cynicism, cruelty, hatred, and frustration. We acquire efficiency in the use of resources and lose humanity.

This is not to say that managers are monsters; on the contrary, they are often gentle people of good intention. Their failures stem from an antiquated system of thought. They persist in believing that past error can be corrected by the same technology of decision making. When liberals expect the next round of salvation to come from measures that increase further the power of government or from a latter day Lancelot descending upon the national capital, they have not gotten the message. New institutions are necessary to shift power to the people; but the managers neither trust nor are able to communicate with them. Although decentralization of power would by no means assure domestic tranquility, we have reached a point where participatory democracy is the only option.

The problem, thus, is the eternal one of power. Those who wield it in the system do not represent the many ethnic groups in the society. They negotiate deals that fail to consider the grievances of different cultural enclaves and impose costs on individuals who do not have representatives at the bargaining table. But aspects of modern society magnify and modify the eternal problem of redressing power. In an age of highly complicated and interrelated technology, change must occur slowly in an orderly process of open inquiry. To tear down everything would put Americans back into the trees. A movement, even one seeking liberation, requires organization, rules, and talent. Man moves forward by using his brain to grasp patterns in the environment and by employing them to promote his purposes. Through a taxing intellectual process of discernment and control, he obtains order and productivity. Our options are confined to a range of organization purpose and to the manner in which we devise and interpret rules.

A controversy exists as to whether this forward movement can be achieved through a deliberate redesigning of institutions or by a change of heart spreading into the society from the posture of the new college generation. Will change come from men exercising their intellect to impose reason on the system or from the sheer presence of the new generation of college youth?

These youths include political activists of the right, traditionalists, political activists of the left, and, for lack of a more discriminating term, hippies rejecting the dominant values of the society. The relatively small band of rightists have little to offer, unless the dismantling of government and fancy verbiage can be said to provide new alternatives. Traditionalists, in the majority, keep their nose to the grindstone and, soon after graduation, disappear into the system; their contribution to a higher order is minimal. The new leftists, encouraged by radical professors, play at revolution. A number of the new leftists play clumsy politics in the new left wing of the Democratic Party. A few have graduated to bombs and arson. They are incapable of creating organization that extends its influence accumulatively into the society. Their illusions trigger repressive law.

The term hippie, used originally to refer to youth rebelling against society, has lost precision in meaning. It now covers many species: aging gurus, freaks, plastics, ego trippers, anarchists, loving grass sitters, individuals with acute mental disorders including melancholia and violent impulse. Hippies now include within their ranks a heavy contingent of persons united against the exercise of the intellect, on whose festoonery of dress can be amblazoned: SLOBS—Students Lovingly Organized against Brain Stress. Their disengagement from the system is subsidized by the toilers they deride. They use drugs to escape from themselves and to obtain instant revelation through a quick drunk in color. But they end up with more problems than before. By basing their communication on noise, color, pictures, and movement, they transport themselves back to the Stone Age. Their life style is a romp in slow motion like the commercials on the idiot box, dictated by the system just as much as that of the middle class they ridicule. The culture they extol is managed by young exploiters who make the more colorful robber barons in the early days of the system seem like a bunch of amateurs. Professors assign to this culture a sublime mission.

But a pursuit of subsidized joy ill deserves the label culture. Take away the subsidy and the culture is threatened. A judge in the Appellate Division of the New York State Supreme Court has ruled that a father cannot be compelled to underwrite the romping life style of his child, a ruling which has caused much brooding in hippy ranks. The hippy life is a fragile vestment easily destroyed by predatory humans; a game of egoism that readily turns into cannibalism; a litany of futile existence. Hardly a single commune of these non-toilers is self-sustaining; if only they took up something, even the digging variety of anthropology at least. The successful dissemination of the idea that upper middle class children will lead us toward a better world is a beautiful finesse of the system; its mass media have been used to circulate a hilarious joke.

These subsidized dropouts ridicule adults for conforming to the system's rules yet enslave themselves to the expectancies of their peers.

Their reluctance to leave the child world is given the aura of revolution; and when they venture into adult life, they botch it. If one yields to their offer of assistance in action programs, they love you on Friday and leave you on Monday. By seeking instant perception through the intake of chemicals, they destroy their capacity to perceive. Their religion is a maximum stretching of the senses. They contribute little to changing the system.

A common denominator runs through the ranks: a conviction of disparity between what they think the society is and what they feel it can be. The extent of their competence in posing barriers to the intrusion of knowledge into their intellects has an effect on both of these perceptions. To a lesser degree, a pessimistic outlook pervades hippydom as to the possibility of closing this gap, a skepticism that reflects a picture of reality based on fact and fantasy. Professors who liberally underwrite hippy perceptions assist them in building their structure of false images. Hippies differ in the manner they relate to this Pirandellian awareness. Some do not give a damn one way or the other about the contrast in portraits; some are troubled by the disparity; some, engulfed by an insecurity fed by a materialistic and loveless family life, seek relief in drugs and alcohol; and some grope for a commitment to protest and change.

In short, hippie behavior often issues from delusion, weakness of character, and escapism. The hippie grows up in a sheltered and fraudulent environment. He describes a society that does not exist. He is unaware of himself and frequently criticizes other hippies of his own image. He finds it difficult to commit himself to a tough and sustained course of action. He is difficult to educate. His supporters are his worst enemies. He is the mirror of a corrupt society, not of a humanistic attempt to reform it.

For society must be so reformed. It is a demonstrable fact that using human and economic resources for profit now leads to self-destruction. Man is likely to survive only to the extent that he assumes responsibility for survival of others. Such is the moral lesson that issues from his disorientation from nature, and the institutional implication of this reality is the emergence of a human welfare economy out of the decline of the profits economy. Hippies are too immature to contribute to this emerging era. Adulthood implies sacrifice for future rewards. Subsidized instant gratification is infantile and anarchic.

Such humanism does not exclude the young or the old; there is no generation gap in philosophy. But humanizing the system requires an effort of intellect, courage, and tenacity, and impulsive youths are unprepared for such outlay. To perpetrate the belief that they are is a hoax on those who seek to understand the system and to determine how the desperate position of youth can be remedied. Even assuming that the good will of youth withstands the ravages of time, structural change by the sheer force of love power commands no precedents. The retreat of the lions from the Christians is Hollywood bunk.

This is not to deny the legitimacy of student grievances against their elders. The student has a valid complaint against his professors. His prescribed texts confuse dullness with profundity. They present in humorless fashion assertions that fail to come to grips with the student's perceptions of the system. Books obscure the author's values and are not sensitive to the student's point of view. He sees processes and relationships that his elders do not write about. He needs an underground view that relates to what he observes. Without such a linkage of perceptions, professors strengthen his suspicion that he is being deceived.

Student views of corporate responsibility provide an example. A corporation considers as its social responsibility a concern for such issues as pollution, urban blight, and unemployment. The degree of its uneasiness over these pressures depends upon the extent to which their existence poses a threat to the corporation. Until its interests are significantly threatened, the organization indulges in footdragging.

The student has a broader and more idealistic view of organization responsibilities. He looks upon institutions in terms of how they affect his vision of an idealistic life. He wants to control the corporation rather than have the corporation control the way change takes place and sees the imposition of restraints on the corporation as a moral rather than economic question. These attitudes, however, do not surface in the social science text. Even though social science fundamentally is moral philosophy, the author presents the issues as bland descriptions of existing forces. The pretense of scientism convinces the student that the author is underwriting the status quo.

Authors must communicate with the student. If they want the student to read their material they must use the written word to talk to him as a live human being. They must stir him with words; present their ideas; tell him what they think of him and his ideas. He does not want to be flattered; he wants to know that he is being heard. Then and only then might he listen and learn.

The so-called generation gap poses no insurmountable barrier to such an enterprise. Much time is consumed talking about it. Some deny its existence and others, out of guilt or frustration, lament its presence. Many young people are rebelling not against traditional values as much as against the way government and corporations flout these values. A more useful purpose can be served by viewing generational differences as an opportunity to negotiate a meeting ground. The conflict over differences affords adults new perceptions and assists the young toward maturity.

Such collaboration does not imply flattering students by becoming their buddies in thought. Professors who exalt student opinion no matter how asinine, because they see in instruction an opportunity for working out their own salvation, are baby sitters, not teachers. They should be drummed out of the profession. The price for presenting a subject appealingly is not its adulteration; teaching and pimping are not the same profession.

The development of the non-student begins in the elementary school, where permissiveness creates within the child an aversion to undergo the difficulty of competent thinking. The nausea that attends difficult thinking carries through to college, where the tendency is difficult to reverse. Liberals criticizing the alleged authoritative control of school children promote this attitude toward learning. Psychiatrists who think similarly would have us all swinging happily from tree to tree. They both assist in developing non-students who believe that if there is no fun it is not education. The non-student can be readily spotted. He happily crushes the meaning out of the English language. He cannot connect three simple sentences into a logical whole. He does not engage in dialogue but flashes a series of loosely connected picture stereotypes. If knowledge does not turn him on, he takes the position that it is irrelevant.

America's greening, if indeed it is here, has not come from such youth. It comes rather from structural reforms generated by ethnics of humble origin who challenge the system. It has derived from the Samuel Gompers, Fiorello La Guardias, Ned O'Gormans, Phil Murrays, Julian Bonds, Herman Wrices, Leon Sullivans, Caesar Chavezes, the Naders and even the Tony Anastasios who render the society more humane through their activity as producers. These ethnics create new forms of life among the people; they are social artists. They are individual-oriented generally, disinclined to apply labels to persons. It is among ethnics that passion exists. Even looking at the system through humorist eyes is an ethnic art. Many problems in American society exist merely because Wasps lack humor. Their humor is Yankee humor, which appropriately is called dry. If ethnics could operate training programs teaching Wasps to belly laugh, many of our problems would vanish.

Ethnics are social heroes. They are heroic not in terms of the turn of an elegant phrase or in the Hemingway sense of a good hunter, fisherman, or bullfighter; but in their dogged spirit to transfuse a creative idea into social action. Theirs is the heroism described by Ignazio Silone— of men who do not sacrifice purity to organization; who can act or deliberately choose inaction to impress a point of view; who have a gift for waiting and a characteristic of stubbornness; and who strip naked the organization man.

Ethnics succeed because the unsystem is not entirely impotent. The system is vulnerable to their prodding because of various reasons: the incapacity of a vast system to react monolithically against the threat of innovation; the reliance on law which represents a two-edged sword; the timidity of managers; the sensitivity to publicity; the chronic necessity of communications media to report events sensationally; the vulnerability arising from the need for deception; the imperative to plan long into the future; the remarkable tendency of the system to finance dissent. Even with suppression the system is timid. To call the United States a police state is an exaggeration. The system is even vulnerable to ridicule; laughter in contemplation of the performance of White House royalty could generate a revolution.

But revolution should not be confounded with an interlude of madness. The task of reconstruction requires not waiting for Consciousness III to overwhelm the system but laboring to develop the not-yet Consciousness. The swelling tide from the ranks of affluent college youth is not Con III but Infantilism I. The surge is fed by loving professors, guilt-ridden parents, and timorous college presidents; from professors who philander; from parents who provide money and protection from struggle; from college presidents who play politics with education. It is expressed in the desire for instant gratification, in the cult of instant solutions, in the disinclination to undergo self-denial to acquire craftsmanship, and in the exercise of cruelty when one does not have his way. Consciousness III is more the disease than the cure. Love without will dwindles down to apathy. The assumption one can produce change by a loving force is a final act in the abandonment of personal responsibility.

Indeed, infantilism is a widespread malaise in American society. It is infantile to reject or embrace the system indiscriminately; to want a glamorous life experience in jig time; to think one can love everyone; to blur distinctions among youth; to react credulously to a romantic notion that the system will wither away by the force of subsidized love. It is a middle class puerility born of not having to struggle and create.

Greatness eludes this middle class society. A great society is one sustained by commonly accepted religious ideas that free individuals from the bonds of egocentricity. Man's humanity derives from his ability to construct cooperative relations of community. His greatest display of genius since the dawn of civilization has been in the voluntary formulation of social rules. But in the United States the corporations, the courts, the different governments, each in their own way, have destroyed the religious sense.

Old Christian societies such as the United States and old communist societies such as the Soviet Union have much in common. Christianity aspired to the development of Christian man and communism, to the emergence of communist man; both of whom were envisaged as practicing a brotherhood of man. Both aspirations have failed, for neither Christian nor communist societies can tolerate a religious idea that interferes with the operation of the system they have created. In neither society does the power structure allow religious sentiment to imperil the functioning of their respective systems. In Christian civilization, the belief lingers that Christian man can survive the absence of favorable political-economic institutions. In communist civilization, the delusion lingers that communist man will issue automatically from institutional change. Accordingly, the evolution of Christianity and communism affords lessons on the current controversy.

American society has moved from concepts based on a religious ethic to an interregnum of hedonism that either shifts toward a collective ideal or becomes disabled. The hedonistic life is a life of emptiness. Politicians seem either unaware of the collapse of traditionalism or disposed to distort the facts in order to pursue their ambitions.

Whether offered by government or corporations, every promise of pleasure in the system implies submission to forces outside the individual. If we want a sense of domination we are offered a shiny automobile; if we want beauty we are offered a trip to the Bahamas; and if we wish to strain our senses, we are offered entertainment that turns us on. But we rarely find in any of these pursuits an act of creation. To the contrary, they are acts of submission that add to a denial of self-worth.

The denial of man as creator manifests the curse of determinism that hangs over western society. Western man has disarmed himself by the simplistic truth that he is driven by economic and psychological forces. His role is to make the best of instinctual urges. This denial strips him of individual responsibility for his acts. He is determined and not determining. He is not accountable for what occurs or capable of electing from alternative courses of action as an act of will that leads to a preconceived result. Because his behavior is determined, courage and integrity are the precepts of fools.

The very individuals who seek man's emancipation perpetuate this determinism. It is not freedom intellectuals proclaim when they assert that the presence of youth will cause the system to wither away; rather it is the act of final submission. But by freedom one does not mean the freedom of fools oblivious to the high degree of determinism in organized life, but an awareness of tendencies, which creates thereby the possibilities of choice. Nor does the retreat of intellectuals into intellectualizing and self-analysis provide much understanding. Greater awareness accrues from involvement and from forging workable solutions.

Our crisis thus is a crisis of personal responsibility. The system pursues needs of its own because we confine our interest to heeding its promises of gratification or divorcing ourselves from its excesses. We have little desire to change it by day, by week, by month, and by year. If we are critical of the system, we propose in infantile fashion that the system can be changed by the brandishing of guns, by bombing it out of existence, or by romantic talk. The system thereby acquires a momentum of its own. And the more this movement remains unchallenged, the more difficult it is to alter its course.

Personal responsibility implies care for particular persons and things. And care generates a social will to perform constructively. Men who do not care become sick. To care for the society requires an ability to communicate with it. But the system makes this communication difficult. The restoration of social sanity requires that man have the power to thumb his nose at government and corporations. Such diffusion of power will permit the exercise of individual responsibility and the joy that comes with intelligent commitment.

Contemporary society suggests a contribution to the fables of La Fontaine. Once upon a time there lived a colony of affluent grasshoppers, whose adults spent considerable time examining their way of life and becoming angry with each other over their different misinterpretations. The young grasshoppers, members of Consciousness III, spent their time waiting for food to be brought to them by their admiring parents, who exhausted themselves by predigesting it. Nobody dared ever tell the children how the food was grown because it was not relevant to their experience. The grasshopper psychiatrists warned it would damage their development.

Down the road a little there lived an ant heap whose passages echoed with toil. The ants were too busy to brood over their egos. No ant even knew it had a self-awareness that needed developing. One day the adult grasshoppers died suddenly of circulatory arrest due to affluent living. The young grasshoppers demanded their rights of predigested food.

And the ants obliged by devouring them.

J.A.R.

Acknowledgments

The old world custom of *le belle maniere* suggests to me I list in bold upper case letters the name of every man and woman who made however modest a contribution toward helping me to convert a mass of loosely related ideas into a book. But what in my younger days was considered good style, would seem an exaggeration in these times. So much for contemporary life styles. Therefore, I confine my acknowledgment to a general expression of thanks to the students, colleagues, and friends whose ideas improved the structure and substance of this work: for their contribution to Systemology and to Mafiatectonics, its ancestral father, my everlasting debt.

PART
ONE

THE
ORGANIZATIONAL
FRAMEWORK

1

Problem and Procedure

Marxism is irrelevant as an aid to explaining the conflict that rages in American society. The struggle is not between workers and owners of capital. It lacks a uniform reference either as to function in production or to income level. The conflict issues from cultural groups searching for a power base with which to preserve their identities and managing elites in big organizations seeking to impose their own values on these cultural groups. This strife of culture can be better described in terms of System and Unsystem. Our first chapter presents a summary of this thesis and an outline of procedure.

In order for a modern society to function smoothly, it must strike a balance of negotiated preferences among the different groups that comprise its members. American society faces rapid deterioration because many of its groups feel they are denied access to this negotiating process. We are unlikely to be rescued from this deterioration by the pious egalitarianism of upper class Wasps, the cosmic generalizations of intellectuals, the self-serving elitism of liberals, or the naive utopianism of college youth.

The basis of traditional values upon which such negotiation used to rest is crumbling. These traditional values stemmed from concepts of authority and individual freedom. Americans committed themselves to a code of values for two principal reasons: because accepted symbols of authority asserted the code was good and because of an optimistic philosophy that by the exercise of self-discipline an individual could master his environment and fulfill himself. Both of these strains were tied to a belief in God, and together they provided the fabric necessary for a workable society. With the decline of religious precept and the emergence of pleasure as the highest good this fabric has been seriously weakened.

3

In this state of disarray, the powerful try to maintain those traditional values that sustain their interests, and, in order to manipulate better those with less influence, lay down rules of proper behavior for them to follow. This rule of managing System and manipulated Unsystem has fallen into crisis. For although the managerial elite does serve a function in outlining the instruments and resources needed to reach objectives in life, it is intolerable to deny people control of preferences from which the details of their life emerge. Any sense of community deteriorates by virtue of such a denial.

Accordingly, restoring the sense of community through negotiation of preferences demands serious political attention. The failure of politicians to bring forward this issue attests to their lack of courage and insight. The question must be discussed openly and thoroughly, for if we do not employ our resources to find a life of community whose design is in sympathetic relationship with its users we may witness a growing demoralization. *The major political issue of our time involves a search for processes to implement this new sense of community.*

As the legitimacy of the system's self-serving ideology wanes, the right of negotiating ideological differences must emerge. As the rationale of deference to other individuals crucial to a workable society falters, it must acquire a new legitimacy within the context of American reality.

Consequently, full power of negotiation by all cultural enclaves is central to my thesis. The social restraints needed to hold together elements of a culturally pluralistic society require institutional transformations. Our system of elite management of political and economic institutions must be junked for a society of culturally autonomous groups with the neighborhood as their political base. The thrust behind management of institutions, whether they are firms or public organizations, must change from the imperative of authority to the right of participation and no institutions should be exempted from the system of values; if deceit and violence on the part of an individual are improper, they are improper as well for government and business. Individuals should be given a greater number of options, and minority rights should be provided to groups affected by the choices of those holding the balance of power at any given time. The culturally and politically autonomous neighborhood should become the fount of life.

For the way to a healthier life for the American lies not in playing a part consistent with managed national images but in finding an identity with a particular culture and placing the difference on the bargaining table. A man has the right to be himself and to keep others off his back.

Society can only demand that he be civil and literate. Other social demands should be subject to negotiation.

In short, our prescriptions include: cultural autonomy; territorial rights of neighborhood; participatory democracy; conversion of management into forms of coordination and information dissemination; societal values, including a new transcendent national purpose, emerging from a creative and affectionate life experience. The task is to relate these prescriptions through negotiation so as to produce a workable blend of individual freedom and social constraints. We must construct the social engineering needed to make an orderly transition from the present chaos produced by secularism and hedonism to a civilized existential society.

I propose, therefore, a *negotiation principle,* in which social conduct issues from a system of voluntarily negotiated restraints. A system of behavior in which elites manipulate the individual by rewarding desired conduct is indefensible. No moral sanction exists to treat citizens as children, criminals, psychotics, or pigeons.

By culture I will refer to the beliefs, values, and attitudes which give direction to a particular people's style of living. By cultural pluralism I will intend a society where there is more than one style dimension. By ethnicity I will mean the emergence of cultural strains from the base of the society and their legitimization in the system. I will argue that the institutionalizing of ethnicity is a necessary stepping stone first toward a recognition of cultural pluralism and then toward a greater individuality. I will also argue that in the interest of sanity, both private and public organization in the society should reflect the cultural pluralism of the United States.

Our procedure will be to develop the manner in which the political-economic system comprises a complex of inter-related subsystems and to determine how individual value preferences can be more effectively asserted in a society of such inter-related organizations. By the system will be intended the managers and technicians in government, industrial, and university organizations, whose actions steer the economy's course; by the unsystem is meant a motley army that includes the scattered remnants of the academic community who do not toil for the system's maintenance, the non-technical subcaste of ethnics, single proprietors who do not work for the system, dropouts, young college graduates refusing to enter the system, artists, inmates in educational, penal, mental, and welfare institutions, and those with the talent to operate lucrative rackets but who have not yet gained the official sanction of the system.

After a sketch of System and Unsystem and the nature of organization, we move to a review of culture and institutions. We then proceed to the emergence of ethnic consciousness and conclude with the prospects of change now and in the decades ahead. Each chapter comprises a self-contained unit. Nevertheless, each one adds to the development of our central question: how can the array of values be asserted in civilized fashion in a system buffeted by the decline of authoritative management.

The critical generalizations of the system constitute descriptions of tendencies; that there are men and institutions whose behavior runs counter to these trends is fully conceded. It is also granted that the ethnic posture expressed in this work is not entirely above reproach; some of it I personally reject. Nevertheless, the position should be stated as a beginning in the restoration of sanity in the body politic. The biliousness it provokes is a first stage toward a higher order of perception.

A reservation also accompanies these views: a concern that their attractiveness to the intellectual may bring about their loss of acceptability to the general public. For there is no greater exercise in futility than the intellectual venturing forth to do battle with the system. He does so armed to the teeth with elegant sentences, accepting the rules of the establishment, and frightening himself with the thought of being cut off from a system that provides him with middle class comfort.

Such are the fantasies of the unsystem.

2

System and Unsystem

The American political-economic system works reasonably well within a framework of traditional values. It performs creditably in arriving at solutions consistent with these values. That fraud in human relationships is a basis of its workability is an element which should not be judged harshly. When people accept chicanery in their relations, in fact if not in sermon, such an attribute should be judged solely on whether its use achieves desired ends. Under the rules, the use of chicanery is commendable if successful, deplorable if unsuccessful. Successful use acquires merit by the superior ethic of a workable solution.

But the system that accepts this ethic is now in crisis, for its traditional framework is crumbling. To assert this does not imply a critical judgment of the system; it is rather an observation based on the system's own premises, an observation which some historical background will serve to explicate.

In the 1930's, the Roosevelt New Deal improvised a decision-making system of countervailing power in which a broad clash of interests produced a fair accommodation of viewpoints. Emerging initially as an influence-balancing mechanism for production, prices, and income, this system of countervailing power became a system of broad national policy making. But organizations thereupon became huge; the big organizations, including government, began to coalesce. Bigness, together with the rising complexity of assessing options, served to centralize and mechanize the decision-making process.

Today, power blocs no longer countervail against each other in a way that expresses the prevailing sentiments of a large segment of the population. Rather, princes of power have united into a coterie under the aegis of government, controlling events, as they must, without full knowledge and consent and pronouncing, as they must, what is reality and

7

what is not in a manner consistent with their objectives. This alienation of power centers from the population, accelerated by urbanization and secularization, has produced an ethic among the princes of power that a goal is proper so long as the technology and influence exist to attain it. The new religion has become feasibility: If it works it's O.K. Accordingly, solutions to problems are no longer arrived at through the negotiation of felt inequities by affected groups, solutions which thereby gain a wide moral sanction, but rather through the quiet work of big organizations operating in the belief that what issues from their deliberations represents the social good. A substantial part of the population is either indifferent or hostile to these solutions; a considerable number is excluded from the democratic process. In short, the system shows a tendency to serve primarily the needs of its elites.

This elitism creates inevitable consequences. It encourages society's managers to believe that since pure reason prevails in their deliberations, a minimum of disclosure increases the probability of success and is therefore justifiable; full consensus making is too untidy. Accordingly, mistakes have to be kept hidden. The decision makers lose thereby the guarantee of an assured following; their power lies not in a mass of loyal supporters, but in an ability to command economic and human resources as the population remains passive. The role of the silent majority is to applaud at command.

The system, therefore, prefers minions to independent human beings. But, through neglect on its part, a rising educated class learns to think for itself. What finally evolves from this system of countervailing power is a rebellion against big organization generally—economic, political, educational—by individuals who reject the manipulation of their lives by elites. What issues also is the rationale that since everyone is responsible, no one is responsible.

Thus, Americans operate their society via institutions that have had their day. Rule by organization power fosters estrangement, cynicism, hatred, and violence. College educated individuals with little influence feel frustrated in being unable to change a mechanism whose solutions aggravate tensions; they seek refuge in isolation or relief in obstructionism. The working class, with similar frustrations but dissimilar objectives and risks, seeks remedies in nihilism. The traditional play of liberal and conservative forces produces a clash of illusions. It is like watching a drama producing wrong outcomes and becoming frantic because of the powerlessness to change its course toward Armageddon.

Traditional values did at one time provide the system's underpinning; they no longer do. Furthermore, for its own preservation, the system now resists emerging values. It disenchants, feeds on the people it claims to serve, stifles upward communication, fosters intransigence. For underlying the system's decisions today are not traditional values, but organizational imperatives of power. Organizational power derives from the management of money and talent within the organization; such power must, in turn, control sources of supply and income. Power thus belongs to managers of big corporations receiving and allocating huge sums of money; to labor officials capable of withholding needed labor; to Congressmen controlling the public purse; to university managers providing the skilled manpower for the maintenance of the system. In short, power belongs to the individual with a titular claim to developing and controlling resources in a big organization; removed from office he becomes a ridiculous figure.

In office, the constraints of organization temper the manager's authority. It is affected by technicians whose skill he needs to make a decision; by his responsibility to maintain a predictable flow of resources into the organization, establish internal routine to the maximum extent possible, and market an outward stream of product. These dictates of control impel an organization to become even bigger. Moreover, once such a machinery of decision making is operative, so much is at stake that a manager must behave like a politician and respond to shifting forces that threaten his position. By so doing, he may have to commit fraud. Accordingly, to understand the system we must understand the imperatives of organization.

THE NATURE OF SYSTEM AND UNSYSTEM

The system comprises a network of inter-related big organizations that supply goods and services. Predominant in this network are government, industrial corporations, and universities. This *ménage-à-trois* of managers with their technical subalterns produce the preponderant amount of the nation's goods and technical manpower. Each counts on the other to play ball. Thus, the government expects the universities to tidy up their campuses; and the university managers, under the threat of loss of money and prestige in the system, scurry to do so.

A fundamental generalization applies to the operation of these organizations. As they irrevocably become more complex, the application of increasing resources to improve their services produces diminishing returns. The older an organization becomes, the greater the amount of bad it produces relative to good. As a corollary, the intervention of government to improve performance may serve to aggravate the problem. It can also be inferred that as these marginal benefits in relation to costs tend toward zero, each organization could profitably be decentralized into smaller units of production by breaking up the constricting grip of its managers. This generalization, which for the sake of brevity can be called the law of increasing badness, implies that life in a society of big organization is a continuum not of rising goods, but of mounting bads. The antidote to such a tendency is ever new forms of counter organization, which under present realities must be supported but kept separate of government.

As we have already stated, the remainder of society comprises an army of subcastes that can be called the unsystem. It incorporates those who fail to meet qualifications set by the system for entrance into its exalted bodies. Through lack of such qualification, these groups fail to acquire the money, power, and social prestige bestowed by the system upon its elites; their inferiority is increased by the system's ability to point out incessantly that in fact they are a flop. Through the educational establishment and the job market, the system develops in members of the unsystem the conviction that they amount to little. The system is dominated by Wasps and quasi-Wasps; the unsystem by white and black ethnics.

The system molds the society to serve its needs first and those of the unsystem thereafter. It seeks the best brains of the society, trains them to serve faithfully, and amply rewards them for such service. Not all who draw wages within organizations of the system are among the chosen; hopefully, those at the fringe will be phased out by technology and dumped into the unsystem.

Modern technology provides the system a guiding dynamic in its philosophy of idolatry for feasible technique. The modern faith is that problems succumb to alternatives proposed by technicians and chosen by managers. The technicians, however, are not professional men in the sense that they are individuals who serve the needs of man. The options they offer reflect the needs of those who hire them for profit and power; their adeptness in using their slide rule is for sale to the highest bidder. The first to know of the system's depredations, technicians perceive what goes on but remain silent. When approached to state the facts, they demur; for their primary loyalty is not to their profession but to their employer in the system. All the advancements made to contain the horrors produced by government and corporate technology do not issue by virtue of these persons raising protests. The information locked in their minds becomes available only from other sources when the unsystem laboriously mounts an offensive generated by the system's excesses. This is not to say that technicians are beyond redemption. They bring to problems a discipline in analysis which their intellectual critics, who prefer seeing as reality what soothes their tensions, infrequently do. The issue is not whether technicians have talent, for they do, but who has the power to buy it.

System and unsystem are discontinuous. The one has the resources and skills of individuals who select themselves as experts in solving problems of the other; but the unsystem rejects the allocation of these resources and talents. A discontinuity exists also in communication. The system, both government and corporations, controls communication. It concedes the right to be heard but not to bargain. Only when the unsystem produces a jolt does upward communication begin to flow. Accordingly, it is a game in which one side deals a serve patronizingly while the other deliberately returns the ball out of the court.

System requires manipulation and suppression in order to manage; it works best by exploiting the misinformation and weakness of the mass. Unsystem needs disruption and sabotage in order to communicate. The system distinguishes between two kinds of violence: that of the system, which is legitimate, and that of the unsystem, which is lawless. The system employs violence as a tool of making profits, as an instrument of amusing the populace, and as a means of solving differences. The unsystem uses violent tactics including bombing and arson as a way of venting frustration generated by the system; and by so doing it invites self-destruction.

The system abhors truth and employs deception and palliative as a means of escape from it. Thus, the government's covering up of the blunders and deception of its officials acquires the label of promoting the national interest. And in the case of drug addiction, a problem reaching epidemic proportions, the first reaction of the system is to provide more funds for legal enforcement; the next, begrudgingly, is to amass money to rehabilitate addicts. Only if the unsystem musters sufficient power will the causes of addiction be looked into.

The system makes ever steady progress in the faculty of telling lies; the unsystem adheres foolishly to the criterion of candor. In the system, success comes by being clever, and failure, by being honest. Those who wish to rise rapidly must practice deceit to do so; the greatest honors fall on the most fraudulent. A measure of the system's success is the incapacity of its most distinguished members to perceive the difference between fraud and integrity. Those who profess to support the system in the name of a higher morality are often the most immoral. The universal panacea of the system is: let us eat cake; and if conscience obstructs euphoria, let us find acceptable ways of stoning ourselves.

Because of the considerable outlay of resources, the system must plan. But the system's planning can tolerate neither spontaneity, nor disruption of the planned, nor honest dealing by the planners. Too much is at stake. The system needs acquiescence to planned goals and obtains this through the offer of material comfort. With the adroit employment of symbolism and traditional values, the system maintains a holding operation. This tenacity nurtures subsocieties and conflicts between system and unsystem.

Labor specialization, an indispensable requisite for the maintenance of the system, fosters its uncompromising elitism. Every major toiler dedicates his life to the development and use of a narrow specialization that commands a market in the system. Accordingly, the specialist who expresses an opinion in someone else's area can easily be placed on the defensive; not having the information which is at the finger tips of elites in whose jurisdiction the particular subject falls, he can effectively be attacked. Even if he seeks such information, he must rely on suspicious elites disinclined to give it to him straight. Consequently, a hero within his area of specialization, he can be an unknown or a fool outside. Unless he can muster counterpower to confront elites outside his field, he finds that passivity outside his area of production provides better assurance of a sane existence. Thus many technicians exist in the system and few educated individuals. The human being in the system is a programmed technician. If natural history provides a clue in the evolution of man, it alerts us to the possibility that specialization may be the road to his extinction.

Every major task in the society is performed by specialists in big organizations. The toil in such organization centers on group analysis of problems and the uniform application of resources through command generalizations that serve as controls. Whether it be in problem analysis, application of resources, or control of responses, individual relationships are on a bargaining basis. That is to say, the persons in each unit of the organization negotiate an accommodation of their interests. Their bargaining power reflects knowledge and the market value of their product. Each contributor to decisions brings to bear an observance of reality through the eyes of his specialization. Occasionally, decisions are affected by specialists who also happen to be philosophers; but such an occurrence is rare.

Under the system, the law is a political weapon that promotes those interests that can most effectively muster money, talent, and organization. Most victories are those of organization. To those who lose, the system teaches: If you feel swindled, go out and get yours.

The arguments brought forward in support of the system's goals often comprise anti-reason. In both the public and the private sector, the application of reason to the objectives of organization would foster a collapse of the system. Therefore, managers in industry and government must manipulate the public for the sake of survival. An outstanding achievement in this area is the development of the individual as a machine of marketable production and rising consumption and of a monetary mechanism to sustain this creation. As a producer, the individual makes his contribution on the basis of labor specialization; as a consumer, he chooses either submission to the tune of producers or strategies to shield himself from them. For the system to succeed, it must convince people that consuming an ever greater amount of goods is the mark of human achievement; to propagate this faith, government and industry employ the media. Government, for example, encourages economic pessimism or optimism depending upon its objectives, and firms inculcate an orientation that serves their pecuniary interests.

Individuals who produce and consume creatively are thus enemies of the system; they can subvert the planning of firms and government. Erratic changes in consumption patterns must be discouraged. Any marked assertion of individuality cannot be brooked for modern technology abhors distinctiveness. The human being must be brainwashed so that he behaves consonant with the system's needs of mass consumption.

Individuals who cannot produce under the rules must be isolated and kept politically quiescent. The rules provide that they be shunted out of the system and furnished with a subsistence income. Should these subcastes become a source of irritation, the system's impulse is to mix palaver with chicanery. The facts cannot be fully developed and disseminated for the system may then be undermined.

Rackets are not confined solely to the unsystem; they flourish in both orders. The essence of system is organization and domination to practice exclusiveness of product and exclusion of competitors. These same goals are sought by racketeers in the unsystem, who differ from those in the system in their lack of respectability and in their forms of violence. These differences are due to a quirk of history. The knaves in the families of Wasps who manage the system are to be found in the distant past; control of a respectable corporation today often has as its foundation the questionable practices of generations back. The now affluent Wasps can afford to practice greater finesse in their crookedness.

Each corporation within the system is itself a system comprising interrelated parts. Each part interacts within itself and with other parts of the corporation; and the corporation itself interacts externally with other organizations. The corporation seeks control internally through routine procedures and externally through seeking to dominate other organizations with whom it deals. Its principal external relationships are with other corporations, government, labor, the general public, and the media.

Whereas big corporations often deal with each other as equals, they generally have tamed government, transferred the costs of dealing with labor to their customers, developed a mass culture consistent with their needs, and subdued community challenges.

To a considerable degree, income in the system reflects the amount of pressure successfully exerted on government to grant subsidies. These take the form of price guarantees, tax concessions, and the underwriting of technological innovation. As a rule, government offers its most generous bounties to executives of big firms, big farmers, and managers of big universities, as producers of goods and skills, and to the well-to-do, as recipients of income. These subsidized producers, together with high ranking government officials who serve their interests, comprise the princes of the system. Shared by all of them is an antipathy toward granting like subsidies to the unsystem.

Change is either decreed by these princes to serve their needs or forced by the unsystem as it vents its frustrations. The princes confer on others the rights of entrance into the system and on themselves the mantle of worthy purpose. From time to time they or their spokesmen will encourage their critics in the unsystem to seek reform through the orderly processes of the system. But should the use of such processes effectively undermine the system, the same rhetoricians will look for new measures to plug the dike. Thus consumer organizations pose serious challenges to the system and the princes are busy mounting the ramparts against the enemy.

In summary, the liberal society of multiple coexisting countervailing groups recedes and makes way for the new order—System and Unsystem. In a clash of these orders, the predictable solution is that which will maintain the power of those managing the system and get the unsystem off their backs. The system comprises an enormous commitment of talent and money in the planned development of production and consumption. Its products, be they of firms or government, are merchandised by attaching fantasies to them. Some fantasy always pays off, for the consumer plays the game with cards stacked by the house in its favor. Although the system's technology is self-serving, the idea is merchandised and accepted that technological advance and the advance of civilization are identical.

The madmen of modern society, the system's managers, must perpetuate escapism. An effective rebellion against this madness would cause chaos. A retreat from escapism must be planned consistent with political and technological necessities, for a modern technological system cannot allow a rise in values that impairs its orderly retreat from one technology to the next. Thus, the air, the water, the noise, the esthetic, and the social pollution, should they pose a threat to the system, must be contained in a manner consistent with the system's orderly movement toward sanity. To do so requires the maintenance of illusion.

To achieve this end, men must be made the system's unknowing subalterns. They must be managed to relate to each other not directly, but indirectly via the system's artifacts; they must be dominated not by ideas, but by objects to which the system attaches fantasies. In short, human beings must be educated to think in conformity with the needs of the system.

Consequently, the system reorders human needs in a manner that plugs individuals into its operations. In some cases the restriction in individuality produces aberrations in the form of private styles of existence in which expression is improvised within consenting groups. Many such groups erroneously think that their derivations are the remedy rather than the disease. Their improvisations—their accoutrements of dress, drugs, improvised play, erotica, anarchical protest, adoration of shock—are triggered by the system and border on sickness. These aberrations amount so far only to an irritation, for the genius of the system lies in its capacity to induce passivity.

Accordingly, an oligarchic system has emerged of cooperating elites who formerly were adversaries, with the government as chairman of the board. At the base of the system, a passive suburban class, preoccupied with keeping its balance on the treadmill of more income and consumption, neutralizes itself as a positive force; in rising numbers, the young revolt against middle class values and shun positions in the system; government pacifies the middle class with techniques that keep the gross national product rising, for rising GNP is the indicator of progress. Bedded together comfortably, these elites shy away from structural change.

Organized labor is no longer a countervailing force. To state, however, that the trade unions retreat, more or less permanently, into the shadows is an exaggeration.[1] They have not retreated so much as blended into the system, where they perform yeomanry service in return for concessions to their terms. Thus, Walter Reuther, the former president of the United Auto Workers Union and a man with a reputation as a reformer, did not in his lifetime commit the indiscretion of mounting an attack against the motor vehicle.

The war industry exemplifies this unity among the princes of power. Guaranteed income and influence, the industrial and labor princes acquiesce to the needs of the military machine. The record reveals not

1 John K. Galbraith, *The New Industrial State*, Boston: Houghton Mifflin, 1967, pp. 274–276.

one speech made by a prominent member of either group against contemporary militarism. The military establishment has so integrated the public and private sector as to make a line of demarcation between them impossible. A particular aircraft for a foreign country may result from the political influence of the labor organization in the plant where the aircraft is built, pressure from the firm's managers, the military mania to convert technological feasibility into hardware, the groups promoting the interests of a foreign country, including intellectuals who under normal circumstances are peace loving.

Challenges issue against these princes of power from an educated class that does not identify with them, a white urban class that feels swindled, an emerging black urban proletariat, and festooned revolutionaries more skilled in playing frisbee than in successful revolution. These challenges are unlikely to have a substantial impact so long as the suburban middle class supports the system.

In such circumstances, shifts in political power between Democrats and Republicans have little effect on institutional change, for shifts in administration do not alter the commitment of government to the system. The system allows a replacement of incumbents with another set only on its own terms. Institutional change requires a political movement led by competent strategists who can muster the systems' own weapons: money, talent, and organization.

THE RELEVANCE OF ECONOMICS AND SOCIAL THEORY

The fragmentary knowledge of system and unsystem is scattered among the many areas of social science; economics, sociology, cultural anthropology, organization theory, decision-making theory, and political science all bring pertinent information to bear upon an understanding of the system. This dispersal of information serves the needs of specialists more than those of social analysts. In none of these areas of social science can an adequate explanation be found of what produces change within its claimed jurisdiction. To understand modern man, one has to read the works of poets, novelists, and philosophers.

The forces that produced the Protestant Reformation have reached a new stage in contemporary life. The secularization of man triggered by the reformation has destroyed the foundations of a system based on elitism. Contemporary man recoils from a life under the baton of elites. Alarmed by his self-inflicted loss of a transcendental purpose, he searches for an earthly substitute within the context of his individuality. These words sound like a far cry from economics; but in actuality they are not. Culture, politics, and economics are all intertwined; economic transactions are political processes in a cultural setting. If the modern American elects to control his wordly destiny by asserting his individuality, a drastic change in economic organization will occur through a political contest at centers of government.

With its present devotion to mathematical models, economics provides no tool with which to understand these transformations. All the basic mathematical tools used by economists have been constructed by mathematicians; which raises the suspicion that economic facts are made to fit their math. The mafia bosses of the social science discipline produce with their mathematical models a reality corresponding with the equations they employ; their impressive algebra obscures the questionable assumptions underlying it. Energies are expended on behalf of mathematical technique at the sacrifice of coming to terms with reality— with the dominating role of corporations and government in the economy and the manner in which they make decisions. Facts must dictate models. Information must be gathered on decision-making centers, including the family as well as firms and government. Economists must apply pressure on government for such information because it will not become available otherwise. The economic policies of the Nixon administration with their overlay of public relations gimickry suggest how badly this information is needed.

The major areas of economics comprise: *traditional suppy and demand analysis,* in which price determination and resource allocation are developed with impeccable logic, but with little basis in reality; *behavioral economics,* which discusses inadequately the way in which people make economic decisions; *social welfare economics,* which has somewhat to do with the determination and balancing of the welfare expectations of different groups in the society. Economics just scratches the surface in the last two of these areas, although it is precisely here that the most vital concerns lie. The improvement of analytical models depends upon acquiring a greater knowledge as to how economic decisions are actually made. With such information, society becomes better prepared to respond to a vital need of returning power to the people. Development of the third branch of economics would help in serving the second most urgent requirement, the need for government, which has become the prime determinant of resource allocation, to analyze and bring into balance the welfare expectations of the society's subgroups.

Although some of the best minds in the social sciences are drawn to the discipline of economics, they are not attracted primarily to these two areas. These are questions that trouble young sensitive minds.

In looking at the tradeoff between inflation and unemployment, a conventional economist would consider this to be a technical problem of quantifying a functional relationship, which might be solved with good data and appropriate econometric techniques. He would, therefore, spend most of his time in trying to get the data into the best form for rigorous testing or some hypothesis about this tradeoff, and in the interpretation of his results.

A radical political economist, looking at the same problem, would also be interested in its quantitative and theoretical aspects, but in addition he would ask why it is that the institutional arrangements of advanced capitalism require that we have either inflation and unemployment, and he would assume conflicts of interest among groups in the society and a highly unequal distribution of power among these groups to influence decision making in this area. These thoughts might lead him to investigate whether the Nixon administration's strong emphasis on stopping the inflation, at the cost of more unemployment, might not serve a powerful group of bankers and industrialists whose financial interests heavily depend on the continuing dominance of the United States in the world capitalist system and hence on the enduring strength of the dollar. He would, of course, at the same time reflect that unemployed blacks and chicanos have very little power over such decisions compared to, say, David Rockefeller.[2]

Such is not to consider sacrosanct the sweeping condemnation made by radical economists; good intentions are no license for sloppy thinking. Crucial is the maintenance of the traditional rigor in thinking. Gurley's is top-rate. If orthodox technique obscures issues, valid alternatives must be prepared.

In orthodox economic theory, the welfare of the consumer is the goal being maximized. This welfare—or, to reduce the word to simple terms, happiness—is maximized when, given the free choice of individuals, the economic system produces and distributes at ever rising efficiency the goods they demand. By such efficiency is intended a labor-capital combination that results in producing this output at lower unit costs. Destroy this crucial assumption of consumer welfare, and economic theory would collapse like a house of cards.

Like princes of power, many economists arrange reality in conformity with obsolete theory; those who do in conflicting ways say nasty things to each other. With today's dire need for analysis as to how to allocate scarce resources in order to raise the quality of life, many good minds are busy debating whether controlling the money supply or government tax-spending policy would better achieve a rise in the gross national product. They participate in this discussion as if the allocation of economic resources has nothing to do with who holds power in the nation. They do so insensitive to the fact that a rise in GNP may be a measure

2 John G. Gurley, The State of Political Economics, Papers and Proceedings, Eighty-Third Annual Meeting, *American Economic Association*, May 1971, p. 55.

of progress toward extinction. The GNP is bloated with activities of individuals seeking protection and rehabilitation from the system's beneficence, and the solutions of economics to maintain it are often at the expense of members of the unsystem. Secure in their positions, economists manipulate people's lives by tinkering with the economy.

Accordingly, the system has outgrown the clothes provided by economics. Its concepts and explanations of economic decisions are obsolete; maximizing welfare by increased consumption is a delusion; the GNP is useless as a measure of progress. Moreover, the consumer is not autonomous; he is determined as well as determining. Economic concepts are not only mute as to the impact of the system on people, but also as to its effect on environment. Economic calculus ignores human and environmental costs imposed by the system, dismissing them as external diseconomies.

Since the latter part of the 18th century, social scientists with a talent for describing the economic system in lucid prose have periodically emerged. John K. Galbraith is such a person in contemporary American economic literature. No one has produced an equally clear and valid description of the workings of our economic system. Consequently, to proffer even the blandest criticism of Professor Galbraith makes one tremble. Five billion years ago the earth was formed. Three billion years later life emerged. In the last decile of these 5 billenia *homo sapiens* came forward, and in the 600,000th year of contemporary man's existence, Galbraith began to intone the new revelation.

Galbraith's contribution is his attack on the fundamental idea of economics that economic organization serves individual wants. He correctly observes that this frame is obsolete since the system employs individuals to serve itself and that this evolution takes place in an economy that raises the consumer above the subsistence level. He points out this basic truth in a clear manner. His severest critics indulge in bad manners. The venemous attacks seem to be inspired by motives other than scholarship.

A more valid criticism of Galbraith can be found in when he cautiously revises description and prescription. In order to work, the system of cooperating oligarchies requires from the population a high degree of uniformity in responses that are consistent with the maintenance of oligarchic power; it corrupts and hoodwinks to gain this allegiance to not fully disclosed objectives. When Mr. Galbraith, in the course of a decade, switches his description from one of countervailing power to one founded on this principle of consistency, there is cause for some alarm.

Galbraith's principle of consistency affirms that there must be a consistency in the goals of society, the organization, and the individual; moreover, there must be a consistency in the motives that induce organizations and individuals to pursue these goals. Accordingly, the goals and motives of the society, organization, and individual tend to be identical. As each entity seeks to impose its goals on the other, through a process of adaptation goals become consistent with each other. Mutual causality is implied; but the elucidation of the principle suggests that the needs of corporate managers are a dominating factor. Thus, the principle of consistency appears to be a truism that rediscovers sociologists' theory of social balance. The principle depicts a fool's world in which managers, convinced they labor for the social good, manipulate individuals, who in turn, as they are being manipulated, are persuaded of the beneficence of the managers. The society deteriorates as consistency prevails.

Galbraith dismisses the question of where this system leads us by stating it is not as important as his determination of where it has already brought us. Had he faced this question, the principle of consistency might have been modified to fit the manipulating state facing subsocieties composed of those successfully hoodwinked, those acquiescing out of no discernible option, and those subverting the system. This picture of the duped, the resigned, and the subverters is not one of a grateful flock being watched over by a wedding of elites in happy union. Thus, for working purposes in the coming decades, the principle of consistency is less useful than one of struggle between elites and people.

His happy vision of a future in the hands of intellectual elites and his failure to acknowledge the alarming disdain for intellectuality in the society are causes also for some alarm. Galbraith bestows goodness upon prophecy: He moves in his use of verbs from "is," to "might be," to "ought to be." He sees the emergence of technical elites in decision making roles and gives them his blessing. But a society governed by technicians is from experience a society of blindness and deceit. American society is already controlled by such elites; but Professor Galbraith has faith in incumbents who are more after his image. The reaction of people to technicians does not seem to enter their calculations. People decide not to dance to the tune of elites. Nevertheless, book by book, academic intellectuals tread down the path toward the Intellectual State.

To restore relevance to their discipline, economists face a difficult task of replacing their obsolete theory of the firm with a theory of the imperatives of organization. With such a new interpretation, they will be at the threshold of relating the analysis of the individual firm with that of the economic system generally, and in turn, with that of the political system. The new theory would have to contain as its core the premise that big organizations in the economic-political system *manage* their output, input, and environment, and prefer *control* or *accommodation* rather than competition between themselves. Furthermore, in such management, the individual tends to be viewed more as a minion unworthy of enlightenment than as a sovereign consumer, toiler, or citizen.

FROM DESCRIPTION TOWARD PRESCRIPTION

Honesty demands recognition of the system's accomplishments as well as of its weaknesses. The system has produced an unprecedented prosperity in a world whose majority lives in the shadow of abject poverty. Its problems arise from an antiquated elite decision making system shored up by an obsolescent profit motive. The system is vulnerable in that it does not comprise an organic whole with a consistent logic. It contains rather a bundle of inconsistencies whose existence has a benign effect. To cite an example, television is a vital instrument of propaganda to sustain the demand for goods. Yet, its relentless advertising leads to a vulnerable irrationality and its need to report sensationally reveals the weaknesses of government.

Other vulnerabilities abound. The need of the system for loyalties requires concessions to obtain them. The system requires the administration of law for its operation, but the law provides the means for a counterattack. Moreover, the system is vulnerable in that the very language used to describe it is no longer precise and thus is subject to criticism. The system's vulnerability, in short, is its contradictoriness. Its conflict is evidence of the successful challenge of power.

Moreover, to assert that the choice is between system and individualism raises a false dilemma. Individualism cannot exist without a system, unless it is reserved for an elite. To deny American society's accomplishments in human redemption is a monumental distortion of history. The system allows an area of permissiveness that would not be tolerated by many champions of individualism were they in power. It must also be conceded that the system's demand for routine is required in any society. The exercise of creativity and imagination needs orderliness in the environment and in the artist himself; completely free spirits are usually parasites, not creators. One should not be beguiled by the rhetoric of intellects. Individual creativity requires self-discipline and the expectation of self-discipline in society.

The system entertains novelty that does not menace its smooth flow. It does not wish to homogenize everyone, so long as those who resist homogenization cop out unobtrusively and do not seriously disrupt the system. This indulgence provides the opportunity for the pursuit of more individualism.

Nevertheless, it cannot be denied that the judicial system's notion of inalienable individual rights lingers only in ritual and not in fact. Rights accrue to the individual by virtue of his ability to employ organizational power. What is right depends upon the relative power of those who claim it. Thus, the courts behave consistent with an old Sicilian adage that he who has the greater power has the greater logic. The courts tend to assign to ascendant power the mantle of universal justice. This they do with or without a statute as a springboard, legislating the new morality riding the crest of power. The system's judicial custodians of morality prescribe how individuals should behave in their communities, in their living rooms, and in their beds. The crime rate would collapse if the system minded its own business.

The system, generally, seeks planned responses. Its desire for uniform behavior has a historical origin. The blacks excepted, America was populated by an incredible assortment of European castaways, those gaining the shore first judging those following more ignoble. Inevitably, a philosophy of social conduct arose in accordance with which Americans in power today busy themselves legislating the behavior of lesser Americans. It seeks such uniformity through a bland form of machiavellianism. Politics is thus corrupted into a technology of manipulation, a corruption which if not checked marks a transitory stage toward sadism.

Some noteworthy options have been suggested as the means of reforming these tendencies of the system. One is the classical reliance by intellectuals of employing intellectuals to lead the society toward a better day. Since the first book of genesis of Karl Marx, intellectuals have assigned missions to the population that the population takes lightly; thereupon the intellectuals brood. They compress reality into neat generalizations with eye-catching titles; in contemporary society the rhetoric has progressed from the society of countervailing power, to the affluent society, the technotronic society, the one-dimensional society, the industrial state, the State of Consciousness III. Exaggeration sustains a unitary point of view.

But reality is multi-dimensional and time variant. Decisions emerge from shifting power configurations, incomplete knowledge, the degree of fear of those who make them, past solutions, the state of the body chemistry, sadism, empathy, the desire to survive, the institutions through which they are funneled. The insights and solutions of today are possible by virtue of the mistakes and solutions of the past. The system shifts not through intellectual rhetoric but in dramatic testimony to the talent of persons to capitalize upon its destructive tendencies.

An intellectual alleges that the individual will triumph in the contest between the demands of organization and those of individualism because of the efforts of idealistic youth. In this view, older people compromise their ideals while young persons maintain a continuity of ideals. The different consciousness of the young is described as resulting from the promise of life that is made to them and their reaction to the threat to that promise.

How does one recognize this idealistic youth? According to this notion, they can be spotted by their earthy clothes, which express individuality and wholeness, in contrast to the business suit, which is at odds with the organization man all day; by the rock music which brings out the poetry in them; by their criticism of a society that is run just for a privileged few; by the way they assume personal responsibility in contrast to the immaturity of adults; and by their use of drugs. And how will the young freedom lovers change the system? They will do so not by a political challenge, but by the sheer force of their superior values and their understanding of reality. They will change the system for the better by stepping outside it *en masse*. The law as a means of reform is useless because the purpose of law is to compel obedience to the state. The nation is close to being a police state; the people are powerless.

The contagion spreading from such youth is everywhere: in the women's liberation movement, in black militancy, in discontented young blue collar workers, in subway collisions, power failures, and even in the way a beauty queen cast away her title because she was required by male chauvinist pigs to be apolitical. The contagion spreads into all institutions.

In sum, when the youth take over as death claims the present managers, the system will perish. Do nothing and the system will slowly ascend toward heaven. And then everyone will find that nobody really wants or needs poverty. Organizations will wither away and so will conflicts of interest between men. Thus, to the literature of doom and gloom of intellectuals, the hippy intellectual adds the literature of transfiguration.

We have presented in this second chapter a general frame of system and unsystem and have indicated thereby the crucial importance of organization. Therefore, we move next to a summary discussion concerning characteristics and issues of corporate organization. Such a preliminary clarification is important to the development of our fundamental question: how the system can be reformed to respond to the cultural diversity of our society. The feasibility of the options brought forward here and another to be presented later will be affected by facts a more thorough examination yields.

3

Modern Corporate Organization:
An Overview

Big organization imposes restraints upon the ferment of cultural autonomy in contemporary American society, restraints that are a prime cause of the social problems that beset it. It is therefore important that the characteristics of modern organization, together with issues that these characteristics raise, be understood. We must understand organization to make it respond to the inclusion of the unsystem into the system.

The values on which organization rest are in a state of transition. An increasing number of dissidents rejects the authority of elites as to how life should be conducted. The weakening of this linkage destroys clear notions of what individuals should and should not do. The life of moral imperative declines, choked by the policies of government and business and by an educational system void of philosophy.

Our crisis of self-confidence, inspired by this change in values, pushes the technology of mass control of individuals past its zenith. An army of rising numbers rejects management by elites and stumbles toward populist institutions. Governments and corporations are put on the defensive. A demand arises that institutions become more responsive to the cultural diversity of the society.

Of the institutions challenged by this quest for cultural pluralism, the traditional corporation breaks down at the fastest pace. The single most important determinant of urban life, the corporation prescribes choices of work; determines the kinds of food we eat; influences the policies that govern education; shapes community and environment; limits the range of political options; shapes cultural tastes. The private corporation is thus anything but private. Moreover, by the end of the de-

25

cade, a mere one hundred multinational corporations will be producing the proponderant amount of the world's manufactured goods.[1]

Created initially under the protective cover of limited liability, corporations find themselves increasingly exposed to demands for unlimited social liability that are open-ended and ill-defined. In ever rising crescendo, managers are called to task for the effects of their products and processes. Under the force of public pressure, government passes a rash of laws and implements new administrative procedures to impose a greater social sensitivity on corporate performance. Although the measures against deleterious effects of consumption of corporate products lag, it is certain that this retardation will not linger indefinitely.

Government hesitates to create structures to accommodate this pressure for cultural autonomy. However, such events as the drawn-out conflict in Indochina, the failure of local government to keep the cities viable, and the surging disillusionment over political leadership push government into the mainstream of this quest. Out of this ferment a cultural pluralism that moves the society toward a federation of subsocieties emerges haltingly. The right of cultural self-determination seeks an ascendancy over universally applied standards of performance.

This ferment feeds on itself. Once values under which the corporation operates change in the society, the reaction in new corporate policies and structures speeds up the alteration. The corporation provides the communication lines with which to undermine further its traditional position. In addition, the new attitudes interpret traditional corporate responses, no matter how benign, as wicked reaction, which adds to the strength of the movement seeking to alter the value base of the corporation. This reaction also feeds the process of change.

How we view the corporation affects our ability to anticipate the effects of this unfolding drama. A popular notion is that corporations comprise a network of interlocking directorates whose members operate in conspiratorial fashion, an idea which persists because it contains a semblance of truth. Managers do hold multiple posts in different organizations and do move freely between them; too, managers in the same industry often come from the same ethnic group. Nevertheless, conflicts of interest exist internally among corporate subunits and externally among corporations in their control of markets and in their contest within and between industries to influence government priorities. The conflict prevailing within the organization limits the capacity of top man-

---

[1] A study of multinational corporations with a minimum of 15 percent in sales or production outside the home country indicates that these firms contribute 40 percent of the non-communist world's national product. See Stefan Robock, "International Business: How Big is It?," Vol. 5, *The Columbia Journal of World Business*, May–June 1970, pp. 6–19.

agers to impose their points of view unilaterally, and conflict external to the organization makes it impossible to sustain the view of the corporation as conspirator.

A more useful concept of the corporation is that of a subsystem of related subsystems in the larger society, existing in an environment of fluid cultural values that emanate from particular groups. Thus viewed, the corporation is a major species of organization. An organization comprises internally a system of inter-related subdivisions and externally a subsystem with a myriad of relationships with other organizations in the larger society. The relationship between organization and larger society is interactive and symbiotic.

These organizations have a variety of noteworthy characteristics which a strategy of social change must consider. What follows holds true generally for organizations in both the profit and non-profit sector.

Modern organizations are big and formal. Their imports and exports of men, product, and information run the gauntlet of the characteristic features of bureaucracy. The subsystems within each of them are staffed by educated and cautious bureaucrats who in their management of affairs perceive matters within the context of their specialization and desire for security. Massive organization in government, industry, leisure activity, research, is a common fact of life. No single subsystem can unilaterally impose its views on any other. Many of the individuals working in one have little or no grasp of the relationship of their work to that being performed in another. Moreover, individuals in the organization have competing interests as to the inputs entering therein, as do the claimants of the organization's outputs. A principal weakness in predicting organization behavior lies in the inability to ascertain factors in the environment that affect this flow of imports and exports.

Big organization implies an internal flow of considerable sums of money. Once this flow is established and maintained through external receipts, to change it significantly is unlikely. Only a gross error in management could do so. In economic terms, once the die is cast on the economics of the organization, it is difficult to alter the pattern either quickly or drastically. Consequently, the behavior of these organizations, like that of individuals, is emergent. It should be understood as a flow rather than as a portrait. The perverse view of organization and individuals as static phenomena leads men to make many errors in understanding.

In addition, the product of the organization, its size, market competition, and the goal behind the product influence its artifacts, processes, and characteristics of its human capital. Intimately related to each other in a mutually casual fashion, the maintenance of this technology of hardware, process, and human beings are important determinants of inputs going into the organization.

An organization's decisions are also affected by the bureaucratic process and by the motives and perceptions of players at its different layers. Most noteworthy are the motives and perceptions of its managers. A principle of agency fixing responsibility of organization acts on these managers is valid: It is they who allocate and control the resources going into decisions. A practical solution to the problem of accountability allows no other means of assigning responsibility.

Large scale organizations must plan; they cannot lead a life of improvisation. A plan is a calculated hope, representing a compromise of the content brought forward by subunits through the reconciliation efforts of middle management and the final imprint of top management. It comprises a collective statement of the possible realized by a series of progressive readjustments which narrow the gap between aspiration and accruing reality. Planning entails not only the *measurement* of market potential, but also, with varying degree of success, its *control*.

A plan is successful to the degree that managers understand and play well the politics of planning in its initial stages. The top manager can apply unrevealed tactics calculated to move men toward the kind of plan he desires. In these maneuvers, he has the advantage of surprise and power of punishment. He also has as tools the ambition of men to be successful in their career by moving toward the top. Ambition makes men easy to manipulate. Moreover, the degree of subunit participation in planning depends to a considerable extent upon the depth to which top management comprehends the operations of the organization. As a generalist in an enterprise staffed by technical specialists, the manager may be at their mercy. By not allowing his personality to become a source of irritation and by strategically placing esoteric terms in his dialogue, the technician may outmaneuver the manager and influence policy.

Although resistant to massive change in direction, these organizations do shift slowly in style of governance, product, and processes. They change as they face an uncertain and potentially hostile societal environment. A major change in any one part of the interrelated internal structure of organizations extends outward into other parts and may eventually cause disequilibrium in the general system of the larger society. This disequilibrium is ever present, because organizations have the will to grow and shift their objectives. Conflict is a tool of mediating the differences that arise between them in consequence of the shift in objectives.

Lastly, we should ever keep in mind that what a corporation is and does is rarely what a corporation says it is and does. The purpose of corporate information is not to give a well-rounded picture of the facts but to convey an impression. The annual reports of firms are testimonials of this rule.

Our view or organization as emergent behavior necessitates placing the course of the corporation in historical perspective. Over time, a corporation tends to produce a collection of goods and bads for the society. By seeking to maintain momentum in profit making, it has been seen that the organization's bads tend to rise relative to its goods. These increasing bads generate public attitudes toward the corporation that are cyclical in character, whose phases include indifference, concern, control, and a return to indifference.

Thus, in the early history of the corporation, the ruthless pursuit of profits was rationalized as productive of benefits for the society as a whole. The interests of society would be fulfilled as the corporation pursued its own interests. Many people believed it; to this day, some academics still do. In the next stage of corporate evolution, as public attitudes changed from indifference to concern, the image of the civic-minded manager emerged. It was considered good business to appear to be socially responsible; good works and good profits became reconcilable. To bring about this accommodation, it would at times be necessary to give up short term profits for long term gains.

In the third stage, the amount of corporate bads had accumulated sufficiently to place managers on the defensive. Their quivers of conscience reflected a shift in public sentiment. Society relieved the corporate manager of the necessity for soul searching and sought to control his organization by imposing upon him specific responsibilities. The manager was expected to come up with more than after-dinner affirmations. A round of negotiation took place between protesting elements in the society and corporation, either directly or indirectly through government.

This cyclical relationship between corporation and society goes on continually. Emerging values that change the corporation become traditional values; a new level of indifference appears; firms switch from defensiveness to dominance; the bads relative to the goods begin to rise; a new round of control appears.

Several issues emerge from these characteristics of big organizations. Of foremost importance is the question of social responsibility, for underlying this issue is whether cultural groups in the unsystem can place their imprint upon the system. Some apologists of the system argue that corporations should not decrease their profits by assuming social responsibilities. Among those who assume they should, honest differences exist as to what constitutes such responsibility; what one person may consider responsible another may think irrelevant. Even if agreement could be obtained on social goals of corporations, conflicts would likely arise as to the priorities these goals command. Moreover, the social response to corporate acts is pluralistic. Whereas some groups in society may feel a product or process is anti-social and should be modified or prohibited, some may be all for it, and others may be indifferent.

Confronted by such a range of views, the social morality of the corporation tends to be whatever it can get away with in the pursuit of its interests. So long as the public remains indifferent to such promotion, for example, a firm may cultivate the idea that drugs are the sure way to bliss. In an economy of mass markets, truth is whatever organization persuades the public it is. At times, the public must be prodded into the proper consciousness; always, the public must not be told by the corporation the full consequences of consuming its product.

Academic apologists for traditional business philosophy stress that business is in business for profit and not for the promotion of social goals. But they thereby raise a false issue. Firms pursue social objectives as the public demands them. Their costs are thereupon imposed on the public and such pursuit becomes good business. Big business has the human resources and analytical tools to reconcile their interests with the social goals deemed worthy by the public.

The General Electric Company defines its social responsibility as follows:

> The corporation is a creation of society whose purpose is the production and distribution of needed goods and services, to the profit of society and itself.[2]

In amplification of this statement, the firm asserts the existence of a mutuality of interest between company and society. If society sees no benefit to itself from a corporation's activities, then in the long run that business will not be profitable. Furthermore, a corporation must reflect all of the society's values. It must change as society changes, but it can also seek to influence the ultimate form and expression of those changes.

These assertions suggest that if public expectancies of the corporation change, General Electric will seek to strike the expected new postures. Indeed, to anticipate these challenges, the firm employs a business environment unit to conduct environmental forecasting as an input in corporate planning, adding a social and political dimension to economic and technological planning. Accordingly, the firm sees itself as belonging to a system of constantly shifting values.

---

2 Virgil B. Day, Vice President Industrial Relations, General Electric Company, "The Social Relevance of Business," 1969.

At times, the desire of firms to feel the pulse of society promotes self-deception. Managers shop around for the right university professors to assist them in the collection of information. Mindful not to bite the hand that feeds them, some of these scholars serve up information which will not be unduly unpalatable to their patrons, and slant the arguments of business critics in a manner that suggests these commentators are either falsifiers or fools. Accordingly, in their concern with their self-images, both firms and professors distort the information they avowedly seek from the base of society.

The question of organizational responsibility raises the broader philosophical problem of functional morality: should the individual change his code of conduct with each organizational role he plays, or should he apply the same rules regardless of the organizational role he performs? Some youths of sensitive intelligence reject the notion of functional morality: if it is wrong to exercise violence, it is wrong to do it for an organization directly or indirectly. Morality should transcend organizational roles. If taken seriously, this position would undermine the exploitative basis upon which goods are produced and sold. Such a consistency in human conduct may be a worthy ideal. To survive, however, the individual reconciles his conscience with particular externalities. He makes transactions between the various parts of his intellect, including his conscience, needs, and early experience, and the subsystems of his environment. He makes choices so as to avoid his self-destruction.

As noted above, the organization is difficult to control internally on the basis of a universally specified moral prescription because of the many internal and external constituencies to which it responds. The many subunits operated by generalists and specialists each perform tasks that collectively produce the organization's thrust. A command coming into the organization from the outside undergoes a shakedown consistent with the needs of these subunits. The top manager responds to their shifting power. His dictates may be subverted. It would be easier to control the organization for specific social objectives if in fact a centrally directed conspiracy existed that issued directives to be obeyed at command. All that would then have to be done would be to hold a gun to the head of the boss and impart instruction as to what he must do.

Moreover, a corporate executive is often not conscious of the relationship between social needs and his organization because he is removed from the activity of the community in which these needs exist. His children may be in private schools or away at college, which tends to make him indifferent to the local school system. His corporate reassignments come with such frequency that he leads a gypsy life, which makes him feel like a transient in the community. When he makes his next move, he buys a house in a neighborhood of executives who feel the same way he does, with whom he shares this indifference. To an increasing extent, his firm follows him into the suburbs. In such circumstances, social issues may be abstractions which have little meaning in his life. It would be interesting, for example, to determine how many corporate executives know where the seat of local government is located in the towns where they camp.

The self-image of a manager responsible for a social goal also affects the extent of its realization. Usually, his corporate performance is judged according to short-term specific economic and technical criteria such as production and efficiency.[3] Frequently, the judgment of whether he is a good company man rests on intangible factors that make him insecure and impel him to pull off a show of loyalty to his superior; he may have to like playing golf if the boss does. His discharge of vaguely defined social objectives may add to his sense of insecurity.

The issue of corporate social responsibility is likely to arouse the interest of institutional stockholders. Universities with enormous corporate holdings are vulnerable to student pressure on the issue. These universities may be pressured into looking at the corporation beyond their financial interests. It is reasonable to assume that universities will yield increasingly to such pressure.[4]

In the area of government intervention to increase corporate social responsibility, two avenues of direct action suggest themselves. The government can hold hearings to nationalize a corporation when by some yardstick it appears the firm has acquired an over-riding social interest. Or the corporation can be required to apply for a national charter when it reaches such a point of social interest. In the second case, specific social controls can be imposed on issuance of the charter, whereas the first alternative of nationalization is likely to produce the greater bureaucracy; we have reached a point where solutions increasing the government bureaucracy are the least desirable. An added merit of the charter

[3] In a study covering over a thousand corporate managers, rated highest by respondents as indicators of success were efficiency and profit maximization and lowest employee and social welfare. (G. W. England, "Organizational Goals and Expected Behavior of American Managers," Vol. 10, *Academy of Management Journal*, 1967.

[4] For the emergence of such policy at Yale University, see John J. Simon, Charles W. Powers, and Jon P. Gunneman, *The Ethical Investor*, New Haven, Conn.: Yale University Press, 1972. The book defines corporate social injury as behavior violating norms meant to afford protection of health, safety, and basic freedoms. The guidelines appear to draw a distinction between voting stock in order to correct a social injury and voting stock to pursue a social goal.

approach is the opportunity it affords for stipulating social controls through participatory democracy.

The government could also take indirect initiatives to encourage socialization of production. It could require television networks to present consumer information programs. It could bring forward the issue of whether social benefits are individual benefits. Because people are so closely quartered and so liable to the effects of mass culture, the government could take steps to protect the rights of the minority from the cultural tyranny of the majority. However, it is unlikely that government would take such measures without organized public pressure. Greater socialization of production could also be gained through the deployment of research and development funds. Government could use such funds to develop socially useful products, consistent with some yardstick measuring priorities.

Within the organization, the corporate official could be made individually responsible for the social consequences of his acts. He could be judged by a system of rewards applied to the manner in which he pursues well-defined social goals and be made accountable to higher levels of management as to the extent to which he fulfills them. The social objective will be ignored by the manager who knows he is being judged on other terms. Employees who report anti-social corporate behavior could be protected by the law. Lastly, social objectives could be incorporated into the standards for the measurement of the overall performance of subunits in the organization.

The individual firm is limited as to the extent to which it can make a social commitment and survive. Restraints on the profit motive must be applied uniformly among competing firms. An appreciable rise in the level of corporate social responsibility can best be generated on an industry-wide basis. Whether this broader application should come from industry, government, or community initiative is a question which will be explored later. In any case, the end result must be industry-wide standards.

Analysis of the corporation's responsibility to society leads to a consideration of its responsibility to the individual and thus to our second issue. Does organization stifle the growth of individuality? A question far too complex to be treated adequately in summary fashion, it is discussed at this juncture in its broad dimensions.

To assert categorically that organization suppresses individual expression at all its levels is to oversimplify. An appreciable decline has occurred in arbitrariness on the job. An educated toiler who likes to be given the opportunity to make decisions within his area of technical competence is often provided the opportunity by big corporations in their own self-interest. The talents required to operate a big firm are so many and so diverse as to provide imaginative managers with considerable leeway in matching jobs and workers. As technology converts work into analysis, these opportunities increase. There are few Leonardo da Vincis in organizations employing thousands of white-collar workers; the problem of giving these employees a chance to do their pirouette is surmountable. The biggest cruelties of anti-individuality are inflicted upon blue-collar workers. The fine subdivision and simplification of their labor crushes their creativity and initiative. Blue-collar workers excepted—they are considered fair game as automatons—the issue of man versus organization seems to be more urgent and complex in man's function as a consumer and citizen and in the tempo with which he discharges these roles.

For those who see in the deemphasis on productivity as a criterion of employment more opportunities for self-actualization, the rise in public employment brings good tidings. As law and political influence become a basis for hiring, the opportunity for quick euphoria early in one's career increases for those with political connections. In New York City, for example, a young black Vietnam war veteran was assigned the post of director in charge of pest control at $22,000 annually. The young man's sponsors, friends of the mayor, point out that the practice of hiring a person with political connections is sound since so much government work involves liking people. Since the man was hired, they add, reported rat bites declined 30 percent.[5]

As a consumer in society, the individual's impulses must be plugged into a system of profit making. It would be unprofitable if the individual were to acquire satisfaction from his inner self alone. The structuring of desires consistent with the needs of profit making is facilitated by mass communications media acting as conduits for commercial interests. For the system to work, advertising propaganda must make man feel impoverished. Because he feels deprived, he cannot be loving; and because he cannot be loving he cannot be happy.

As a citizen, the individual's mind must be managed in a way that promotes the orderly operation of government organization. The contest over the right of information between government and mass media is one of whether the individual should be manipulated for political or commercial interests. Both employ the same strategy: the dissemination of fantasy over reality. Moreover, the subdivision of work as an employee tends to impose blinders on his view of the collective impact of his corporation on society and environment.

5 *The New York Times,* November 29, 1971.

These remarks do not mean to dismiss out of hand the issue of individuality in a person's role as employee. Certainly, the sense of self-worth acquired even by workers of professional status is tempered by the realities of being an employee. But the gaff a professional employee takes can often be reduced by effective labor organization. An employee who wishes to promote greater individual satisfaction in work must organize and force the firm to adopt such a goal. Exhortation is unlikely to do it. He may acquire greater individual satisfaction through forcing an increase both in the operation each employee performs and in the collaboration and independent decisions he makes. But these goals are likely to curtail productivity in the short run, and firms abhor such a result.

In some instances a technician's self-satisfying contribution as an employee may curtail his role as a citizen. An engineer, for instance, may know the impact of his corporation on the environment and may thus be able to assist community groups to defend themselves. But because he is afraid of jeopardizing his job, he keeps his mouth shut.

Moreover, it should not be assumed that the extent of individuality or the nature of the organization in which it unfolds is a constant. As a social entity, the organization imposes itself upon the individual via a shifting set of constraints. In turn, the individual presents a different personality to each organization personality. What may be a constraint for one individual may be a stimulant for another; what is one man's meat may be another man's poison. Who dominates whom varies with each organization-individual confrontation. An individual's ability to control his organization and to find one that best fits his personality tends to vary. Competition between organizations and equality of opportunity are important factors in determining this ability.

Accordingly, the extent of accommodation between organization and individual varies to some degree according to characteristics of the person. The difficulties individuals have in organizations at times mirror their incapacity to relate to the personalities of others. With the exception of those trained for such a purpose, many persons do not listen effectively; their sense of inadequacy affects what they hear. They commit violence on others as they lament the other person's lack of sensitivity. The iconoclast may find the generation of these irritations tolerable if necessary in order to gain structural changes in the organization. But he is faced with the reality that peers and superiors prefer being associated with persons who abide by procedures.

The third issue to be considered has to do with the nature of corporate thought processes. A corporation tries to think systematically. Academics tend to provide as many systems of thought as the number of promotions available in their institutions. The crop of techniques in systematic thinking proliferates like a nuclear chain reaction that has gone out of control. They include Simulation Technique, Multivariate Analysis, Classical Regression Analysis, and Bayesian Decision Theory Applied to Two-Tail Testing. The fad is harmless if not taken seriously; it fills a need of technicians to promote their careers. It has been pointed out that had a management specialist applied Simulation Technique in 1890 on the urban transportation problem, he might well have concluded that by 1970 the cities would be inundated with horse manure.

Corporations acquire respectability by adopting these systems. The firm gains a reputation for applying a rigorous analysis, whatever its fashionable title, to the identification and solution of problems. In broad terms, these bodies of thought comprise a systematic way in which to observe a particular subsystem. The area of observation can range from a particular subunit of the organization to the corporation in relation to other subsystems in the larger society.

These observations are summarized in terms of inputs going into the particular system, which in combination produce a particular result. The inputs, or explanatory variables, comprise a state, object, or event whose absence or presence produces observable behavior. By employing variables that capture causal factors and that lend themselves to conversion into numbers, the organization can ascertain what combination of variables would produce a desired result. By fixing the objective, the firm ascertains the values of variables necessary to achieve a predetermined goal.

Management specialists try to adapt these models to an explanation of human behavior. By summarizing a behavioral matrix in terms of the personality of the individuals involved, the characteristics of the environment in which they act, and their perception of that environment, it can be speculated as to what combination of explanatory variables are required to gain a desired social result. Such a human behavior matrix could conceivably be used to determine what public policy would command a broad consensus. This determination can be achieved by a system of trial and error by which tentative policy proposals are examined so as to anticipate possible outcomes.

Such systems of thought generate horror in some quarters, an abhorrence which stems from the conviction that they are employed to manipulate individuals for purposes not fully disclosed. Such concern has some substance. The inputs fed into the system and the stipulated goals reflect the ideology of those who control it. They may have an enlightened view that desired behavior should be sought in a system of open negotiation, or they may be concerned primarily with serving the not fully disclosed purposes of top management. But the role these systems play in decision making should not be given undue importance. Organization decision making emerges less from the techniques of university professors catering to the needs of managers and more as an act of politics within the organization.

Another issue of note derives from the imperative of continuing and ever increasing production. A big organization faces the prospect of mounting costs progressively eroding its net income and threatening its long term stability. It is therefore compelled to develop new markets and to advertise its products. This compulsion of bigness is often tied to the manager's joy in exercising power. He acquires prestige and a sense of self-importance by virtue of playing with an increasing number of chess pieces. When shorn of his badge of office or when caught in unfavorable publicity, he often emerges as a man of small stature.

The imperative of bigness produces increasing bads for the individual and society. To sell more often requires deceiving the public into thinking it is getting a new product as well as burdening society with the costs of such products. The drive for bigness manifested in the agglomeration of firms crossing industry lines frequently ends in undue political influence and corruption. Sooner or later society is forced to intervene and control these excesses.

The imperative of continuing production has a special wrinkle in the case of defense firms. Government must underwrite their continued existence. If these firms fall into crisis several options are available: Government can take a laissez-faire posture, which it doesn't; the government can provide funds for the continuance of customary production; or these firms can be required to shift production to forms more in keeping with social priorities.

If the public elects to arrest the rise in non-defense production, can it be done without destroying the viability of the firm? The system would become chaotic if corporate life were not maintained. To accomplish the goal of a shift toward social production, the firm may be required to convert its advertising into information, including the social costs of product and processes. If such information causes unemployment, planning would be necessary to shift the resources of the organization into more socially useful production.

Television could be employed to stimulate such a change in production. Programs could dwell on the full costs of the automobile. Foreign as well as domestic comparisons could be made. If, for example, people in Philadelphia were made aware of subway systems in such cities as Stockholm, Montreal, and Mexico City, they may be more disposed to exert pressure for similar transportation. So employed, television could become a tool of participatory democracy.

The last issue to be raised has to do with the sensitivity of organizational power to individual initiative. When one looks closely at power in the United States, a paradox appears. Not entirely without merit, the idea that political and economic power is concentrated in the hands of a few has been drummed by intellectuals into the public consciousness. But it has also been observed that at times an intelligent and courageous person can effectively challenge these huge concentrations of power. Armed only with brains and a law degree, for example, one person was able to shake up the biggest corporation in the world and make its chief executive render a public apology.

There are many reasons why this is so. The biggest one probably lies in a combination of two realities: the way in which instant communication dramatically exposes and distorts the failings of the managerial class and the disposition of people not to knuckle under to power.

The necessary diffusion of power within organizations has something to do with this optimistic attitude. The increasingly complex factors that must be weighed to make a decision require the employment of specialists who cannot be dictated to. The manager who refers to a decision *he* made suffers from delusion. Moreover, the production of a variety of products and services by the same organization serves to intensify the cooperative nature of decision making and thus the diffusion as opposed to the concentration of power.

Other factors contribute to the decline of awe for power. Trade unions for a century have whittled down unilateral decision making on the part of the employer. Managers themselves are products of institutions of higher learning that foster an attitude of tolerance. And the decline in the cultural chasm between Wasp manager and inferior ethnic has brought the image of the manager down a peg.

Nevertheless, it is not entirely clear how this democratization in production affects the attitude of the individual as to his position relative to power in his function as consumer and citizen. His specialization cannot be used as a leverage in this role. Thus, he may feel an equal in his producer organization but bewildered when confronting the myriad consumer and citizen organizations that claim to promote his interests.

We have thus observed the big corporate organization in its response to both social and individual needs, in its use of systems of thought in the identification and solution of problems, in its reaction to the imperatives of production, and in the nature of the power it wields. To conclude, we bring forward estimates of the future within the frame of these organization characteristics and issues. The big corporations are likely to respond to new challenges by structuring into their organizations a scanning mechanism that incorporates these challenges into their planning. While corporations seek to control the values of society to better pursue their interests, they also rally around emergent ones in the interest of survival. As the society's values change, corporate managers pragmatically accommodate to them. Such is not to say that some corporations will not continue to seek a new coloration through pretense. The advertising profession is always disposed to provide such a service. But such improvisation is unlikely to endure.

In view of this accommodation to new ideas, an intensive revolt against organization is unlikely. An attitude change may surface slowly that may produce a relative decline in the importance of quantity of goods and a rise in the value of quality. As government is forced by public pressure to make such a shift through a variety of prescriptions, the private profits system could be converted into the social profits system. The change from a profit economy to a social economy may take place as resources are increasingly allocated consistent with preconceived social goals. A revolt against quantity would undermine the foundations of the corporation and the economy as a whole.

Contrary to past, in the new attitudes that emerge is a deep mistrust of government. The general decline of belief in elitism, the grievous errors made by government, weaken the image of public institutions as seats of wisdom and justice. The behavior of government employees in seeking changes in their terms of employment increases further the contempt for government. Without acceptable institutions with which to channel the protest, a populist reaction against big organization may border on the chaotic. Therefore what may issue is the imposition of social accountability upon organization through the emergence of participatory democracy as a tool for controlling the decision making of big organization, including industrial firms, public organizations, and government itself.

Consequently, the United States emerges as a revolutionary nation in the capitalist camp. Its capacity for revolution derives from a blend of a penchant for excess, a reaction in a sense of outrage, and an optimistic faith in the capacity to change things for the better. The absence of an ideological commitment by the firm weakens its resistance to such a groundswell for change. While a firm may conceive of man as an unredeemable object to be used for the promotion of its interests, it promptly changes its outlook if people in significant numbers acquire a vision of a better life and seek it. And they do, despite corporate blandishments that blur the vision. As they do, the corporations abandon the old-time faith for the new; they adjust their operations consistent with the new ideology. During the reconstruction of these relationships, the conflict so quickly and dramatically recorded in an open society such as the

United States should not be construed as the manifestation of an oppressive order. Open conflict is rather a process of acquisition of consensus as a revolution proceeds in course.

The big defense corporations straddling the public and private sectors are most susceptible to such a revolution. More sensitive to public pressure, they have the mechanism to analyze social problems. As new opportunities in the private sector become scarce and as defense production declines, their markets lie in social production. As they move into such production, they are likely to affect firms in the private sector both in outlook and structure. In this way, the emerging values of the society may be structured into the system.

This brings us to our fundamental question: what are the social responsibilities of corporations. The contemporary attack against the corporation is not the traditional one of disaffection with particular practices of firms in pursuing their role as an economic institution. Rather, the assault raises fundamental questions on the relationship of individual and organization. It poses the challenge that the entire array of corporate behavior and effects should be consistent with what the individual feels is proper in his relations with other individuals. It poses an unprecedented demand that the morality of the corporation should be in harmony with the morality of the individual. It requests that the individual be given a sense of personal responsibility and dominance over the system. The criticism is leveled at the propriety of a dual system of norms: one for organization behavior and another for individual behavior. Furthermore, this posture is directed not only at corporations, but at big organization generally including government.

If this observation is correct, only some form of mass participation in decision making is likely to bring a new era of reconciliation between corporation and society. The individual who believes organization to be corrupt is unlikely to accept domination of his life by unilaterally made decisions of organization, no matter how equitable these decisions may be. Moreover, if corporate self-policing will not be taken seriously, more government regulation would be even less so.

Therefore, no amount of internal corporate changes in structures and policies may achieve a new stage of stability. Yet, the literature that dwells on this contemporary challenge sees the accommodation in terms not of institutional changes external to the corporation but in terms of corporate changes within.

These are possible avenues by which individuals may seek more dominance over organization:

> demand greater and more reliable information be disseminated by organizations, including estimates of bads created by their product and processes;

voting of corporate blocs of stock owned by institutions not primarily motivated by profit;

local monitoring of corporations by community alliances tied to urban universities as a source of technical information;

federal chartering of firms that acquire an overriding social interest;

protect the right of corporate employees to disseminate information on anti-social practices of the corporation;

require the government to convert consumer advertising into informational advertising;

organization of corporate employees for purposes of collective bargaining;

develop colleges of business that educate in addition to training technicians;

charter community broadcasting corporations under public subscription with existing stations required to donate time and facilities for broadcasting of local and national issues;

national planning of priorities including deploying of research and development funds by a board with public representatives making recommendations to the Congress;

in new land development, accepting corporate plants on condition the firm recognizes by charter its obligations to the community in which it locates.

The corporation lives by sufferance of the society. It tends to become an embodiment of the values of those segments of the larger society from which it draws personnel, demand, information, and prescriptions. Its social responsibilities are whatever the education process and the public make them. Education instructs the business not only in technique but also in what is proper and improper in corporate behavior. The instruction varies, depending on whether it emanates from a Harvard Business School, a Columbia University School of Business, or one of the institutional mills that grind out degrees in business administration. At the same time, through government and other forms of collective actions such as community initiatives, the public prescribes and proscribes corporate behavior. Such is not to say the public dictates terms; rather it expects the corporation to negotiate. Emerging policies, as in pluralistic settlements generally, reflect differences in the power to persuade. Furthermore, as these corporations structure their listening posts in self-defense, they provide better channels of communication through which the public can impress its point of view.

Thus, the constraint of education, directly or indirectly, progressively increases its power over the yardstick of doing whatever the market will bear. The constraint of education is not just that provided by schools, but also that of the learning process generally. In school, if a manager pursues studies in business administration to promote his career, he cannot escape the impact of some of his instructors on his sense of social responsibility. In some colleges of business he buys not just a degree but a conscience.

It would therefore seem imperative that schools of business focus their attention on the *why* of business as well as on the *what* of business, that they teach analytical theory and explore human values. For we live in an age that questions critically the performance of business. Should this disparity of viewpoint between school and society prevail, the most intelligent students are likely to shun business education and the schools may become homes for dullards.

Our view of the corporation applies in its essentials to big organizations generally, including government. The differences in sources of income and in profit making versus budget balancing of non-profit organization are not of sufficient importance to justify separating for purposes of discussion profit from non-profit organizations. Business becomes more and more like any organization, and organization becomes more and more like business.

This sketch of the corporation as organization elucidates the contemporary realities of management in society. The modern American corporation has considerable power. It controls human and economic resources, consumer tastes, the relative distribution of income, the environment, technology markets; it is not simply a business. The corporation is the tool with which modern life is managed. Therefore, it is essential that it be understood within its context of the larger society. To this end, we next turn to life at the base of this societal structure.

PART
TWO

THE
SOCIAL
FRAMEWORK

4

The Demoralization
of American Life

*The characteristic of the time is that the vulgar spirit,
conscious of its vulgarity, has the gall to affirm the right
of vulgarity and to impose it everywhere.*
                                        Ortega y Gasset

Americans lead the world in consumption. Correspondingly, they are also the world's champion polluters. For years, Americans have used air and waterways as garbage receptacles. Now, like the Sicilian *mafioso* who spat at heaven, they get it right back. Even employing the ocean as a dump poses limits. Close to land, waste causes pollution. Out at sea, low temperatures and low oxygen preserve wastes in a state of refrigeration. Were a tidal wave suddenly to stir the ocean bottom, New Yorkers could get 70 years of waste back in their faces. Our attention first turns to the culture of this affluent people threatened by their own waste.

It is difficult, even presumptuous, to make general observations about all Americans. American society comprises many different social groups, and in each one, individual differences exist. To discuss these groups at length falls beyond our purpose. Our concern instead will be confined to the examination of 5 segments of the population that do not fall into neat scholarly classifications, but which nevertheless exert a noteworthy influence on the system. They comprise college students, members of the corporate middle class, intellectuals, white blue-collar workers, and urban blacks. These 5 groups often have different positions on major issues. Thus, on the Vietnam intervention, the students were the most

45

privileged and the most critical; the corporate class would rather not have thought about it; the intellectuals manifested their general peace loving nature, save Israel and Bangladesh; white blue-collarites were so frustrated generally that they would have had the war over by obliterating the enemy outright; and the blacks furnished more than their relative share of sacrifice. Both urban blacks and college students together with their faculties and administrators are discussed later in an institutional setting. In this section, after an overview of the social setting, we discuss the corporate class, white ethnics, and intellectuals.

THE DEMORALIZATION OF AMERICAN LIFE

The evolution of traditional patterns of western culture has come to a halt in American society. In its place there has arisen a mass marketed culture of sight, feeling, and sound. With this change the deference to the man of culture traditional in western populations has been replaced with esteem for images of consumption and money making. The deterioration of traditional restraints generated by the emerging shift and the resulting conflict between cultural groups fosters demoralization. We present in this chapter evidence of this demoralization as seen in certain aspects of modern American life.

Literature and the Arts. Deviation in human behavior preoccupies the mind of the American intelligentsia. In the social and behavioral sciences, in the performing arts, in mass media, in literature, the focus falls on aberration in human experience. The lewdness for sale evidences the deterioration of the social fabric that holds together American society.

The assault on human worth is under the generalship of writers of limited artistry and credit card revolutionaries who would be held in contempt by those with a legitimate claim to the title of revolutionary. A psychology journal has a cover that vies with that of *Playboy Magazine.* A movie reaches a climax with a resounding fart. A play presents sexual intercourse without love in a manner that poses a problem of what to do if the public demands an encore. Unencumbered by a sense of self-worth, writers disgorge a stream of sexual fantasies which they market as literature. Some even acquire reputations as intellectuals. One writer earns for the nation the reputation of having raised the world's best masturbator. Coarseness and artlessness are chic; they gain mass markets. The cult of mass marketed vulgarity that goes under the name of culture nurtures a generation incapable of drawing a distinction between art and fraud. Its purveyors look down their noses at the folk tastes of ethnics. Underwritten by liberals, the cult of aberration strips man of his unique qualities. The culture describes a community playing encounter at the bottom of an active privy.

The cult of shock is a form of violence needed by the apathetic to jar themselves into feeling. They require this violence and the society obligingly mass produces it for them in literature, in pornography, in art, and even in the vicarious experience of warfare. The need to shock and be shocked expresses the need to be sadistic; and beneath that need is self-hatred. If the public unexpectedly became bored with sexual gymnastics and denigrating words in books, movies, and theater, the gross national product would be dealt a serious blow.[1]

Firms publish non-books that focus on shock at the expense of truth. Their authors have mastered the art of catering profitably to the society's corruption and thereby make loads of money. Sex as a gymnastic technique commands more money than sex as an act of love. Sex is never the object of laughter.

The New York Times carries these ads:

> The book revolves around the trial of a Los Angeles bookstore owner charged with selling the most obscene piece of pornography ever written. The long banned work (telling a women's thoughts during seven minutes of sexual intercourse) is condemned not only for obscenity, but for having driven a respectable college student to rape and murder.
>
> *A Man for the Asking* has been banned in Italy, the German magazine *Stern* called it the most indecent book of the year. The teenage Catherine writes of sex with such whorehouse candor that the image of Francoise Sagan may yet be reshaped into something resembling, say, Louisa May Alcott.
>
> To her family, she was a saloon slut, unfit ever to enter their home again. To her ex-husband, she was a white nigger. To the countless men she had known, she was the perfect lover, bold in the bedroom, shy in public.[2]

Trade in erotica is one of the most booming businesses in the United States. Annual sales estimated at over a billion dollars serve the needs of the consumer in books, magazines, movies, pictures, and artificial penises. The right to his pornography becomes an intellectual cause.

[1] The report by the Commission on Obscenity and Pornography in 1970 recommending the removal of statutory restraints on pornography was rejected by President Nixon. As a piece of research, it deserved no better fate. By the use of dubious research methods, the report suggsts that whatever little effect pornography may have tends to be a good one, as evidenced by the superior positions consumers of pornography have. It goes to the point of suggesting that persons who consume erotica are superior to those who do not. The report exemplifies a common practice of using research to give respectability to conclusions previously arrived at.

[2] *The New York Times,* Sunday Book Review, September 28, 1969.

Books making best seller lists are defended on the basis of freedom by those making money on them. Tastes divide along social lines. Those of intellectuals converge on these best sellers, amply illustrated tracts, and expensive nude theater. Those of the working class focus on hard core pornography and peep shows. Intellectuals ignoring these social distinctions run the risk of becoming *declassé*. As sales in erotica break records, so does the venereal disease rate. In California, the state public health director asserts that the rate has reached epidemic proportions and that the government is unable to cope with the problem.

Pundits claim that it is not that the aberration has actually risen, but that it is only more accurately reported, more concentrated, and hence more visible. The Greenwich Village neighborhood in New York City is cited as an example. Formerly attractive because of its light touch and authenticity as an Italian ethnic enclave, the village now has the heavy presence of derelicts, neurotics, guitar-plucking hippies, addicts, and panhandlers. Its largest Italian parish, Our Lady of Pompei, reports that its confessionals are used for defecation.

The mass marketing of sex affirms the genius of the system in converting human needs into forms conducive to profit making; even Jesus falls within the bounds of legitimacy. To maximize profits, the arts move from the fanciful to the bizarre and from the bizarre to the fraudulent. Movie and theater producers, book and newspaper publishers are purveyors of sensation. The ultimate success of the profit motive will be achieved when man no longer can or wants to discern the truth and when the distinction between man and the other primates will have blurred. In this regimen of pleasure instantly concocted and instantly consumed the last scene will be one in which artist and mass consumer would be locked in an embrace of equality.[3]

Education and Religion.   The educational system contributes to the estrangement and demoralization in society. American education knows no middle ground between creating immature anarchists of little use to themselves and to others and developing crippled children resigned to their imposed impairment. Permissive liberals equate liberation with the avoidance of making intellectual demands on youth, and thus children grew up without authoritative images. Adults are not symbols of wisdom, but buddies or rejects who have no youth and hence have nothing. The heroes of children are the false personalities perpetrated by mass media developing the cult of youth for profit. Teachers dwell

---

3 The scandal reaches beyond unscrupulous publishing houses with an established reputation for sensation mongering. Reputable firms including McGraw-Hill, Harper & Row, Stein & Day, and Little-Brown have published books that have acquired a reputation of spuriousness, cavalier treatment of facts, and questionable authenticity.

on respect for child society and norms at the expense of encouraging emulation of adults who are images of worthy persons. Adolescents, mostly black males, are converting Philadelphia into one vast privy house, while the liberal minded hesitate to criticize or rebuke out of fear of stifling individuality. There is little likelihood that a Michelangelo will issue from the ranks of these muralists.

It is difficult to have a cohesive society without a common respect for symbols of informed authority. The lack of cohesiveness reflects the absence of common purpose. American education has yet to reconcile the goal of individual expression with the demands society can legitimately make for the use of its resources.

Religion as a rule of living declines as norms of behavior are inculcated by commercial interests. Through their reading of the constitution, the courts contribute to the decline of religion. The idea of accommodation to a universal will vanishes. Politicians do not permit religious principle to interfere with their decisions. They relegate religion to the last sentence of their speeches which places God on the side of the policies. Christianity as a norm of behavior in the system is dead, its demise brought about by the imperatives of the system. A practicing Christian might end up in jail or in a lunatic asylum.

Morality comprises acts of individuals. The reduction of religion to statements of lofty principle converts religion into nothing. In the face of the atrocities in Vietnam, the Roman Catholic hierarchy maintains an awkward silence. It professes a morality of words only. By so doing, the Church becomes a discredited voice in its own community.

The system reduces religion to ceremony and socializing. Taking religion seriously would cause chaos, for it would conflict with the system's hedonistic foundation. The current fashion of converting faith into pleasant sensation poses no threat, nor does the effort of intellectuals to convert God into another intellectual. If religious success is measured in numbers, the faith of greatest prominence is a simplistic one that gives its adherents an emotional experience and preserves obsolete views on how the system works.

Man successfully reaches out for a higher order of life by becoming servant to a transcendental vision. He becomes a better man as he rises above an ego adjusting to his social environment. But a famine exists in the affluent society: a famine of human purpose.

The Law. The law, and its interpretation, is the portrait at a given moment of the power relationships in the society. The law is administered by judges who serve on the bench principally because of political connections. In these circumstances, the law tends to become a game of power. Activists show contempt for law; crooks say the hell with it;

politicians place it at the disposal of the powerful; and business men pervert it to serve their interests. Government ignores law in international relations; trade unions rise above the law; and little people, like damn fools, abide by it.

Traditionally, the law has been used an an instrument of containing the poor in the interest of promoting the workability of the system. The poor would tip the balance of law in their favor when they threatened political instability. The antipoverty program providing legal services for the poor provided to the unsystem the use of law against the system. Consequently, the innovation incurred the wrath of its elites.

The hideous futility running through the unrestrained use of the system's legal power is a major strand running through American life. Americans are sensitive to the use of power but harsh as they employ it themselves. There is a touch of infantilism in this show of power. If the English have a flair for using power with a light touch, it has not rubbed off on their American cousins.

For law enforcement is heavy handed. A black student on his way to the United States from Canada is ordered by American customs officials to descend from his bus on suspicion of possessing subversive literature. (If the student were taking a course in Soviet economics, he could easily possess material the law may consider subversive.) The officials call the FBI to make a check on the man, which turns out to be negative. While awaiting this reply, they order that the man be searched. The black panics, wounds three of the officials with a pistol, and kills himself.[4]

A mentally retarded boy in Los Angeles is seen by the police running along a sidewalk and suddenly slowing down. He is frisked and reaches for his wallet. One of the two policemen shouts: "He has a gun!" The boy is killed. No gun is found. The fear reaction has some basis in fact. In 1968, the importation of low price guns was barred. Within one year, the system's manufacture of hand guns rose from 75,000 to 500,000. Police killings have risen sharply in the big cities. In 1969, the figure went over a hundred. Further increases occurred in the next two years.[5]

Doctor Raymond Raglund, a black pharmacologist, is walking through his integrated middle class neighborhood in Philadelphia on his way to buy cigarettes. He is stopped by two highway patrolmen who order him to identify himself. He remonstrates. He is hauled off to jail after being hit with a nightstick and punched in the abdomen.

---

[4] *The New York Times*, September 27, 1969.
[5] The data on guns are from *The New York Times*, April 29, 1969. Police killing data are from *Uniform Crime Reports for the United States*, Federal Bureau of Investigation, Washington, D.C.

A white man of 21 strikes a bus with his car in a tense racially mixed New York neighborhood. A black in civilian clothes demands to see his registration. The youth remonstrates; a scuffle ensues. The Negro, who turns out to be a policeman on vacation, holds the youth by the neck with one hand and with the other shoots him dead in the heart. No riot.[6]

Willie Stewart, a 17-year old black convicted of burglary, is sentenced to serve a one-day sentence in a Little Rock, Arkansas prison, a punishment which is supposed to convince him that crime does not pay. After a day of hazing, including having shots fired at his feet and doing pushups outside the chaplain's office, he dies.[7]

In some metropolitan areas, police strip women for misdemeanors and search their bodies. A society matron received the treatment during the 1968 Chicago police riot. In New York State, two suburbanite secretaries were given the same processing after protesting delays in train schedules on the Long Island Railroad by refusing to show their commuter tickets.

It may be futile to lodge a protest against the police in big cities. The police may respond by placing a disorderly conduct charge against you, or beat you up and charge you with resisting arrest. Philadelphia's former police commissioner, Frank Rizzo, states that a policeman should have the security of knowing he will be supported by his fellow police if he makes a mistake, a sentiment often popularly attributed to the mafia. To defend themselves in litigation involving the integrity of the police force, the police are disposed to lie through their teeth. And neither judges nor jurors are inclined to hold them to account. Police who abuse their power go off scot free. Thus, the overseers of the law appear to be highly immune from law enforcement.

The federal cops, the late J. Edgar Hoover's beloved FBI, are busily establishing a network of stool pigeons who inform on associates in the name of maintaining a free society. In a Philadelphia suburb college, the switchboard operator got a professor on an FBI 3 by 5 index card because of his odd behavior. In a nearby university, an elderly priest informed the FBI that his young colleague had taken off in an automobile for the weekend just prior to the bombing of the national capitol building. The young priest's name is now on file too.

A policeman's role is undeniably a difficult one. He must oversee the behavior of citizens and bring to court those who overstep the bounds set by the system. The job's complexity is enhanced, first because overseeing the behavior of people attracts a type of personality inclined to

6 *The New York Times*, July 6, 1971.
7 *The New York Times*, December 12, 1971.

abuse such authority and second because the policeman feels pressure from the system to impose restrictions on change. As preserver of the status quo, he becomes a scapegoat.

Police are a measure of the community's deficiencies. Whereas they are duty bound to uphold the law, a majority of police-reported crimes go unpunished. Their efforts are undermined by a judicial system that moves criminal repeaters in and out of courts like through a revolving door. The police are vilified by aggressive minority groups supported by white liberals looking for causes. The mechanization of police work and their assumption of traffic violation duties makes it difficult for people in the community to identify with them. If elements in society have a grievance against the police, the policeman has a valid grievance against the society. It is easy to point out police excesses. But little is done to remove the conditions causing them.

Variation does exist in police behavior. Most of them are neither stupid nor sadistic. They reflect the fears and aspirations of social groups with whom they identify. Some are professional males whose sense of masculinity is strengthened by their armament of blackjack, handcuffs, nightstick, and gun. When these latent aggressors meet head-on with persons whose values appear different or who are a threat to their power, some policemen become a law unto themselves. Policemen are at their best when they seek to cool social conflict rather than suppress it. There is no such thing as an imposed solution to emotionally charged social conflict; competent policemen sense this. These variations in their behavior generate hope of an overall rise in the level of their performance.

The changing nature of violence in the metropolitan areas compounds the complex problems facing the police. Violence has become more an act of irrationality. A lawyer writes:

> I wish to report that my brother has been murdered on the afternoon of September 2, 1971. My brother Seymour Schneider who in his lifetime had never raised a hand in violence against another, was shot in the head twice and robbed.
>
> Murder has become commonplace. It has joined the crimes of mugging and rape in occurring with such frequency that newspapers seldom report them.
>
> When I went to the medical examiner's office to identify his body, I was given a number to await my turn, as we are given numbers in a busy retail shop.
>
> The grotesque, the monstrous, the aberrant, the perverted have become the common and the commonplace, the usual—and God help us— the expected.[8]

8 *The New York Times*, October 16, 1971.

Traditionally, violent crime in the United States has been handed down from one ethnic group to another like an old suit of clothes. The Irish and Jews had their day so long ago that it takes a far-reaching nostalgia to remember a Legs Diamond or a Lepke. The Italians who took over next have also passed their zenith, yielding the crown to the blacks, who have now assumed the record for violent crimes. The blacks have a beautiful ongoing racket; there is a certain novelty attached to their crimes. Supported by high-minded liberals, they are difficult to convict when they claim their violence was politically inspired. Sadly, as they rise up the social ladder and claim equal right of embezzlement with Wasps, crookedness will lose its ethnicity.

But the violence of these times has the new element of the joy of cruelty. It permeates more than just the working class. Violence is romanticized. A survey by the *Christian Science Monitor* of 7 days of television programs on the 3 major networks reveals 84 killings in as many hours of programming. Three hundred and seventy-two acts of violence or threats of violence were recorded, almost half on Saturday morning when most of the audience consists of children. The most violent evening hours were between seven-thirty and nine when some 27 million children are watching.[9] With the acquiescence of the national government, research suggesting the association of television crime with violence has been played down.

The United States is more violent than other western nations of similar economic standards. It leads the world in homicide after Guatemala and Nicaragua. For a long time, American sociologists have been critical of statistics of rising crime published by the Federal Bureau of Investigation, statistics that indicate increases since 1960. In 1970, under the Nixon's law and order administration, the crime rate increased by 11 percent. These increases used to be shrugged off on grounds that they were inflated by more accurate reporting and by petty property offenses such as auto thefts. Two specialists in criminology, Lloyd E. Ohlin of Harvard University and Marvin E. Wolfgang of the University of Pennsylvania, now concede that violent crime in the United States is indeed rising.[10] The judicial system cannot cope with the causes behind these new patterns of violence.

Justice can have a light touch also. In Philadelphia, Judge Joseph Sloane ordered the Electric Factory, a midcity psychedelic music spot

9 *The New York Times,* July 25, 1968.
10 The FBI annual crime report of 1970 states a 148 percent rise in crime during the decade 1960–1969. During the period, the number of murders rose to 14,950, for a rate of 7.2 per 1000, the highest in the South. Sixty-five percent of the murders are committed with firearms. Rapes, generally underestimated because of undisclosure by victims, increased 93 percent. *Crime in the United States,* 1970, Federal Bureau of Investigation, Washington, D.C.

closed as a public nuisance. The suit was instituted after Police Commissioner Rizzo visited the club and found it wanting. Judge Sloane found that the club was replete with monkey bars and sliding boards. Donald C. Goldberg, attorney, stated that he had gone down the sliding board twice and all he got out of the experience was flashing pictures. In a learned opinion, Judge Sloane wrote:

> Unlike the Academy of Music, where one hears the orchestra of Toscanini or Stokowski, or Ormandy, the Electric Factory caters to other groups known variously as Peanut Butter Conspiracy, the Jefferson Airplane, or Country Joe and the Fish.
>
> Such a place of amusement is not a place of quiet mirth.[11]

Justice can be injustice when used as a tool for business interests. After paying his mortgage for 14 years, and with less than $200 to go, Frank Saunders, a semi-skilled worker, falls sick and loses his job. He misinterprets and ignores a letter threatening to take action against him under the law. His house is placed on sheriff sale and is bought by his mortgagee. Mr. Saunders is ordered to pay rent or get out.[12]

The use of the judicial system to dun the working class is a multi-million dollar business comprising evictions, wage-garnishee actions, and attachments of personal property. Under the aegis of local government, city marshals armed with summonses obtained from the courts derive their income from the misfortune of the poor. In New York City there is on record one such marshal who grossed an income of $167,000 in 1967.[13] The marshal business is a legitimate racket fostered by a system that employs government to serve private economic interests. The system cons individuals into buying what they cannot afford and then punishes them for so doing. Respectable bankers are often part of the swindle. Employers selling a product or service to a customer on the installment plan can sell the financing to a bank. The bank is interested in collecting the money and not in the fraudulent character of the sale.

To a considerable degree, the image of government held by the working class emerges from its harassment by the judicial system.

> The courts are very political. Garnishment redistributes millions of dollars each year from the wages of debtors to the accounts of creditors. The use of these courts involves frequent harassment and considerable stigmatization. Court actions color people's perception of the government.[14]

---

11 The Philadelphia *Evening Bulletin*, April 2, 1969.
12 The Philadelphia *Inquirer*, January 23, 1971.
13 *The New York Times*, January 2, 1969.
14 Herbert Jacob, "Winners and Losers: Garnishment and Bankruptcy in Wisconsin," Reprint 33, Institute for Research on Poverty, *The University of Wisconsin*, 1969.

Justice rendered on the young of the working class is out of proportion to their contribution to crime. They are more visible. For adults, law enforcement at times is reduced to a truce between police who shut their eyes at infractions and adults who are expected to be unobtrusive in their law violations. As a corollary, an individual who solicits the police to enforce the law against adults may be considered a nuisance. When the son of a middle-class father gets in trouble with the police, he gets an admonishment and papa goes down to pick him up. When the son of a worker, especially a black worker, gets involved with the police, he may get banged up; and sometimes papa may have to go down to the morgue to claim his body.

Justice is giving a priest 6 years in jail for pouring goat's blood on draft records; letting a policeman go free for murdering a man in a bar brawl; giving a socialite a year in prison for using his government position to bilk the public.

Justice is often a clod. Bradley Cook, 17-year old runaway son of a minister, gets hungry and homesick and steals a car to head for home. He is caught and placed in a Miami cell 18 by 36 feet with 19 hardened criminals. Cook is found dead the next morning, strangled by two blacks for an alleged racial slur.[15] Roy Gawf, of the same age, indulging in fantasy over becoming an Air Force cadet, is surprised by policemen trying to enter a Kansas City high school where the Air Force examination was kept. He tries to run away; the police shoot him dead. The judge rules the shooting justifiable homicide.[16]

At times, justice takes a turn inconsistent with critical doctrinaire attitudes, such as freeing Black Panthers when the liberal line is that the judicial system oppresses them. This kind of justice suggests that the United States is not a monolith as is so often claimed today, and that the system is subject both to groundswells of counterpower and to the individual conscience of those who man the courts.

Judge Tim Murphy of the national capital's Superior Court states:

We do not know much about judges in the United States. We are not even sure how many there are. We think there are about 15,000 limited jurisdiction judges, but some estimates of the latter go as high as 50,000. We think that about 6,000 of the limited jurisdiction judges are lawyers, but we are not certain. We have no idea, for example, how many judges there are in Texas because we do not know who performs judicial functions there.

We do know that most of the judges and the people who perform judicial functions in the United States are not lawyers. I suspect that most

15 The New York Times, January 28, 1971.
16 The Philadelphia Evening Bulletin, March 3, 1972.

are not even high-school graduates. We know that most of them are tied in very closely with the local political system. For the federal judges there is only an indirect political connection. But in Georgia, a candidate for a judgeship must pay over $3,000 as a filing fee. It is common talk that a judgeship in the lower courts in the city of New York costs one year's salary paid to the party.[17]

Many of the clerks in our courts are the brothers, uncles, and friends of politicians who simply cannot earn a living in a competitive situation. Our clerks don't know anything, we don't pay them anything and for the most part, they don't do anything.[18]

Bureaucracy. The system tends to convert humans into an abstraction for the purpose of their efficient control. A person comprises a series of numbers each of which elicits a coded response. Those aspects of the individual that are computerizable are relevant; the rest are not. He becomes managed in this fashion as a producer, citizen, or consumer, and when the corporate manipulators persuade him to buy goods he does not need and cannot afford, he is dunned as an abstraction. He is expected to behave in a way consistent with the computerized judgment made of him; he must perform in keeping with the system's needs.

Computerization of the individual provides bureaucrats with opportunities for growth. They weave a network of detail in which the individual becomes trapped and which renders staying alive increasingly more complicated. Moreover, they possess fertile minds with which to make the complexity ever greater. The individual tilts with the Internal Revenue Service, the bank, the credit agencies, the auto shop, the traffic court. He clears up outstanding mammoth bills. If he manages to remain sane and keeps the chores of daily living within bounds, he must search for life's meaning in tense metropolitan areas. Sometimes he gives up and seeks refuge in alcoholic stupor.

A bank puts out what it calls an easy explanation of a new checking system. Each one hundred dollars of collective balance earns 15 cents. Costs are 5 cents on each deposit slip plus 3 cents for each check listed, 5 cents for each check drawn, plus one dollar. And what is more, one can choose deluxe checks (in 10 cover styles), custom (only 3 colors available), and stock, which is available in one color only, but for no extra charge. The bank's highly educated suburban customers have not even written a letter to the editor.

In another example, the Blue Cross allegedly pays for hospital care.

---

[17] Tim Murphy, "His Honor Has Problems Too," Vol. 3, *The Center Magazine,* May–June 1971. In words of understatement, the article describes the horror the judicial system has become.
[18] *The New York Times,* May 27, 1971.

In practice, Blue Cross represents a collusive duopoly with the hospitals as a partner, in which mammoth price increases are negotiated periodically and then passed on to the consumer. Hospital bills can assume such enormous proportions that it is often in the interest of the patient not to survive. In Philadelphia, the Blue Cross issued a simplified description of a better plan. Elderly persons, says the announcement, will find it advantageous to go into their reserve plan if in hospital for 90 days or more, on the grounds that they are unlikely to be hospitalized again for that period of time. Accordingly, says Blue Cross, it will pay 5 dollars daily from the 61st to the 90th day, 20 dollars daily from the 91st to the 150th, and then all reasonable hospital charges from there on to the 180th. On certain clinical services, however, Blue Cross will continue to pay up to $50 yearly, and 20 percent thereafter to special subscribers who do not carry Medicare Part B which costs $4 monthly. But those who carry Part B will have those charges paid *only if they also carry Blue Shield 65 special*. And on it goes like a sadistic joke.

The bureaucrats in charge of waste disposal are quickly weaving a web of detail to match that of the managers of consumption. Americans accumulate waste faster than the capacity of existing facilities to dispose of them adequately. An environmental engineer calculates that the contemporary American accumulates 50 percent more waste than did his predecessor of 50 years ago. In one year alone, he discards 188 pounds of paper, 250 metal cans, 135 jars and bottles, and 338 caps and crowns. The annual growth of solid waste affords via recycling opportunities for returning the material to the gross national product. Since traditional methods of disposal are no longer tolerable, and since industry increasingly produces goods and wastes difficult to dispose, the solution says the engineer is to get Americans to consume their wastes.[19]

Evasiveness is the acme of perfection in bureaucratic response. It marks the triumph of bull over substance. The following letter supports this thesis.

We would be pleased to give every consideration to your request for a teaching and publication grant. Quite candidly, balancing the overwhelming backlog of pending appeals against reduced prospective resources, there is little likelihood of our participation. This does not reflect disinterest in your program so much as comment upon the difficulties of administering finite funds.

Although a more positive response is not possible, hopefully you can appreciate our position. Thank you for writing, and may others not so fully committed be encouraged to provide desired support.

19 The Philadelphia *Evening Bulletin*, September 30, 1969.

Bureaucratization fosters alienation between princes of power and rank and file. The alienation exists between trade union members and their officials, students and educational bureaucrats, citizens and governors, catholics and bishops. Not even the promise of heaven maintains the traditional bond. The led, by way of retribution, make a hobby of giving their managers a jolt. Polls indicate the disillusion and cynicism. The rank and file does not believe that managers are being candid. George Gallup states:

> I think the mood of America today is one of rather great confusion and disillusionment. All the time we have been operating, 32 years now, I have never known a time like this when people were so disillusioned and cynical. I think this goes back much to their feeling of the inadequacy of the leadership of the country.[20]

It is erroneous, however, to infer that bureaucrats are monsters; they are not. Away from their desks, they are often *simpatici*. At their posts, they must exercise vigilance over the tendency of human beings to disrupt routine. Of necessity, the system comprises a faceless machine impervious to individualistic expression. Like a robot, once plugged into its programmed cycle, it cannot be stopped. He who complains is like a person shouting his protestations in a hollow wilderness and receiving back only his voice in a series of reverberations that diminish in intensity to the final silence of defeat.

Consumption. Production and consumption are equalizers in life. Their effects are spread uniformly through all levels of society. Killing, maiming, and poisoning without bias, the motor vehicle is a prime force in the general movement toward the equal right to maladies. In production, as the hernia rate for the working class declines, the ulcer rate for the managerial class rises. As the working class approaches maximum free time and guaranteed income, the governing class spends more time manning the machinery of the system. Managers and workers breathe the same polluted air. Violence, once confined to working class districts, moves into fashionable areas. Women are raped without reference to social distinctions. The rising consumption of cigarettes by women serves to reduce the inequality of the lung cancer rate between the sexes. In volume of sales, men have closed the gap in the scenting of bodies. Males and females become increasingly indistinguishable.

The motor vehicle expresses American consumer values par excellence. The car provides Americans with an obscenity to hurl at their society. Public health officials call it public enemy number one. It con-

[20] *The New York Times*, February 10, 1968.

verts pink lungs into gray-black, produces more than half the total number of disabling accidents, provides lawyers with a substantial income, and guarantees undertakers a minimum of 60,000 funerals annually. Although a motor car powered by something other than the conventional engine is technologically feasible, it is difficult to persuade Americans to sacrifice their jazzed-up autos in the interest of the collective society. Nor is the auto industry, or oil and construction, or even the President of the United States inclined to lead them toward such a persuasion.

For the auto mirrors the sanctity bestowed by the system on major contributors to the gross national product. The highway construction it demands, the legal actions brought about to disentangle its effects, the costs in both time and labor of its production and maintenance, make the motor vehicle the dominant component of American energies. But if the actual economic, social, and esthetic costs of the automobile were calculated and taken seriously, reason alone would dictate a drastic curtailment of its use; nevertheless its employment is not only relatively unrestricted, it is encouraged by economic managers.

No other single object has such an adverse impact on the environment and on man's attitude toward his fellow man as does the automobile. Oil firms providing the fuel for cars are a major source of visual and respiratory pollution. They have destroyed the beauty of the traditional American town cluster with gas stations that make these centers look like a permanently ensconced carnival and side show. Wherever the car goes, pressures quickly mount for a hideous collection of these stations, together with used car lots, new car lots, junk car lots, car washes, beaneries, mammoth advertising signs readable by the slow-witted at 60 miles an hour, and that typical finishing touch: a generous sprinkling of trash. New stores no longer use ribbon-cutting ceremonies. Americans baptize them continually by emptying their car ash trays on the parking lots.

Americans with a modicum of empathy lose it quickly as they slide under the steering wheel. They communicate with each other via stickers and decals on their automobiles. The stickers signal in what manner the car owner feels superior to other Americans. Thus, when a motorist states via his rear bumper: America love it or leave it, it is clear whom he feels is worthy of staying. And when he displays the flag, his judgment as to his own patriotism compared to lesser Americans is evident.

The pitch of the auto industry is toward the power conscious male. If one gives a young man of modest intellect 400 horsepower, he uses it. Six thousand dollars of automobile is more economical than $25,000 of psychiatric care. He becomes a man when enthroned in two tons of gleaming steel. He sleeps, eats, works, makes love, and dies in it like a dog. His car's equipment includes snack bars, telephones, and tape transmissions. For his immortality and to solve the ecological crisis, he should with appropriate honors be buried in his automobile.

Cars are the offspring of frivolous marketeers and emasculated engineers. If the lines of an automobile impale pedestrians, if cars without bumpers cause horrendous repair bills, both effects contribute to the GNP. In the official view, the progressive elimination of the bumper as a means of absorbing impact expresses consumer preference and hence freedom. The auto industry argues that the consumer has the right to choose between a design that lowers damage risk and one that offers a gain in appearance. Under pressure to modify design so as to increase protection, the industry announced early in 1972 an improved bumper. The Insurance Institute for Highway Safety, a non-profit organization, tested the improved bumper and found that the average damage in frontal crashes into a standard barrier at 5 miles per hour was in excess of two hundred dollars. Later that year, after intensive lobbying by the auto industry, the United States House of Representatives Commerce Committee killed legislation designed to encourage the production of cars less prone to damage.

An automobile has the right of eminent domain. The burden of proof rests with those who seek to take it away. For example, in a labor of decades, the city of Philadelphia developed a small neighborhood known as Society Hill. After a protest from its upper middle-class residents, the city proposed to the national government that a new expressway passing the fringe of the neighborhood go underground for some 600 feet of its length. The government engineer stated that it would inconvenience the motorist to travel from the sunshine to the artificial lighting of the tunnel. Moreover, pollution level permitting, he would be denied the pleasures of viewing at 60 miles per hour the beauty of Society Hill.

Should American civilization vanish, the car will have played a major causal role. In addition to its bads of environment pollution, noise, and ugliness, scientists assert that the motor vehicle demonstrates an ability for mental pollution through its destruction of the sense of empathy of people for each other. One can imagine the demise. All of erstwhile America the beautiful will have been converted into concrete highways and consumption stations. Cars will be locked in a love grip, bumper to bumper, in the last traffic jam. Then the rumor would spread that the outstanding engineering contribution to esthetics, the highway mercury vapor lamp, shining from overhead on expressionless faces, is causing galloping cancer. And in the future, a digging anthropologist, sifting through the remains of this American civilization, would unearth the information that a people had focused its life on the veneration of the automobile.

The Conspiracy Syndrome. An overview of the social setting would be deficient if it did not call attention to the conspiracy syndrome that afflicts the nation. Americans are enthusiastic believers in demons. The thought that conspiracy prevails in the land—of war lords, assassins, communists, the mafia—excites the people. That a conspiracy is afoot and that government officials are dragging their feet over it provides sensations like those derived from reading ghost stories, sensations which comprise a useful remedy for afflictions including difficult menopause. The first modern emergence of the conspiracy syndrome, with the debauchery of justice that often attends it, appeared in the way peace-loving Wasps ganged up on and executed two innocent Italian workers: Nicola Sacco and Bartolomeo Vanzetti. The year of that justice was 1927.

The communist conspiracy erupted in earnest after World War II, fanned by the communications media and clergymen. In early 1947, for example, *Time Magazine* underwrote the view of a Congressional Committee that David Lilienthal, President Truman's choice for the chairmanship of the Atomic Energy Commission, if not a Red, loved Reds.

> There is at work in the United States an active, aggressive malignant thing —conspiratorial communism—which must be rooted out. If the Congressional investigations (of the House Un-American Activities Committee) achieved nothing else, they were dramatizing one fact: a man can be a Communist or a totalitarian liberal and call himself a good American, but he cannot expect his fellow Americans to agree.[21]

In the same issue, the magazine cites Monsignor Fulton J. Sheen as announcing the revival of Christianity. The magazine, happily, affirmed Sheen's proclamation of a new era that might be called the religious phase of history. Neither the magazine nor Sheen turned out to be good prophets. The religion that emerged against the communist devil was hedonism.

A short time after this joint proclamation, the Chairman of the House Un-American Activities Committee was convicted as a crook. But that

21 *Time Magazine*, February 17, 1947, p. 27.

did not stop the forward march of the communist conspiracy. It came into full bloom in the next decade under the guidance of Senator Joseph McCarthy. Many politicians, starring Richard Nixon as Tricky Dick, rose to prominence on its crest.

The communist conspiracy became shopworn in the decade following, but new conspiracies appeared: the Kennedy conspiracy, the Martin Luther King conspiracy, the baby doctor conspiracy, the government world-wide conspiracy, the central heating-Kissinger conspiracy, together with a perennial favorite, the mafia conspiracy. In the conspiracy to turn off the central heating in the national capital and kidnap presidential advisor Henry Kissinger, the government could have shown a sense of humor. But it could not resist the temptation. It indicted some anti-war intellectuals and came up with a conviction against a priest and a nun of passing clandestine letters in and out of prison, a practice so common it is ignored by authorities.[22]

The conspiracy doctrine in American law permits a man to be jailed not only for committing a crime in concert, but also for appearing to plan to commit one. If it is demonstrated that two or more individuals have agreed to commit a crime, a subsequent overt act, if judged to be in furtherance of the conspiracy, can be prosecuted; the same act, if committed by an individual acting alone, may be lawful. The government has used the conspiracy doctrine in many areas, from going after thieves to suppressing protest challenging the established order. If the government has clear evidence, as it must under the law, that an illegal act is being planned, how much more economical it would be to so advise the plotters.

What constitutes a conspiracy is vague both as to the characteristics of a conspirator and as to who can be considered a co-conspirator. This vagueness affords government the opportunity to take action against troublesome persons when no other logical course of action is available. For example, the government decided to proceed against some activists

[22] In 1970, with much fanfare, President Nixon signed the Organized Crime Control Act. The legislation perpetuates the myth of organized crime of non-Wasp origin, consistent with the adage that a myth repeated frequently becomes a self-evident truth.

The law requires a witness to testify against himself, gives the federal court the power to place a recalcitrant witness summarily into jail; finds syndicated gambling to have an effect on interstate commerce; provides for a commission to determine its effect on interstate commerce; makes its difficult for a respectable racketeer to invest his money; gives federal judges the power to mete out 25-year sentences to "dangerous special offenders"; provides penalties up to death for the sale and distribution of explosives.

Much in the style of a football coach exhorting his players, the president told his law and order team that now that they had the tools to go to it. One senator voted against the law. Since the legislation was passed, the crime rate has risen.

against the Vietnam war, including Doctor Spock, the well-known pedia-
trician, on a conspiracy charge. The 5 conspirators met each other only
after the indictment, which stated that the defendants did combine, con-
spire, confederate, and agree together and with each other, and with
diverse other persons, some known and other unknown. During the
trial, the judge was heard whispering to his clerk: "Tell (the prosecutor) that son of a bitch to cut it out. He'll blow the case if he keeps
this up and get us all in trouble." In the judgment of a Harvard law
professor, the purpose of the government in this case was to frighten
people away from active participation in protest against the war.[23]

Vested interests can ill-afford the extinction of the mafia conspiracy.
Politicians, judges, policemen, writers, and journalists would otherwise
be deprived of their sustenance. Informers would be denied the opportunity of telling their employers what they like to hear. The film industry
would be denied the chance to pander to the sick elements in American
society. And the game of pursuit of the mafia by the forces of law and
order as a tranquillizer for the general public would thereby vanish.
The ritual of gilding the lily must be preserved in the interest of the
GNP.

Every day millions of members of the working class bet on guessing
a 3-digit number between 000 and 999. Each player has a thousand
to one chance of guessing right, odds much more favorable than those
granted in lotteries of the government. The game has a background of
Italian tradition. Each week Italians in the old country play *Totocalcio,*
trying to guess the results of soccer matches. In the United States, the
managers operating this service are referred to as the mafia. Without
college degrees in Business Administration, they perform miracles in
management; they comprise the remnants of ebbing American entrepreneurship.

For decades, the mafia conspiracy has made fascinating press and
television copy. The term originally referred to Sicilian criminal elements, but it has now come to be used to refer to "organized crime"
in the United States. The implication is made by *The New York Times*
that organized crime is under the management of individuals of Italian
ancestry.[24] This alone—lumping together Sicilians with ordinary Italians
—is enough to make legitimate mafia blood boil. The President of the
United States himself, in a message to Congress, got into the game by

23 Alan Dershowitz in a book review of a work by Jessica Mitford, *The Trial
of Dr. Spock,* New York: Knopf, 1969, in *The New York Times,* September 14,
1969.
24 *The New York Times,* April 24, 1969.

mentioning the 5,000 members of the 24 mafia families as constituting the hard core criminals in the United States. Nixon went on to state that many Americans contribute to organized crime by illegal betting, but these Americans the president called decent.

A rose, then, is not a rose by any other name. In alluding to the activity of the mafia, *The New York Times* describes an intricate organization of some 5,000 persons that culminates in a national commission to adjudicate disputes. An impartial student looking at the same facts, assuming they are, would marvel at the mafia's civilized procedures and its profound comprehension of modern management methods. The same *Times* points out that the mafia is getting into legitimate business. An impartial sociologist might describe this outcome as upward social movement. Such interpretations, however, lack drama.

In a more modest account, *Time Magazine* reports that the nucleus of American organized crime comprises 4,000 persons doing a $30 billion annual business managed by Italians. The figure amounts to the gross national product of many nations. How persons of such limited education can handle such business is vague. What stands out in the article by inference is the extensive corruption of managers in the system. Such accounts are self-perpetuating because of their glamor and because they cannot be challenged since the persons they vituperate cannot join the debate.

The mafia provides a service catering to American values. Its organizational techniques are solid American virtues. The Italians who migrated to Argentina are of the same origin as those who came to the United States. But no mafia exists in Argentina.

According to the newspapers, the mafia has integrated its forces. They report a gentleman by the name of Myer Lansky as a top associate and Negroes as collectors. A newspaper ad associates Air Freight thefts with a mafia type by the name of Davidoff. A belief thereby gains currency that the syndicate should be renamed Kosher Nostra. A solution to the problem emerges: pass an equal opportunity law requiring the syndicate to train Jews and Negroes for top administrative posts. However, the disappearance of ethnic uniqueness would be lamentable. An opportunity would be lost for Americans to transfer their deficiencies to nefarious foreign forces.[25]

---

[25] In late 1969, newspapers reported a "mafia linked" firm as having received $12 million in defense contracts. The story is cited as an example of how the mafia penetrates legitimate business. The company, it seems, was described by Senator John J. McClellan as a hangout for what his Committee refers to as a ruthless head of the mafia. The owner of the firm concedes having an association with this individual by virtue of the fact that the character is one of his customers. The Philadelphia *Evening Bulletin*, October 29, 1969.

In mid-1970, *The New York Times* reported that 130 individuals had been seized by federal agents in drug operations, a field reputedly controlled by the mafia. A beaming Attorney General is shown photographed with a chart indicating place and number of persons arrested. With a sense of nostalgia one must report that no Italian names appear on the list; the field apparently has been pre-empted by Cubans and Puerto Ricans.[26]

The whole conspiracy syndrome should be placed in the context of the state's obsession with surveillance of non-conformist behavior. In preparation for the day when the panic button must be pushed, a law abiding American can fall under the surveillance of the Central Intelligence Agency, the FBI, the United States Army, the local police, and the espionage systems of the different states. This should only happen in communist countries.

In the same year of 1970, the Un-American Activities Committee of the House of Representatives sent a letter to 179 colleges and universities asking for the names of its campus speakers. Only 7 institutions saw fit not to reply. From this correspondence the Committee compiled a blacklist of enemies of the state, including characters committing the heinous crime of advocating the abolishment of the Committee.

Government surveillance has its aspects of comic opera. In the surveillance of Mrs. Martin Luther King in a public address after her husbands' death, the Army snooper was instructed by headquarters to find out the full significance of her quote: "I have a dream."

Human Relations. Americans have made enormous accomplishments in mass technology, but are primitives in mature interpersonal relations. The two phenomena are related. The strongest evidence of the demoralization of American life is to be observed in the way men relate to one another. As a result of man's denigration by the forces of the system

---

[26] A serious study indicates that the Sicilian family in the United States undergoes a process of legitimization over the generations. The families are held together not by fear as is commonly supposed, but by a genuine concept of honor. Furthermore, as the legitimization goes on, the crime is taken over by other minorities, including Cubans and Puerto Ricans. The poor are the criminals; pressed with the necessity of acquisition and the absence of a skill commanding a price in the legitimate market, they find that the illegitimate services they provide society pay off handsomely.

The study indicates a mafia does exist as a web of moral code peculiar to the Sicilian sense of personal dignity and the value of cooperative relationships. A traditional Sicilian to whom an appeal is made to cooperate will do so at considerable personal sacrifice. The alleged ritual and ceremony of the mafia is bunk.

My experience accords with these findings. (Francis A. J. Ianni, *A Family Business: Kinship and Social Control in Organized Crime*, New York: Russell Sage Foundation, 1972.)

that envelop him, a decline has taken place in his ability to communicate with his fellow man. People are symbols of insensitivity and cruelty. The cult of aberration, prolonged diet of sensation, narcissism, and anti-reason produces persons incapable of empathy. Instead, they make caricatures of one another.

The knack of making a person feel prosperous by small acts of humanity is lost. A writer notes how American visitors in England remark on English civility. Whereas the English appear to be sensitive to the particular situation of a person, urban Americans are more angry, more abrasive, more oblivious of the feelings of others. Individual Americans, universities, and firms spend considerable sums of money in training for the reacquisition of sensitivity.[27]

Le belle maniere, the faculty of making a person feel prosperous through dialogue, is uncommon. In the cities, much of the population divides between those indulging in the rhetoric of hatred and those who are disposed to do so but hold back. With little provocation, they denigrate. In trying to compensate, they devise talk that mistakes confession for intimacy. It is compulsive; not artistic. It is declamatory; not intimate. For these failures in communication, Americans pay fees to quacks who promise to correct them in jig time.

People are unable to laugh at themselves. Italian self-mockery is alien to their character. They look grim and deprived despite their affluence. The faces of young women suggest that the reward of their attractiveness is only a daily onslaught. American adolescents do not convey an image of self-assurance; their posture, rather, is one of indifference or self-deprecation. This submergence of individuality carries over into adulthood.

Concepts of right and wrong are eroded. We are either the feeble children of the unconscious mind or the bland issue of nanny psychiatrists. Our conduct is sick or adjusted. We are not heroic or cowardly, but slick or naive. We are not free men but protoplasm pushed this way and that way by deep-seated impulses or by the environment.

We seem at odds with ourselves and with others. Bureaucracy creates a society of strangers seceding from each other. The educated with no vested interests in the system feel disenfranchised and secede; the new middle class, preoccupied with making money and consuming new varieties of goods, secedes from the body politic; the intellectuals secede from each other by fracturing their organizations; the young secede by

---

[27] Americans have not always been grumpy. In a book written in the late 1930's, Albert Einstein describes the positive attitude of Americans and their friendly smiles.

converting themselves into caricatures. No one is in a conciliatory mood. The system docs not fulfill, and the public tunes out.

Urban life contributes to this alienation. Managers and rank and file used to be linked together in the cities through attachments of paternalism, cultural identity, and highly personal human relationships. Such is no longer the case. The separation of work place from home contributes to the decline of neighborhood loyalty; lack of identity with a group produces a loss of loyalty to the society as a whole. At times, the alienation assumes macabre proportions. A newspaper reports an auto accident leaving two dead. When the police arrive, some youngsters are busily removing the hubcaps. They scatter and drop their loot in an alley.

The urban dweller feels impotent and frustrated in the face of life's irritations: the deterioration of his neighborhood; the noise of planes, transportation equipment, and industry; the violence; the rat-race pace; the lack of trust in government to do anything about them. All he seems to get from government officials is double talk. He feels smothered not only by unfulfilled expectations, but by the meaninglessness of his very accomplishments.

In the city, human beings are phantoms indistinguishable from the environment. They do not approach each other in a way that delights the spirit. They are indifferent, fearful, or cruel. They do not seem to be conscious of the image they convey to others, nor are they even concerned with their own self-image. Their lives are a series of well-managed tasks whose reward is boredom.

The bureaucratization, the manipulation, the estrangement in life, the consumption rat-race, trigger expenditures in the hundreds of billions of dollars on means of escape from society and from oneself. What is done naturally in backward societies—going to sleep, having a bowel movement, digesting food, making love, experiencing tranquillity—is facilitated in the system by the use of drugs. Respectable Wasps in large firms lead the drug culture.

Each year Americans spend an estimated $100 million on marijuana, $225 million on heroin, and an incalculable amount on hallucinogens. Moreover, if television provides a clue, the habitual use of commercial drugs amounts to a national pastime; the line between their use for short term relief and their abuse leading to deterioration of the individual using them is uncertain. A more acceptable form of escapism, alcohol drinking, is indulged in by some two-fifths of the population. For ten million of this number, drinking amounts to an addiction. Half of the more than one thousand-a-week deaths in auto accidents are ascribed to individuals under the influence of alcohol. These outlays afford a quantitative measure of the degree of escapism and self-destruction in society.[28]

We next turn to several social groups in American society. Corporate man, the white ethnic, and the intellectual are brought forward to show in more detail how their life styles either evidence or contribute to the demoralization that prevails.

[28] *The New York Times*, January 8, 9, 10, 11, 12, 1968. From press reports, drug addiction is common even among children. A 10-year old child is on record as a heroin user. The *Times* (December 22, 1969) reports 210 children and teenagers were killed by heroin in 1969. Drug addiction is not confined to the urban poor. Middle-class Nassau County on Long Island reports the number of addicts seeking assistance rose from 202 to 989 in the 3-year period 1967–1969. A belief exists that television advertising encourages the use of illicit drugs. It should be also noted that the prohibition of cigarette advertising on television may push the industry to increase drug commercials.

A popular notion that marijuana users are forward looking types searching for a vision of perfection is not borne out by research. In a study of users in Vietnam, the vast majority were found to be incompetent passive personalities who thereby complicated the many problems they already had. (*The New York Times*, April 3, 1970.)

Studies reported in the press covering New Jersey, California, and Toronto link drug use by adolescents to use of drugs by their parents. (*The New York Times*, July 23, 1971.)

The Inhabitants

CORPORATE MAN

Corporate man rushes through life wearing a mask on a face whose laughter is programmed. William Whyte's "organization man"[1] in the flesh, he is more disposed than is the blue collar worker to accommodate to the demands of organization. It is indeed difficult to find in his social behavior anything not programmed consistent with the needs of organization.

Our corporate man is a white with an annual income over $15,000 and more than likely living in the suburbs. On the Main Line, he is the fellow reading the Philadelphia *Inquirer* or the *Wall Street Journal* (the fellow with *The New York Times* is likely to be a college professor) on the way in to Philadelphia, and the *Evening Bulletin* on the way back. If television shows are valid indicators of social stereotypes, he is a fool, but a nice guy nevertheless. The willing minion of the women in his household as well as of the system, he moves through life from one sensation to the next, devoid of historical and religious perspective. Politically, he makes a fitting prop which the system's managers can use to pursue their operations successfully. With an incapacity or a disinclination to come to grips with social realities, he elects to exercise his responsibilities of citizenship by giving politicians a blank check. He concedes American society is in trouble but believes it is the fault of agitators. Not wanting to offend, he is non-committal, yet he is receptive to hearing from politicians the vituperation of persons who offend his sensibilities. Easily bamboozled, he is repeatedly deceived by politicians who do not fully reveal their cards and by writers who zoom to the top of best seller lists with instant comprehension of complex

1 William H. Whyte. *The Organization Man*, New York: Doubleday, 1956.

matters. He is adept in making money. Corporate man is an individual, stout because of excessive eating and little exercise, at the helm of an aggressive-looking automobile, with an impassive look screwed on to his face. As a super salesman, he is a vital cog in the machinery of consumption.

His passivity surfaces at times in a frenzied pursuit of goods. His wife makes going to the shopping center a many hour ritual. She does not buy necessarily, but to know all the goodies that can be bought comforts her spirit. On Saturdays, she is joined by her husband, who spends relatively more time in the hardware and sporting goods departments.

In one's fantasy, the biggest sale ever occurs in a shopping center featuring a 20 percent price cut throughout its stores. The sale is triggered by the wail of a siren signaling permission to allow the excited men, women, and children to rush into the shops. Overhead in the parking area floats a huge pink balloon with the inscription: SPEND FOR THE GNP. Amplifiers shriek the tune of Yankee Doodle. Within minutes, the first wave of enraptured spenders pour out of the stores hauling clothing, jewelry, color television sets, cosmetics, shoes, hardware, sporting goods, cameras, and exotic merchandise. A young man blasts through the incoming waves with the first of 10 raffled automobiles: a 400 HP Ford Jet Stream Super. The crowd scatters successfully, with the exception of two who become mangled beneath the wheels. The Volunteer Wayne Ambulance Brigade quietly and efficiently carts them away to a hospital that looks like a summer resort. A New York intellectual with a sign stating "Keynesian Economics Is Obsolete" is led through a jeering throng of Nixon Republicans by two burly policemen. At the end of a fabulously successful day, in a background of litter galore, the partners of the shopping center distribute their profits: one for you and one for me; two for you and one, two for me.

These acquisitions serve to make life more complex. They rarely satisfy emotional needs. It is not, therefore, surprising that sick youth are often the children of well-to-do suburbanites. Corporate man is mediocre and that is his right. But he also claims the right to impose his mediocrity on the society.

Thus, hippies are generally the offspring of corporate man. They play a part in a script that calls for unconventional regalia and a studious contempt for money, the liberation from which is subsidized by their corporate fathers. They do not reject the society so much as they prey on its beneficence. The hippie meets the challenge of the system by squatting, playing the sole chord he knows on the guitar, and moodily contemplating his navel. He turns in on himself by attachment to a coterie of mutual admiration. Often cerebrally underprivileged, the hippie affects a posture of wisdom. He represents a tendency of the system to generate individuals of little use to themselves and to others.

Their principal source of subsidy, corporate man, struggles to maintain his precarious balance on the treadmill of income, consumption, relief from both, and more income. He spends most of his time buying goods, consuming them, struggling to pay for them, recuperating from their use. At times, the futility of an ever-rising level of consumption makes him irritable. His offspring react by creating an avant garde that makes a fetish of unproductivity. They wear the paraphernalia of rejection and pursue the inner self. After some search, they, too, find little.

Corporate man is so busy making transactions that he does not have the time to think of where he came from and where he is headed. He cannot face death realistically; humans do not die, but pass away. His major preoccupations, judging from his conversation are babes, booze, baseball, and bullion. Food, televsion, cars, and orgasms round out the good life. He is trained to respond dutifully to planned obsolescence, consistent with the philosophy of the former Board chairman of General Motors who stated that planned obsolescence means progress. He sustains the system's need for the proliferation of goods which now include powered back scratchers, pink cigarettes for weddings and blue for bar mitzvahs, and Cupid's quiver liquid douche concentrates in floral scents (orange blossom and jasmine) and flavor scents in raspberry and champagne.[2] For corporate man, the Great American Society consists of a third scoop of ice cream, a guarantee against not having to leave childhood for the rigors of adulthood. Under corporate direction, Nirvana will come when American man becomes well-fed, well-clothed, well-housed, and well-titillated. For pleasure mechanized is the suburbanite's ethic; he is tuned into an erotic utopia that makes him incapable of fine judgment.

His gypsy life dutifully following the orders of his corporation allows suburban governments to operate as private clubs serving the interests of realtors, builders, and land speculators. Together with the highway consortium, these groups form a private circle within government, destroying what first attracted corporate man to the suburbs in their beginning.

In the upper layers of the corporate class one finds the Wasp preservers of the traditional American faith. Armed with money and political connections, they select those Americans who have supported

2 According to *Time Magazine*, sales reached $290,000 in the first two months. (December 26, 1970.)

the faith in a manner worthy of being bestowed with immortality in stone. On a hill at Valley Forge they have listed in granite the 17 political and economic rights of Americans, which protect the dignity and freedom of the individual. The corporations in which they place their investments have destroyed many of these freedoms.

Those in this group of rural town origin fancy themselves as self-made men in contrast with present day ethnics. Preacher Billy Graham states:

> We also wrestled with poverty except we did not know we were poor. We did not have sociologists, educators, and newscasters constantly reminding us of how poor we were. We also had the problem of rats. The only difference between then and now is we did not call upon the government to kill them. We killed our own.[3]

Suburban corporate man runs up the flag on a holiday, and then spends his time in chores such as shining the car or mowing the grass, and in pleasure pursuits such as cocktail and dinner parties or a swim at the all-white club. The next morning he brings down the flag (sensitive to the ritual prescribed by custom), and then ventures forth in his car to make a killing in sales. Though not exacting intellectually, he certainly is patriotic, fun-loving, and wholesome. His heroes are John Wayne, Joe Namath, and Billy Graham.

His wife looks upon feminist organizations such as Women's liberation as way out. Milder forms of male envy are found within the hierarchy of the League of Women Voters. The aggressive Gung-ho types in the League manage to channel their neuroticisms into service of country through a system of organized superficiality. For the wife who considers the League of Women Voters too risky, there are many social affairs that regularly make the suburban society page. She appears photographed at a charity ball, horse show, antiques auction, in a variety of poses including ascending a staircase, descending a staircase, on a horse, beside a horse, grasping a cocktail, or holding a silver cup.

Both are registered Republicans since affiliation with the other party runs the risk of becoming *declassé*. It also might hurt the husband's business. In a Philadelphia suburban community, for example, the preponderant majority of the voters automatically reach for the Republican master lever even though the party is in control of a corrupt machine. Most of the voters have college degrees and doubtlessly consider themselves more informed than urban ethnics. In a Republican primary for the school board, the incumbent came out vigorously in support of quality education, a profound move calculated to gain the support of

---

[3] The Philadelphia *Evening Bulletin*, October 16, 1971.

fellow Republicans who believe in progress; a woman candidate placed her sex and membership in the League of Women Voters on the line and shopped for support among the party hacks; a third candidate presented as his platform his happy public school children; and a fourth, a maverick economist, foolishly tackled issues and scorned making his peace with the party hacks. The first 3 candidates won handsomely. The process discourages candidates from running for office who are disinclined to show reverence to individuals whose primary interest is choosing a candidate that would maintain their power and prestige.

His empty-headed hippie offspring is not the only cross that corporate man has to bear. Suburbanites are constantly fleeing from other Americans just entering the middle class, but their flight is futile. They sneak off to the same places and create another mess. Nature was bountiful to the United States, but upper middle class values and the profit motive convert the bounty into a honky-tonk.

For the profit motive shapes the contours of the suburban community. In suburban Philadelphia on the Main line, 25 gas stations line a two-mile stretch of highway, which amounts roughly to one for every 500 linear feet. In a suit brought by the Gulf Oil Corporation, owners of 5 of the stations, the court asserted that the community could not control their number. In effect, the criterion stipulated by the judge was the ability of the firm to make a profit. Dispersed among the hideous gas stations are hamburger joints including Gino's, Hot Shoppes, McDonalds, and Hamburger King, symbols of the successful subordination of family life to the imperatives of mass marketing. Shopping centers and auto dealerships complete the scene on a stretch of road that once was among the most attractive in the nation.

The supremacy of the rule of profit making in the suburbs creates rows of housing enclaves segregated by income group, accessible only by motor vehicle, and strips of commercial establishments. The commercial strips represent a potential for spreading decay. Their standing advertising signs resemble gods of industry perched on their pedestals. The residential zoning differentiated by land size and construction costs serves to guarantee the isolation of different socio-economic groups from each other. Liberals could achieve voluntary integration if they would persuade local government to develop raw land on a comprehensive basis with housing for different income groups. But the profit motive would have to be subordinated to social goals.

A believer in progress and the private enterprise system, corporate man hesitates to protest this spreading vulgarity. The courts join the alliance for progress by taking the view that local government can concern itself only with the health, safety, and morals of the public, and not with its esthetic and psychological needs. The supremacy of the rule of money making over the rule of a life of quality can be exemplified *ad nauseam*.

Suburban governments are manipulated by money makers who manage to obtain political decisions that often conflict with the community's wishes. Politicians count on apathy and resent the sporadic backlash of community residents. The stakes are high. An investment can be quadrupled by getting a local government to change the zoning after the purchase of land.[4] The community thereby develops according to actions of individuals holding land for speculative purposes. Such speculation could be controlled by taxing the capital appreciation and using receipts to buy land for controlled development; but the organization against such a proposal would be formidable.

The land speculating has been going on ever since the British kings gave out parcels to their bosom buddies.

> When the Duke of York received the grant, he separated them and divided the least of the two, called New Jersey, between two of his favourites. Carteret and Berkley, the first of whom had received the eastern and the other the western part of the province, had solicited this vast territory with no other view but to put it up for sale. Several adventurers bought large districts of them at a low price, which they divided and sold again in smaller parcels.[5]

The control of suburban governments by one political party makes winning the primary tantamount to election. The primary candidate's chance of winning depends on his acceptability to an entrenched clique. A product of this control is a disease that often afflicts the offspring of first cousin marriages. A challenger to the chosen candidate of the political machine need not necessarily be a move toward better politics. One such challenger in a Philadelphia suburb, loaded with money and Madison Avenue techniques, brought forward as his major themes his name and anti-pollution. He polluted the community with his name, plastering it on every available utility pole and traffic sign. He seemed to want to outdo the handiwork of the graffiti artists in the city. His radio commercial comprised mostly a repetition of his name in a backdrop of muffled tympani. Holt lost by a whisker, and says he is coming back.

A basic statistical technique used by planners in controlling the sub-

---

[4] A builder in Suburban Philadelphia bought a piece of land for $35,000, ran successfully for the township board of commissioners, and got the land rezoned a week afterward. The land was sold for $800,000. (The Philadelphia *Evening Bulletin*, March 14, 1971). In a Baltimore, Maryland, suburb, a lawyer bought a house from a Negro woman for $500, turned around and sold it to a new housing authority for $35,000 (*The New York Times*, May 2, 1971).

[5] Abbè Raynal. *Philosophical and Political History of the British Settlements, and Trade in North America*, Edinburgh, Scotland: C. Denovan, 1779, p. 87.

urban sprawl is to measure trends such as population, motor vehicle use, and industrial growth. In Pennsylvania, these studies are used by a State Highway Department staffed by individuals who could not possibly make it in a competitive society, and who oscillate between a paralysis of inaction and a stubborn position having no semblance of rationality. The research, so-called, on transportation problems serves to promote particular interests. Thus, a traffic engineering firm may conclude that a particular artery contains predominantly local traffic when local funds are available and interstate traffic when federal money is more likely to be forthcoming. Land speculators and highway interests use these trends to force political decisions that make these projections a reality. For example, a population rise is projected, which creates the rationale for more road construction, which in turn contributes to bringing about the predicted rise in population. The highway is supposed to relieve the traffic congestion, but in fact creates more vehicular flow by its existence. So more money has to be spent on roads in order to ease what the prior expenditure was meant to cure. Accordingly, the undesirable is planned and the remedy for the planned outcome aggravates the disease.

Suburbanites cannot escape this progress. Highways, jet planes, commercial establishments pursue them in their flight. Zoning laws which they believed would give them a guarantee of privacy are easily subverted by individuals tackling the government and judicial system with money, astute lawyers, and political connections. The engineers who could provide counsel to the community are employed by the vested interests and are therefore reluctant to say anything that might jeopardize their jobs. Those affiliated with universities also hesitate to give technical assistance to members of the community because of the danger of losing contracts.

The suburban circus can be costly. In a Philadelphia suburban community with a population of 29,000, the taxpayers feed 141 full-time government employees. Its budget, excluding school costs, amounts to $2.4 million. With salaries comparable to those of big cities, a quarter of the budget goes to a police department of 49 men, whose primary duties include controlling traffic moving in and out of the township, and running down complaints of women irritated by children, adult neighbors, and dogs. The operation is listed in the budget as police protection. The substantial terms of employment for police jobs of little or no skill or risk reflect political influence. Boredom provokes the police to indulge in petty harassment. To avoid the disabilities that may occur from overwork, township employees enjoy a 37-hour work week, 4 weeks vacation with pay, and 13 paid holidays each year.

Adding a school budget of $7.2 million, local government costs amount to approximately $330 for each man, woman, and child in local taxes paid by the community. The school board grinds out tax increases each year. Corporate man takes it without a murmer. The little people complain, but they lack the technical information, organization, and money to react effectively against the school board barony. The management principle that can best explain this mafia-like operation in the suburbs is that the amount of money a local government needs is a function of its degree of astuteness in extracting money from docile taxpayers.

The suburb, then, dramatizes the reality that a livable community cannot be built on elitism and the profit motive. Nevertheless, the suburbs have a potential for an existence of quality. Their small political subdivisions can afford greater opportunity for citizen participation than do cities, and suburbanites have the money and the education with which to participate. Suburban areas that manage to create a town core or to preserve the traditional one that existed prior to the arrival of the new corporate class have a basis for sound planning. A cluster of shops among which one can walk without the intervention of the motor vehicle, surrounded by a variety of amenities and housing within walking distance of the core, would together provide a base for developing a sense of stability and identity. A local newspaper can encourage a feeling of attachment by discussion of local issues and by exerting pressure on politicians to protect the community against exploiting interests. The suburban town can serve as a model of how to convert the cities into civilized areas, but people must be educated to think that social benefit means individual benefit—an unlikely prospect. The ravaging continues without any apparent abatement. The traditional town core of the suburbs continues to be systematically destroyed by the profit motive, and communities emerge not on the basis of what the community wants but what the profit makers want.

The resources the spoilers can muster in decision making are formidable. Most importantly, they can rely on the timidity of corporate man and on his disposition to resign himself to organized forces that push him this way and that. He submits to the manner in which the judicial system prepares an urban onslaught on the suburbs against their zoning in the name of equality for blacks. For the fundamental characteristic of corporate man is his lack of courage.

THE WHITE ETHNIC

The white ethnic blue-collar worker belongs to the most abused group in society. Maligned by so-called intellectuals, and used as an object of social experimentation by liberals, he represents the most exploited class in the United States. The liberal managers of public policy impose the costs of their social policies upon the white ethnic in his housing, schools, taxes, loss of political leverage, and inability to make earnings rise as fast as prices. Government policy created the middle class flight to the suburbs, the pauperization of the rural Negro and his march to the cities. The brunt of these phenomena falls on urban white ethnics.

The profile of Caucasian blue collarites, more typical of those with no craft skills, indicates the following characteristics: first or second generation American at a higher occupational level than that of his immigrant antecedents; performs a rudimentary skill within the broad spectrum of industrial labor; a strong ethnic attachment; a non-protestant christian; education not beyond high school; sensitive to the low status accorded him by society; conservative and indisposed to social activism. The skilled craftsman, particularly the one in construction, is more secure. His skill and wages affirm his manhood. He has arrived in the mass culture and his arrival makes him more conservative than the factory worker. The white ethnic dislikes pushy blacks, hippies, welfare riders, and intellectuals. Intellectuals call him a racist. But studies indicate he is a moralist more than he is a racist.

He has seen his neighborhood deteriorate physically and socially. The increase in crime by urban blacks outside of their community falls most heavily upon him. But liberals do not talk about this and ethnics are supposed to be magnanimous. In exchange for this deterioration, his taxes have risen three times faster than his wages. About a third of his modest income is taken from him directly or indirectly in federal, state, and local taxes. He pays for the day care of his children while his government plans to tax him for the free day care of the children of unmarried welfare mothers. He is vexed, troubled, frustrated. The white ethnic is the slob who adheres to the ethic of work in order to subsidize the ethic of welfare.

The descendent of Irishmen, Italians, Poles, Southeastern Europeans, and other white ethnics, his income hovers around $9,000 and his kind numbers some 65 million. His life unfolds from a long history of venable folk culture, which affords him a psychological satisfaction denied him by the system. A valid portrait of him suggests restlessness, edginess, escape seeking, envy. It indicates a sense of manhood shaken by the decline of traditional values in contemporary society.

A radical change has taken place in his political thinking. Traditionally, he has followed the leadership of liberals. Now he no longer thinks they can be trusted with the future course of the nation. Politicians are crooks and intellectuals are fools. He sees big organization as an instrument of promoting the interests of those who manage them.

Out of this disenchantment arises a suspicion of proposals that increase the role of government.

> The position of the white lower middle class American is one of seeing the organized poor, militant Blacks, and upper middle class whites effectively creating new bureaucratic entities and manipulating them in their interests. They also see governmental and business structures acting in directions that deny major value premises of middle Americans.[6]

The white ethnic's confidence in the survival of his way of life has been shaken to its very foundations. His beliefs in hard work, sacrifice, family, religion, and ethnic neighborhoods are under attack by the liberals he now despises. He is appalled at their esprit critique over what he thinks is just. He senses that the so-called educated think he is an inferior, a bigoted dope. The very language scholars use suggests that his culture is inferior rather than one in a diverse array. He is the lower class. His aspirations have been betrayed and even his children seem to have been lost. Uncertainty marks his life. He is made insecure even by his own church as traditional ritual is abandoned to support the tastes of college graduates. Because of uncertainty, he seeks desperately to maintain his traditions, and because of this reflex intellectuals label him a reactionary. What makes it so frustrating is that he does not know how to state his point of view openly without feeling defensive about it; and nobody tries to help him.

> Where once the enshrinement of value consistency, adherence to principle, and trust in decisions of those in authority represented key elements of life, Middle Americans do find schism instead of certitude. Whether the area is child rearing or doing business with "Red China," Middle Americans face adherence to their values as a battle against prevailing forces of change. Someone appears to have moved the finish line. The standards of what is good have changed. These are people who ran the extra mile—who really carried out the beliefs others only spoke in behalf of. They never shirked their duty. They tried hard to conform to the values and it is precisely this conformity that now results in punishment for what at one time was seen as a virtue.[7]

His ethnic orientation is a mark of sanity rather than bigotry; if the worker did not develop his own ethnic base, he would become a cultural freak. The American managing class is not disposed to think proletariat culture has much substance. Scholars play into its hands by writing books on the culture of poverty. But without the develop-

[6] Donald I. Warren. "Anomia and Middle Class Americans: Some Observations on Normative Flexibility," Winter 1971 Meeting, *Industrial Relations Research Association*, December 28, 1971, p. 376.
[7] *Ibid.* p. 378.

ment of their own cultures, which gave them a sense of purpose and status, the laboring classes of minority origin would have felt even more keenly their sense of isolation. The blue collarites succeeded in developing ethnic enclaves whose human relationships were anchored in feelings of mutual trust. The Wasps and quasi-Wasps have destroyed these enclaves in the name of progress; the wise guys have taken even that away from them in the name of Negro rights.[8]

The white ethnic wears the hat in patriotic ceremonies of veterans organizations; goes to church on Sundays or at least gets the family there; feels bitter about the Negro protest movement; plays the horses, the numbers, and the lottery in a constant search for a killing; tries to break the social barrier by getting at least one of his children into college, but is persuaded he is being discriminated against in favor of blacks. Intellectuals interpreting this posture conclude he is bigoted, naive, and unsophisticated. Change, to the urban white ethnic, is not progress, but change for the worse. The least pure of Americans, he is the remaining remnant of puritanism in American society.[9]

He has lost the status acquired in the era of Franklin Delano Roosevelt. Because of this loss, he develops a fatalism and cynicism; society for him comprises one big racket. His job gives little satisfaction; its value is often related to the opportunities it affords to goof off. His complaints are most prominently associated with jobs that allow little opportunity for autonomy and creativity.[10] The little skill remaining in his work he feels is being destroyed by pressures from government to open up jobs for blacks.

Thus, the white ethnic needs to find status beyond the confines of his job. Few do. Social change and the political system invoke his derision because they are someone else's doings designed to take away his modest conquests. His frustrations dispose him to bursts of authoritarianism. He needs to shove something down the throat of the wise guys in society. The political demagogue who promises to do so becomes his hero. What ails the blue collar is that the system has made him a second class citizen.

The neighborhood was the biggest antidote to the abuse the white ethnic has to take. But that was taken away by the managers in the

---

8 The working class intuitively grasps the psychological importance of cultural tradition. In Philadelphia, the mummers parade, a one-day extravaganza requiring a year of preparation, is the product of white ethnics.

9 For a brief description of the urban white collar, see Peter Schrag, "The Forgotten American," *Harper's Magazine*, August 1969. For a thorough analysis, see Arthur B. Shostak, *Blue Collar Life*, New York: Random House, 1969.

10 See Stanley E. Seashore and J. Thad Barhome, "Behind the Averages: A Closer Look at America's Lower-Middle Income Workers," 24th Annual Meeting, *Industrial Relations Research Association*, December 1971.

name of equality of opportunity. The liberals dictating public policy assign to him the role of villain. He is expected to react with equanimity to accusations of racism and bigotry as his accusers use his money and promotional opportunities to raise the income of blacks. His trade union leaders are wedded to the system. While the nation prospers generally and blacks experience upward movement, the white ethnic does not succeed in increasing his real take-home pay. As his taxes rise, the relative corporate share of the federal income tax declines.[11] Thus, the well-to-do transfer their guilt and the costs of their policies to the white ethnic. They take from the have-little to give to the have-not.

The blue collar works off the boredom of his work, the frustration over his loss of status, and the inequities of the system through the aggression afforded by spectator sports; through gaming; through escapist television shows; through drink. More frequently emotional and hotheaded than the intellectuals, he is far less spiteful and malicious. We should learn to take his Donnybrooks in stride and to incorporate them into the democratic process. To cite a possibility: an encounter between ethnics on issues such as civil rights is bound to trigger emotions, and at a meeting called by the Chairman of the United States Commission on Civil Rights it did. The meeting was held in the Brotherhood in Action building and somebody threw a chair at one of the brothers. The chairman, a quasi-Wasp, was appalled and adjourned the hearing. To have thrown out the chair hurler bodily would have been more appropriate procedure—a liberal interpretation of Robert's rules of order, but suitable under the circumstances. In this fashion, democracy acquires greater cultural authenticity.

Some ethnics obtain relief through maligning people more wretched, hopefully, than they. Some of the crime recorded by the courts issue from members of ethnic groups committing minor offenses against each other. Cracking each other's bodies and stealing each other's property

---

[11] Using 1957–1959 prices as a base, the typical blue collar worker with a wife and two children had a real weekly take-home pay of $78.77 in 1968 compared to $77.30 5 years previously. Figures for 1970 indicate a slight decline. As a group, construction workers and organized truck drivers have done better. If they are removed from the data, the decline in the economic position of the semi-skilled industrial worker would be reflected more dramatically. The figures are from the U.S. Bureau of Labor Statistics.

The price-wage freeze in 1971 and the thaw thereafter promoted the interests of the corporate class at the expense of the industrial worker. The announcement of the freeze triggered a $50 billion rise in stock market values. Stabilization had the effect of providing a windfall income to employers by restricting committed increases in wages. In a Philadelphia study, about half of corporate executives covered received raises in excess of the limit fixed by the Pay Board. One executive doubled his compensation in a one-year period. No reason exists to think that this bias is not nation-wide.

In 1972, after minimum real gains in 6 years, a moderate rise occurred in the real wages of production workers.

are traditional practices in the ranks of the urban proletariat, behavior which should be viewed as cathartic; it reduces tensions. The more gentle middle class experiencing shock over this old fashioned tradition demonstrates a culture bias. A good portion of thsi recorded crime stems from police interfering with the social mores of the working class instead of minding their own business.

While these peccadillos of the working class are labeled crimes, those of the college educated class are often given euphemistic terms such as transgressions and do not enter into statistical tabulations. High caste Wasps and quasi-Wasps have their own brand of crime—embezzlement, falsification of product claims, bribery, securities fraud, and misleading accounting—which comes from stealth; that of the working class issues from passion.

The Wasp caste becomes less enmeshed with the judicial system. They are more law abiding—because of their command of money and legal talent to interpret and pass laws consistent with their preferences —and they stay out of reach. If the system becomes troublesome, they can seek refuge in far away places such as Switzerland. If political pressure on Congress prevents such flight to the country of happy yodelers, they can hire clever lawyers to circumvent the new law.

As an example, a lawyer who became mayor of a big city paid back $700,000 to the Attorney General of the State of Washington after the official made an agreement with him for $2.3 million in legal fees to represent municipally owned utility plants in their suits against electrical equipment firms violating anti-trust laws. Both gentlemen denied doing anything illegal. They turned out to be right.[12]

The alleged irresponsibility of the white ethnic reflects the failure of managers to communicate with him. This failing occurs in politics, in employment, and in community affairs. Despite the abuse, he takes the gaff with hardly more than tap room complaining. The managers of government policy speak of individual rights without giving too much consideration to what the white ethnic considers to be his rights. He reads how the same persons, out on bail, commit most of the crime, and he encounters such statements as:

> The cornerstone of our democracy is the protection of individual rights as well as the rights of the community.[13]

The statement, from a member of the educated class, would be meaningless were it not so provoking. It is easy to make such statements when one does not have to confront the victim.

[12] The transaction was reported in *The New York Times,* December 20, 1969.
[13] A statement attributed to the Chancellor of the Philadelphia Bar Association.

Outside of the fancy artifacts of consumption in his home, what has the blue collarite gained? Very little. He is more insecure than ever before. He relies on a self-imposed apathy to protect himself from the system and yields occasionally to the joy of irresponsibility at work and in his community. His work has lost its meaningfulness; and he has lost also the feeling of self-esteem that comes with a sense of neighborhood.

Criticisms leveled against blue collarites often reflect the values of the critic. In turn, these values are frequently viewed by ethnics as inferior. For example, erudite intellectuals criticize Italian ethnics for their lack of competitive drive and organization. But Italians may consider the competitive spirit as a form of greed and possibly an indication of madness. Jewishness is a convincing commodity to Jews, but a cult of Italianness would be ridiculous. The organization of Italianness is not likely to make it. The person who tries to arouse interest in one may be pushing a not fully disclosed racket. Italians are disinclined to organize either for differences or against differences. The abuse they take over the mafia business reflects their tolerance.

Sadists do exist in the ranks of white ethnics. But they are by far outnumbered by individuals perplexed by the change imposed on them by others. Nevertheless, they are inclined more than many other groups in society to make sacrifices in the interest of the whole. There is probably more joy, more honesty, more affection in the lives of white ethnics than in those of the "superior" intellectuals.

White ethnics need reorganization to reacquire their lost position. Once they organize, if by some miracle they ever do, they may want to steal a chapter from the blacks and impose percentage quotas on the system. They will find Wasps receptive if they threaten disruption. If they could reach an accommodation with blacks, the boredom in American life would vanish.

But the white ethnic's view of the black obstructs this accommodation. He converts his perception of the black sub-proletariat into a stereotype of all Negroes and sees thereby men of no ambition and loose morals. He is unaware of the distinction made between members of his own ethnic group by his father or grandfather. Working class Italians, for example, looked upon those who had little to do but hang around corners as *cafoni*. But this similarity should not obscure the fact that the Wasp policies took a much greater toll upon the blacks than they did upon the Italians. The problem of the sub-proletariat is far more acute today than it was in the days of the Italian *cafoni*.

The low tolerance of ethnics for political and ideological differences, as in the case of Americans generally, stems partly from the absence in their lives of intensive and informal interpersonal relations beyond the family. Such relationships would generate acceptance or tolerance of different points of view. A second contributing factor is the high degree of instability in their lives, much more than in those of the college educated class. The clichè that more education generates more tolerance distorts the truth.

THE INTELLECTUALS

We next move to consideration of the intellectual element in our society. Intellectuals are persons with high convictions of their mental powers and their ability to provide enlightenment; to white ethnics, however, they are jerks. We present them within this frame of disaffection, conscious, nevertheless, of our responsibility to scholarship.

In discussing such a disparate group a problem of classification immediately arises. The term intellectual is often loosely used and undeservedly bestowed. The classification encompasses a great range of individuals—from writers critical of American society to persons included in such category by virtue of a mere undergraduate degree, from persons who delight incorporating obscenities into their speech and writing, rendering themselves *au courant*, to well-groomed citizens of restrained language who move in the system's more conservative circles.

The problem of classification is compounded by the fact that most intellectuals have exclusionist views of themselves. To avoid contamination with lesser intellectuals, they assume such titles as conservative liberals, democratic socialists, passive anarchists, theoretical radicals, or just leftists. The problem seems to be one of difficulty in finding another intellectual of comparable erudition. Nevertheless, a common bond exists: bitching and a preference for the complex explanation over the simple one.

Take the Manhattan Jewish school of intellectuals, reputed to talk mostly to each other and occasionally to God. They live piled high on one another in the stench of their wastes. In 1756, the population of their island numbered 10,498 whites and 2,275 blacks.

> There is not any town where the air is better or where there is a more general appearance of ease.[14]

Two hundred and sixteen years later, the population of the Jewish intellectuals' oasis numbers 1,509,327. And the air is most foul. As their eyes scan a vista of garbage, they conjure up highfalutin words and disgorge them on bond paper in the hope of marketing their sufferings in literary works. Many a battle has been fought and won on their

---

14 Abbé Raynal. *Philosophical and Political History of the British Settlements and Trade in North America,* Edinburgh: C. Denovan, 1779, p. 84.

typewriters. They consider themselves cosmopolitan, but their life experience is confined mostly to an area bounded on the East by Nassau County in Long Island and on the West by the Hudson River. Their global generalizations issue from mid-Manhattan neuroticisms.

The *New York Review* is a major source of erudite information for Manhattan intellectuals. The *Review* pimps for a particular audience much in the same way popular magazines do for theirs, with the advantage of ascribing to its pandering a superior social purpose. The thrust of the journal is anti-Americanism, and its analysis of social problems reflects this bias. Its writers profess the good guys versus the bad guys theory of social analysis, the one comprising mostly Jewish intellectuals together with a few redeemed Wasps and the other, the American establishment. Of less headiness than the *Review, The New York Times* is also an indispensable part of their *vade mecum*. The sunday issue on the door mat in front of the apartment door is a symbol of intellectuality.

Many such subspecies of intellectual prevail. Today's list is obsolete tomorrow as groups divide and sub-divide. One can mention intellectuals such as Eric Hoffer, the anti-intellectual who has gained notoriety as the poor man's intellectual; intellectuals whose causes amount to slumming; lackey intellectuals (a term invented by the brethren) who sell their brains to the highest bidder in the system and who assuage their torment with drink, sex, and psychiatry; scholarly intellectuals who cannot let well enough alone like, for example, the one at Brandeis University who says the Jews discovered America before the first Italian ethnic: Cristoforo Colombo; intellectuals who play war games for a livelihood, who devastate entire nations like children knocking over a line of toy soldiers, but who have not been within earshot of a bullet bent on destruction. Some claim awesome titles. In a speculative book on China, 3 parlor warriors are listed as Deputy Assistant Secretary of Defense for Policy Planning and Arms Control, Specialist in Weapons Systems Choice, and Director of Guerrilla Warfare. Big deal.

Intellectuals believe that a life of cerebral abstraction is superior to one of the spirit. The malaise resulting from this attitude catapults them in hot pursuit of psychocures and worthy causes. This visceral deficiency also disposes them to embrace sweeping criticisms of the society. By so doing, they forfeit the use of intelligence. Sweeping condemnation currently fashionable among intellectuals is the view that individuals are obsequious servants of the system. This observation brings the cross of determinism in American society to its logical end result: the individual is the product of forces beyond his control. But at this point a paradox emerges. Somehow a consciousness unfolds that is independent and critical of the system and individuals elect to behave in a manner inconsistent with the system's demands. Thus, there emerges the philosophy that although the system is not the consequence of individual choice, individual choice will cause the system's collapse.

The vast abstraction inherent in the language of intellectuals is often accompanied and perhaps caused by a scrupulous avoidance of defining terms. For example, Gerald Meier wrote a book on world poverty, but the term poverty does not even appear in his index. And Gunnar Myrdal, of wider reputation, who also focuses the problem of economic development on poverty, not only does not tell us what the word means but does not even bother indexing his ideas. One must take their abstractions on faith.

Some intellectuals are real tough. They are realists, despite their intellectual standing. Walt W. Rostow falls into such a subspecies. Far be it from this brand of intellectual to brood over the fact that the rationale he sells to a prince of power does not place *his* life on the line. Their decision making cannot be cluttered with questions of moral decency. While the contribution of these gentlemen to the collapse of United States prestige abroad is by no means minor, they nevertheless garner many laurels and pass on to positions of even greater eminence in the system. Princes of power shield this variety of thinker from the working class, whose suspicion of such a type manifests political acumen.

Within the array of intellectuals is a small band which comprises the American new left. Their revolutionary role is prudently confined to giving moral and financial support to protesting white and black youth. Theirs is a quixotic kind of logic. The violence committed by the American system, they assert, is similar to that of Nazi Germany. Therefore, to commit acts of violence against the system comprises a worthy moral act. Analagously, the propriety of an act of violence depends on the sympathy one has for the individual who exercises it. Once you decide an official is a baddy, it is all right to label him a criminal without due process. Once he is so labeled, committing violence against him constitutes a superior moral act.

Of all the intellectual varieties in the United States, the Roman Catholic leftist is probably the most bizarre. He and his disciples possess an awe for pure moral posture and a disdain for political strategy; if one asks them for specifics on their assertions, they fall into shock. Comprised mainly of elements of British origin, they are the eternal wonder of the Italian and Slavic contingents. They have discovered sin in the society and the discovery is a heavy burden. In observing their enactment of a morality play, one must restrain the urge to applaud. Come the revolution, they will provide its backdrop of poetry and lyre.

Scratch a Catholic leftist and one finds a man who believes his thought is of a very high moral order. Convinced of his righteousness, he arrogates to himself the task of determining who in society promotes goodness and who fosters badness. He goes further. The conduct of goodies is more excusable than that of baddies. Goodies earn a sweeping moral approbation, and baddies, utter condemnation. For the mischievous conduct of the virtuous is the fault of the depraved. The Catholic leftist decides whose conduct is more worthy and hence entitled to exemption from the rules. He starts from lofty universal principles and then bestows rights of exception to the chosen. He begins with the principle of non-violence and proceeds to corrupt it; he starts with individual responsibility and corrupts that too.

His contribution to the New Logic runs as follows: If a cause is just, then all actions performed to further the cause are non-violent. A cause is just if its adherents sincerely believe it is so. Conclusion: Critics of the cause commit acts of violence when they take action against the cause; thus, Kant's Categorical Imperative has been rediscovered.

The conspiracy syndrome has not spared intellectuals. Conspirators, according to the intellectuals, are the United States government and American management. The Catholic left sees in any oppression anywhere, foreign and domestic, the United States as the neo-colonial oppressor. Restraining their traditional penchant for cosmic generalization, the Catholics limit their accusation against the U.S. government as a conspiracy against the world.

Non-Catholic types tend to limit the range of the conspiracy and make it most lusty. Discussing technology, for instance, Professor Theodore Roszak states:

> Such statements, (i.e. of Former Secretary of Defense McNamara), uttered by obviously competent, obviously enlightened leadership, make abundantly clear the prime strategy of the technocracy. It is to level life down to a standard of so-called living that technical expertise can cope with—and then, on that false and exclusive basis, to claim an intimidating omnicompetence over us by its monopoly of the experts.[15]

[15] Theodore Roszak. *The Making of a Counter Culture*, New York: Doubleday, 1969. Roszak does not affirm life. He deploys an abstract vocabulary to display delusions on the nature of science and technology and on the mission of the counter culture to inject mysticism into society. He exemplifies the inverse relationship existing between the talent to make complex generalizations reinforcing personal prejudices and the capacity to comprehend human life.

In another passage of the same book, he states:

> To liberate sexuality would be to create a society in which technocratic discipline would be impossible. But to thwart sexuality outright would create a widespread, explosive resentment that requires constant policing; and besides, this would associate the technocracy with various puritanical traditions that enlightened men cannot but regard as superstitious. The strategy chosen, therefore, is not harsh repression, but rather the Playboy version of total permissiveness. In the affluent society, we have sex and sex galore—or so we are to believe. But when we look more closely we see that this sybaritic promiscuity wears a special social coloring. It has been assimilated to an income level and social status available only to our well-heeled junior executives and the jet set.

It is my observation that the young Roszak champions acquire more sex galore than do junior executives—at considerably less cost.

Of the militant Catholic left, Ned O'Gorman writes as follows:

> In the militant Catholic left—and in the Black militant left, too—there is an irrationality that taints the revolution and limits its chances of success. I write of that crippled, howling, petulant, spoiled brat anger, and the self-importance that traps revolutionaries in their own will and leaves their zeal, their visions and their hope abandoned to their egos and to the collective egos of their followers. I am not sure if I can bear any more the small voice crying alone in the wilderness. One seeks the solitary, searing voice of the prophet, but I want to hear it in the street, in the world, in schools, in politics where change is still possible. The Catholic left has nurtured a community of parasites who free-load off the Gospels.[16]

Many of the general propositions lofted by intellectuals are unassailable; while their terms lack precision, they convey nevertheless unquestionably good intent. For example, when it is asserted that Consciousness III is the recovery of self, who dares criticize such a worthy restoration? But they too often do not let well enough alone; they indulge in exposition. By so doing, as when they cite that the recovery of self by hippy youth involves freedom from parents, school, and career, they take a massive step toward the brink of absurdity. And when they go on to suggest that such youth, so pitiably unable to communicate in effective language, will lead the working class toward the same redemption, they plunge in head first.

Most intellectuals are liberals. Few of them would quarrel with such an assertion. But not all liberals are intellectuals. For example, a man not disposed to shock when hearing an obscenity is liberal minded, but not necessarily intellectual. But if he uses 4 letter words in his own

16 *The New York Times*, May 30, 1971.

dialogue, he merits the title of intellectual. The confusion raised by this distinction diminishes as liberals, out of frustration, become intellectuals. For a liberal in these times is weighted down with pessimistic thoughts. He bears the heavy burden of fighting oppression, racism, and police brutality. He confronts a world of racists, fascists, and anti-semites.

Liberals are heavy contributors to the social ills they lament. Those who fight for community integration are principals in its destruction, for within their ranks are men who are racist, intolerant, and ill-informed. Driven up the wall, they hurl down darts of accusation against their critics of lack of compassion and intellectual strength, qualities which, by inference, they possess in abundance. They are dead serious and do not take lightly the sting of criticism.

Liberals often make their fire and thunder revelations in the press. Down at the bottom of the editorial information, under a formidable list of underwriters of the new faith, non-luminaries can indicate their spiritual and financial allegiance by marking the appropriate square and sending a check. No space is provided for rebuttal. The *Review* provides such a meeting ground for liberals promoting high minded causes. A full page ad lists academics in support of Angela Davis. Their proclamation alerts the reader to the special importance of the Davis case to the academic community because of her dismissal by the Regents in California. It goes on to assert that the charges against her in connection with the Marion County Courthouse shootout, "at which she was not present and with which she denies any connection," are part of the continuing persecution she has suffered for her liberation activities.

> The attack upon Angela Davis is part of an attempt by the repressive forces in the country to move it in a reactionary direction. The focus of the attack at this moment is something they believe is most vulnerable— a Black, Communist woman academic.
>
> In making charges of this magnitude against her, these forces count upon the racism and anti-communism of our society to inhibit people from coming to her defense, to deny her the presumption of innocence and to convict her before trial.[17]

This statement is signed by individuals the academic profession refers to as scholars.

At times, the distinction between liberalism and conservatism seems to be one of disposition arising from dissimilarity in body chemistry. One is tempted to think body enzymes trigger differences in perceiving the same phenomena. Thus, in observing a noisy group of black demonstrators, a liberal uses the term *boisterous* for what a conservative would

[17] *The New York Review*, July 22, 1971.

describe as a *howling mob;* in referring to a teenage rioter, one might say *impressionable youngster;* the other, *hoodlum.* Final judgments differ also. Thus, the liberal may state *we have to relate,* and the conservative, *call the cops.*[18]

Despite its lack of precision, the term liberal is useful as a generic description of persons disposed to see things change. As a general classification, it serves the purpose of lumping together the dissenters: from pragmatists who are receptive to new courses of action, generally at someone else's expense, to neurotics whose perturbations incline them to be critical.

Therefore, we launch the hypothesis that intellectuals are mostly liberal, but liberals cannot automatically claim the title of intellectual, nor would they want to. We must keep in mind as well the many categories of the subspecies. Thus, the general class "university professor" divides into "instructor in absentia" and two sub-categories of liberals: the "dutiful," taking their cues from administrators, and the "dissenters," stirring things up at faculty meetings. The dutiful prepare their lessons religiously and periodically publish the same findings. The dissenters rarely hazard bringing forth their own proposals, but stand ever ready to pounce on the ideas of others. They are not competent strategists in dealing with power, nor are they effective advisors to princes of power or able analysts of social events. To use the term of Harvard professor Crane Brinton, they can be classified as the subspecies "bellyacher."

The most profound of liberals, certainly, are those who talk and write extensively on social movements without ever referring to any one social problem in particular. Their ability to produce highly abstract words is inversely proportional to their capacity to make a social movement come off. Their writing strategy includes the invention of new terms for old phenomena and the use of charged words to control meaning. Thus, for instance, a liberal would term genocide society's restrictions on a woman copulating at public expense. And he would refer to a black neighborhood as a ghetto.

In a clash of opinion between themselves, liberals often behave like infants, accusing each other of ideological error and insulting each other with highly worked-on prose. Their competitive spirit asserts itself not only in the exchange of verbal assaults, but also in one-upmanship in the scope of their liberation movements. A New York liberal presently wears the crown: he is working for the liberation of all individuals imprisoned for political, racial, or religious reasons anywhere in the world.

---

[18] The same verbiage can convey entirely different meanings to different specialists. A Chemistry professor colleague stated at lunch he was going to lecture on heavily doped semi-conductors. I assumed he was referring to hippies.

Although much of the pursuit of liberal causes is harmless, some of this activity, such as that on behalf of Negroes, freedom of religion, and international causes, affects many individuals who do not think similarly and creates an impact out of proportion to the relative number of persons participating in it.

Major political, social, and economic decisions in the United States issue from liberal thinking. Even conservatives, once they acquire decision-making posts, are frequently forced into liberal thinking as they enter the system; Republican fiscal responsibility becomes Keynesian economics once its advocates assume political office. The common procedure is to rely on teams of technicians to come up with options and to choose one that minimizes risk; what is considered good politics prescribes the ultimate choice. Regardless of the label of those who make them, decisions tend to be the same when the circumstances are the same. The liberals who deplore the excesses produced by the decisions of others are likely to make the same decisions as those who are making the choices at the moment.

This style of decision making suggests an over-reaction theory of social change. To cite a hypothetical example: In stage one, liberals start beating the hustings over society's cruel treatment of homosexuals. They acquire support from high minded politicians and from progressive organizations such as Women's Lib. A liberal law is passed. In stage two, the homosexuals reach such a level of daring that a man cannot move his bowels peacefully in a public toilet without being propositioned by one of their number. Conservatives become indignant over this turn of events and in the next stage muster sufficient strength to pass another law. The law, under the vigorous leadership of the FBI, places police guards at all public toilets in the United States. And on it goes, the next stage being police brutality.

Liberals delight in platitudes. The specifics of a situation do not interest them. Thus, the liberal candidate for mayor of a large city declared during his campaign that the only solution to racial unrest was a community in which all races lived together in peace. He thereby aligned himself on the side of virtue. When someone in the audience suggested that integration could be achieved by limiting the influx of Negroes in white communities, he appeared shocked. The mayor won to lead a city in a cycle of integration that runs from separation to integration and back to separation.

Liberals also have an abiding faith in the ability of government to reform individuals. Coercive law is the means of prodding people into a higher level of virtue. But they are disillusioned regarding the ability of the labor movement to reconstruct the working class. Nevertheless, many still feel squeamish about crossing a picket line.

Liberals gain employment in the upper echelons of the public bureaucracies. Some seek jobs in government as a shield against the rigors of life. If their ideas for a better world cannot be brought into fruition, government at least provides them a sanctuary from the inequities of the larger society, and in its higher echelons, they are afforded the opportunity to apply their analytical frameworks on global scale. In government, then, the liberal is formulating policies; in the educational system he is pushing it this way and that with the latest fad. In industry, he is providing the techniques with which to manipulate the consumer. One post becomes a springboard for another. He moves together with his colleagues from one letter head to the next as he proceeds from one cause to the next. The list used to run from Roger Baldwin to Norman Thomas, but due to ravaging time and the decline of the Wasps, the order now is Bernstein to Yarmolinsky. In short, they are the standard bearers of ideas crystalized in the Big Depression of over 3 decades ago. Inside government, they are prudent. Outside, they pronounce the truth and pour out books that lament the errors of their successors. Their influence does not derive from a mass following, although some are so deluded; it comes, rather, from the princes who pick and choose. When their sway is terminated, there is always another set of liberals eager to take over. If Galbraith, Goldman, and Schlesinger are disengaged and pouting, there is always a Roche, a Rostow, or a Kissinger available. With some shopping around, a set of liberals can be found for every mood.

The liberal judges himself to be a humanitarian and man of universal principle. But consistency is not his virtue. Some of the same liberals who find war barbaric want the United States to do some sabre rattling in another. The horrors of war are seemingly more bearable when directed against baddies. Thus, the liberal discriminates in his love for humanity: he loves some people more than others. He has a sublime feeling for the whole human race, but a special affection for particular members with whom he identifies out of personal needs. He is readily disposed to abandon the use of intellect when a just cause demands it. He shares with the society generally a penchant for anti-intellectualism under pressure of self-interest, but he gives the switch the name of justice.

His intellectuality blocks him from relating to one person at a time. With a profound understanding of mankind, he finds it difficult to grasp the character of any one person. He victimizes himself by stereotypes of his own creation. Once the liberal assigns virtue to a particular group, its members can do no wrong. He panders to their every impulse; those who oppose represent evil. Once a liberal makes up his mind on an issue, he in effect loses his liberalism. A person expressing a contrary view may be a demagogue, misguided, or incompetent. Thus, in referring to liberals in the Congress who voted against busing of school children, Tom Wicker of *The New York Times* writes:

> It was also, for those numerous liberals who knew better, rank demagoguery. Some others may only have been caught up in a stampede. Still others may have acted from genuine, if misplaced, concern. All of them failed, in one way or another, to meet the ordinary standards of leadership and vision that ought to be expected of members of Congress.[19]

The liberal selects and embellishes those phenomena that are consistent with his ideological outlook. Once the sought-for generalization is found to be sustained by selected facts, the generalization acquires universality.

The liberal evidences characteristics of youth: a need to worship charismatic figures, confidence in one's own wisdom, and ignorance of the facts. The newspaper ad liberals who make their pronouncements on issues suggest that the most bitter enemies of liberals are other liberals. They denounce each other by exchanging letters via publications. They even state for the record how they denounced each other on the telephone.[20]

His current angel is the Negro. The Negro is his guru. No matter how atrocious the black man's behavior, it is understandable. The posture is tinged with masochism. Some blacks are not loathe to take advantage of the halo provided them. The liberal's view of the race problem as an abstraction labeled racism, joined with the posture of middle-class blacks, provides a major thrust to social policy. Protest against this posture is not considered virtuous. The involvement of virtue in decision making inhibits pure political flows upward, and its consequence is bitterness and backlash. Allegedly fighting for consensus and egalitarianism, liberals reap a harvest of divisiveness and separatism. They even incur the contempt of Negroes they champion.

Liberals have lost their rank and file, and politicians accordingly ignore their positions with impunity. For example, the Americans for Democratic Action, a dry bones relic of World War II, repeatedly demonstrates an inability to capture mass support for its proposals. When the Kerner Commission on the Negro riots trumpeted its finding that white racism was responsible for the conflict, liberals reacted with

---

[19] *The New York Times,* November 9, 1971.
[20] Daniel P. Moynihan, formerly of the staff of the Nixon administration, is viewed as an apostate by other liberals. Mr. Moynihan is one of those rare individuals who knows how to acquire political power while continuing to state the facts. But his thinking on Negroes is unacceptable to liberals. The Machiavellian stunts used to discredit him reflect the decadence of American liberalism.

enthusiasm. They took the delightfully global conclusion to their bosom in a spirit of *mea culpa,* assuaged their sense of guilt, and thereby alienated large numbers of white ethnics who traditionally had voted liberal in the United States.

Liberals pontificate in the city about tolerance and then go home to their suburban dwellings, while white ethnics whom they exhort go to bed in the city afraid. Liberals push educational opportunities for Negroes to the point where a black high school graduate is sought after with promises of financial assistance by politically minded college presidents, while white ethnics, most of whom lack a college education as do Negro parents, undergo sacrifices to get one child into and through college without the same subsidy. In constant hot pursuit of the current underdog, more out of vexation with American society than because of the merit of the position of the individuals they champion, liberals flit from the white working class, to the poor, to black South Africans, to Soviet Jews, and to the Israelis, for whom the label of underdog is a misnomer. One gets the gnawing feeling that liberal politicians who demand justice for the Israelis may be inspired by the greater number of Jewish over Arab votes in their constituencies.

White and black liberals are similar in many respects. Both are middle-class minded. Similarly, the position of middle-class blacks on racial issues reflects their own needs more than those of the urban black proletariat. Their posture on housing, education, and employment demonstrates a personal position that often produces more political stress than substantive return to the blacks they champion. The leaders rising out of the urban ranks have a markedly different mentality from that of their middle-class brethren. The black liberal imposes borrowed ideologies on the Negro working classes and gives them a mission to perform that may have little to do with their pressing needs. He shares with his well-heeled white colleagues a disinclination to see matters as they are. There are exceptions to this posture, but the black liberals who take them run the risk of being accused of racial disloyalty by other liberals.

Power fascinates us all. Liberal intellectuals denied power pout and become critical of those who acquire it. They are not against the use of power so much as the manner and condition of its employment. By criticizing its use, they compensate for their inability to gain it. A sumptuous lunch in the ornate private dining room of a prince of power is enough to give an intellectual a sense of euphoria; aware of this weakness, industry and government take advantage of it. They hire intellectuals to perform tasks, interested not in the end product of their toil so much as in the aura of respectability given their questionable dealings. Undoubtedly, some of these employers may have a genuine interest in his product; undoubtedly also, some consider the intellectual a naive person who can be used for purposes not fully disclosed.

CONCLUSIONS

Our discussion of the intellectual concludes this section on the social setting in modern America. A few observations, however, bear repetition, in order to crystallize the picture presented and to suggest the implications indicated.

The social fabric that holds together American society is a delicate one. No other nation at a similar level of economic growth has had to face problems in a similar context of social differences. Issues have to be resolved in a precarious nexus that was formerly held together by the national government as a symbol of justice. That symbol was damaged severely by men who have held government posts since the Second World War. In a society where a large segment of the population mistrusts its government, which propagandizes people into believing that happiness derives from acquisition of goods, the dominating thrust behind life becomes the pursuit of power and pleasure, and the highest pleasure, sex; when that wanes, there remains only the terror of death.

The system of mass pleasure seeking requires conditioning behavior to serve its needs. The conditioning necessitates the use of deception. The deception conflicts with the need for an environment that stimulates individual expression. The conflict frustrates the life cycle of individualistic outpouring, intake, and accommodation. The frustration manifests itself in aberration, cruelty, and sabotage.

Individuals who have to be instructed in how to express their feelings are symptomatic of the society's deficiency. So are the advocates of such training when they sell their programs as the sure road to happiness. For a massive decline in the sense of community has emerged from this materialistic base. Americans are less generous with each other, less inclined to make concessions to different points of view. Traditional romantic idealism has vanished and infantilism has taken its place. Americans are mistrustful persons of limited courage who play their role cautiously. They are disinclined to hear what is in conflict with their views. They commit cruelty in the name of fair play. The esprit de corps that arises from shared values is lost; accompanying this loss is a rise in social tensions.

Life reeks with falsehood and hatred, and Americans know it. They keep a troubled silence or react violently at the suggestion of such qualities in their lives. Intellectuals and corporate men make their contributions to the rise of hatred. They have an aristocratic condescending attitude toward the workingman, a hauteur which the worker quickly senses. It is this aristocracy that comprises the vulgar crowd. It is they who peddle vulgarization of the spirit; they who provide a harvest of disastrous policies and a generation of child men; they who cloak their interests with lofty principles of service; they who have succeeded in destroying the traditional life.

An American intellectual does not convey an image of a man of culture. A more typical portrait is that of an insecure, humorless egoist, aristocratic in outlook, using shock to gain prominence, lacking courage to concede his mistakes, unable to talk man to man to an individual outside his .class, incapable of bringing forward a substitute for the traditional philosophy he assisted in destroying. His cleverness does not extend to bringing forth an alternative, not even for his own salvation. He is trapped in a life cycle of futility, searching desperately for gurus. The intellectual has destroyed his image as a man of learning and yielded to the working class the hope of a new creation.

It is axiomatic that intellectuals who never have managed social conflict come up with solutions on the basis of applying their own universal principles. Whether it be a Herbert Marcuse or a Skinner, they are all fascinated by the wisdom of their intellectual discoveries and impressed with the foolishness of their intellectual rivals. Theirs are authoritarian minds. They do not affirm life. The more remote their craft from the management of social conflict, the more authoritarian they seem to be; if man lived consistent with their objective knowledge he would acquire a kingdom of serenity and authenticity. But if, by some genetic coup, everybody became an intellectual, we would more likely achieve a kingdom of chaos and abuse. Although no precise knowledge exists as to man's fundamental nature, intellectuals are ever ready to promote their universal principles of human behavior.

In short, few intellectuals exist in the ranks of American intellectuals. They are obsolete in their political and analytical role. Their inability to command respect is their own doing. History gave them the chance to lead an accommodation of social differences, but they blew it with their ego tripping. The working class has relegated them to the trash can.

From this sea of egocentricity in American society one can thus detect a faint smell of change. Its fomenters are not exclusively from any one class. It moves not in accordance with an overall design. The rebels of humble origin who appear at its forefront ride the crest of attitudinal and institutional ferment issuing from the emergence of ethnic identity, the rejection of the Wasp image as a model of behavior, and the clash generated by the position of different groups. Elite decision making seems to be ebbing. The new order emerging may be cultural pluralism.

PART THREE

THE INSTITUTIONS

Toward a Mafia Theory
of Economics

The modern world is a Machiavellian world.
Moravia

A revolutionary change in decision making has taken place in the American economy. The political-economic system of countervailing power has blossomed into an oligarchy of conservative managers in government and industry. They enjoy flying in each other's company in corporate aircraft. They exchange positions periodically in a game of musical chairs. They are all-purpose heroes. A manager may be an executive in industry today; a top official in the military establishment tomorrow; the day after a battler against world poverty in an international organization. The corporate lawyer who advises his firm one day on how to promote its interests with government may be a government official the next purportedly defending the public trough against corporate incursions. No major movement occurs in any one direction. However, a trickle moves from firms and government to foundations and universities in order to pursue a sublime mission before retirement; they perform as elder statesmen and purveyors of truth after the rough-house and deception of industry and government. Thus, roving managers discharge the burden of administering the economy. As they do, they periodically congregate and bestow honors on each other.

We present information in this chapter on how this system is mafia-like in its methods. And we conclude with an appropriate mafia theory of economics.

The managers operate a system of cooperating baronies given direction by several thrusts: the imperative of becoming big in order to become secure, the need of the government-industry combine to rub each other's back so as to maintain orderliness in their respective function; the powerful hunger for money and power; the pursuit of sensuous pleasure by an ever growing middle class. The managers are favored by the passivity of this middle class and by the existence of effective mechanisms with which to manipulate it.

Engineers and lawyers are among the crucial professionals hired by these managers. Engineers provide them with technological options. Lawyers are essential if only as a defense against other lawyers; the possibility always exists that a rival lawyer will try to exploit a semicolon. Few decisions are made without consulting legal staff; most decisions require their imprimatur. Managers rely on law to promote their interests. A major mission of attorneys thus is to ascertain how the law can be subverted to this end.

A *menage à trois* beds together industrial, political, and educational institutions. The bureaucrats think alike, look alike, act alike. On the whole, they keep their cards close to the chest and avoid the expression of provocative ideas. Some, even college presidents, manage to achieve the formidable record of not uttering a non-conforming idea for decades. This attribute is by no means considered a deficiency within the managerial coterie. In fact, peers reward this accomplishment as a mark of administrative statesmanship. They do not collude. It is not necessary. They live and let live so long as rising income and power are guaranteed them. The issues that bind the managers are greater than those which divide them. Former dissidents are bought by government, directly or indirectly, overtly or covertly. Government makes them docile by hiring them, honoring them, bending the law in their favor, guaranteeing them rising income, and generally placing the state apparatus at their disposal. The dialogue of managers in the private sector, which is no longer private, does not differ in essentials from that of government officials. No effective power bloc exists with a line markedly different from that of the bureaucrats. Even labor union officials have joined the circle. Their view of war is as solidly American as that of the super-Americans. The oligarchs are not selfish men; they are given to bursts of generosity so long as the system runs smoothly.

At administrative summits unanimity and sense of duty prevail; at the base frustration and irreverence. A feeble gesture in countervailance is made by a few Congressmen powerless to alter the course of events. The system of countervailing power dies. The new order is rule by monied aligarchs and the new slogan to each according to his ability to manipulate.[1]

With this change in the relationships of organized blocs has come a shift in the traditional meaning of conservatism and liberalism. In one respect, the words have exchanged meaning. A conservative now may be an individual who believes in the right of cultural pluralism and a liberal one who seeks to maintain traditional values through the force of law. They both believe in elitism and in the use of the state as a tool of manipulating the economy and its people. They differ, however, as to whom they represent. The conservatives generally are the spokesman of corporate leaders; the liberals, spokesmen of organized pressure groups of the middle class.

Events in the two decades following the Second World War have hastened these changes. Enormous military budgets have forged an alliance of government and corporations, many of which have never competed in the private market. International crises have sanctioned deception of the people by the State in the interest of the people. The people are computerized by state and corporation to better serve them. Laws that control the relationship between organized labor and management have created bureaucracies that cooperate often at the expense of the individual for whom the laws were intended. Regulatory agencies of government, created to control particular industries, are controlled by the organizations the agencies are supposed to regulate. Laws passed to foster competition stifle it. In short, foreign and domestic challenges place the control of resources in the hands of a coterie whose rule appears sanctioned by the divine right of kings.

The power clusters in the system are big industrial firms, big Labor,

---

[1] The cozy relationship exists also at local government levels. In New York, a former city administrator, as president of a consulting firm, obtained $15 million in consulting contracts from the city in one year. A former rent administrator receives $200 daily as a consultant to the new rent administrator. An executive of another consulting firm, formerly an official of the City Planning Commission, has some $8.4 million in consulting contracts with the Commission (*The New York Times*, July 4, 1970). In one instance, the head of a consulting firm was obtaining contracts at the time he was heading the city agency. (*The New York Times*, July 7, 1970).

In another example, the consultant fee of Mrs. Eugenia M. Flatow, former executive director of the Model Cities program, comes to $650 weekly, or more than her former salary. Mrs. Flatow used to be a member of the Riverside Democratic Club, whose leader is a special assistant of the mayor. Mrs. Flatow is quoted as stating she was working on the relationship of the budget process to the total work program of the City Planning Commission, so that it becomes a year-round part of the total agency work (*The New York Times*, February 10, 1971). Much of the consultant work involves repeated studies of the same problem. Ten such studies were made on one bridge in New York City within a 20-year period. None of the recommendations were implemented. (*The New York Times*, July 14, 1970).

big foundations, big communications media, and government machinery controlled by a small number of patriots, principally from the confederate states.[2] By controlling men and money, they seek to propagate the values necessary for the system to work. Formerly, a dissimilarity of interests among the princes of power would produce varying allegiances and alliances that would change with the scope and strategy of particular issues. A continuous process of organizing and counter-organizing would shift conflict between the economic and political arena. However, today new trends are notable. On major political and economic questions, the princes unite so as to impose the price of their settlement on those in the unsystem. Second, the distinction as to what is politics and what economics becomes increasingly blurred. Major economic decisions become an act of politics. Third, solutions tend to concentrate power further.

In short, no neat distinction exists between economic and political power. Each is a tool or generator of the other. Government is at the disposal of those with the power to control its processes in the pursuit of their interests. The mercantilist state dispenses favors to those with the money and talent to claim them. In some instances, as in the case of oil refining, the propaganda is disseminated that what is good for the industry is also good for the state. Capitalism having been overthrown by this oligarchic state, the people are no longer oppressed but tethered.

The humanistic arm of the obsolete system of countervailing power used to be organized labor. But the days of trade unionism as the voice of social idealism have long since gone. Union members tolerate the system's depredations so long as their organization produces jobs and pay checks. Unions tolerate hideous advertising signs so long as they produce union jobs, bigger and better munitions if they produce jobs, and destruction of the environment if that brings jobs. The system gives them no alternative. Accordingly, trade officials share points of view with corporate managers. They no longer countervail but join forces, as in the Commonwealth of Pennsylvania where the union and employers combined to push through legislation allowing trucks 65 feet long on the highways. Or they acquiesce to the crunch of inflation on members of the unsystem so long as it it not in their interest to take effective measures against it. Such cooperation cannot be beaten.

In short, the values of American labor officials have become integrated with those of employers. The necessities of playing an institu-

[2] In 1971, Organized Labor, the United States Chamber of Commerce, and the National Association of Manufacturers elected jointly to take exception to a question on an Internal Revenue tax form listing lobbying activities. The government asked the 3 groups how the question should be removed and accepted their suggestion. (*The New York Times*, February 19, 1971.)

tional role in the preliminary stages of labor management relations hide
the extent to which this integration has taken place. To those participating in the day-by-day resolution of management union conflicts, the
extent to which labor officials acquiesce to employer criteria for decision
making is obvious. Employer prices provide union members with income. Therefore, unionists share an interest with employers in maintaining prices. Trade unionists exert their influence on prices indirectly
by exerting pressure for uniform employment standards and technology
among employers. The parallel interests of employers and unionists,
nurtured by the government, can be observed readily in the construction
industry.

A major concern of these employers is the perennial one of the mafia:
how to maintain power within their respective duchies and how to guard
them from outside encroachment. This concern demands fealty to the
chief. Within each organization, a subordinate is judged on the basis of
whether his relations with his superiors and outside bargainers favorably
affect the position of his superior. What is proper is that which maintains and enhances position in the hierarchy of command and what is
improper is that which undermines it. At the same time, top managers
must appear to govern in the name of promoting the needs of their
respective constituents.

Managerial decisions are an amalgam of points of view held by sub-
monopolies within the organization. Each sub-monopoly carries weight
to the degree it can undermine the position of the chief. A frontal
attack on a threatening position is not prudent; it is more effective for
the top man to isolate and weaken the standard bearer who challenges
him. Hypocrisy is his most valuable asset. Whether in political office
or in competition for one, whether an official in the public or private
sector or a university administrator, a competent manager does not
make the fatal error of describing matters as they are. Rather, he depicts a reality consistent with the maintenance of his power. Thus,
when a university president's policy is challenged by a professor, it is
prudent to curtail the professor's initiative in the name of unknown
sub-monopolies in the organization which sustain the president's views.
Accordingly, the president can appear to be managing on the criterion
of democratic consent.

Some princes are beholden to nobles in their organization, a depend-
ency that is undesirable even though it may rest simply on sentimental
grounds. These nobles may be carryovers from a previous administration or new incumbents hired to assist the prince in his acquisition of
power. To consolidate their influences, princes must eliminate those by
whose sufferance they live and replace them with obsequious subordi-

nates. This elimination can be carried out with impunity so long as the prince convinces the nobles he acts in their interest, maintains in the course of eliminating them the support of the nobles' rank and file, and avoids forcing the nobles to organize out of fear for their future.

All princes of power, in government or out—corporate managers, managers of foundations, and university presidents—are essentially politicians. They have to manipulate communications in a way that maintains their position. From their political promontory, the princes utter platitudes, sometimes even in brilliant fashion. They have been known to talk for a decade without saying anything. In fact, a prominent national politician has managed this feat since World War II.

Accordingly, government can be lumped together with corporate organization. Differences there are, obviously. Corporations do not print money; their killing is much less obvious; nor do they levy taxes. However, both are political-economic institutions that must control resources in a manner that sustains their organization. The same internal rivalries have to be faced. Although the imperative of profitability seems to be a difference, the distinction is actually not as sharp as appears at first blush. Governments in the long run have to maintain a balance between revenue and expenditure as do corporations. However, the forces of competition do compel corporations to be more efficient. Only in a government office can an employee proceed from morning newspaper to extended coffee klatch to early lunch without repercussions.

On the surface, the pose of oligarchs is that of benefactor; underneath, they practice the art of extinguishing the careers of those who threaten them. Thus, the outstanding prince is one who appears as a great humanist at the level of visibility while prudently neutralizing rivals below. This latter role he can perform wisely by assigning it to an expendable subordinate. For the sake of appearances, hatchet men are called assistant or Vice President for Academic Affairs. In the mafia they are called *consiglieri*.

The managers of organizations maintain vigilance on each other, propose and dispose, and quietly bargain out their differences. The government official, formerly the exponent of the public, is now their alter ego. No significant change in policy occurs without their agreement or acquiescence. Managers allocate employment opportunities, shape public tastes, administer the armed state, in effect set the general tone of American life. Their common source of irritation is an unmalleable constituency. Organized labor has not penetrated this circle to the same degree, but not because of lack of aspiration; with greater responsiveness to the needs of the establishment, a deeped breakthrough is likely. Infiltrating the establishment are university entrepreneurs, a tribe of professor that increases by the exercise of discretion and by convincing the managerial coterie that they possess needed technical skills. Occasionally, minority groups penetrate the circle, should they possess the physical and mental attributes that make them respectable. The managers are so closely tied to the apparatus of state, it is difficult to determine on whose payroll they should be. They share the problem of how to render ineffective the protestations of constituents, be they voters, consumers, taxpayers, employees, students, or rank and file unionists.

Who are these managers? Preeminently of Wasp origin, those who administer large firms or who choose those who do are the holders of big blocks of corporate stock. In a study of the nation's largest 250 firms, Don Villarejo concludes: "A relatively small group of persons, the propertied rich, both own and substantially control the giant enterprises of the nation.[3] According to Robert J. Lampman, the wealthiest one percent of adults has actually increased its percentage of stock ownership to 76 percent.[4] Robert L. Heilbroner judges that some 45,000 families (one tenth of one percent of American families) receive an average income of over $100,000 yearly. Some 90,000 families own three quarters of the corporate stock. The relative income going to this upper class has risen. Professor Heilbroner notes that for the half century beginning in 1910 no change occurred in the relative income (30 percent) of the top 10 percent of income recipients. Since 1960, their share has increased.[5]

This upper middle class furnishes 50 percent of the directors of the top corporations. The remainder comprise individuals who have amassed credentials to enter the upper class from the niche directly below.[6]
The upper class dominates the top executive structure of big firms, into a sport for millionaires.

[3] Earl F. Cheit, "Why Managers Cultivate Social Responsibility," in John G. Maurer (ed.) *Readings in Organization Theory: Open System Approaches*, New York: Random House, 1971, pp. 365–387.

[4] Robert J. Lampman. *Changes in the Share of Wealth Held By Top Wealth Holders, 1922–1956*, New York: National Bureau of Economic Research, 1960, p. 26.

[5] *The New York Times*, November 28, 1971. The relative importance of the upper middle class income as a proportion of the total income should not be exaggerated. In 1969, income recipients of $50,000 or more received $38.5 billion compared to $603.5 billion for others. The tax liability amounted to $13.8 billion and $96.6 billion respectively. If the entire remaining income of the well-to-do were confiscated, it would amount to 10 percent of the national government budget. (Statistics of Income 1969, Individual Income Tax Returns, U. S. Government Printing Office, 1970). Much of the income inequality represents inequality in the fortunes of birth, differences in the desire to make money, and in luck. Equal opportunity in education is unlikely to remove the inequality to any great extent, while reducing income inequality by tax law has only a short run effect.

[6] *New York Review*, January 4, 1968.

In 1950, 85 percent of the business elite were of native born fathers of the Protestant faith, especially Presbyterian and Episcopalian. The remainder were predominantly self-made men of Jewish or Catholic origin. The Jews tended to enter the elite by first achieving middle class positions after graduating from prestigious schools and the Catholics, by leap frogging from the bottom of the labor force. Ninety percent of the generals and admirals derived from native born parents of Protestant faith, principally Presbyterian and Episcopalian. The same study indicates that the majority of senators are native born, third generation white Protestants of Northwest European descent. Of the 92 members of the Supreme Court from 1789 to the date of the study, only 9 justices rose out of the working class. Of this number, 8 were either British or Northwest European Protestants.[7]

Historically, Wasps have claimed the right to govern by virtue of their self-determined superiority. In the early part of the century, Senator Albert J. Beveridge from Indiana was stating that God had been preparing the English and Teutonic people for a thousand years to govern inferior peoples. John W. Burgess, professor of Political Science at Columbia University, was asserting at the same time the right of the Anglo-Saxon race to assume leadership. Sociologist Edward A. Ross, disturbed by the immigrant waves of white ethnics, was saying:

> To the practiced eye, the physiognomy of certain groups unmistakably proclaims inferiority of type. I have seen gatherings of the Foreign born in which narrow and sloping foreheads were the rule. The shortness and smallness of the crania were very noticeable.[8]

In sum, not all of the upper middle class rules, but those who do are upper middle class. They hold positions by virtue of the advantages of birth. The higher the post, the rarer the appearance of a non-Wasp name on the nameplate. Alien blood filters through occasionally, principally in new corporations and industrial areas that experience sharp increases in economic growth. However, the closer to the apex, the more likely the top posts are manned by upper class Wasps. In a belated show of conscience, the Wasp managers are seeking by means of percentage quotas to induce a movement of blacks into the occupational ranks of white ethnics. They can ease the pressure attending this movement by magnanimously vacating some of their posts to white ethnics.

The very American Americans have an influence in domestic and

[7] Suzanne Keller, *Beyond The Ruling Class*, New York: Random House, 1963, pp. 307–325.

[8] George H. Daniels. *Science in American Society*, New York: Knopf, 1971, p. 254.

foreign affairs considerably greater than their numbers in the population. They are constantly threatened by an invasion of lesser Americans of their neighborhoods, schools, clubs, and political organizations. And while they lament the passing of traditional values, their investments in business contribute to their destruction.

As stated, the class identity of these managers does not imply rule by conspiratorial decision making; they are not organized into a cabal. They must reckon with the turmoil their decisions may create and the persistence of the lower classes such as Blacks, Jews, and Southern Europeans seeking to enter the club. The princely decisions are conservative ones, a conservatism which seeks to maintain obsolescent institutions and traditional rights of wealth. The ethnic pecking order for entrance into their ranks is Wasp, facsimile Wasp, Northern European, and, when the labor supply becomes scarce in relation to demand, just White Christian. Under acute stress, the power structure accepts not too-Jewish Jews and non-Negro Negroes.[9] Top posts being in short supply, Wasps predominate. Although Americans dislike talking about it, this pecking order is a fact of life.

Any significant ideological differences between aspirants to high decision-making posts and incumbents diminish as the aspirants approach entrance into the circle. Upon admittance, the decision-making structure completes the conformism. Candidates present credentials to top incumbents who choose self-images; the technicians who feed them information with which to make decisions remain essentially the same; and the same view of the American way of life enters their calculations. A dissident generation rejects such managers and pushes for significant change. But barring convulsions in the society such change will not occur, for faces and nameplates change but not points of view.

The key group of decision makers in the United States is thus a small group of super-Americans of Anglo-Saxon stock and facsimiles of such stock. They are in Congress, the military, top government posts, finance, foreign policy, and in both political parties. Not to be confused with patriots of a lower order, such as those of the American Legion variety who quibble over trifles such as how to raise and lower the flag, these patriots shuffle around dollars by the billions. The affluent custodians of traditional American values and champions of the armed services, they are suspicious of latter-day Americans and by extension foreigners,

---

[9] For 10 years, I placed into a folder newspaper accounts with pictures of Negroes assuming managerial responsibilities in the system. Not one of the photos is of an individual with Negroid features. The possibility of bias is discounted by the fact that the motive in starting the folder had nothing to do with the message it conveyed a decade later.

and have a nostalgia for the old days. They are ambivalent. Spurred by noble feeling, convinced of the superior virtue of their position, they are also disposed to use money and power to subvert democratic institutions, corrupt the young, condone the assassination of foreign citizens, all in the pursuit of noble ends.

The patriots have considerable power in Congress. While deploring excessive government spending, they can obtain passage in jig time of a $3 billion pay increase for the military and block passage of a $10 million subsidy for low income housing. They can succeed in forcing a president to cut welfare appropriations in return for increasing taxes for the Vietnam War. They are well represented in investigatory committees of Congress, whose revealed facts are designed to support pre-established conclusions. In the work of these committees, the patriots manage to demonstrate how their opponents are lacking in solid American virtues and are therefore unworthy of protection under the democratic process. They are amply represented in the State Department, in the propaganda organizations supporting its policy line, and in the espionage agency of the government. The lineage they have built in government vies with that of the Roman emperors. The majority of patriots are Southerners, demonstrating that those who lose a war can still win the peace.

These patriots form part of an assortment of bedfellows brought together by war and the preparation for war. Many industrialists have fed at the public trough for so long that to enter the market looking for work would be a traumatic experience. The life of a big firm in the East is typical. The company was created out of World War II government contracts. Since that time it has ventured into the private market only once and the disastrous experience has not tried again. According to some economists, such firms can be easily converted into non-war production, but such optimism is unwarranted. Their managers prosper from a booming military establishment and together with the patriots represent a substantial political-economic force in the United States.

The princes of power derive their influence from controlling substantial quantities of resources. These include money, productive property, marketable skills, and effective organized blocs. Their interests are diverse. In Philadelphia, for example, the president of a big corporation and member of the board of trustees of one of its institutions of higher learning also owns part of a heavyweight prizefighter. Money is the most important of all of these assets; if one is astute, money can buy the others. The amount of assets managers control has a direct bearing on the acceptability of the opinion they utter. Thus, the reasoning of Mr. Smith who controls two times as much as Mr. Jones is twice as weighty. An expression of idiocy by a prominent prince of power is treated in the same manner as the fabled populace handling the emperor's new clothes.

Thus, controlling large sums of money is the supreme weapon of these managers. For practically everyone and everything in the economy there is a price. With money, friendships are bought, governments manipulated, and the professional with the right views purchased. Money can be used to induce fears in the consumer and thereupon to persuade him that the right product will allay them. Money shapes public tastes, fixes what is reality and what is not, and determines in what way the frontiers of knowledge will be extended. Big money disbursers have the greater privileges and honors and can buy influence, justice, men, beautiful women, and honorary degrees. With money, they control communication lines to make themsedves immortal and to bestow honors on themselves for self-recognized accomplishments.

The system uses money as a tool of obtaining mass behavior consistent with its needs. Thus, as the draft fails, military manpower is sought through the incentive of money. Consistent with the employment of euphemisms to obscure the truth, the proposal for a mercenary army is called a proposal for a volunteer army.

Accomplishment is measured in terms of money; the way in which it is made is of little importance. Even anguish is for sale. A clever young man with color slide pictures of the Mylai massacre in Vietnam instinctively saw the possibilities of selling world rights to his atrocity pictures and set up a market in a New York hotel room. Shooting for a hundred thousand, he had to settle sadly for a modest forty thousand.[10] The controllers of budgets are judged by their ability to obtain maximum bang per buck. There is a presumption that the bigger the bang the greater accomplishment. The greater the money behind a transaction, the greater is its importance. The greater the talents are of money controllers the more the amount of money needed to purchase them in the market.

Money fixes the quality of justice. There is very good justice for those with a lot of money, and modest justice for those with modest sums. Of course, all individuals with tidy amounts of money do not necessarily increase their judicial clout by such holdings. But the power to control judicial decisions is inconceivable without money.

Most relations between Americans issues from monetary transactions that involve the sale and purchase of goods and services. The importance of these relations is measurable in terms of the amount of money involved. In pursuing their interests, producers are more effectively

10 *The New York Times*, November 29, 1969.

organized than consumers. The consumer can get his pound of flesh more efficiently as a seller. Of primary importance to the producer is an expansion of sales regardless of the welfare of the consumer. Consumption must be increased to keep his production machinery going. This imperative requires the perpetration of fraud. The most effective weapon against producer duplicity for the consumer is to practice it himself as a seller. The consumer is supposed to make choices after rationally weighing alternatives. He must decide, for example, whether toothpaste, mints, gum, or mouth wash would most effectively weaken the lady's resistance. In fact, his choice is conditioned by managers who seek through stimuli to obtain the response necessary to maintain profit levels. Intelligence, education, and experience serve to build up resistance to such manipulation. Therefore, the young and not-too-bright, and an educational system attuned to producer values, facilitate maximum returns for the manipulating dollar.

The billions of dollars poured into advertising serve to foster the chicanery necessary for the maintenance of the system. Once income rises above the level of subsistence, the individual must be made to respond mechanically in the interest of the system in order for it to survive. Government agencies regulating advertising propaganda are forced to raise their tolerance levels of deceptive practices for the orderly running of the system. In 1969, for example, the Federal Communications Commission extended the license of a radio station that had admitted fraudulent billing and fake advertising contests during the period when it was on probation for earlier infractions.[11] The deception is practiced by the most respectable of firms. Thus, General Electric defended an ad claiming its 10 inch color TV set cost only half the price of many color sets on the basis it was actually comparing its portable with a 25 inch console.[12]

The art of deception, developed to a consummate degree by corporate managers, penetrates the larger society. The populace reduces the falsification of reality by responding to it in behavior. The government asserts that the right to lie is fundamental to the preservation of the system. The university joins forces in the creation of imagery under the euphemistic term of public relations. The unreal becomes real as the population is successfully managed into failing to see the distinction.

Producers must convince buyers that their products are needed, that no better ones exist, and that they would suffer deprivation if the offer were not accepted. Whether the offer is genuine is not relevant. The valid consideration is not whether the product increases the welfare of

11 *The New York Times*, October 3, 1969.
12 The Philadelphia *Evening Bulletin*, April 21, 1972.

the buyer, but whether the buyer is convinced that it does. In a sense, government represents the ideal world of the seller. It sells services whether the buyer wants them or not and punishes him if he does not pay for them. Such a relationship between producer and buyer would be the corporation's highest mark of accomplishment.

Nevertheless, to say that seller and buyer in the United States confront each other in a Svengali-Trilby relations would be an exaggeration. But to state, as the government does, that the consumer is king is nonsense.[13] Sellers have considerable resources with which to develop captive audiences. Competitors in a particular industry have a common interest in persuading the consumer to buy its product. In the auto industry, for example, they share the function of manipulating the psyche of the consumer until he begins to drool at the sight of a shiny car. Having each made their contribution in the interest of all, whether he heeds the call of a Tempest, Tornado, or Barracuda is irrelevant; he must succumb to one to reduce his palpitations. Furthermore, government monetary and fiscal policy assures the seller that once the scramble has taken place, every competitor will enjoy an annual rise in income.

The university in the system provides the auto industry with assistance also. To give an example, industry designs cater to young male thrill seekers. Auto engineers rationalize these designs; louvres over rear windows to reduce wind drag at high speeds are billed as a device to keep snow off rear windows. The University of Michigan Highway Safety Research Center has concluded that these drivers are dangerous, but the industry financed unit has gone out of its way not to criticize industry policy.

The success of a single industry such as autos provides guarantees of consumption in other sectors. Billions of dollars in highway construction are spent so as to correct jams created by prior construction. The rising number of roads also provides employment in other industries. Undertakers, plastic surgeons, physicians, insurance carriers, pharmacists, lawyers, auto repairmen, and advertising sign makers rely heavily on auto sales. The 13 million auto accidents annually make a heavy contribution to the gross national product. A precipitous decline in auto sales would be a disaster.

The gross national product that totals these goods and services is used by the government as a testimonial of progress. The GNP has been called the holy grail of economists. To some the gross national product

---

13 In addition to this claim, the U. S. Department of Commerce also asserts that "consumerism" (consumer demand for government protection) can destroy freedom. The statement was made by the Secretary of Commerce in 1969.

refers to an elected official prominent in government; to others an over-
flowing garbage can; and to still others a symbol of forestalling the day of
shifting from childhood to maturity. The GNP includes to the tune of
billions of dollars such items as cigarettes, booze, and expenditures on
household pets which, including such services as special foods, groom-
ing, and animal cosmetics, amount to more than the United States allocation for the war against poverty. Beautification of the human body,
excluding clothing, accounts for another $5 billion. Entertainment in
violence, sadism, and sexual voyeurism makes another significant contribution to the GNP. If the psychological costs incurred by producing
and consuming this bounty were discounted from the dollar amounts
of the product, the GNP would probably decrease annually thereafter.
The $50 billion expenditure on advertising to maintain the GNP is a
measure of the public's disinclination to buy what is good for them.

This product of the system emerges out of political-economic communication between technical elites. On a particular issue, elites assume
a self-serving position and seek to promote it on the basis of fostering
the common good. Chicanery is employed to promote the validity of
one's view and to undermine contrary views. Usage is commendable
to the degree it achieves a desired result. Truth is not relevant. Impact is.

In these transactions between elites, bargaining groups seek to place
the costs of their settlement upon those lacking the organization to with-
stand such settlement. Stress between elements of the power elite diminishes as rising income and status is assured them. As such guarantees
materialize, restraint between themselves is a preferable course of procedure because of the uncertainty as to what conflict would produce.

Presumably, the solutions emerging from these transactions are
affected by liberal and conservative alignments within and between organizations. To what extent, however, these alignments are an ideological
pose of little consequence in the forthcoming decisions is a difficult
question. As opinion makers, conservatives and liberals express differences that may have little effect on the decisions they ultimately work
out. In their transactions, their problem lies not so much in how to
resolve ideological differences among themselves as in how to jointly
protect themselves from the unsystem.

A fundamental characteristic of the system is the manner in which
policy proposals enter into this elite decision making process. It is important that a decision maker anticipate alternatives he may find repugnant
and make them illegitimate as early as possible. For example, an issue
can be posed in a manner which implies that those who are likely to bring
forth contrary proposals are irrational. A foreign policy maker, for instance, trying to defend government intervention could suggest the only

alternatives to be isolationism or abdication of responsibility; his critics could thereby be impaled. Correspondingly, he could seek out university professors with views similar to his own and present their output as objective analysis.

If an issue has moral overtones, it is always advisable to consult with prominent churchmen. If distinguished (which is to say acceptable) clergymen are not asked for their point of view they may become piqued and stir things up among their parishioners. The opinion of the clergyman may vary from that of his flock, but the difference is not important so long as there appears to be unanimity over the right opinion. The clergyman may not always come through, however, as when a protestant minister criticized the Vietnam policy of the United States President, as the chief executive sat defenseless in his pew. The effective course of action was to indicate under a more favorable setting that the clergyman's opinion had no rational constituency; in keeping with the high dignity of the presidential office, the indication was made by a White House aide.

The mass communications media constitute an important element in the system's decision making by the way they describe facts, by the portrait they convey of elites, and by the opinion presented in both description and portrait. Their need for sensationalism is a major concern of princes of power; it intrudes into their cozy relations. This need for sensationalism is cloaked at times within the mantle of the right of the public to know. However, the right to know frequently does not clarify issues as much as it generates a contest of imagery. In such a contest, the one who allows honesty and unskillful use of resources to tarnish his own image is often a loser. The media encourages a contest of fantasy and one succeeds or fails on the basis of devising winning images.

Sensitive to adverse publicity, princes of power court the favor of the mass media. At times, the democratic process is confined to a contest between managers and media. The media purport to speak for the people, but actually have institutional needs of their own to which managers respond. It is important to managers that they control which issues enter the democratic process, how they are posed, the manner in which they enter, and who the protagonists are. However, the media may elect to play their own game. The managers who court their favor are often made to appear superficial and evasive, which serves to increase the cynicism of the population.

It is important that princes of power who make announcements to the newspapers try to color them with a self-serving interpretation. In the late months of 1969, for example, the unemployment rate rose sharply, an increase which in substance amounted to the transference of the cost of the war to the working class. The government properly announced that the rise demonstrated the effectiveness of its anti-inflation policies.

Unlike newspapers, radio and television are less sources of information on public matters than they are an arm of the advertising business. In theory, the airwaves in the United States belong to the people, but in practice, the overriding criterion of their programming is how to maintain high profits through advertising. The worth of a program depends on the numbers in its listening audience, for this is the basis of advertising income. Television dramatizes a characteristic of the age: the obsolescence of reason. Brainwashing via suggestive imagery works better. The medium is at its dullest when it is used as an exercise in reason; its vacuity can be fully appreciated when listening with eyes closed. It is most effective when it operates under the assumption that the mobs of people who watch programs are not worth educating.

Nevertheless, the media have ambivalent effects on the system. Although not in a uniform manner, they generate by inadvertence pressures for change. Major institutional changes are often inspired by the clamor of the media. By sensationalizing the decisions of managers, the media undermine their authority in the eyes of the public and produce a desire for change. But they are also a vehicle of mass propaganda in the interest of the system. Government and industry use them to promote a self-serving reality. Because users and managers of media exercise a self-serving censorship, the frustration of the population, often not allowed to rise above a whisper in the media, produces a rampant cynicism as to the workings of the system and the possibilities for change.

The system's structure and processes inhibit a bold response to this cynicism. Each idea becomes diluted by the opinion of technical sub-monopolies and the opposition of some organized bloc. The contest of imagery between elites submerges the rise of truth. The system drifts slowly away from mistaken policy and labors toward the new; at times, prudence dictates that anything new not even be revealed. The sub-groups within and between organizations gear their reaction consistent with the preservation of their interests. New policy rarely represents a substantial departure from current operations, because it tends to be tied to what is already known. The manager perched at the top of a group of sub-monopolies cannot choose an option that brings on a marked change in direction. Such a choice would meet a stiff resistance. Hence decisions are political; change is confined to a magnitude that minimizes instability.

In summary, then, how does the system work? Its principal power clusters include government, industry, and the universities supplying them with technical skills and proper attitudes. Its principal support is a war economy. The big organizations control instruments of power: money, productive property, and human skills. They exercise influence within a maze of communication pipelines through which initiating challenges, responses, and accommodations flow in a never-ceasing series of transactions. Their decisions reflect a reconciliation of views shaped by the degree of influence each commands.

Manipulation is a crucial ingredient of the system; the public has to be deceived in order to be served. Managers do not provide the full facts as they know them, for a considerable commitment in resources produces stakes too high to permit honesty. The truth upsets planning. Appearances are important, facts to the contrary notwithstanding. At a moment when a role player states his desire to be frank, it is prudent to assume he will be devious. As this manipulation unfolds, players maintain the fiction of freedom of choice. The fabrication hides the fact that what is right is usually what those with the greatest influence can achieve.

Obsolescence pervades this system. The universal fact of life is obsolescence of cities, corporate structures, family, trade unions, of political and economic institutions generally. Institutions do not meet the purposes for which they were created, nor do they show a capacity to restructure themselves to fill human needs. No such impulse comes from the managers. Those who shape tastes and environment—the big producers of goods, the oil firms, the trucking companies, the auto industry, the land speculators, the managers of universities—are not disposed to reforms that may damage their interests. And no disengaged force exists that can act as a leverage.

Obsolete, too, is the traditional theory of private enterprise. It no longer, obviously, explains the reality of American economic life. We propose, therefore, a mafia theory of economy, an interpretation of American society which may lack the elegance of prevailing theories but which is certainly more up-to-date. Its merit is simplicity. In essence, the theory holds that every activity in the economy tends to be converted by Americans into a syndicated racket. A program to correct a social problem, for example, is soon transformed into a mafia-like operation calculated to serve primarily those who control it and secondarily those for whom it was originally intended. Parent-teacher associations, trade unions ,transportation authorities, military establishments, anti-poverty organizations, Congressional committees—you name it— are latched onto by *mafiosi* who operate them quietly as self-serving rackets ostensibly in the interest of their respective publics. The young Machiavellians who feed techniques of manipulation to presidents of government, firms, and universities are obviously mafia types. University professors have their syndicates too. They conduct on-going rackets in government and industry. The initial problem of new aspirants is acceptance by the appropriate syndicate. With proper obsequies to the mafia chief, they enter the club. Step by step the economy moves with the history of the mafia in Sicily.

The key to consistent success is creating and defending an exclusive racket. This is a universal practice, employed even by intellectuals, who reassemble old ideas, give them a differently arranged language, and thereupon protect the alleged new thought from poachers. The idea can be nonsense and yet survive, provided it acquires a reputation of profundity. Some intellectuals, in fact, having acquired a renown for unique ideas, dare not arrange them in any intelligible order. Clarity would be their undoing.

Syndicates each have their customary level of violence. What is appropriate for the representative of a truck drivers unions is hardly the proper style of a college president. More sophistication is required. A disequilibrium may take place with the passing of the boss, but once the infighting caused by the power scramble dissipates with the choice of a successor, matters simmer down into the customary routine racket operation. Each group of *mafiosi* delineates its area of interest, respects the duchies of others, lives and lets live. To maintain decorum, each chief uses a lieutenant who is given the title of vice president or executive director. His responsibility is constant vigilance against foragers moseying around the power jurisdiction of the chief.

Periodically, syndicate members congregate, ascribe a sublime mission to their activities, and bestow honors upon each other. Honors are in the form of scrolls, medals, plaques, keys, and university honorary degrees. As some are less respectable than others, a few syndicates have to meet in secluded areas.

The mafia pervades the entire economy. It exists in the auto industry, in basic steel, in pharmaceuticals, in construction, in the police forces. The highway consortium comprises a mafia of honorable gentlemen. In the handling of automobile insurance, lawyers have one of the more lucrative rackets in the United States. The talent of Americans to sense a good deal is highlighted in the sudden emergence of the abortion referral services; their annual turnover is estimated in the millions of dollars. There is even a mafia in the Republican Party, which like the *amici* in industry deplores social change that menaces its interests.

The attraction of the legitimate mafia to the illegitimate mafia is suggested in the behavior of the Mobil Oil Corporation. In the latter part of 1971, the firm, one of the 5 biggest in the industry, hired 3 reputed members of organized crime as strikebreakers. The firm agreed to pay $120 for each truckload of gasoline, a finder's fee of $100 for each driver, and payment of $10 hourly to each driver for a 16-hour day. The deal entered the public record when the 3 thugs, all convicted criminals, tried to extort money from the oil company.[14]

There are mafia cliques in university organization structures too. An Eastern university has one nesting in its college of business. Its formal organization chart reveals neither who the members are nor who make the crucial decisions. The gang complises a chief, two *consiglieri*, and 4 workers recruited from the instructor staff assigned to the dirty tricks department. They call the shots on promotions and awards. Their techniques include *sub-rosa* dealings and character assissination. Advisory services of the *consiglieri* are in behavioral science and law. What is good for the clique is good for the college of business. They operate successfully because the staff outside the circle does not use similar tactics.

Routine procedures characteristic of the mafia are common throughout the system. Agreements over prices and spheres of influence are tacit; spelling out an accord only invites complications under the law. Accommodation with political authorities is achieved through such procedure as going to parties, sharing rides in private planes, and meeting quietly in far away places. Even solutions of last resort—wiping out the competition by the most feasible means—can be found as a tool of operation in the highest economic and political circles of American life.

To summarize, the essence of the system is the substance of mafia philosophy—organization to practice exclusion and control in a manner that guarantees steady profits. But the exclusion and control that is exercised by the system has the effect of channeling new entrepreneurs into the illegitimate mafia on the unsystem. The legitimate mafia in government and corporations spawns a Wasp nepotism that produces disabling mutations. The illegitimate mafia is a remnant of ebbing entrepreneurship and a tonic for tired Wasp blood. A corollary of the mafia theory of economy is that the Sicilians who made such a successful transplant from their island had fertile soil with which to work. Another corollary is that the differences between system and unsystem can be reduced by making legitimate the services in the unsystem.

The difference in type of production between these two sectors is an accident of history. It should not obscure the fact that the system is mafia oriented. The extent to which illegitimate mafiosi find sympathetic spirits in the system is a measure of the affinity of both. The tacit

14 *The New York Times*, December 10, 1971.

agreement of the former Attorney General in the Nixon administration to drop pejorative terms in referring to Italian criminals supports this hypothesis. While the illegitimate mafia makes little pretense as to the nature of the services it renders, the Wasp mafia, while getting their share, do so in a posture of public service. Should this pose be insufficient to soften the perturbations of conscience, they support church and boys' organizations. A critical difference between a Wasp crook and an ethnic crook lies in the fact that the Wasp, having worked at it longer over the generations, has more finesse and more competence in getting the law to promote his interests.

Perceptions as to what comprises good and evil often arise from habits of thinking. The evil associated with the unsystem can be reduced by forcing a redefinition of the system. What was considered evil can thereupon seem good. In the case of the illegitimate mafia, we may reorient our thinking by looking upon the work as an acronym for *Make A Friend with an Italian Association*. To assist in the attainment of this worthy social objective of benign thinking, we may borrow a lesson from Negroes and organize a NAAIP: the National Association for the Advancement of Italian People. Is there a compelling reason, for instance, why Italians as well as Negroes and Jews should not organize to grab a few bank vice-presidencies? Equity demands that every group in the economy be given its quota of top positions. The Chinese in the United States have exceeded theirs and should be cut back.

As a gesture of logical consistency and in a spirit of self-sacrifice, the university professors who advocate precentage quotas should demand the quota system be applied to their profession. This move would evict many Jews and Wasps, including a prominent advocate of the percentage game, John Kenneth Galbraith, and provide new opportunities for Catholic ethnics. They would claim 30 percent of all professorial posts and university presidencies.

Since illegitimate *mafiosi* provide services more freely chosen by their customers, in contrast to producers in the system who employ manipulation to create markets for their wares, the sub-economy behaves more consistently according to traditional economic theory. Long run equilibrium would be attained as the two economies move toward each other. By extension, however, as the legitimate and illegitimate economies approach each other, the illegitimate economy will lose its responsiveness to the wants of consumers.

In short, the difference between the mafia in the system and that in the unsystem is a lag in respectability. What other difference, for example, is there between an auto executive who makes souped-up cars for impressionable youth of modest intellect and a mafia entrepreneur who runs a numbers racket? Who is the greater perpetrator of violence? Although members of the unsystem progress in their amicable relations with local government officials to legitimatize their violence, they have devoted insufficient time to cultivating an understanding attitude among national officials. Their public relations are wanting. To achieve greater respectability, they must apply themselves more.

For the sake of brevity, we can call the legitimate mafia economy LME and its illegitimate offspring IME. Production, either in its processes or products, produces goods and bads in both LME and IME. A noteworthy contrast between both economies lies in their good/bad relationships. In LME the bad tends to rise relative to its good; in IME, the reverse occurs. Thus, the auto business produces good in flexible means of transportation and mounting bads in air pollution, noise, ugliness, and mechanized human relationships. And the numbers racket produces good in promoting expectations among the poor and bad in an occasional fracas. A primary factor causing the bads to rise disproportionately in LME is the inexorable pressure to maintain consumer demand. Thus, the need to prop up demand created bumperless cars, polluting soap detergents to clean whiter than white, and advertising to persuade the public that intake of chemicals is the sure road to happiness. It can be seen, therefore, that the maintenance of profits relates directly to a firm's ability to maximize bads, or social costs. To assure profits, the firm must be able to increase social costs without incurring the retaliation of society. An upper limit on profits is reached as social costs kill off a rising number of consumers and force society's intervention.

In LME, the bads are sustained by the society until society musters enough strength to curtail them. In IME, since the goods are outlawed, the bads, even though of less proportion, are employed as a means of defending the outlawing of the goods. Moreover, the bads in IME are almost exclusively imposed on producers in the form of intensive kinds of competition such as beatings and homicides.

A high demand for an outlawed good increases the resources necessary to curtail the demand. The control of its bad, as for example in the case of prostitution, can be achieved more efficiently by legalizing the good. Assuming rationality on the part of society, this legalization occurs when the costs of prohibiting the illegitimate goods exceed the costs of allowing them to enter LME.

The system tends to resolve the problem of bads in LME in a manner that imposes its greatest costs on the poor. By any pollution index, the poor have lived in pollution long before the suburbanites and their child revolutionaries discovered it. The revolutionaries are too committed to preocccupy themselves with fundamental causes of poverty. They are too busy singing anti-pollution songs to the earsplitting accompaniment of instruments amplified by power coming from polluting plants.

The poor are likely to get caught in two ways: by a deflection of government resources away from them and by a rise in the costs of their goods and services. Ecology has emerged as the antidote to suburban boredom. Who knows if a new point of view on poverty may emerge reflected in such slogans as: Don't flatten that cockroach brother. You may be ruining the ecological balance.

The Goddess Technology

Technique! The very word is
like the shriek of outraged Art.
Leonard Bacon

The meaning of technology often eludes both its advocates and its detractors. Its partisans and critics load their writing with propaganda. Yet, a clear understanding of technology is vital to a comprehension of the system, for it is the dominant driving force behind modern American life. In varying degree, it shapes the course of most sectors in the economy, including government and the knowledge industries. Nevertheless, technology is not fully integrated into behavioral science and often merits no more than a postscript.

This elusiveness arises partly from the fact that technology is bound up with a way of thinking. It is an application of the intellect with consequences in hardware, human skills, and processes that derive from how people think. This frame of mind has produced a consumption revolution of unprecedented proportions and a deterioration of environment. The contest over technological innovation between manager, scientist, and humanist comprises a struggle whose outcome is the promise or scourge of a life of quality.

Some humanists tend to overemphasize the inexorability of technology,[1] while others view the future more optimistically.[2] The motives behind technology of profit and power are learned patterns of behavior, and the process of resource allocation implicit in innovation involves

[1] See Jacques Ellul, *The Technological Society*, New York: Vintage Book, 1964.
[2] See Emmanuel G. Mesthene, *Technological Change: Its Impact on Man and Society*, Cambridge, Harvard University Press, 1970.

social relationships that can change also. Thus, while the course of technology should give us concern, there is a danger in being too deterministic in its analysis. The course of this chapter steers, therefore, between pessimism and optimism in discussing the nature of technology, its effects and its control.

NATURE OF TECHNOLOGY

Technology consists of know-how developed from the findings of science, ranging from making and selling automobiles to placing a man on the moon and bringing back rocks. Know-how constitutes using men, hardware, and processes to gain an objective. The process of technologizing involves tentatively defining the goal, gathering facts in a search for the most feasible know-how to pursue the goal, locking in definition and know-how, and pursuing the goal at maximum efficiency by application of know-how. What is feasible involves a reconciliation of the technical, political, and economic realities facing the decision maker. The search and application may be routine, comprising at times little more than choosing and applying a minor incremental change such as hiring a particular skill; or it may be non-routine in character, such as the search for new know-how. Routine is related inversely to the variability of problems coming into the organization. To cite an example, processes in a research organization may be highly non-routine in character compared to those involved in the operation of a motel.

A judgment of what comprises efficiency is limited by time and space. What is efficient today may not be tomorrow; and what comprises efficiency for the organization may constitute inefficiency for the society as a whole. In addition, the bias and intelligence of the participants in decision making affect the facts collected relative to the problem.

In summary, technology constitutes search and application of technique. The technological sequence comprises discovery, testing, application of choice, and discard. Technique depends upon the kind and purposes of work. Choice affects organization, including its structure and the individuals who labor therein; moreover, choice in one organization affects the structure and labor force of other organizations related to its processes. The key elements of technological thought are goals, facts, options, applications, and evaluation. The crucial strand running through these elements is feasibility. Lastly, whenever an organization makes a technological choice, someone benefits and someone is hurt—in income, status, and quality of environment. Without structured community and government controls, technological assessment is made by the potential user on the basis of what innovation best suits his economic and institutional interests.

The distinction between technology and science must be kept clearly in mind. It is in technology where the extensive advances since the Second World War have been made. The new discoveries made by science, particularly social and behavioral science, during the same period have been few. Many so-called scientists are technicians. Mass-communications media make a noteworthy contribution to the confusion.

It is also important to reiterate the overriding influence of feasibility upon choice. The individual making decisions on technologies, like the politician, the university administrator, and other power strategists, makes his choices on the basis of feasibility. If it is feasible, it is proper. If the most feasible technology does not quite fit the goal, the goal may have to be changed to fit the technology. Progress comprises what is technologically feasible. The morality of method and objective is relevant insofar as moral attitudes may affect favorably or adversely the use of methods and the pursuit of objectives. It is the feasibility philosophy of the decision maker and the moral sense of the population that cause much of the stress in contemporary society.

Accordingly, the norm of what man can be becomes less important than the norm of what is possible at the moment. Technologists thereby gain a reputation for being pragmatists. If their choices turn out to be successful and dramatic in their impact, they even acquire a fame for statesmanship. The morality of feasibility dominates not only economic choices, but political choices as well, such as those involved in the Indo-china intervention. When a course of action is judged to be feasible, pressures arise to adopt it. And when in time the course of action proves to be unfeasible, the individual who recommended the initial choice on the basis of feasibility is likely to advise its abandonment on the same basis.

Managing men, hardware, and processes in this way has ambivalent effects. On the one hand, modern technology tends to create a dual society, of toilers who respond to the demands of the production machine, and of drones not wanted by the machine, who live on subsidies. On the other, it shows promise of creating a society of independent technicians with the intelligence, money, freedom, and free time for greater participation. On the one hand, technology, creates its own demands which individuals acquiesce to but which may have little to do with human needs. On the other, technology frees men from the drudgery of mere survival.

In short, technology gives direction to change. In a primitive society, man's responses accommodate to the demands of the physical environment. In a modern society, he responds to the demands of deteriorating and ascending technologies. Technology fixes the occupation modern man prepares himself for, as well as the manner in which he performs the work in his occupation; it steers the course of his life. Consequently, technology controls the options available to man; and these options are shaped to a considerable degree by government policy. Thus, the differences in government expenditures facilitating private automobile use and those providing for public transportation have an effect on the options available to the traveling public. In sum, technology orchestrates the symphony of life.[3]

The subdivision of labor implicit in modern technology prolongs the period of gestation from the conception of the task to delivery of the end result.[4] If somehow, for example, a speck of iron ore were to be followed from its emergence from the mine in the mouth of a mechanical shovel to its appearance in a suburban garage as a particle of the choke of a lawn mower, it would be found that its facelift took a considerable amount of time. The subdivision of labor required by modern technology affords efficiency and high degree of organization in the use of manpower. As such use of human capital becomes more costly, an increasing amount of tangible capital can be efficiently employed in performing the task.

This roundaboutness of production requires planned innovation and planned obsolescence. It demands a society in which men and government serve its needs of planned creation, use, obsolescence, and replacement; if these needs are not served, the economic consequences are serious. The use, obsolescence, and replacement of technology creates a climate of continuous change. As individuals who fall within its impact area finally accommodate to innovation, a new round creates a new disequilibrium.

Understanding this process helps to dispel the confusion which prevails in the distinction between technology, mechanization, and automation. It is all technology. Mechanization, the use of machines and equipment in production, constitutes a major strand in the historical evolution of technology while automation is its contemporary child; each developed from the process of discarding and adding methods and artifacts which comprises each phase of technology. Thus, from the 12th to the 16th centuries, western man reached new levels of technological attain-

---

[3] Modern technology may even affect the battle of the sexes. The ability to predict sex of a new human being may produce the know-how to increase the relative number of males. The rising scarcity of females would make them a commodity of short supply. Thereupon, the feminist movement may dictate its own terms.

[4] For a vivid analysis of this aspect of technology, see John K. Galbraith, *The Industrial State*, Boston: Houghton Mifflin, 1967. Before Galbraith, Bohm Bawerk explained the nature of roundabout production, concluding that it is more productive and therefore justifies an income payment called interest.

ments through the construction of churches. Two centuries then elapsed before the fortuitous convergence of rational liberal philosophy and mechanical power ushered in a new era of technology whose motivating force shifted from a transcendent purpose rallying together members of the community to individual gain. Later, the automobile and mass marketing brought forth mass production techniques, which in turn became the basis of the automatic control of the quantity and quality of production. With the risk of some simplification, therefore, we can state that western technology was founded by the ancient Romans, re-activated by the medieval churchmen, launched on a basis of mechanized power by the British-Americans, and ushered into modernity by the Americans.

The sequence from early mechanization to contemporary automation then, took place in three stages of development. First came the discoveries of the industrial revolution replacing human and animal muscle with mechanical power. In the second stage, mass production brought forward simplification of work methods and subdivision of semi-skilled labor. In the third, automation brought the mechanical control of quantity, quality and production flow. Thus, it is all technology, the new terms being useful to describe the thrust of a new phase.

What is meant precisely by the label automation? It refers to the mechanization of sensory, thought, and control processes in production. The machine perceives, analyzes, and acts. It does so by man's programming into a machine a specific sequence of these mental processes in order to achieve an intended production goal. The computer, a product of technological evolution, reaches a new zenith in the mechanization of mental processes. It stores information as the mind does, analyzes the information, decides what has to be done, and even commands machines to do it. Neither automation nor the computer would have been possible without the related artifacts produced by the technology which preceded them.

The computer has possibilities for good and evil. The machine is a tool that does what men who control it want it to do. It replaces tedious work. It has considerable possibilities for social advancement through instruction, community consensus, and analysis of the city. On the other hand, the computer also provides the means for a mushrooming of enterprise devoted to the compilation of individual dossiers to serve the needs of government and business. But more important, the machine's very limitations determine what is to be considered relevant behavior in social affairs. Whatever the computer can compile tends to be considered useful information; whatever information can be compiled becomes gospel. In a nation founded on individual rights, the computer cannot operate on the basis of the uniqueness of each individual.

Automation can also be seen as the result of the objective of maximum efficiency, the crux of the philosophy of technology. This objective is a common thread which runs through different methods of management. For example, operations research is a systematic search by a team of specialists in different disciplines for all factors in a given situation so as to determine what new combinations would produce the goal at greatest efficiency. Systems engineering, another popular term, alludes to the determination of the components of a system and the realignment of these components so as to obtain a desired solution. Information systems, of which the digital computer is a major component, involve the collection, analysis, and dissemination of information at maximum efficiency. A system posits a problem, collects pertinent information, analyzes it, and presents alternatives to the manager as to how to proceed with the solution. The process is characterized by centralization, speed, and high volume. These methods change in the interest of those who market them, but the basic tool remains the same: analytical method.

Modern technology can be applied with maximum efficiency under the following conditions. All factors in the problem to be solved (technicians call them variables) can be measured and their relative importance determined in numbers. In addition, the problem should be of sufficient scale so that the available know-how can be efficiently employed through reaching a point in size that obtains the greatest return out of resources expended. Moreover, the human factors operating within the framework of the problem should be so systematized that a particular stimulus produces a desired response in a uniform manner. Only those human characteristics compatible with the system are relevant. Like Pavlov's dog, given the stimulus, the response should be predictable and uniform. Human qualities that adversely affect the desired response should be neutralized.

To cite some examples, the desired objective in television advertising is to capture the largest audiences possible and to manipulate them with maximum efficiency. The *summum bonum* is obtaining the greatest consumption bang per buck of expenditure. In education, success is often measured in terms of cost per student hour of education, a criterion that often has little to do with the quality of education and which produces a backlash from the student body. In highway engineering, the criterion is the number of motor vehicles that can be moved from one point to the next at a minimum expenditure of resources. In the sale of a book, given unit production costs, one selling a hundred thousand copies is a hundred times better than one selling a thousand. Consequently, the individual in modern society falls into a classification, his value comprising the characteristics of that classification usable to the technologist in gaining his objective. Modern technology thus is a kind of 20th century Marxism.[5] The Marxists are the managers of the system viewing human beings within their field of operations as an abstract mass whose successful manipulation produces profits.

A marked contrast exists between the slowness of roundabout production on the one hand and the manner in which technology accelerates the tempo of life for a particular individual on the other. Technology telescopes time for the individual. One should observe closely the urban young to note this effect. They rarely experience the life cycle of hope, investment, and harvest in a slow groundswell of experience. Rather, they bounce from one instant gratification to another without experiencing the entire process of fulfillment, a loss in life's meaning further aggravated by their divorcement from the rhythm of nature. Habit sustains this tempo of life until death.

With the coming of industrialism, life became geared to the artificial pace of technology. At first, that merely meant that if one worked in a factory, one had to adjust oneself to the rate of the machine.

Gradually, however, the ever-accelerating inhuman pace of technology has invaded every domain of life. The values of the factory—efficiency, speed, total use of available resources—have become the values of the home and of leisure.

Television replaced books and radio as the dominant cultural force. It is often criticized for its violence and banality. But television's most subtle debilitating influence is that it makes audiences passive and accustoms them to expect instant gratifications.

The children of the television age see politics as a happening, a demonstration, a dramatic confrontation. They do not realize how much time and effort are needed to alter the character and direction of a large, mature, complex society like the United States.

Resenting death, we murdered time. Now, time vanquished, we lie ex-

[5] The two classical points of view on the relation between values and the economic system are those of Marx and Weber. Marx maintained that values were determined by systems of production. The Weber tradition reverses the relationship by stating that economic growth is shaped by values. Since this traditional development, sociologists have never bothered to study seriously how a hierarchy of values is related to the economic system and how the hierarchy changes. Non-sociologists, economists especially, view technology and values as interacting learned processes affected by the speed and historical period of change. Institutional economists, looking at the United States today, tend to make modern technology more a cause than an effect. Many of the non-economic social scientists concentrate on the spurious issue of the discontinuity between man and technology.

For a superb discussion by an economist, see Kenneth Boulding, "The Interplay of Technology and Values," in Kurt Baier and Nicholas Rescher (eds.) *Values and the Future: The Impact of Technological Change in American Values,* New York: Free Press, 1969.

hausted alongside our victim. Almost too late, we see that what we have slain is not time but our sense of ourselves as humans.[6]

Technologists are organized more effectively than are those defending themselves from the technologists. Much more research money goes into creating the technology desired by government and industry than into controlling its effects. The government agency regulating air transportation is more effective in promoting the interests of the airlines than in protecting the public from these interests. The government is more at the service of the lumber interests than the preservers of the wilderness. The individual protesting against jet noise and the destruction of the forest is likely to obtain a weasel-worded letter from the government in reply, whereas the producer pursuing his interests is apt to be granted a serious hearing. With the acquiescence and at times the assistance of government, the user of modern technology for profit transfers his costs to the community. A consequence of this subsidy is the deterioration of the environment on an unprecedented scale. It has created a force of engineers to combat the depredations of another set of engineers. But the innovators have more power than the conservationists. Thus, the problem of technology boils down to a problem of power.

To a considerable degree, government develops and shapes the course of modern technology. The war machine and the space program are prime factors in technological change. Overall, the government's imprint derives from its allocation of billions of dollars annually in research and development programs.

One such development, the SST supersonic plane, dramatizes the clash between government-sponsored technology and popular will as to technological choice. Vested interests in the aircraft included the military, the quasi-public firms who rely on government contracts for their survival, the commercial airlines, and university groups with an interest in its development. At the time of the political contest over the plane in the United States Congress the government commitment was estimated at $2.5 billion, in sharp contrast to the commitment of the government to protect the public against jet noise. The government lined up on the side of a formidable array of power in support of the plane. Its propaganda was of high quality. It was argued that the SST would create jobs. But a dramatic counterattack was launched by professionally prepared organizations. The idea was brought forward that technological change does not necessarily mean progress. The proposal on the SST was defeated by the U.S. Senate. Even if the plane eventually goes into

[6] William V. Shannon, *The New York Times*, July 8, 1971.

production, it will emerge a better aircraft from an environmental point of view.

The SST episode brings forth lessons on the containment of technology. Counter voices are effective when brought forward in publicized dramatic fashion. The more quietly an issue is raised the more able are organized interests to control legislation. In this respect, the U.S. House of Representatives, originally designed by the founding fathers as an expression of populism, is in fact especially sensitive to the interests of organized blocs. In 1972, for example, a water bill that gained little public notice came to the House from the Senate. Lobbyists with the cooperation of the White House succeeded in weakening the pollution standards proposed by the Senate. The success reflected the lack of drama over the issue compared to that generated by the SST.[7]

SOME PARTICULAR POINTS OF IMPACT

As stated, technology is a powerful motivating force throughout the economy. It affects the evolution of firms, characteristics of labor supply and demand, type and design of consumer products, relations between managers and rank and file, social relationships outside work, government policies, mass communications, physical environment, and even the education industry. We turn next to an examination of some of these major points of impact.

Effects on the Firm.   Since the end of the Second World War, a marked rise in counter-ecological technology has taken place in industry. An important factor behind this increase is the thrust to maintain profit rates. Moreover, an overwhelming portion of this innovation is introduced by a relatively small number of big corporations using public money to do so. In 1960, approximately 85 percent of all research and development money allocated in industry was spent by some 400 firms. About 65 percent of these funds came from the national government. By providing these funds, the government underwrites the prices and markets of these corporations.[8]

This innovation affects the firm's internal management. By accepting the expert in technology as a partner in decision making, the manager subordinates himself to technical points of view which he often fails to understand in all their dimensions. Traditional lines of managerial authority thus break down. The intellectual with a technical skill ac-

[7] *The New York Times*, March 29, 1972.
[8] John K. Galbraith, *op. cit.*, p. 32, citing hearings before the Subcommittee on Antitrust and Monopoly, 89th Congress, First Session.

quires status. He does so not as a manager calling the shots, but as an information monopolist instructing managers who often pretend to comprehend what he is doing.

By making possible the supervision of large masses of employees and because of the imperative to speed up the collection, analysis, and transmission of information, modern technology has the effect of both dissolving and consolidating management activity. Standardization and mechanized control of work places supervisory responsibility in the hands of relatively fewer supervisors. Information demands have consolidating effects in such areas as marketing, manufacturing, purchasing, and material control. Accordingly, organization structure changes through shifts in the dispersion of managers, particularly middle management, and through the creation of an increasing army of technicians working semi-autonomously. While the long term consequences of this shift are not entirely clear, the old days of authoritarian managers and passive employers have vanished.

Such is not to say that all organization structures are evolving in this manner. They do where considerable knowledge exists about the nature of the production transformation, where the variability of operating problems is small, and where the technology thus tends to become routine. A routine operation places greater control in the hands of top level managers, decreases the interdependence of groups in the organization, and programs the coordination between groups. Accordingly, direct supervision becomes more light-handed. A non-routine operation has an opposite effect on organization structure. However, since most firms tend to evolve into routine operations, many organization structures move in the same direction.[9]

In summary, we can state as a general rule the following relationship between technology and organization. An intimate relationship exists between a firm's product, the structure of its organization, and technological innovation. A firm making a technical product in a competitive market tends to create an organization structure conducive to quickly changing technologies. The greater the uncertainty of the market, the lower in the organization structure will a system of cooperation and conflict resolution be found. Thus, market uncertainty stimulates a

---

[9] See Charles Perrow, "Technology and Organizational Structure," *Proceedings of the 19th Annual Meeting Industrial Relations Research Association*, 1966. I am aware that such variables as culture and social classes affect organization structure. Behavioral scientists, however, ignore the effect of technology. As Perrow states, too much stress is placed also on firm size, type of firm, and philosophy of managers. Similar scale and firm classification does not necessarily produce similar technology. Two mental hospitals may have different technology if one stresses custody and the other cure. The overriding factor is the state of the art vis-a-vis the objective.

search for technologies that would maintain profit; and a rapid rate of innovation tends to decentralize the authority to make decisions. Such is not to say that the rate of innovation relates solely to market competitiveness. The number of "bugs" in a production process, the age of the individuals making technological decisions, firm size, and the industry's stage of growth have similar relevance. The computer by itself does not appear to generate strong pressures either for centralization or decentralization of authority. The managers accountable for profits still have to make the same set of decisions. And market uncertainties may require a high degree of autonomy regardless of the availability of computer technology. What the computer does is to centralize menial tasks, to permit more complex analyses and to make them more quickly available.

Effect on Jobs. Modern technology changes the labor force pyramid into the shape of a diamond. This results as the relative number of unskilled workers at the low end of the occupation distribution declines. At the same time, a new class of technical and professional employees emerges that will shortly comprise some 25 percent of the labor force. Consequently, since the requisite for these technical and professional jobs is a college degree, technology tends to create a moat separating this elite from a group of blue collarites at the bottom of the diamond destined to be limited in their opportunities for advancement.

Traditionally, three broad types of blue-collar jobs existed: craft, semiskilled assembly work, and unskilled operations. Modern technology has mixed effects on this spectrum of blue collar work. Whereas some craft skills in industry are diluted, they persist in building and construction because of labor organization. In some industries, the mass production jobs give way to those of specialists doing more work of an integrated nature. The rise of blue collar technicians in conjunction with automated operations creates a fuzzy line between the bottom of the white collar class and the top of the blue collar class. Thus, technology destroys the smooth progression of blue collar jobs and blurs the distinction between the end of blue collar work and the beginning of white collar work.

Out of this job ferment issues the controversy over whether modern technology creates or destroys jobs. Optimists state that at least as many jobs are created as destroyed. Pessimists assert that modern technology shuts out persons from work because of the highly structured labor demands of employers and that no amount of government monetary and fiscal measures can cure such unemployment. In economic terms, if the technological process reduces unit labor costs and the demand for the product is elastic, the effect should be a rise rather than a decline in employment. But such may not be the case. It is no longer fashionable to reduce prices in the expectation of a rise in demand. A rise in demand, should it occur, may be managed by unused plant. Third, the new jobs may not be available to the unemployed. Modern technology shifts plants away from old industrial centers to the suburbs and small towns. Concomitant with this change in location, the relative decline in goods production compared to services causes a drop in the traditional semi-skilled and unskilled jobs that formerly provided positions for workers of limited education. A generation ago, for example, a minority teenager with little formal education got himself a job at a bowling alley setting up pins. Today, his job is mechanized. His contemporary representative is out on the streets getting into trouble, for plants with sophisticated technology and government minimum wages lower demand for his services. At the same time, however, jobs have been created for the manufacture, installation, and maintenance of pin equipment. But these jobs do not provide opportunities to the teenager. Only full employment and concomitant institutional reforms will do so. When the labor market has a surplus, employers want high school graduates at the least; but when the market is tight, they seek able bodied men.

Consequently, technology eliminates jobs, combines old ones, creates new ones, and places jobs in new geographical areas. By so doing, the spectrum of jobs and the content of jobs change. The services industries—education, public administration, finance, and travel—increase relative to the manufacturing industries. At the top of the labor force are the managers and technicians who control the deployment of human and economic resources. Below this top level are professional workers in service organizations charged with educating and maintaining manpower. At the middle are found the administrative bureaucracies supporting the efforts of managers. At the first blue collar level are the craftsmen and technicians, and below them, the second class industrial workers performing tasks that cannot be mechanized. At the bottom are the casual laborers making little or no contribution to modern production, and living in the cities as part of an emerging institution of organized poverty under the baton of government.

This change in the labor force has its greatest adverse impact upon the Negro. He does not have the unskilled entrance jobs that immigrants from Europe, such as the Italians, did. In the old days, a man with no industrial skill could go to the factory gate and land a job. However, the traditional assembly line of the 1920's has vanished. And it has disappeared in the cities to which the Negro has migrated as a consequence of his having been phased out of rural employment by agricultural technology. Moreover, the inflexibility of the big employer in setting up qualifications and the inflexibility of the small employers in setting up jobs aggravate his difficulty. The job demands on educational achievement outpace his educational attainment. And the training potential of the Negro urban proletariat is unknown.

It is held by some that in the long view technology will not create enough jobs for the number of men who want to work. Such a pessimistic outlook is unwarranted. The relative decline in goods production is offset partially by the rise in services, as we have noted. It is conceivable that a leveling of goods demand may occur as marketeers find their selling efforts less successful, and that a job crisis may ensue should technology invade the services. But should there be a slackening in the private sector, the rebuilding of cities and the decontamination of the environment alone would provide decades of employment. These activities, moreover, would have a pump priming effect on employment in the private sector. Modern technology, assuming wisdom on the part of government, should have the effect of recasting employment rather than of creating overall losses.

A side, but nonetheless important, job issue is the impact of technology on the satisfaction derived from a job. Investigators differ in their assessment as to whether jobs become more or less satisfying. In blue collar work, an inverse relation exists between work satisfaction and technology based on minute subdivision of labor. The classical assembly line exemplifies such labor specialization. Low level clerical jobs are subject to similar standardization. Mass production technology appears to meet stiffening resistance from young blue collar workers. Should their resistance and sabotage increase further, the employer may be forced to design work for semi-autonomous groups making their own production decisions and performing an increasing number of operations formerly done by sub-assembly lines. Trends outside the United States sustain this view. Should such a trend materialize, the job skill and satisfaction derived from the job are likely to rise.

Technology has always posed an employment threat to the workingman who has made sacrifices to acquire a marketable skill:

> Come all ye bold wag'ners, turn out man by man
> That's opposed to the railroad or any such a plan.
> 'Tis once I made money by driving my team
> But the goods are now hauled on the railroad by steam.[10]

While the threat of technological displacement has been present since the start of the modern industrial era, the social implications of contem-

---

10 John Smith. *Travels and Works of Captain John Smith,* Edinburgh: John Grant, 1910, in J. C. Furnas, *The Americans: A Social History of The United States 1587–1914,* New York: G. P. Putnam's Sons, 1969, p. 354.

porary change are unprecedented. A man used to be paid for his individual effort in production. Now men are compensated on the promise that they not show up for work. The machine does not need them and the solution is an improvisation. If the manager and his robot produced all the material bounty demanded in the market we may have solved the production problem and created two others of distribution and leisure.

The manner in which innovation affects noise in blue collar work is ambivalent. In some instances, technology reduces noise and produces a cooperative talking relationship between workers and supervisors. Changes have taken place from an environment of deafening noise to one where men can talk to each other. In some industries, new technology brings more noise as well as lower skills.

Much of the literature in this area of technology and jobs emphasizes the emergence of working elites in the future society. Some writers even suggest that the queen bees be given favored treatment so that they can better concentrate on their work. But this is to state in effect that the affliction of modern society, elitism, should be subsidized. It is like prescribing green apples to a boy ailing from eating too many of them. Elite rule is ever enticing to the intellectuals. The persistence of this idea, despite a steady accumulation of facts to the contrary, suggests that individuals who work hard to produce a generalization fall in love with their creation.

Effects on Trade Unions.   Modern technology poses a variety of challenges to trade unions. Blue-collar trade union membership in the goods manufacturing sector has stabilized; the increase in the number of unionized workers comes to a substantial degree from the public sector of government and the teaching profession. As the labor force changes into a force of white collar employees, so must the style of unionism. Even trade union leaders today have doctoral degrees, a change which makes a trade union official such as George Meany a symbol of a bygone era. His style does little to persuade educated white collar employees to rush to the union office.

As technology produces changes in the labor force we have noted, it also affects the size and composition of collective bargaining units as well as the bargaining power of unions. In the stage of mass production, the labor complement ran from a group of unskilled workers to a larger number of semi-skilled operatives, and thence to a small group of craftsmen with clearly defined skills. Technical innovation moves jobs out of the bargaining unit entirely, decimates the ranks of the semi-skilled, and dilutes the skills of some of the remaining blue collar craftsmen. Accordingly, innovation reduces the mainstay of industrial unionism, the semi-skilled worker, and moves some technicians out from under union control and into the white collar ranks. For example, when a union during the Second World War organized an aircraft assembly plant, it captured the overwhelming majority of the employees. Now, successful organization of its descendant plant means the unionization of a small fraction of the total number of employees.

On the question of union bargaining power, modern technology reduces unit wage costs but curtails the coercive power of the strike. By decreasing the amount of blue collar labor required per unit of production, the impact of a wage increase on average cost is reduced. Thus, the effect of a wage boost is much less when labor costs are 20 percent of total expense than when they are 60 percent. The union obtaining a 20 cents per hour increase in the first instance has less impact on overall costs than a union in the second category. On the other hand, technology gives management the opportunity in many instances to resist more effectively the wage demands of unions because of its capacity to operate a plant during the course of the strike. The automation of work in such industries as power and communication increases the possibility of continuing production with a small supervisory force. For example, most long distance telephone calls are dialed directly; the remainder during a strike are easily handled by supervisors.

Technology and Education. The transfer of technology into education comprises a record of fadism and ineffective use of funds. No marked improvement has occurred in learning by virtue of technological innovation. Many factors account for this result. The school competes with other institutions such as the mass media, which shape values and perceptions the school has difficulty modifying. Second, an aversion exists among teachers against compiling a large aggregation of educational consumption units, a distaste supported by an inability either to agree on educational goals or to determine precisely the results of such aggregation. No consensus exists as to what educational outlays should achieve. Should the goal be the transmission of past knowledge, adaptation to the society, or generation of a process of changing the society and the individual? Some teachers believe the goal should be the creation of good feeling in the classroom. The absence of acceptable goals and clear measures of results create strains and miscalculations. Thus, the use of lower unit costs as a criterion of achievement without reference to output provokes dissension. And the absence of precise measures of product tends to preserve for an educational institution a reputation it may no longer merit. Third, school administrators lack competence in the management of resources. Fourth, teachers as specialists lack either the skill or the inclination to participate in a cooperative movement toward goals. Fifth, even if these factors were met successfully, the attainment of a desirable educational product at low unit cost does not readily produce quick rewards in income and prestige as in the case of industry.

Sixth, the new technologies are inspired more by the profit motive than by an informed public concensus as to what educational objectives should be sought. The profit motive generates a quest for techniques that can reach a mass audience at the lowest unit cost. For example, cable television is emerging not in terms of how best to serve a social need, but in terms of which technology can provide the greatest profit. Accordingly, we tend more to adapt the learning problem to the most profitable technology than the technology to the learning problem. A conflict exists between maximizing the rate of profit and maximizing the rate of social return.

These factors produce appalling results. They inhibit a systematic process of development, testing, and adoption of innovation. The education establishment indulges in a fadism whose stages comprise an exuberant introduction of innovation, disillusionment, discard, and a crash program introducing the next panacea.

Mass Communications Media. The United States has some 10,000 newspapers, 8,000 magazines, 7,000 radio and television stations, publishes millions of books annually, and releases some 7 million words daily on the newswires. But are Americans as a consequence well-informed? If the answer is no, it may be that these media do not have information as their primary goal.

The communications media exemplify the tendency of modern technology to impose their own demands. The industries represent the biggest agglomeration of power in the private sector. They shape cultural tastes in the interest of their advertisers and assemble for the populace their version of reality. The media claim to be the voice of the public; but they fail to come forth with a mechanism to muster effectively those voices that protest against the system. The information contest between government and press is a battle over the prerogatives of elites as to who should manage the public. The direction of their communication is essentially downward.

To the mass media in general, individuals are a statistic to rationalize advertising expenditure. The greater the number of potential consumer votes, the more defensible a higher expenditure. The United States is the only major nation in the world that uses television essentially in the interest of advertisers. No other nation tolerates the presentation of a film on the medium with interruptions every 12 minutes for several or more commercials. Much of what passes for news on the screen is entertainment geared to getting the commercial message across to a mass audience. The crucial task of the media commonly is to manipulate so as to gain a mass allegiance that commands advertising income.

Newspapers require sensationalism to gain such allegiance; many have become chronicles of aberration. Hopefully, the audience captured by the sensationalism reads and reacts favorably to the ads. Protagonists in newspaper accounts of events often sense a description of reality at variance with the facts. The phenomenon frequently has little to do with deliberate distortion, but comprises the price for the speed with which events are reported and the imperative to make the report readable to a mass audience. We thus draw judgments and make decisions based on what we think exists but often does not. Trapped by the necessity to frame reality within the familiar rather than within the newly discovered, journalism underwrites outmoded ideas and paints a day by day picture that does not reveal the emerging society.

The bloody Attica prison riot in 1971 suggests how the need for sensationalism draws the media into making news. The inmates played for the television cameras, as did the chief negotiator for officialdom. At one point, because of a bad camera angle, the negotiator was asked to repeat a crucial statement he had just made to the prisoners. He complied.

This need of the media poses a constant threat to the tranquil operation of the system. The press creates and discards issues and makes or destroys prominent decision makers. Managers in government and industry are sensitive to publicity. Firms hire public relations men to plant stories in newspapers with the purpose of promoting the interests of the organization. Aware of the manner in which the press manages the news, government officials seek to do some managing of their own by issuing releases and currying the favor of news men. The military establishment has developed the management of reality to a fine art. The department of airplane drivers alone has scores of public relations officers carrying the message to the wild blue yonder.

In early 1972 the press reported an FBI investigation of Daniel Schorr, a television newsman. The investigation was requested by the White House allegedly for the purpose of considering Mr. Schorr for a job. In testimony before the U.S. Senate Subcommittee on Constitutional Rights, Schorr stated that on at least five occasions President Nixon and senior officials of his administration had criticized his reporting. On one occasion, he was asked to come to the White House to hear an objection to his report. The following day he was interviewed by FBI agents, as were his neighbors and previous employers.[11]

Such is not to deny the legitimate grievances of government over the sensation mongering of the press. However, if it does not join forces, the government allows itself to be placed on the defensive instead of presenting the public with contrary facts and figures.

Newspapers are all sensational; they differ only in the type of sensationalism they peddle, which depends in turn upon the tastes of their audiences. Thus, *The New York Times* can orchestrate the pilfering of government papers by a reconstructed intellectual, the sensation mongering of a publishing house, and the insidious ways of the mafia, while the New York *Daily News* must focus on matters more titillating to its readers. While this penchant occasionally serves to maintain a vigilance over the system, the character of particular individuals is often damaged in the process. In the name of freedom of the press, the courts impose an increasing number of restrictions on libel suits brought by persons against the news media for slanderous statements. In No. 64 Rosenbloom v. Metromedia, the United States Supreme Court held that a radio station that acted without any malice could not be held liable for damages to a magazine distributor who was erroneously called a smut peddler in a newscast. The tendency of the Court is to progressively remove the press from accountability.

News in papers, to a greater extent than that on television, produces some analysis of issues. Television technology does not allow clarification in depth. A newspaper can count on holding an individual's attention for about a half hour on a couple of major issues without incurring prohibitive costs. Television must rely on quick picture impact rather than sustained reasoning. Television therefore tends to create fraudulent human beings, models which young people thereupon imitate.

Television rests on a cost structure that makes mandatory delivering a complex message in a minute. To enjoy above average fare, viewers must rouse themselves at dawn; its limited audience does not justify the use of prime time. The necessity of using showmanship to attract massive audiences pushes aside the very articulate individuals that the industry needs in its contest with government. Even television news commentators are showmen in the sense that they are judged commensurate with the numbers they attract to their program. There is less langauge in their half hour programs than there is on one page of a newspaper, yet on the basis of these words, a television viewer makes his judgment on foreign affairs, drugs, the Indochina War, poverty, inflation, pollution, unemployment, and race relations.

11 *The New York Times*, February 2, 1972.

Educational television comprises a contradiction in terms. The tube conveys a biased impression by the pictures it employs as an instrument of analysis. Its purpose is to enthrall. Many of our college youth, the first television generation, reason by mustering a collection of words that flash a series of pictures. They are not analyzing so much as describing feeling and experience. Educational value accrues to those who present a television show rather than those who watch it. For the latter, a possible gain may occur if the program motivates them to determine what the facts actually are; but one can safely surmise that few individuals rush to the library after watching a show on poverty.

In a typical example of the imperatives of television technology, an important address in Philadelphia by former Secretary of State Dean Rusk received 90 seconds in a half hour news program. The minute and a half of reporting included pictures of a demonstration going on during the talk. In handling the Negro protest movement, as another example, television news focused on sensational events and statements taken out of context. Whittling down an entire statement to an emotionally charged phrase and then turning the camera to a commercial reflects the medium's penchant for distortion. If a foreigner had to rely on television for his understanding of American race relations he would gain the impression of a relationship in constant turmoil. Yet, despite this superficiality, an increasing number of Americans rely on television for their knowledge of public issues.

Television is mamma's third breast. A post World War II child reaching the age of 18 will have logged some 22,000 hours before the TV screen listening to messages which teach that drugs, autos, and deodorants provide well-being and that violence is a desirable mode of conduct if it gains one's objective.[12] Television advertisers spend $2.5 billion annually to influence mass audiences. Because of the greater potential life span, capturing the mind of the young maximizes returns on this investment. The industry's major source of income derives from autos and drugs. Its restraint on these products suggests how institutions become corrupted by the necessity of assuring a steady flow of funds.

Television's rule of sensationalism does not apply to the expression of way-out political views. The medium is uptight about presenting minority ideologies unless they are rebutted by a conservative but is un-

[12] In a report on television violence, the Presidential Commission on the Causes and Prevention of Violence found that violence is generally presented not as unacceptable conduct, but as a legitimate means of attaining desired ends. The report states that within low income families, 40 percent of poor black adolescents and 30 percent of poor white adolescents believe that television portrays a true picture of life. "The preponderance of the available evidence strongly suggests that violence in television programs can and does have adverse effects upon audiences. Television enters powerfully into the learning process of children." *The New York Times*, September 25, 1969.

perturbed about giving a full 90 minutes to the uncontested views of a thief who wrote a fraudulent book, and who timed his show with the publication of a new work of true confessions.

To be critical of television is not to say it is ineffective as a tool of controlling government excesses. It sometimes reports government blunders even before the government finds out. Television news can frustrate government manipulation of the public. To cite an example, an effective way for a United States president to gain quickly the support of the electorate for his point of view is to dramatically present well selected facts on television without opportunity for them to be challenged. The speech made by President Nixon on November 3, 1969 was intended to serve such a purpose. In the third paragraph of his remarks, the president asserted that the American people were entitled to know the truth. Soon thereafter he stated that the war was Johnson's and not his, but quickly added that whose war it was assuredly was not the issue. Then the president delineated in general terms what has come to be known as the policy of Vietnamization. He explained that the war began with North Vietnam launching a campaign to impose a communist government on South Vietnam and that assistance was granted to the South Vietnamese government to help its people in stopping a communist takeover. Anything is negotiable, he stated, except the right of the South Vietnamese people to determine their own future. He referred to a letter of Ho Chi Minh to indicate the inflexibility of the adversary and inferred that those Americans not supporting his position were working for a United States defeat.

The scenario did not come off in the manner intended. The networks were poised on the ready with their commentators. One asserted that Mr. Nixon wasn't much of a politician; another announced that Ho Chi Minh's letter was actually conciliatory; a top government official, the chairman of the Federal Communications Commission, entered the fray by making personal telephone calls requesting transcripts of the comments on the speech; the Vice President accused the networks of imposing a monolithic and conspiratorial point of view on the public. In the ensuing exchange between government and media officials, the argument ended in a draw.

In another similar context, a government official lamented the high proportion of liberals among television commentators. In substance, he stated that hiring individuals on the basis of ability tends to weight staffs in the direction of liberals. The answer to the dilemma is clear: hire ignoramuses to come up with a fair share of conservatives.

In summary, the media employ sensationalism with their particular publics to fill their role as organs of the economic system. Within the constrictions of its technique, each medium must titillate to command an audience. Their fare presents American life with few, if any, redeeming features. If Americans have compassion, it is not reflected in mass communications. As a conduit for commercial interests, the function of mass media is first to amuse and then to orient aspirations to serve the needs of profit making. Because they determine how people should think, they represent the most powerful institution in the society outside of government. The contest between the government and the media comprises a struggle over whether the individual should be manipulated for political or commercial motives. It represents a contest over which institution should have the overriding power in mind management.

The media enjoy a monopoly over such management. Eighty-five percent of American cities have only one daily newspaper. When cities with two dailies under joint management or ownership are included, the figure rises to 97 percent.[13] What the radio and television stations lack in such a degree of control they make up in network programming and in uniform policies in the management of information. This massive concentration and uniformity of control explains to a considerable degree the decline of the media as instruments of mirroring the cultural diversity of Americans.

The future prospects for the expression of this diversity are bleak. Government and the media seek methods to improve their ability to manage the American mind. They share a common objective of conveying illusion in the guise of reality. They play the game with cards stacked against the public. This, in turn, raises the level of frustration in the body politic, a frustration that can be arrested only if a new institution can break the monopoly.

MAKING TECHNOLOGY MORE HUMANE

Technology thus serves the system as well as the individual. How can technology be made more humane, more responsive to the needs of each member of society? To answer this question, we will note first its tendencies and second the problems involved in their containment.

A lesson arbitrators of labor management disputes learn about technology is that innovation always hurts someone and that it hurts most those with no effective voice in the making of technological choices. There is no doubt that innovation often increases well being; it is also true that technology can destroy a man's job career, corrupt institutions,

---

[13] Schiller, H. I "Mind Management: Mass Media in the Advanced Industrial State," Vol. 11. *Quarterly Review of Economics and Business*, Spring 1971.

invade one's privacy, and damage the ecological balance. The enormous resources technology commands, its inexplicability to many men, and its drama, render the layman an easy prey for propaganda on behalf of innovation and make the managers of modern technology self-styled heroes. In the technological revolutions of our time, including the jet engine, computers, aerospace, and atomic energy, a relevant question is, then, what have these accomplishments done for man and with what costs.

One has to exaggerate technological tendencies to discern their direction. If technologists can reduce human behavior to a fixed response to a particular stimuli, the complete machine is possible. The individuals with the power of free choice would be the managers. The *summum bonum* would be reached when all the managers but one, a behavioral psychologist, would be planning consistent with a master plan imposed by him without their awareness. The planner's dream, the total imposition of commands while giving the appearance of free choice, will have been consummated.

Modern technology seems to be heading toward this robot society. It eschews man as a single human worth and relegates him to a mass who should behave consistent with organizational imperatives. It employs a stream of fantasies to defend this allegedly superior state. It converts the society into a goldfish society in which the kingfishers watch the behavior of the toilers to see that they perform consistent with an overall plan. Privacy is obsolete. The only tolerable behavior is the open and computerizable. Anything short of such behavior is irrelevant and suspicious. As Erich Fromm asserts, if the sick can be defined as passive and dependent individuals, modern technology has to produce sick people in order to have a healthy economy.[14]

But some human beings rebel at this sort of thing. They view managers not as heroes but as moral eunuchs with a franchise to manipulate in order to reach self-serving objectives. By rejecting positions in government and industry they aggravate the tendencies they abhor. Modern technology is thus a principal factor in the creation of a society of big brother, minions, and cop-outs.

It is fashionable in academic circles, especially in institutes of technology, to talk about the development of the engineer humanist who would make modern technology more humane. Purportedly, such an individual would temper his choices consistent with a humanistic vision of man. But no engineer, unless he wants to lose his job, can afford to be a visionary in a competitive profit making economy. His solutions must

14 Erich Fromm, *The Revolution of Hope,* New York: Harper & Row, 1968, p. 2.

be consistent rather with motives of profit and power. At best, he can serve in some government post seeking ineffectually to contain the destruction wrought by other engineers. Without a powerful organization supported by law and funds, the engineer humanist is impotent. Expected by managers to perorm as a hired engineer and not as a humanist his task is to suggest profitable alternatives in accordance with prevailing engineering practices. His training in humanism is of little use in his role as hired engineer. His services are available to the highest bidder, to be applied like a book of formulas. Such treatment is not offensive to him. Surveys demonstrate that engineers have self-deprecating images of themselves; they rate their technical abilities somewhat above those of electricians and compare their management responsibilities to those of shop foremen. They are amenable to being told what to do. Left to their own devices, they often create chaotic human relationships. Their vision of the needed technology of the future amounts to an extrapolation of existing trends.

In such a course, technology evolves not from a philosophical vision of a better man but as patchwork that pushes man hither and yon by power and profit. If the managers of technology are not pursuing money, they are after power, or both. A new jet engine is designed primarily on the basis of transporting more weight more profitably and not for the well being of the communities around airports. A major technological choice is partly based on the extent to which the producer can impose the costs of pursuing his objectives on to the community. Those who resist such a basis of decision making are cranks. The typical cycle of innovation is the introduction of change, hostile reaction, and acquiescence in a spirit of resentment and frustration.

Is there reason to think that change can be introduced in some other way? The evidence is mixed in this respect. Collective bargaining and the use of third parties suggest how technological decisions can be reconciled with human values. The protestor, the union, has the right to challenge the management decision and management can maintain its position at the risk of sustaining losses and forcing an adjudication of the conflict outside the firm. This industrial jurisprudence superimposes itself on the law of a society that protects the right of an individual to make money rather than the right of an individual to protect himself from the effects of such a pursuit. Collective bargaining history is a history of challenging this bias in the law. In addition, the union, by virtue of organizing the competitors of an employer, does not restrict technology at the expense of any single employer. A labor organization does not commonly seek to impose technical modifications to the disadvantage of any one employer. There are exceptions, but the union generally does not want the employer to go out of business and seeks rather to impose standards uniformly on competing employers. Because of such uniformity, an employer can more effectively reconcile technological demands with human values. And in the absence of a union, the employer who shows concern for the human consequences of his policies is generally not faced with intensive competition. The lesson of such experience is clear: the community must become the labor union and organize to control technology without placing a particular employer at a competitive disadvantage.

From time to time, suburbanites organize against technology adversely affecting their way of life. These attempts are generally an exercise in futility. Their improvised organization arises out of the emotions stirred by a particular issue and disintegrates thereafter. The contest with producers is on uneven terms. Their protest against the railroad is no match for the legal talent of the firm and the legerdemain of its accountants. When the chips are down in a conflict between a big corporation and an indignant community, the odds are strongly in favor of the producer. In the attempts of suburbanites to protect esthetic values against the inroads of highway and land interests, the courts take the position that esthetic values are not valid criteria in controlling the pursuit of profit shaping the community. And when suburbanites try to find engineers to muster an informed rebuttal against the engineering gobbledegook brought forth by producers, the engineers disappear. They are reluctant to testify against those who feed them. The void is filled by government technicians who cannot earn a living in competitive industry. Thus, the experience in suburbia provides further evidence of the problems involved in containing modern technology.

It is sometimes suggested that artists could generate a movement against technology's excesses by blending art with technology. Artists and engineers working closely together would develop forms suggesting the dehumanizing effects of technology. Thereupon, these persons could focus their attention on artistic forms conveying a transcendent human purpose. The idea, however, requires considerable money and maverick engineers, both of which are in short supply.

Can an initiative come from college student protest? Facts do not support such a possibility. The issues raised by technology are subtle and complex, requiring a sustained effort in inquiry and organizational strategy. Students today do not have the time or the inclination to undergo such an effort. They are more concerned with issues that provide opportunities for showmanship. The protesting undergraduate student is inclined to do his pirouette before his homework. He is at his best when walking for poverty on a mild Spring day. His rebellion against the subordination of the individual is ill-defined. He has a way of graduating and his organization thereby succumbs to a crippling annual turnover, much to the relief of administrators. The activism of the undergraduate student at times resembles an unstructured course in achieving maturity.

Professors and staffs of technological universities are in a position to infuse humane technology into the society. They are technically informed. But they are accustomed to working for government and industry rather than the community. It would take strong incentives supported by administrations to persuade these individuals to place their technical competence at the service of community organizations tied to the university. The role of such a group might include: providing information for the control of technology in the community; developing graduate students as monitors of technology in the community with skills in maneuvering within the system; with the assistance of representatives of the community, planning the introduction of technology into the community. It would be fatal if such a center became converted into a quasi-government agency. Government is not a neutral in technology but an advocate.

Can the initiative to contain technology in the interest of social goals come from traditional sources of reform such as organized labor and consumer groups? The evangelical days of the American labor movement have long since past. It has neither the structure nor the interest to promote social values through containment of producers. The labor movement is inclined to see a landscape converted into a honky-tonk if the conversion is performed by union labor. As far as consumer groups go, they are not prepared to undergo a sustained pursuit of strategies requiring high technical competence that would create a groundswell of support from Congressmen.

For in Congress lies the source of funds and legislative sanction for change. Populist centers of technology control tied to universities require Congressional support. A sustained organizational effort and the mobilization of scientific judgment on technology are required to so move Congress. What is necessary is a populist strategy of power, not just academic papers. The payoff for informed action at the community level is Congressional support.

POSSIBILITIES FOR THE FUTURE

Will modern technology be placed at the service of social ideals or will man remain its servant? Will technology for profit be replaced by technology for individual development? The initiative presently belongs to those who control technology with money, power, and prestige. They view men more as a means than an end, and no organization exists

powerful enough to counteract this tendency. But man has never resigned himself permanently to institutions of his own creation. Nor is
it ever precisely known into what new institutional areas he will elect
to enter.

Should man choose to contain modern technology, he would have to
impose on government a system of social goals planning. Government
sides with producer values unless powerful forces are mustered to the
contrary; it cannot be otherwise expected to provide an initiative in the
pursuit of human values. Such a hope is not reflected in the manner
government machinery to control producer excesses becomes readily
converted into a mechanism to control the government in the interest
of producers. The record of government against the excesses of technology, even after strong public indignation, is one of foot dragging.

The control of human values has shifted from family and religion to
the market place. The market demonstrates an ability to produce goods
in abundance and to promote a culture to sell these goods, but little
ability to produce a life of quality. The university, one would think, is
the logical source of inspiration and strategy for such an objective. But
those in the university who understand the scope of the problem are too
busy working as paid advisors to producers.

The initiative, accordingly, rests with professors and students with no
vested interest in the use of producer technology. But they have to get
away from the global manner in which they pose the problem of technology. To state that technology and human values are in conflict is an
imprecise statement. The objection by intellectuals to modern technology is often based on the disguised assumption that their values are
superior. In a values democracy, the problem is how to disseminate
knowledge on technological options and how to develop bargaining
power for the entire array of value preferences in the society.

Such a change in the *process of valuing* would have the effect of sub-
jecting value structures to open inquiry and change to bargaining among
all affected groups. The technological initiative held by producers would
be subject to social control. The new democracy would be value democracy. Elite planning would shift to populist planning. A new era would
emerge in which values become more cause than effect.[15]

Not all the effects of prevailing technologies are inconsistent with
ascendant human values. The trends in innovation create a rising

---

[15] In the Second World War, a group of young technicians working on Japanese code breaking decided to break a Coca-Cola machine programmed to deliver one cup of coke for each nickel. They succeeded. But the machine kept
on delivering filled cups, which created a new problem of how to dispose of them
discreetly. The incident has symbolic meaning as to the nature of machines,
intellectuals, and social control.

number of independent technicians who may elect to free themselves of the demands of the system. A class of technicians with intelligence, money, job security, and organization could, through political pressure, impose greater social control on technological choice. The latent power of these technicians is underestimated because of their modest position in organization charts.

A contest may emerge between the managerial elites operating the system, who seek to control values consistent with its smooth operation, and an increasing group of technicians who search for life styles not in conformity with the system's demands. Should the libertines acquire bargaining competence, we may see a rise in institutions that negotiate norms for technological innovation. We may want to think, therefore, that modern technology creates its own forces of control. Reason dictates, however, that social control would be enhanced by competence in bargaining. In the absence of such skill, the deleterious effects of technology are likely to prevail. Thus, the humanist must become a competent bargainer.

At times, modern society appears to betray a death wish. To place its technology more at the service of man, the impulses of society must be at the same time more *scientific* and more *humanistic,* in the 19th century meaning of these words and not in their contemporary popular sense of hardware on the one hand and neurotic activism on the other. However, the management of decisions has more to do with questions of money and power than with scientific honesty and humane outlook. Moreover, these qualities of scientism and humanism rarely exist in the same individual. The scientist infrequently works with a vision of transcendent man, and the deeply felt values of the humanist often serve to blind him to the reality of life. The manager tends to think that what can be should be; the humanist, that what should be can be. But he has no plan with which to bring that about. He rarely goes beyond complaining and poetizing.

The manager, the scientist, and the humanist perform consistent with the demands of their role. The manager plays technological choice as a political game in conformity with not fully disclosed ambitions. The scientist and the humanist allow themselves to be persuaded by the manager to play the game, in contrast with the manager, according to altruistic objectives. In such a game with a manager who does not reveal his cards one does not know what to counsel: despair, hope, or withdrawal.

The tendency for the Goddess of Technology to replace the traditional God is suggested by those who managed the Indochina war and who subsequently left for other posts of at least equal eminence. For these managers, the war was proper so long as it was technologically feasible.

The war became improper when cost-benefit analysis deemed it so. If such thinking prevails within the high echelons of the system, assuredly God is dead.

Once a massive commitment is made in modern technology, dissent cannot be allowed to jeopardize it. Only a slow transitional change is tolerable. If the technology employed to change the old technology threatens the system, a tactic of suppression and vilification may be necessary to stop such a threat. Thus, the abandonment of modern technology as a process in problem solving is unforeseeable. What lies in the realm of possibility for the future is a shift in choice of techniques and objectives through greater participation in decision making. In essence, the fundamental problem raised by modern technology is a reordering of power. Symbolically, the contest is between the power of the owner of the jet plane overhead and that of the individual in the house below. And the thought of the individual that he could redress that power by writing a letter to a government agency is sheer foolishness.

SUMMATION

A subject so vast and complex as modern technology is difficult to summarize. There are, however, several basic ideas about modern technology that suggest its dimensions and should therefore be reviewed.

Technology comprises tools in analytical thinking, hardware, human capital, and processes used to achieve a precisely defined end. These tools provide the options available in resolving a problem and the costs in human and economic resources for each of the options.

The configuration of these tools are related to the level and rate of economic growth and the size and dispersion of the population.

Technology is not an intruder independent of the society from which it arises. Those who deplore modern American technology deplore the values of Americans.

Technology has an impact on the array and content of jobs. While its effects are mixed, technology appears to be creating two principal orders of a professional-technical class and a subcaste tolerated because they cannot, yet, be mechanized out of existence.

Technology generates social change, the resolution of which occurs in the political arena. The sequence of events takes place in the following manner: The new technology, motivated by the pursuit of profit, power, or other preferred goals, clashes with traditional values. The conflict produces social change, or change in the relationships and functions of groups. Questions are thereby raised as to the proper goals of society and ways to pursue these goals. These questions become resolved through politics, using the term in its broad sense. The resolution reflects the bargaining power of the groups affected.

Therefore, technology raises a fundamental problem of power. Technological choice reflects the relative distribution of power in society. Equity demands that all affected groups be able to negotiate effectively. The need to reallocate power between government, firms, and community necessitates new institutions, institutions which themselves are a form of technology. For government or firms to be responsive to the array of cultural values in society, social action is necessary. To reconcile the needs of elites with the posture of diverse cultural groups is a major problem for the remainder of this century. The reconciliation of elitism and participatory democracy is undeniably difficult, but the problem must be faced because modern technology fosters centralization of power at a time when a rising educated class is scornful of authority and demands a share in decision making.

Government is not a neutral in the power contest but an advocate. The fundamental motive of firms in technological choice is profit. The fundamental motive of government is to serve the preferences of those who control it.

Technology increases the range of choices available to society. By broadening options, it generates a contest of value preferences. Modern technology thus not only curtails but expands individual freedom. The problem centers on organizing in a way that expresses all possible options and masses the costs and benefits of each of these options. Again, the solution that emerges from this need is a technological bargaining society.

Modern technology has caught the private enterprise system in a vise and is destroying it. One jaw is represented by contemporary goals that require expensive technologies underwritten by government; the other is technology for profit making so pervasive in its effects and requiring such a vast concentration of power as to generate public concern and government intervention.

Modern technology gives some individuals a sense of helplessness with regard to their ability to control decisions affecting their lives. Some resign themselves. Some rebel. Some seek new institutional forms of control. Technological change has always created conflict and social disruption. The difference today is that technology is supported by enormous public funds, is more pervasive in its effects, and faces a public less willing to acquiesce to its demands.

Firms and government introduce new technology based on economy studies which ascertain whether benefits will exceed costs. Firms, as well as government to a lesser degree, ignore social and environmental costs in making such studies. The system tends either to ignore or suppress aberrations from the routine of technology, depending upon the extent of their threat. Once a movement becomes massive, the system acquires the dimension necessary to modify and exploit it as part of the system's orderly processes. Thenceforward, the life of the new process depends on the propagandizing capacities of its managers, the amount of bads it generates, and the extent of competition with other processes. Producer reaction to innovation is more effective than consumer and citizen reaction. The quicker and more effective the social reaction, the greater the likelihood that options will be kept open.

Modern technology forces man to live in the future. Technological choice is so expensive and so difficult to revoke once made that society holds steadfast to choices even though they may not be the right ones. With some imagination, man can actually see where he will be into the future. He seems caught in a grip between the technological imperative of living for the future and the psychological need of living for the present.

Precise knowledge is a requisite for fulfillment now. If the controversy over the effects of technology is to avoid sweeping generalizations, more has to be known of the manner in which technological decisions are made and the way in which these decisions yield social effects. Only through technological analysis can society be rescued from the futility of so-called progress. Only technology can save us from technology. We should, moreover, keep the problem in historical focus. Technology freed man from an animal existence. The problem is not the machine, but the control of those who design and use it. The intellectuals who damn technology out of hand are as much distorters of the truth as those who praise it indiscriminately.

A time lag exists between the introduction of technological innovation and the application of social controls required to contain its bads. The amount of lag is related to the degree of information available concerning the bads, the extent to which the innovation is motivated by the profit motive, and the relative political power of the innovators. This time lag in social control is a major determinant of the intensity of resentments against the society.

To achieve social control of technology, all major decision structures, both public and private, all major economic institutions, in short, whose decisions affect the allocation of human and economic resources, have to be monitored by organization independent of government. But such monitoring is difficult because non-elites simplify problems and elites are incapable of relating to a non-technical public. Furthermore, to make such monitoring effective, corporations and government should be required to make public their technological plans. The social control should be performed by quasi-public bodies in the form of *assessment of proposed technology* and *evaluation of operating technology*. A similar but separate mechanism should be set up for military technology.

The rate of technological innovation has not increased as much as the overall pace with which we do things. The rate of innovation in the first 3 and a half decades of the present century was as much as that of the next equivalent time period. Thus, the rate of increase is approximately constant. But over time, the tempo of life rises considerably. We travel faster, communicate more frequently at longer distances, try to absorb an ever-increasing amount of information, analyze more problems, and even treat our leisure with dispatch. As we become better technicians and get more things done, we become less educated. We do things so efficiently, apparently, that we try to do more. We rush through life and lack the time to ask why we do what we do. We pay a price for this tempo of life in our superficiality and in our loss of life's meaning. And we reap a rebellion for this alleged efficiency.

These costs of modern technology create support for a conversion of the economy into a social profits economy of severely limited population growth. Such a state implies a system of priorities calculated to improve the quality of life and maintain the ecological balance. In such a state one would suppose that the high bads industries such as autos, chemicals, and oil would be down-graded and the frivolous use of electrical energy reduced through a system of incentives. A minimum standard index would also be established on goods and services such as food, housing, health services, and environment.

The advantages of zero population growth include: more investment per person; more parental attention per child; termination of the pollution rise attributable to a greater population and a rise in returns per anti-pollution outlay; an arrest of the increase in population density of metropolitan areas. Its problems include: where to find jobs for the new entrants to the labor force; how to contain inflationary pressures as the population shifts its demand to services; how to protect a rising number of elderly from the inflation. Limiting population growth would not produce a payoff until well into the future. If, for example, the goal of no more than two children per family, were achieved, it would take more than a half century for the population to level off. By that time, the population will have increased by an additional one hundred million.

Despite the fact that technology is the dominating force in American society, no comprehensive and integrated body of information exists how innovation is transferred to the society and how social controls contain such tranference. The individual who makes the sacrifice to write such a book will render an outstanding service to the society.

To conclude, Americans doubtlessly pay a considerable cost for a technological advancement whose mainspring is the profit motive. But do Americans consider technology a Goddess or do they acquiesce to change in the conviction they are helpless in controlling it? Without more facts, this fundamental question cannot be answered.

8

Unions and Labor Relations

*I'm armed with more than complete
steel—the justice of my quarrel.*
Christopher Marlowe

Labor management relations in contemporary America are in many ways a microcosm of political and economic decision making in the society as a whole. They depict vividly the class nature of conflict and the way this conflict can be reconciled. Much can thus be learned about social organization by observing how this relationship works and how it has been adversely affected by current trends. Moreover, by examining how negotiation operates to reduce conflict in this microcosmic situation, we may be able to discern a means of arriving at equitable solutions of the conflict in the larger society.

TRADE UNIONISM

In trade unionism can be seen both the needs and conquests of ethnic groups. The union has been an attempt to respond to their desire for status, creativity, and justice. But today trade unionists are fed up. They are fed up with trying to make ends meet; with the deterioration of their neighborhoods and values; with a political process that mocks their anxieties. The decline in their support of the Democratic party and their rejection of agreements negotiated for them by the top brass reflect their frustrations. Their leaders' suggestion that a law be passed empowering the government to set aside rank and file votes on labor agreements reflects how alienated these managers are from their membership. Trade unionists are in the ranks of a hostile force that affords politicians in and out of government the opportunity to manipulate.

153

Considerable change has occurred in the past decade at both the union leader and rank and file level. The organization bureaucracy has grown old; increasingly unimaginative in outlook; more detached from the membership. The rank and file is younger than that of a decade ago; more dissatisfied with modest gains; less inclined to defer to the initiative of their leaders. Because of irresponsible political as well as trade union leadership, union members are ignorant of the economic realities behind an agreement and care less. To compound the difficulty, they transfer their social irritations on to the shoulders of their officials who make collective bargaining settlements for them. Moreover, public authorities discourage the strike; its use as a means of teaching realities to a young and impatient rank and file is thus lost.

Industrial workers expect their union officials to provide them with rising income and job security. With the exception of the Teamsters and the construction crafts, most unions fail to fulfill either of these aspirations. Union leaders have lost the initiative to the officialdom of government and firms. Nevertheless, the little security industrial workers have, they owe to trade unionism.

To an industrial worker in affluent America, the loss of his job is a disaster. Employer personnel policies foster job insecurity. The employer, as an example, places a high importance on maintaining a young work force. More than any other of the world's advanced nations, the United States throws its toilers on the scrap heap as they age, a policy which strips men of their income and self-respect. In backward nations, an old man has status; in the United States, he is a reject.

Unions are accused of a variety of peccadilloes including causing inflation, distorting wages, lowering efficiency, and indulging in corrupt practices. The indictment is exaggerated, as an examination will show.

The prime cause of inflation is the institution that pontificates most against it: the national government. National policies generate a surge in the money supply, which is subsequently fed by state and local governments, the construction and service industries, and other groups seeking to maintain their real wages without raising their productivity.[1] With a tradition of fiscal responsibility, the Republican administration compiled the biggest deficit since the Second World War. Initially, the Nixon administration relied on monetary and fiscal policies to arrest the surge in prices and signaled to employers to raise prices by public statements

[1] With the acquiescence of government officials and university professors serving as public members, the construction industry operates like a barony indifferent to the public conscience on inflation. The committee that oversees construction wages has secretly approved wage settlements in an effort to conceal increases substantially above national guidelines. (*The New York Times*, January 28, 1972.)

against wage and price controls. The price and wage controls it ultimately instituted had a bias in favor of the upper class.

Traditional anti-inflation policies rely on fostering unemployment to stem the price rise. The approach commands intellectual respectability through economists' so-called Phillips curve, which associates a given amount of inflation with unemployment. Thus, using hypothetical figures, if one wants to confine inflation to a rate of 3 percent, an unemployment rate of 6 percent must be generated. The Nixon administration produced both: high inflation and high unemployment. At mid-year 1972 the inflation was running at an annual rate of approximately 3.5 percent and unemployment 5.6 percent. Its economic policy is managed with an overlay of propaganda that counts on short memories for its effectiveness.

Trading unemployment for price stability is class oriented. The persons who play with Phillips curves are not the ones who lose their jobs. When the Chairman of the President's Council of Economic Advisors announces with satisfaction a high rate of unemployment, the abstraction is a solution to him since he is not out of a job either. Inflation has become so institutionalized that only a system of tough selective wage and price controls with concomitant protection to social groups, such as fixed income recipients, will alleviate its burden. Inflation is more a political than an economic problem, both as to its cause and remedy. In the 1930's Keynesian economics became a liberating force for the working man; in the 1970's its interpreters use it to oppress the working man.

Employers do the price raising. Managers of big industrial firms duck behind the platitude that unions are to blame for the inflation and that the solution lies in urging them to confine their wage demands to increases in productivity. But some price raising employers are in industries where unions are weak or non-existing. The major culprits are in such industries as construction, health care, and in local government. They yield to price increases because of the lack of competition, the lesser ability to raise productivity, or, in the case of government, because of the tendency to pass along increased costs to the taxpayer so long as he does not raise a stiff resistance. If an employer increases prices in consequence of a wage settlement that raises unit costs, he should be taxed for so doing. If, for example, an employer boosts wages two percent above an agreed-to measure of productivity, an additional two percent should be levied on his profits. If, in any event, the price level does rise, groups unable to match the increase because of little political power should be protected by a government incomes policy.

Caught in an inflation not of their doing, workers are not going to ease their pressure on wages on the promise that firms or the government will exercise statesmanship in their policies. The best policy against inflation is full productive employment. Thereafter, it is up to managing elites to exercise their skills in monetary and fiscal restraint and in legislating against social inequities caused by such a full employment objective. Such policies require, however, less presidential jawbone and more presidential backbone.

On examination, the wage distortion thesis turns out to be an academic exercise demonstrating that wages would not be what they are in the absence of unions. Big deal. That is the unions' reason for being: to change wages in the immediate interest of its members. Unionists are not concerned with the long term effects of their actions because in the long term they will be dead. Nevertheless, unions do bring rationality to wage structures. They tend to reduce the number of classifications and the spread between top and bottom. Their influence in narrowing differences between industries is minimal; such differences reflect more the dissimilarities in economic constraints. In addition, the allegation that industrial efficiency would be greater in the absence of unions certainly has not been convincingly demonstrated. By their pressures, unions motivate employers to greater efficiency. When a labor organization sets standards of craftsmanship, it is often promoting efficiency in the use of labor.

The corruption thesis alludes to practices not considered "nice" in middle class Wasp society. These include means of maintaining order at Teamster meetings more forceful than those suggested in Roberts Rules of order as well as the imaginative use of union funds by union officials. Not all unions indulge in such practices; the unions that do, lean toward the Republican party. It does not follow, however, that all republicans are corrupt. Moreover, sin is not only a matter of proclivity, but opportunity. The virtuous who earn the reward of heaven are often those denied equal opportunity to temptation. One would imagine that most of the residents up there are members of the system and those below members of the unsystem.

For ethnics, labor management relations signify their means to the acquisition of freedom. Although this conquest tends to be ignored in academic discussion, it is real. The failures in labor management relations are to a considerable degree those of the bureaucrats in labor organizations and firms who allege to be leaders in the field. In an age when the moon was conquered in a decade, these administrators have been uttering the same hackneyed ideas for far more than one decade and have been confining their spirit of inquiry in the main to ridiculing the new ideas of others. Their dialogue is between themselves, and, expressed or implied, it is conducted in terms of their own institutional interests. It has reached a point where a new institution is needed to protect the unionists from labor management institutions created in their interest.

As labor management relations in the public sector acquire greater importance, and even more cautious bureaucracy enters the field. As this shift takes place, these relations become ever more a political process; what is "economic" and what is "political" becomes increasingly blurred. A basic flaw in such public sector labor relations is that the negotiating parties, including the mediators and arbitrators, are disbursing other people's money and that the decisions of these elites are not subject to a direct review by the public that pays for them. The strike in the public sector produces too many costs relative to its benefits. Issues are too technical to be handled in an atmosphere of crisis. In addition, the strike unleashes complex forces beyond the competence of parties to manage. A continuous dialogue involving the rank and file, the general public, and the leadership, must be encouraged, or the playing of politics to the exclusion of competent analysis can be anticipated.

The decision-making process in union management relations provides rich insights into the general problem of power in the system. Containing technology to serve human purposes is an ever present problem in these relations, as is the concern with linking power to a rule of reason. Arbitrators and mediators by virtue of their experience in labor conflicts are expert in their understanding of problems of power. They tend to view conflict as a tool of problem solving and are less afraid of it than is the general public, a view that can justifiably be generalized from the area of labor relations to that of American society as a whole.

Unfortunately, however, these experts are disinclined to express what they know. Despite the fact that settling disputes is an exciting human experience, much of the literature on the subject is dull, smacking more of an unimaginative sales promotion than of precise analysis. It gives the impression of having been authored by people who either know little about labor relations or are not being candid. Labor management relations, microcosmic as they are of the operation of the system as a whole, are deserving of a less varnished treatment.

HOW LABOR RELATIONS WORK

Labor relations take place within the framework of the larger industrial system, which comprises multiple associations between government, management, unions, and neutrals such as mediators and arbitrators. Its scope shifts with the nature of the problem being solved. The subsystem represents the single most important management of political and economic power in the broader social system. While industrial relations principals are interested primarily in employment standards, they also negotiate social and economic questions of wider scope. The relationship represents a mechanism of civilized conflict in which parties establish and interpret the rules of the game. They stand ready to offer something to each other in expectation of concessions in return. Each can exercise coercive power on the other. Each expects to obtain returns within the context of a structured exchange system. A study of labor relations is indispensable for an attempt to improve the technology of public policy making.

The rules making function of the parties in labor relations has characteristics that bear upon operations of the broader system. Rules are tailor-made to fit particular situations. They are made by participatory democracy. They can be complicated and overwhelming to the rank and file. And the rules can serve more those who manage institutions than the individuals for whom the institutions are created.

The major constraints in labor management relations include the values of the parties, technology, marketable labor power, the particular product market they serve, and money. These components are interrelated in much the same way as are the organs of the human body. But as much as the players in the relationship accommodate to forces, they create them also as they pursue their interests. In the confrontation of the parties, the primary interest of government is power and minimization of conflict; of management, the efficient uses of resources so as to maintain profits; of the union, worker and institutional security. The more asymmetrical their values, the greater is the likelihood of conflict. As the parties consummate exchange, however, their value differences narrow.

As bargaining relationships produce returns to negotiators and their respective constituents, a community of values emerges that diminishes conflict. Barring the appearance of external disequilibria such as inflation, the parties develop a philosophy of live and let live. Trade and the development of a consensus on the rules of trade by negotiation tend to destroy warring relationships. Whatever the parties agree to is equitable. In effect, trading partners establish a church that democratically legislates what is moral. The lion in the relationship exercises restraint and does not fleece the lambs lest the shorn develop a desire to sabotage the rules of the game. The game they play is one of balancing real and imagined inequities. A party that is hurting must be soothed by the other regardless of whether it has the power to command such salve. And if the cost of the game can be levied on other than direct participants, so much the better.

The function of the strike in labor relations is to achieve this meeting of minds. Conflict generates clarity of thought, empathy for the other party's point of view, catharsis. The release is analogous to that of spouses indulging in an old fashioned Donnybrook or well-heeled individuals performing on psychiatric couches. Carried to excess, the conflict is counterproductive. Nevertheless, a mature labor management relationship often issues from a long conflict; and many immature relationships are frequently the result of politicians, motivated by the desire to become heroes in the eyes of the public, preventing strikes from occurring or arresting them in their course.

Generally, labor arbitration in these relationships is a voluntary means of settling a dispute between a firm and a trade union on a final and binding basis. The process usually grows out of a complaint by an employee over what management has done or has failed to do. The arbitrator has two employers: the firm and the labor union. Since he has to be acceptable to those whom he judges, he is more subject to the pressure of contending parties than is a jurist presiding in a court of law. He has no judicial robe by which to detach himself from the disputants and no official body of law with which to defend himself. In effect, the parties hire him to render a decision that reflects the felt inequities of each. He must address himself to institutional needs as well as to those of the rank and file for whom the institution was originally created. Consequently, comparing an arbitrator with a judge is misleading. The arbitrator can bring to bear on the parties the stature that he earns over the years. But he executes his office at the sufferance of the parties involved. He must discard quickly any false notions of being a potentate.

In many ways, the arbitrator's justice based on consent is superior to the system's justice. Coercion is not justice, but knuckling under. Moreover, as it cannot be precisely known why a person does what he does, how can he be judged? The alternative to an elusive search for factors behind a person's behavior is an examination confined to the conduct itself. But this restricted viewpoint presents difficulties also. If, for example, two individuals report to work intoxicated, one an elderly person with terminal cancer and another a young man back from an all-night date, would justice be rendered by firing them both? "To Make the Punishment Fit the Crime" is a good melody but questionable justice.

Justice is more temperate when the judge identifies sympathetically with the judged, as is often the case in arbitration. It is difficult to be severe for conduct one might also have performed under similar circumstances. Justice responding sympathetically to the one whose conduct is being assessed is better justice. A Wasp politician passing judgment on an ethnic union official in a holier-than-thou spirit metes out not justice but vindictiveness.

Collective bargaining is the rules making machinery in which the arbitrator operates. How collective bargaining works in theory can be described in simple terms. If an approximate equality of power exists between firm and union, the decisions on employment terms are not dominated by the point of view of either party. The threat of a strike and the strike itself play a functional role by generating pressures that force agreement or acquiescence to a set of employment terms. A strike coalesces in the minds of disputants the uncertainties confronting them and moves them quickly to a common area of expectations. Furthermore, neither the strike nor the agreement affects adversely the public interest to any great degree. Both are private matters, the strike having a greater impact on the parties and the costs of settlement falling on the disputants rather than on the general public.

The ritual of collective bargaining comprises a series of stages. In the first, the pre-bargaining probe, the union makes excessive demands and the firm expresses shock and dismay. Each side brings forward so-called facts to maintain the validity of their extreme positions. An atmosphere of crisis emerges. The parties agree to a suspension of negotiations to think matters over.

Next come the feigned "real" position stage, in which both sides make a show of backing away from their initial posture to a simulated take it or leave it stance. They rest on the superiority of their respective positions.

In the third stage, each side plays chicken. Each states: accept my reasonable offer or break off negotiations. The party that does must know how to institute bargaining once more without weakening its defenses. The real issues begin to crystallize.

The fourth stage comprises estimating the other party's losses if its position is maintained. A process begins of whittling down extreme positions by demonstrating their unreasonableness.

In the fifth stage of bargaining, trading commences. A concession is made if the other party accepts a newly modified position. Trading takes place between economic and non-economic issues, and many demands are washed out in the process.

The sixth stage is that of statesmanship. As the differences narrow, each side gives up something in a show of largesse in the interest of promoting a settlement. The parties reach a common ground.

In the event of a strike, the process reverts back to the early stages of bargaining; each side publicizes the unreasonable position of the other. But at the point of deadlock and gloom, the bargaining moves forward again.

To an alarming degree, a breakdown is occurring in this theory of bargaining. Bargainers no longer negotiate in the framework of private markets. They often represent public agencies seeking more public money or firms not producing in competitive markets. Trading partners do not knuckle under to the forces of the market place but rather expect the public to adjust to their decisions. The price to the parties for maintaining rigid positions is less than the cost of making concessions. Their position forces the intervention of politicians motivated to seek settlements by their political ambitions. The absence of market restraints thus shifts the game to a play of political power. In this way, the system, in a hand-me-down process of bargaining, shifts ultimately the burden of its decisions to inferior castes in the unsystem.

Government involvement in collective bargaining often assures the unfolding of these preordained tableaus. The government issues pronouncements of noninterference in collective bargaining and expresses a hope for non-inflationary settlements. But parties plan their strategies in the expectation of government intervention. The statements of neutrality by officialdom, by affecting the position of the adversaries, assure eventual intervention. A party adversely affected by a hands-off position seeks to force intercession in its behalf. Frequently, bargaining does not occur until the government steps into the picture. Both firm and union want autonomy of action. Therefore, each seeks to elect the time and kind of government intervention. All 3 play their respective game of image making, and none of the scenes in their play are easy to eliminate. Each appears necessary for the development and denouement of their drama. To take their script at face value, however, is misleading. Each scene in the unfolding play promotes an undisclosed objective.

Each party may gain its sustenance at the expense of some other segment of society. If the burden of the ultimate bargain does fall on others, imagery is employed to obscure such a result. Thus, "true believers" issue pronouncements on the wonders of the democratic process and thereupon disarm their critics.

As this system of collective bargaining evolves there arises another group of individuals who, while remaining at the periphery, manage nevertheless to exert considerable influence in labor relations. They include not only arbitrators, but also mediators, lawyers, consultants, and practicing social scientists using universities as a base of operations. In seeking an understanding of what collective bargaining actually is, it is to these technicians one must go; once involved, it is difficult for clients to wean themselves of their services.

Of these practitioners, lawyers are among the most enterprising. Through the role of advocate that they are duty bound to assume, lawyers acquire a taste for winning cases rather than for solving problems. Their employment increases geometrically as Congress writes new laws; one set of attorneys is needed to seek ways to counteract the legal guile of another set interpreting the new law. Parties often hire lawyers skilled in delay and obfuscation, who at times appear not to want a decision so much as an opportunity to play legal sophistry. They use gimickry that nettles; they win a point through legalistic mumbo jumbo and thereby loss of faith in the law. They seem insensitive to the fact that men are morally inspired human beings, in terms not of abstract principle but of homilies applied to particular circumstances. A man insists that others respond to what he feels is the decent thing to do in a specific case, and the wise lawyer builds his case on such a judgment. He avoids irritating man's sense of moral judgment. Most lawyers, as do technicians generally, run roughshod over this moral sense. As occupational specialization increases, a technician's capacity to empathize with those on whom his judgment falls seems to decline.

Many labor arbitrators have organized their own ongoing racket also. Entrance into the trade is not simple. Their continued success is predicated upon an ability to avoid making decisions that may induce a party to terminate their services. The field of arbitration is sustained and its long term growth assured to the degree that every grievance is made a crisis and the use of reason deemed impossible. This state of affairs is nurtured by the parties themselves who insist on hiring star performers who sell their wisdom at high prices and who surround it with the ritual and ceremony that makes for reverence. Arbitrators, like lawyers, want to survive. New business must be planned, and the failure in direct problem solving helps. Such is not to say that arbitrators do not serve a role. The prospect of having a college professor as an arbitrator is often frightening enough to bring about a direct meeting of minds between the parties themselves.

As arbitration becomes established, it inhibits reliance on common consent. Its quasi-legalistic procedures sharpen differences rather than reveal similarities; to avoid a clash of reason, parties can shop for arbitrators whose views approximate their own. By forcing parties into a game of contending positions, arbitration imposes on the neutral a choice of two positions, either of which reason would not accept. In making his choice, the arbitrator has to lean a little in the direction of the party more likely to terminate his services. By so doing, he underwrites decisions based on power.

Originally, the function of the arbitrator in labor relations was of limited scope. It was designed as a substitute for the use of economic power in the settlement of differences. The arbitrator was a referee called upon from time to time to determine whether an act of omission or commission by a manager violated the agreement. In exchange for this power of review, the union gave up the right to strike. By its acceptance of the right of review, management gained stability and control of the future; management could thereby plan. As a referee, the arbitrator was not hired to administer therapy on the basis of a superior-inferior relationship with those he was to serve.

However, with the passage of time, arbitration as an institution acquired its own needs. By interpreting agreements, arbitrators found in them meaning that was not in the minds of the parties who wrote them. Interpretation became legislation, often with the acquiescence of the union, who found in arbitration an opportunity to acquire what it could not obtain directly at the bargaining table. As the institution developed, a kind of arbitration was imposed on the employer that he originally had little intention of purchasing. His ultimate acceptance of the institution was in part a calculation that the alternative would be more costly, and his calculation was affected by a lack of understanding as to what he was buying in the process. In part, he accepted because of the fear produced by uncertainty. Accordingly, powerful competing institutions accede to the power of a new institution if by so doing no differential disadvantage occurs and if uncertainty is reduced.

The arbitrator is thus a manager. He is a manager in the sense that he chooses one of several possible courses of action and creates an allocation of resources that exists by virtue of his decision. He is hired to make a decision for the parties, and the benchmarks he uses in weighing alternatives are complicated and are neither apparent nor universal. To minimize friction, he best not divulge them. The reality he faces in making a choice is not what it appears to be at the moment. It includes the human impulses of those affected by the decision, each of whom assumes a different view of reality. His decision is also influenced by what he expects of men. The facts from which his choice emerges become more apparent after the affected parties and the arbitrator begin to play their roles. Facts come forth after a full expression by affected individuals. It is thus naive to think one can obtain all the nuances in a social situation in the detached atmosphere of one's study or from the perch of a judicial bench. It is this fact of life that flaws the solutions of elites.

Each case comprises an emotional and intellectual involvement. The arbitrator has to make up his mind, albeit reluctantly at times, and face up to the consequences of his decision. He pieces together differing and conflicting concepts of justice and fits them to statements of principle of the rules of the game put together by the parties. To give an example, how should he dispose of a case in which an employee deliberately strikes another employee with an automobile when the agreement provides him not only with the return of his job but retroactive pay? Should he yield to his conscience and muster his industrial relations knowledge to prevent the bestowal of such gifts, or should he adhere to the letter of the law? Should he set aside the apparent intent of an agreement in order to placate his feelings of justice?

The arbitrator, therefore, does not simply interpret an agreement. He injects personal values in his decisions. He may want to re-equate the balance of power in favor of the weaker party, or he may decide to give the lion his full share. He may seek to implement what he considers to be equitable. No agreements have yet been written which anticipate fully the nuances of the future situations for which policies are prescribed. Accordingly, the arbitrator has ample opportunity to implement his private benchmarks of decision making.

The goal of organized arbitrators is to make arbitration a laudatory profession. To achieve this goal, the rascals in arbitration have to be made to conform to ethical standards. Many outstanding citizens who like people feel thereby qualified to be arbitrators. Being called an arbitrator is a coveted addition to titles of status such as economist, writer, and world traveler. One individual has claimed competence in arbitration by virtue of his membership in the American Legion. Some arbitrators indulge in ambulance chasing and fee padding. A simple discharge case taking two hours of hearing may require a week of deliberation, each day of reflection costing the parties hundreds of dollars. The differences in zeal for acquiring money creates pressure to standardize fees. As in other professions such as law, medicine, and psychiatry, the plungers in arbitration receive more publicity than those who assume the air of indifference that should be expected of individuals in the professions.

To include arbitration among the professions may indeed be an unwarranted assumption. No assumption of specialist inequality exists between the arbitrator and those to whom he provides his services. Arbitrators live by the consent of contending parties who expect their own expert knowledge to manifest itself in the arbitrator's decision. Parties can dispense with his services by reconciling their differences directly, an alarming possibility that may lead to his extinction. Arbitrators live at the sufferance of unions and management; accordingly they must adapt to the code of behavior of the system in which the parties operate. As an appointee, the arbitrator is subject to the political pressures of those who control his appointment; he is a judge having to fear the power reaction of the individual he judges. Some arbitrators inure themselves against such pressure. Others, particularly those who depend solely upon arbitration for their livelihood, are sensitive to what the union or management can do to their position. At times an arbitrator may even have to sacrifice the needs of an aggrieved individual for the needs of the system in which he operates. If troubled, he has to countervail against his joint employers, who may thereupon terminate his employment.

In contrast to the arbitrator, the mediator in labor relations is the wet nurse of parties writing new agreements. The same individual who performs both functions changes his style considerably when acting as a mediator. He provides parties a much needed cathartic; each is allowed to weep separately on his shoulders. He tells each the great merit of their position, and should an observer point out his inconsistency he would consider his critic absolutely right also. He is concerned with the maintenance of his acceptability to the parties more than the arbitrator. This leads him at times even to seek out disputes before they occur. The mediator is the direct offspring of the parties, born out of wedlock, more the issue of the union than of management. His behavior is expected to be that of the successful person in the system. Inflation, the public interest, moral considerations, all are concepts too abstract for mediators and deemed ineffective tools with which to ply their profession. The abysmal state of the economic arts in measuring the effects of collective bargaining places mediators in a position to ignore them. Imprecise knowledge gives the mediator room for maneuvering.

Like arbitrators, mediators have their own institutional needs. While they defend requests for bigger budgets on the basis of preventing strikes or shortening the duration of those that occur, they sometimes in fact promote the contrary. A drawn out conflict between parties can engender reason and thereby curtail strikes in the long run. But mediators cannot afford such an outcome; their employment requires them to intercede and thereby often to forestall a maturation of relationships. He must convince parties he provides a free consultant service of practical use; he is thus a salesman.

Salesmanship encourages rivalries between mediators and mediating institutions. Some jurisdictional disputes are settled by log rolling and allocation of spheres of influence. In some instances, even when state and federal mediators in a more philosophical mood may feel intercession unwise, they may sadly elect to enter a dispute jointly out of fear that each may do so separately. Sometimes they agree doing so in order to keep out a rival organization. The competition may be keen enough for a mediator to urge a party to withdraw the handling of its dispute from a rival agency on the promise that such a shift would insure a better settlement. Competition doubtlessly produces a greater overall intervention reflecting the needs of the institution more than those of the patient.

Competitive rivalry has also contributed to the downgrading of the national mediation service. By contending with state agencies over trivia, the federal organization has developed a mentality attuned to such disputes. As is often the case of government agencies generally, its image tends to be not that of leader but of finagler. It has found that the notes of a symphony orchestra float over state borders and therefore constitute interstate commerce subject to its control. If the lemons and parsley department of the Waldorf Astoria kitchen were to go out on strike, it is highly conceivable that the federal service might intervene to close the distasteful breach. The service must justify its budget.

Of all professional peace makers, those of the academic community who offer expert opinion for a fee deserve a special mention. The university professor is a sought-after technician. He is employed by parties singly and jointly. An increasing number of his colleagues derive a major portion of their income from employers and labor organizations. Their university posts are a profitable base for an extensive network of industrial operations. As teachers they furnish perceptions of quality in the objective mood, but as practitioners they create hazards in discharging this function. The posture necessary for their gainful pursuit of outside enterprise makes them often more propagandists than analytical observers, with a nonetheless fervid conviction of their complete objectivity. Devoting their time increasingly to the promotion of the system, they acquire partisan perceptions and impose upon themselves a censorship consistent with the maintenance of their business. Unlike the parties in industrial relations, who are often conscious of the way they select facts to support their interests, the university practitioners adhere irrationally to the conviction that their judgment is not affected by their own racket.

The susceptibility of economic organization to this formidable array of advisors, propagandists, and decision makers evolves structures, methods, and policies that would not obtain in their absence. To what extent this is so is difficult to say. Perhaps few changes actually occur as much as the hiring of the particular expertise that matches private interests. These experts do articulate to some degree the opinion of the general public. But to call them representatives of the common good is a strain on credulity. They cannot depart to any great extent from the direct interests of those who pay them. Moreover, the general public is neither organized nor homogeneous. There are different publics rela-

tive to issues and their influence is felt in the system at times not by
what they do as much as by what government is concerned they might
do. Affected publics are not adequately organized to retaliate against
the decisions of power blocs. The communications that emanate from
parties in industrial relations are often intended to mislead rather than
to clarify issues. They are designed to defend an interest or, in the guise
of neutrality, are laden with a mass of data meaning little to the public.
The peripheral army of technicians then cannot be expected to inform
the public or defend its interests. They are specialists in the employ of
the parties, not the public.

Injecting the public point of view via the mass communications media
is also chimerical. Issues not effectively dramatized by media are unlikely to arouse public attention. When issues are so dramatized, the
obscurity produced by the imagery of interested parties is replaced by
the sensationalism and simplification of the media. Changes in public
opinion are often merely changes in the estimate of the media as to what
the public is thinking. The public could organize so as not to rely on
the media's interpretation of what it thinks. It could hire specialists to
decipher the manipulatory data of the parties and disseminate counter-
propaganda. By so doing, it could become part of the system, making
its own contribution as another organ of manipulation.

Again, and from a different direction, we reach the conclusion that
institutions originally created to serve the needs of the individual blend
into the system and promote the interests of those who control them.
Labor relations, together with its processes of arbitration and mediation,
have considerable validity. But they, too, are subject to rising bads, a
tendency which can only be controlled by eternal vigilance.

Moreover, one can also observe that engineering problems are more
easily solved than those in labor relations. The variables in a system
affecting a problem in engineering can be more readily isolated and their
relative importance measured. Induced changes, therefore, are more
easy to calculate and the goals to be reached are less complicated. To
solve an engineering problem takes a good technician. To solve a labor
relations problem takes a good artist with a forceful personality.

THE ETHNIC STAKE IN LABOR RELATIONS

Trade unionism and labor relations have additional merit in that they
provide opportunities for individuals outside the system to rise into influential positions. As in politics, this rise injects new virulence into tired
Wasp blood. Italians, Negroes, Puerto Ricans, Mexicans, and other
forms of low life gain an opportunity to become decision makers. It is
not uncommon for an arbitrator to chair a hearing with a Negro reading

the riot act to a meek Wasp executive on behalf of a white ethnic. The arbitrator himself may be a reconstituted ethnic. The writer has acted as arbitrator in disputes where white ethnics testified against members of their own ethnic group in the interest of blacks. They acted out of a sense of decency. Yet intellectuals assert in their writing that white ethnics are racist.

The tendency of Wasps to resolve conflict by issuing paper edicts serves to accelerate their debilitation. Removed from active involvement in conflict, even United States presidents feel it necessary to practice pouting and thinking vigorously. Tests devised by sociologists indicate that Wasps have become extraordinarily timid. In one test, for example, Wasps measured well below average in their ability to stand on a Harlem Street corner. Sociologists believe that the maladay is not genetic, but one that could respond to socialization training.

Ethnics who rise out of conflict into positions of influence overcome the disadvantages of low birth. Many are the children of immigrants with little formal education. By assuming positions of leadership, they serve to assimilate minorities into the society. Carl Sandburg, a Scandinavian ethnic, observed in his lifetime that an important history could be written on the contribution of the sons of immigrant minorities to the functioning of American society.

To a considerable degree, the New Deal's grant of power to the working man triggered the rise of ethnics outside the system. The bitterness with which those of inherited wealth look back at the New Deal and the nostalgia with which ethnics view the FDR era are a mark of reality and not fantasy. At times, this historical fact escapes the children of ethnics; to their parents, the New Deal comprised a triumph of decency. The Wagner act of 1935, giving blue collar workers protection under the law to organize and bargain collectively, was a prime catalyst in this reallocation of power. Its critics assert that the legislation was one-sided, but law calculated to place power behind a value cannot possibly be neutral.

With this labor relations law, blue collar workers tamed organization by counter organization. They demanded that the system give them the ability to organize so as to acquire their rights. With the law, the unilateral discretion of employers was curtailed. Accordingly, in the system today, a manager can discharge an engineer after many years of service with impunity, but he cannot mete out such abuse to a blue collar worker without creating a fuss.

Tony Anastasio, former boss of the Brooklyn Longshoremen, was an ethnic who came out of the ranks. Tony was a short, stout man who looked much older than his years. He spelled his name with an "o" and used to express his annoyance with the intelligent and good people of the press for spelling his name "Anastasia." He was born in a barren region of Calabria in Southern Italy, where peasants manage through prodigious efforts to maintain a level of subsistence; they grow beans on the stone base of dried-up streams. As nature in Calabria is unresponsive to the efforts of people, so the people are equally unresponsive to each other. They appear, to paraphrase Edwin Markham, as things that grieve not—the emptiness of ages on their faces. Gentle Wasps readily label them criminal types. Tony was such a person.

A Brooklyn waterfront longshoremen local could be hardly more than a table and benches in a former retail store. Tony's operation was bigger. His headquarters used to house what as a boy appeared to me a fortress, but described by my father as a Swedish saloon forbidden to Italians. (All Scandinavians were Swedes to the Italians busting up the block). Where the floor show used to be, the longshoremen played *briscola*. Tony's office, equipped with an expensive mahogany desk and a red leather chair, was in the rear of the hall.

Tony came from a family of 8 brothers, 6 of whom migrated to the United States with their father. They moved into a neighborhood whose departing Scandinavians gave them the stigma of inferiority. The neighborhood was a short walk from the delapidated docks, to which 5 of the brothers—Tony, Joe, Frank, Henry, and Albert—gravitated. Albert's career ended abruptly; he was murdered in a barber chair. Salvatore, the sixth brother, became a Roman Catholic priest. Tony never went to school, but learned fast how to acquire power. He had begun hard labor at the age of eleven, determined to achieve success in the context of his environment.

Tony would give the impression of weariness and hostility, a look often found today in the face of leaders of the black proletariat. Why should he look warm and gregarious? His life was ugly. But with a little prodding he would become animated. He resented the suggestion of criminality which he felt the newspapers fostered, stressing that he never had been convicted of a felony. His most bitter feelings were aroused by what he considered the failure of the national union to recognize his power as a waterfront leader. He pointed out that some 70 percent of the longshoremen on the New York waterfront were of Italian origin, compared to 16 percent Irish, and 6 percent Negro. Although the union had given him the title of vice-president, he was rarely consulted or called to meetings of the executive council. He saw no reason, therefore, to abide by decisions which he had no part in making.

The Italians of Tony's generation considered the word Irish as synonymous with American. Tony enjoyed taking advantage of the opportunity to twit the noses of this superior race; a feeling shared by the dockworkers. They derived a psychological lift in seeing one of their own giving the superior Americans a rough time. In those days it was all right for Italian males to lay a Irish woman; but to bring one into the family through marriage would be a calamity.

Tony's status in the establishment used to shine upon his followers. He could be rough to deal with, but he represented a thorn in the side of those he disliked. He began his rise to power as a stevedoring contractor. He used the job as a means of gaining the loyalty of his fellow countrymen. By getting his *paesani* to join different locals, he captured control of one organization after another. The tactic was simple and effective: He would wait until his followers had a majority of the vote and then propose consolidation of the local with his organization. Through this strategy, he succeeded in putting together an organization of 7 thousand men.

He saw little difference between the job of a labor leader and that of a politician. Both functioned to serve their constituents, not to change their tastes and values. To Tony, the labor leader who suggested such change was a hypocrite, since he would not do it himself and run the risk of being thrown out of office. The labor leader is a servant and not a reformer; he should reflect the personality of the rank and file.

Ask Tony about racketeering in the International Longshoremen Association and he would readily grant its existence. The boys gave what the longshoremen wanted. It got out of hand in small locals and the answer was centralization of leadership. "How else can you try to change an organization?", he would ask. He would also point out that everybody in the system had some sort of racket or other.

Tony wanted his place in the sun. He wanted to be recognized by the labor movement and by the general public as an outstanding leader, but the press treated him like a bum. He had a particular dislike for high-class newspapers like *The New York Times*. Their pretensions were especially irritating. He resented the condescension of the gentle Americans out to see life at the docks and considered them hypocrites as well. One of his great achievements, he thought, was ousting Ryan as the President of the National. Tony would spend 14 hours a day, including Saturdays and Sundays, on the job, because, as he put it, of the necessity to take care of a growing tree.

Italian immigrants produced fewer labor leaders in proportion to their numbers than did other ethnic groups. From the point of view of status, Italians were down at the bottom. Unlike labor leaders of Scotch and Irish origin, they had a language barrier to contend with; they were not as aggressive and competitive. Moreover, they arrived later; the system was already in control of other groups. Their lower educational level posed difficulties in communication. Tony was favored by an Italian milieu. Although he spoke English badly, with an accent that was a blend of Brooklynese and Calabrian dialect, his followers spoke that way too. If some longshoremen did not come from the same *paese,* Tony at least was ITALIAN and not IRISH. His brother Joe was deft with figures and letter writing and thus provided the tools of administration. The blend of awe, respect, anxiety, and shared sense of status which the men felt for Tony was to his advantage. The many conflicts his family had with the system did not bother the rank and file; that was a private affair. As often happens, a favorable combination of circumstances provided Tony with the chance to take control of the Brooklyn waterfront. Tony had the astuteness and guts to grab it.

The second generation of leadership in the outcast ranks of American society has generally made the attempt to achieve respectability on the system's terms. Mr. Anastasio was succeeded by his son-in-law, Anthony M. Scotto, a college-educated man who wanted to inject broad social issues into waterfront trade unionism. Consistent with the system's custom of condemning a man outside the courtroom through guilt by association, and abetted by high class newspapers such as *The New York Times,* the United States Department of Justice released a publication naming Mr. Scotto as a captain in the mafia. Mr. Scotto was put in his place. His effectiveness in public affairs was destroyed. Thus, by predicting an inevitable social truth and giving it a sinister motive, the system brings about the evil it prophesies.

The trade union movement grew out of a conflict of workers with the managerial class. Its social goals were sought through negotiation with that managerial class. As a reconciliation of interests took place in such negotiation, the trade union movement abandoned its critical examination of social goals. Thus, the history of organization of ethnics has been challenge, modification of the rules of the game, rewards, and acceptance of the system once its terms were altered. And when this organization does not respond to new challenges, new organizations emerge. The Negro protest movement is an extension of this process, although most of it lies outside the structure of labor organization. The same phenomenon takes place in the case of white ethnic organization as new needs arise to be fulfilled.

These needs are often grossly misunderstood by intellectuals, who tend to dismiss the ethnic spirit out of hand, missing entirely the important returns that ethnics derive from labor organization. Even as acute an observer as John Kenneth Galbraith shows such tendencies. The trouble with intellectuals is that they have never been in work clothes.

SOME ARBITRATION CASES

Arbitration deals with diverse issues, some of which are highly technical in character. Some cases are not resonant with fine points in worker manners. In addition to the usual politics, psychology, and economics, there are cases which display the crudeness and intensive pressure of social conflict. The arbitrator, by his presence and even by his resignation, makes such conflict more civilized. And often he must use scorn and humor to put over his point.

In one of my cases, a black employee was discharged for using abusive language and committing violence on the person of Mr. Edgar Smith, his foreman. As Jones was enjoying a McIntosh apple while working on the assembly line, it seems that Smith, in his best alliterative English, told Jones to "finish that f----- apple." Jones took umbrage with the foreman's manner of speaking and called Smith a "mother fucker." At this point, the foreman, after calling Jones a goddam Nigger, received a blow on the forehead and fell back into the paint conveyor. After pulling himself together, the supervisor told Jones he was fired.

The grievance has since been filed as the Case of the Forbidden Fruit. The toilet wall words which generated the conflict might in a different context have been considered terms of endearment. Production was lagging, and the foreman had been told to get tough with the men. Jones was ordered back to work with full retroactive pay.

The following journal of a waterfront dispute suggests the intensity and crudity of power play, and indicates to what extent economic affairs are an act of politics. The names are fictitious.

Wednesday May 24th:

After several attempts to reach me during the day, Cruse of the employer association gets me on the telephone at about midnight. He states that the longshoremen have refused to discharge wood pulp with a 22 man gang with 8 in the hold and 3 on deck. They want more men on the pier. It is the third time that the situation has arisen and that the union has knocked off the ship. I suggest he try to work out an agreement with the grievance panel first and he says it is hopeless but he would try. I warn him that an arbitration award may not settle anything.

Thursday May 25th:

Cruse calls again in the morning saying that the union failed to show up for the grievance hearing. He had bumped into the union president who said the men were wrong for refusing to work on the basis of piling up the pulp 3 high. But he was having trouble with the business agents doing ass licking with the men, and he did not want to appear as an Uncle Tom. I call the union president and asked him to attend a meeting at the offices of the association. There the union takes an official position that it is impossible to work the pier with only 11 men. Both parties state the situation calls for negotiation. But each wants the other side to make the first concession. An arbitration is called at shipside at 3 p.m. One of the business agents demonstrates with the help of two pilemen and a trucker the difficulty in piling the bales 3 high. He gives an impressive performance. Cruse states out in the open that the union president had stated privately that the men were wrong. Allen, the president, is placed on the defensive and mumbles he was not aware of all the facts. A decision is handed down against the union at 5:30 p.m. and the union president takes off saying there is nothing more we can do here.

Friday May 26th:

Cruse calls to say the men failed to show up for work on the ship. The local is being advised by telegram that unless the men return by Monday at 8 a.m. the port would be shut down by the association. He would rather do it this way than take court action. The Federal Mediation service says it will take a hands-off position so as to impress the union with the necessity of adhering to the contract. But later that day the labor adviser of the Mayor calls the Service about attending a meeting with the union. The association states its disinclination to participate in a mediation meeting involving an arbitraton award.

Saturday May 27th:

Call from Cruse sayng the union had staged a mass meeting at the waterfront. Later, the labor advisor for the city calls to inform me of the intervention of the mayor. I am told the mayor is on the spot politically and the possibility of a port shutdown could not be risked. I tell him an attempt by the mediation service and the mayor to fill their needs would force me to quit. In another call I'm advised that the mediation service resents the mayor's intervention because the situation lies within the jurisdiction of the federal government. I advise that a way of my getting off the hook is for the union and the association to make an agreement modifying the existing contract. In this way, the union would not appear as having violated the agreement.

Call from Father Smith that the mediation service is smarting over the association's refusal to attend a meeting at city hall. The union, says Smith, is going to accuse the arbitrator of being pro-management and thereupon the Service and the mayor are going to use me as a sacrificial goat. The association wants me to stay on to use me as a club over the head of the union.

Cruse calls me up saying the association had no choice but to attend the meeting at the mayor's office. The mayor stayed there for 12 hours and the association was reluctant to pick up and go. The mayor obtained an agreement that the union and the association would not make statements to the newspapers.

Sunday May 28th:

Call from the mayor's labor adviser. He tells me I am "vindicated." He sounds like he is buttering me up for the kill. The mayor could not have possibly waited until Monday in the face of a possible shutdown. He suggested a cooling off period and would I postpone next Wednesday's scheduled arbitration hearing on another dispute. The mayor got the parties to agree to a statement from him. It would say nothing about arbitration. Why rub it in? [2]

Monday May 29th:

Telephone call from the employer association giving their version of the meeting in the mayor's office. The mayor appeared distressed. The association stated we will not mediate an award. But that fuckin' labor adviser of the mayor set us up to make concessions. The union is using the dispute in order to create jobs. That's the way they operate. On the west coast it took the association $28 million to keep their freedom.

Call from the mayor's labor adviser. He apologizes for the newspaper story placing the arbitrator in an unfavorable light, but that was not the intent of the mayor. Says it is nonsense for an arbitrator to adhere to an agreement and that a contract should be interpreted in a way that keeps production going. When a decision can go either way, it should be given to the union to avoid disruption. The threat of disruption only brings in the government and they are only going to screw the guy with the least power.

Wednesday May 31st:

Receive a letter from the president of the union requesting that all further meetings be postponed indefinitely. The mayor's labor adviser tells me the union president wants to talk to me personally, but it would be suicidal to do so at this time.

Telephone call from the association. Advise Cruse I am resigning.

---

[2] The local morning newspaper of May 29th reported the mayor as praising the work of the mediation service, the employers, and the union for demonstrating their concern for the welfare of the community.

Urges me to stay on because quitting would ruin the arbitration machinery.

Call from the union president. He disavows the accusation of lack of integrity on the part of the arbitrator. Says my award made it difficult for the men to goof off from the pier during the shift. But Cruse is not worth a shit. He is always making it difficult for the union president.

Thursday June 1st:

Allen suggests a luncheon meeting with the association, with the union paying. But he calls up later saying some of the business agents don't think it's a good idea and he has to go along.

Call from the association. The caller states the union president does not have a free hand because he and the union attorney have a racket going on third party claims at the waterfront and he does not want to antagonize anyone. The labor adviser is a liar and the mayor an opportunist. One of the union people told the mayor that the arbitrator had promised the union a win. The trouble is due to the fact that the business agents are out to get the union president.

Friday June 2nd:

Call from one of the stevedoring firms in the association concerning the use of pallets to discharge frozen meat. Says he will resign from the association if a quick decision is not forthcoming. Tell him I'm taking a long vacation and might resign afterwards.

Wednesday June 7th:

Call from Cruse who says they have negotiated an agreement on the discharge of wood pulp. The mayor offered us an air conditioned room but we told him we'd rather go to the association office.

Monday June 12th:

Conversation with Kane, a labor arbitrator. Says the labor adviser is not working for you because he is trying to make the mayor look good. The mediation service is no longer going along because Washington says the longshoremen are within their jurisdiction and not the mayor's office. The employers do not know how to make concessions. Maybe some of them give the union people payola. Everybody is crooked so why shouldn't the business agents make a deal walking along the pier with the employer.

Monday June 19th:

The association advises that there is more trouble with frozen meat on the MS Coral Sea. Some sorting of the meat is necessary by consignee and we told them to do it in the hold, but the union president told the men to do it on the dock. So the Car Loader Union protested and stopped work. Their men are carrying picket signs saying the longshoremen are being unfair to the car loaders.

I talk with the president. He says he will have the men sort in the hold of the ship.

Friday June 30th:

Receive the following letter:

I wish to protest your recent arbitration award 3–61 concerning meat and pineapples. I am of the opinion that you have gone far beyond your powers and are writing into the contract something that is not there. It has been the practice for the last 35 years in the port to the best of knowledge, that when cargo comes out of the ship Local 1291 puts the cargo onto the dock, not onto pallets for storage or shipment.

Friday June 30th:

Call from Cruse. States they are having trouble at Pier 4 North in loading sponge iron. The union delegate ordered the load cut from 48 to 24. The cargo had come in from the plant in pallets of 48. At the pier I ask to see a load of 48. The load buckled noticeably. Each bag weighs 110 pounds so that a draft of 48 runs over 2 tons. The load looks deceptively small. A violent argument ensued between the foreman and one of the longshoremen, belly to belly. I tucked mine between theirs.

August 31:

I submit my resignation to the parties. A representative of the city of Philadelphia calls requesting a copy of the letter. The call is not returned. Either the company or the union leaks the letter to the newspapers. The letter in part reads as follows:

I am submitting my resignation to you as impartial arbitrator for your local unions and the marine trade association. I would also like to present my appraisal of the operation of the grievance system during my term in office.

A detailed assessment of the maneuvering which took place after the longshoremen knocked off the ship must await a later date. Suffice it to say now, the immediate intervention of outside parties after the arbitration award caused the grievance machinery to become inoperative.

The parties are not disposed to a voluntary assumption of the responsibilities involved in processing grievances in a civilized manner. The Union seems to view arbitration as an intrusion and feels it gains nothing from the system above individual political gains. The Employer on his part is inclined to look at arbitration as a gun to hold against the head of the Union. If the employer will accede to political and economic pressures after an arbitration decision is rendered, it is best that concessions be made beforehand within the arbitration process. The arbitration system does not deny the opportunity to any party to make concessions.

The success of a voluntary arbitration system for settling disputes depends on the willingness of parties to abide by arbitration decisions even when it means losing a badly wanted case, and the will and ability to require their constitutents to honor them. It works only under a self-imposed restraint on power.

The parties debase the procedure by using it as a weapon to undermine the sense of dignity of individuals. They have employed the machinery as a means of continuing the running battle between themselves.

If the relationship is to move in the right direction, I believe some time for contemplation may be fruitful. To calm the frightful tempers and growling dispositions of elements on either side, the parties may want to join in some soothing activity such as bird watching.

CONCLUSIONS

There are several interrelated lessons that may be derived from industrial relations experience that apply to the system generally. One has to do with power relations in institutions designed to render justice to individuals. A second relates to the problem of bringing about a movement of power blocs in the direction of social goals. And a third has to do with the exercise of will in American society. The relationships described in this chapter are cruder than most in industrial relations, but they serve to bring these problems into focus.

Institutions created to render a service to individuals soon develop needs of their own to which the served individuals must acquiesce. Justice tends to become elusive, because its processes eventually thwart an effective expression of the point of view of the individual to whom it is being dispensed. Justice indeed can be blind, blind to the set of circumstances for which it is rendered. To contain this tendency, counterorganization is an ever continuing necessity.

Warring organizations tend to accommodate each other so long as the costs of doing so can be transferred onto someone else. This tendency negates the theory that a society of decision making by elite power blocs promotes the interest of the individual. The performance of the so-called neutral in industrial relations furnishes clues as to feasible strategies to achieve the objective of movement of the system toward social goals. To expect government to perform such a role is a delusion of liberals. And when book-writing intellectuals suggest that a combination of government, industry, and university elites would lead us out of the woods, the delusion reaches the edge of madness. Nevertheless, only government by statute can create a system of neutrals to provide an instrument of public accounting and disclosure designed to move the system in the direction of social goals. Without such statutory support, neutrals who are the best informed on how the system works cannot perform a public role. Thus, government must create a powerful force independent of government and industry which would promote social objectives.

Despite its faults, the arbitration process points toward such an independent force. The arbitrator, with an image of reconciliation, and in an exercise of will, perceives, raises in his mind alternative courses of action, and decides. He has faith in acts of will that involve perceiving, acting, and improving. He persists in such faith despite the failures. The outstanding arbitrator sees meaning in a situation external to himself and makes a choice that shapes the future. He has empathy for those involved in the situation, even for those whose acts are repugnant to him. He is an intellectual, not just in the sense of one who observes and describes, but a doer. To survive, he must be a competent observer. He must make up his mind and do something even though its consequences may be disastrous. No one gives this power to him. He acquires it on his own merit. In short, he takes risks in empathetic acts of will in contrast with the wasteland of apathy and infantilism that afflicts much of society today.

Man's greatest display of genius since the beginning of civilization has been his construction of systems of social rules. Man's humanity derives from his ability to construct relations of community. He has developed a system of formulating and interpreting abstractions that issue from a contest of reason and serve to determine the manner in which men consent to relate to each other. These abstractions are symbols of authority to which men acquiesce and which contain their individual inclinations. Without such a system of civilization by rules, man would not have attained his extraordinary level of achievement in science and art.

This system of rules has become disabled in American society. The failure exists with respect to who should devise these rules, what they should be, and how they should be interpreted. Since the beginning of the Nuclear Age in 1945, government has progressively destroyed its image as a wise and civilized leader; its image has become rather one of conniver, sadist, or fool. Today this destruction has reached its zenith in a system that elevates to top positions of national leadership Machiavellians whose motivation is the promotion of their ambitions, who do not believe in honest dealing with the public, who use the media as a means of deception, whose task is not governing but maintaining power.

What is involved is fundamentally a clash of philosophies. The cynical one views the mass as ignorant, mean, self-serving, easily manipulated, governable only by duplicity. The contrasting optimistic philosophy considers men capable of accepting common ideas of equity through a process of dialogue. One considers man as beyond redemption and the other, as capable of ever-higher levels of creation.

Despite its many faults, collective bargaining is based on a philosophy of optimism. It provides many clues as to the ingredients necessary for a new system of rules making. Of fundamental importance among such ingredients is participation. The arbitrator-mediator can perform a crucial role in the rules making of the new society. He can be a crafts-man in the process of change. Of such a role more will be said in the final chapter.

9

Government and the
Political Process

*Political institutions are a superstructure
resting on an economic foundation.*
Lenin

American government has undergone profound changes. If a young
American at the end of World War II had been told that in the name
of freedom his government would soon become a subverter of governments; would condone political assassination; would spy on, bug, and
wire tap its people; would subvert American institutions; that its presidents would start their own private wars and defend them with Machiavellian tactics, he would have been incredulous. The American government began its history without princes, without a military machine, without an established religion, and without a record of oppressing foreigners. Now, after less than two centuries, its princes of state initiate
their own wars, the military establishment operates an inner government
that shapes the course of international relations and the economy, the
state religion is *Machiavellismo,* and foreigners are killed in the national
interest. The same young American, now a mature person, contrary to
his inclinations, teaches his children not to trust government.

Fear of communism was an important factor behind this evolution.
The astute exploitation of this fear catapulted a United States president
and many other politicians to their positions of prominence. Politicians
described the communist challenge as the expansionist tyranny of international communism without moral principle and without honor. After
this conspiracy doctrine gained wide acceptance, they structured a gov-

181

ernment whose conduct resembled that ascribed to the adversary. They left a legacy of government coercion as a tool of controlling values.

Government lacks an inherent warrant to coerce individuals into any prescribed course of behavior beyond that necessary to prevent them from harming each other. Government does not exist independent of the individuals it represents. Rationally, individual actions can be curtailed only through negotiation of a consensus on the extent of the restrictions they wish to impose on themselves. Beyond his potential to harm others, the individual is free to pursue his own course of action. He can be asked to do otherwise through an exchange of information and through an appeal to his sense of equity. The use of government power to exact conduct beyond the minimum social contract encourages employment of counter power to subvert its efforts.

Having acquired an appetite for coercion, government ignores its social limit. Allegedly, its exercise of strength promotes the common good. To this end, government monitors the thoughts and behavior of the citizenry receiving its beneficence. Functions derive increasingly from force and rarely from agreement, which is their only legitimate instrument. Love of country is sometimes mustered into service to obtain acquiescence to policies. An appeal enshrined in emotionally charged palaver is made to forestall the emergence of reason.

The government thus can rightfully demand only that people not be unduly anti-social. It can require that people be civil and literate. Logic cannot project these limits further, not even to prescribe the manner in which these qualities should be acquired. When government insists its citizens adjust to policies not of their making, it curtails the right of man to be maladjusted.

This official preference for automatic response emerges from the needs of organization generally. For the orderly maintenance of policies and institutions, people must be manipulated. This common need for control rather than participation, for rhetoric rather than truth, for fantasy rather than reality, can be easily ascribed to a cabal of devils. But in fact, their necessity emerges from technological imperatives that tend to trap modern society. The manipulating state makes technological commitments that require deception for their orderly evolution. For the sake of maintaining modern organization, an imprisoned minority must control a manipulated majority.

In no small measure the United States Supreme Court contributes to this relationship between government and people. By reading their values into an obsolete constitutional document, the Court instructs the President and the Congress as to the limits of their power. Inspired by a vision of egalitarianism and unencumbered by control from the electorate, the Court contributes to the practice of employing institutional power to coerce individuals to accept high-sounding purposes promoted by individuals with organizational backing. The justices are non-elected politicians who periodically rewrite an antiquated constitution to suit the demands of shifting power configurations. An elite of old men defines its powers and from its sanctuary proceeds to solve complex problems by the issuance of *pronunciamenti*. With an assist from liberals, they have abolished prayer in the schools in the name of freedom of religion. In the guise of judicial review, they have legislated in the field of housing, employment, race relations, and education. Their decisions impose on the executive the obligation to coerce persons into improving their social attitudes. The judges rewrite old law, pass new law, and repeal old law no longer to their liking, all in the name of a social ideal of the in private persuasion and do not even have to persuade the individual of the merit of their edicts. Accordingly, the Supreme Court, through the process of elite decision making, advances the manipulating state.

To cite an example, the Supreme Court in 1971 struck down a Pennsylvania law providing financial assistance to parochial schools on the finding that the relationship between government and organized religion was getting too cozy. The state law comprised a practical populist acknowledgement of the manner in which the parochial schools alleviate the burden of public instruction. The Court found the law unconstitutional. On what basis? On grounds it violated the clause stating that Congress cannot pass a law in establishment of a religion or in prohibition of the free exercise thereof. What do these grounds have to do with the Pennsylvania statute? The answer is that the law is unconstitutional by virtue of the constitutional restriction on Congress because the Court says so. In the same ruling, the Court concluded that providing financial assistance for the construction of a parochial school gym does not violate the constitution. Thus, the law is, in effect, what the judges say it is and the practical way to change it is to shop for the right judges. U.S. Presidents do.

To a considerable degree, the law emerges from judicial stipulation of the rights of criminals and vested interest organizations, with little regard for the people affected by such stipulation. Thus, the relationship between criminal and community is developed in terms of the rights of the criminal, and the relationship between moving organized bloc and community in terms of the rights of the organized bloc. The procedure is guaranteed to frustrate populist will. But the Court is not accountable to such a will and can be contained only by getting the right United States President or by the laborious process of constitutional amendment.

In discussing government, we shall address ourselves to executive and legislative government and to the political process by which elected officials who manage these branches are chosen, keeping in mind, however, the existence of the super-government embodied in the United States Supreme Court. It will be shown how the development of government as a colossus in the service of organized interests has produced a sense of powerlessness and mistrust in people and that the solution lies not in more elitism but in more power to the people. To advance the argument, the nature of government power, the impact of government on the economy, the imperatives of political office, and the watershed national political campaign of 1968 will be considered.

THE NATURE OF GOVERNMENT POWER

American government is an octopus. By conservative estimate, the national government stores 70 billion sheets of paper in 4 million 4-drawer cabinets more at the disposal of producers than the general public. At the bottom of the Big Depression, the federal budget amounted to $3.3 billion. Four decades later, during the lifetime of many Americans, the budget increased to 70 times that amount. One of every 5 individuals in the labor force, or more than twice the number in so-called socialist Britain, works for government or a public agency such as a school system. If one adds individuals whose income derives from government money—armed services personnel, farmers, pensioners, welfare recipients, and workers on government contracts—the United States fast approaches the point where half the population derives its income from tax receipts.

Government buys, sells, fixes the rules, judges whether the rules are violated, mediates, disciplines, encourages and discourages competition. Government establishes the crime rate by legislating what is criminal. Government is the self-styled fighter against poverty. By acceding to the power of industrial groups, government also lowers the living standards of the poor.[1] By official and informal grants of power in the name of the public interest, government fosters inefficiency, limits employers in a particular industry, decides in the interest of public welfare the kinds of output persons can use as soporifics, and sets up customs barriers between the states. Government subsidizes those who have political influence and shapes directly and indirectly the amount and component of the gross national product. By controlling output and transfer of

[1] My neighbors in Washington County, Maine, are poor. They pay a premium on oil for heating their homes because of the ability of oil firms to maintain the fiction that placing import quotas on foreign oil promotes the national security.

money, it affects the distribution of income among the population. Government controls the relationship between unions and management, sets minimum labor standards, affects the prices of half the goods of the economy, issues loans and licenses to private industry, and determines who obtains patents. Through monetary and fiscal policies, it has improvised a system of guaranteed consumption in return for acceptance of the system. It does not always work.

In discharging these functions, government varies in precision, in the speed and variety of effects, and in who is favored and who injured. Each new responsibility is a victory over individualism. Each legislative triumph is a win over man and a day closer to his demise as a free spirit. This power is scattered among a network of semi-autonomous agencies, each seeking to prevent any encroachment upon its prerogatives. Their functions of necessity are decentralized, thereby minimizing the possibility of a concerted move against the individual. Facing each government bureaucrat is an array of representatives of organized blocs guarding the interests of their clients. His most formidable weapon is the ease with which he can confound them as to where responsibility lies in government. The most effective tool used by government to confuse the public is this diffusion of authority. When a half dozen persons are responsible for a decision, no single one is responsible for its outcome.

Government has a tradition of low productivity. It provides a vast training ground for soldiering in which the art of loafing without appearing to be becomes a consummate art. As a general rule, the typical government employee in the United States is less competent than his counterpart in the private sector. In government he finds a comfortable nest away from the rigors of competitive life, often at terms of employment more favorable than his more able correspondent in the private sector.

Government is at the disposal of those with the money and talent to control its processes. Carried to an extreme, such a propensity encourages the purchase of legislation from cooperative legislators. The practice of legislators representing employers as clients and the appointment of businessmen as government officials promotes this tendency in the relationships between government and industry.

Many examples can be cited of this close relationship between government and industry. In one big industrial state, the leaders of the legislature pass laws which favor employers who also happen to be their clients. These leaders are also responsible for developing an ethical practices code for themselves. In the United States Congress, the chairman of a committee considering the curtailment of oil depletion tax allowances is a representative of oil interests. The key Congressmen controlling the flow of subsidy money to shipping firms receive campaign contributions from these shipping lines.[2] In New York, State Supreme Court judges solicit contributions for their campaigns from lawyers who practice before them. In the executive department in Washington, D.C., a member of the cabinet finds nothing unethical about his name being used to solicit money from employers on behalf of a United States senator. The solicitation gives the donor the right of free choice: making a donation and coming to dinner or making a donation and foregoing the meal. In another department, an assistant secretary of agriculture passes information to grain dealers, which provides them with windfall profits, and shortly thereafter becomes an executive in one of the firms. In a third, a heavy contributor to the president's campaign fund acquires a bank charter in less than 3 months.

In Pennsylvania, lobbyists write bills for legislators to promote the interests of their clients. In a tax proposal, the chairman of the Pennsylvania Utilities Commission, a former chairman of the state republican committee, advises a lobbyist on how to write a tax bill that would shift its incidence to the consumer. The same state sells the names and addresses of its motor vehicle registrants to advertisers and thereby presumes to invade a man's privacy.

In the state of New York, the distinction between lobbyist and representative of the people is extinguished entirely. Lobbyists are, in effect, staff members of the legislators, deciding which bills are to be brought forward in the legislature and how they should be voted upon. They deplore direct contact between the electorate and their kept representatives and prefer controlling the political process exclusively themselves. To assure steady employment, lobbyists even encourage other lobbyists to introduce bills against the interests of their clients; they can then be in the prestigious position of slaying the dragon. Moreover, they provide their clients double insurance by overseeing the administration of the bills they pass.

In 1972, the organized trial lawyers of New York State demonstrated *their* clout. They swooped down on the legislature to stop the passage of no-fault insurance. In simple terms, no fault insurance is a plan in which victims of auto accidents are compensated for medical costs and loss of income without regard to fixing fault for the accident. The plan places restrictions on damage suits by the victim. Lawyers make money on such suits through contingency fees of up to one third of the settlement. The legislature, comprised of more than 75 percent lawyers, got the message and killed the legislation.[3]

[2] *The New York Times*, September 9, 1970.
[3] *The New York Times*, May 15, 1972.

In the national capital, the Ford Motor Car Company leased its luxury car to 19 key Congressmen for $750 yearly. For beings of lesser importance, the cost is $3480 for the same period. Among the legislators enjoying the courtesy are persons responsible for auto safety.[4]

Government blurs the distinction between fact and rhetoric. Its monetary and fiscal policies are a principal cause of inflation as it beseeches industry and unions to exercise restraint. No one can accuse the government of setting an example of restraint. One of the first acts of the Congress in 1969 was to grant itself a 41 percent wage increase. The same Congress delayed increases for postal workers for a year as it indulged in power play with the administration over the reorganization of the postal service. In the executive branch of government, the same adage prevails: What is good for princes of power is not necessarily good for the populace. Thus, in Pennsylvania taxpayers contribute close to a half million dollars yearly for the shelter and sustenance of the governor. On the national level, the government has spent a third of a million dollars to build a helicopter landing pad on the waters of the presidential private winter home. The population gets the message by example.

Some industries such as oil refining operate as a government within a government. Thus, for example, Senator Russell B. Long of Louisiana, who collects hundreds of thousands of dollars in tax-free oil royalties, happily presides as Chairman of a committee considering a bill to reduce tax privileges for the oil industry. Senator Long is against the proposal.

Spokesmen of oil firms allege that their interests and those of national security are indistinguishable. In 1968, under the initiative of Robert O. Anderson, chairman of the Atlantic Richfield Company, the major firms began oil exploitation in the state of Alaska. Mr. Anderson was a heavy contributor to the 1968 campaign of Mr. Nixon. The commitment in Alaskan oil amounts to one billion dollars in exploration and land leases. The firms propose building, consistent with the national interest, a 800-mile pipeline from the Alaskan Northern slope to a port on the Southern coast. The proposal has the opposition of conservation groups. In 1972, the Nixon administration approved the plans of the oil firms.

In November of 1970 President Nixon expressed concern over a price rise put into effect by the oil firms. After 6 months of study to determine if the increase was in the national interest, the Office of Emergency Preparedness concluded yes and no. The study found that the rise had no adequate justification on short run national security grounds, but

4 *Bangor Daily News*, August 3, 1970.

that in the long term it was consistent with security considerations. When asked whether he was proposing that the president roll back prices, the Director stated he was not proposing anything. Senator William Proxmire is cited as stating that the oil industry could not have written a better report for itself.[5]

By administrative decision in 1971, the Nixon administration gave to business a $3 billion tax cut through liberalization of depreciation allowances. The cut was placed into effect despite the report of a Treasury official that it would require new legislation. The decision was defended on the theory of percolation: what is good for business barons is good for ethnic peasants.[6]

Officials of government regulatory agencies are regulated by the firms they are supposed to regulate. This switch in role is fostered by different factors. First, government officials are hampered by the insecurity attending the reaction of Congressmen to the handling of their business clients. Second, they are less resourceful than their friendly adversaries. Third, a considerable amount of their energies is dissipated in defending their decisions rather than in planning and evaluation. Fourth, they not only must be concerned with irate Congressmen but also with the White House pulling the rug from under them in support of employer interests. In one such instance, the Food and Drug Administration and the controlled industry disagreed as to the manner in which the sales of drugs should be controlled. Firms took exception to the agency position that drugs should be restricted when other drugs are more effective in alleviating a particular ailment. The director was fired by President Nixon and the conflict was thus resolved.[7]

To acquire influence, these officials have at their disposal involved procedures and buck-passing, which, if astutely employed, can mire down industry representatives. But they prefer a quiet life. In a field investigation of the Federal Trade Commission by Harvard Law School students, a top administrator was discovered asleep in his office in the morning with a newspaper covering his face.

A myth surrounds the nature of American government. Folklore has it that the colonies were founded on high-falutin moral principles, when actually they were established on the opportunity for private gain, and that the economy grew out of the assumption of freedom from government intervention. This myth of the instinct for voluntarism has no historical verification. In part, the error stems from focusing attention on the evolution of federal power rather than looking at the activity of

5 *The New York Times,* May 4, 1971.
6 *The New York Times,* May 4, 1971.
7 *The New York Times,* December 31, 1969.

state and local governments in early economic history. It also derives from interpreting laissez-faire philosophy as hostility to government intervention rather than as determination by industrial spokesmen of the conditions under which government should act in their interest. The rule of minimum intervention, or more accurately consignment to organized power, has created a mercantilist system of considerable complexity. Government is less a positive initiating force and more the handmaiden of organized industrial power. Groups create nests for themselves in particular branches of government from which they oversee their interests. Government thus rules by bloc morality.

Under such conditions, the line between corruption and being at the service of industry becomes obscure. Thus, according to newspaper reports, two associates of a former vice president of the United States were zealously promoting the interests of federal contractors. Five of their romantic friends in a government agency yielded to the caresses of feminine favors underwritten by the contractors. Clearly, economists should gild their supply and demand curves to suggest how government soothes producers while making token gestures to consumers.

Government is a principal violator of its own norms. Thus, the law prohibits hiring on the basis of racial quotas, but government sets up a quota system of employment for its contractors in the construction industry. While it preaches law and order, the government engages in a war in conflict with law. Government prosecutes individuals who lie before its tribunals but claims the right to lie to the public in the national interest. Moral posture is no longer serviceable as a tactic because it would be viewed as hypocrisy. Morality is not relevant. Power is. Thus, the United States Department of Agriculture pays subsidies to the American tobacco industry to support its advertising and the Health, Education, and Welfare Agency holds back a publication on air pollution in fear of offending the coal industry.

In what appears to be a lesson in Keynesian economics, a principal task of government is to create problems that eventually require its intercession. Every major crisis of the past two decades was underwritten by prior policy. The urban crisis was guaranteed by policy in housing and agriculture. Polarization in the cities was underwritten by policy that ignores consent of the governed. The death grip of the motor vehicle on the cities was underwritten by transportation and highway policies. Thus, the government trades in solving problems by first creating them.

The virtue effect in such problem solving assures the rise of tensions requiring further government involvement. As a crisis develops, the position of those demanding change, if they have power, is sensed as virtuous and that of their opponents as evil. Opinion of the baddies is ignored, which in time generates pressures sufficient enough to switch the identity of those who represent virtue and those evil. At this point, government throws into the fray the policy of benign neglect. Thus, the dynamism of government involvement is not a smooth line but a continuous series of oscillatory movements whose effect is a long term rise in national power. Government does not plan change; it remains inert, fulfilling housekeeping duties and responding to action when matters, because of government policy, reach a boiling point.

Accordingly, to describe the government process as representative democracy is inaccurate. Rather, government represents a service organization whose dispensed goodies measure differences in the effectiveness of organization to pursue their private claims. For example, the outdoor advertising lobby has always had a sympathetic ear in the Congress even though opinion polls indicate that a big majority of the American people wants severe controls placed on such advertising. Congressmen can ignore this majority sentiment with impunity so long as it is not supported with money and organization. This tendency to serve organized interests until adverse reaction tips the political balance exists at different levels of government. The marriage terms between government and industry change when they reach predatory levels.

Government as the alter ego of organized interests also expresses organization needs of its own. Officials prefer to control private organizations in a manner that keeps them in business. Bureaucrats prefer cozy relations with power blocs following the rule of thumb of not rocking the boat. However, contention between industrial giants creates tribulation. Each contending party tends to be sympathetic to imposing government restrictions on the other. Unless the parties accommodate their differences, the government may increase its control over both. Cooperation among the three promotes the needs of all. The tendency toward organization accommodation underscores the need for a second set of government regulators to regulate the regulators.

In this game within a game, candor is inadvisable. Censorship of communication provides the means of appearing in the best light. Possibilities are increased, therefore, for a widening gap between reality and the picture drawn of officialdom. Numerous means of deception are available: the misleading anecdote, the false dilemma, evasion, and hinting that one's critics are unpatriotic or effeminate.

An important function of communication is to promote self-serving fantasy. A good deal of government communication is designed to placate power blocs by indulging in such promotion. For example, in a booklet called "Do You Know Your Economic ABC's?", the United

States Department of Commerce describes the economy as a free enterprise system. By reading its message, states the introduction by the Secretary of Commerce, the reader can make himself more economically literate. The tract announces that what makes the country strong and powerful is our reliance on individual choice. The consumer is king and the system works on the basis of the choices he makes. The pamphlet lists as examples of the gross national product, jelly, sports cars, dental services, fur coats, and cans of varnish remover. Later, under purchases of the GNP, we find that government does somehow enter into the picture. But it is a government whose economic policies are determined through ballots at election time.[8]

An uneasy bargaining relationship exists between government and the managers of mass media as to their respective prerogatives in communication. Each party presents its case on the basis of the right of the public to be informed. However, the contest centers on their respective rights to manage their organizational needs. By their management of the news, the media often make it difficult for government to dispose the public to a particular point of view. The media are sensitive to government controls that may dry up their sources of information and curtail the sensational reporting to maintain public interest.

Normally, however, the relationship between the two institutions is cozy. Newspapermen quietly provide information to government and the government seeks to avoid making a public issue of its frustrations caused by the media's management of the news. In 1969, however, the government's petulance surfaced. Its resident intellectual, the Vice President, presented the thesis that the media did not adequately express the posture of the government and hinted that a conspiracy was afoot. He stirred a flurry of ideas, including one from a government official that the solution lay in the media employing a quota of individuals who could demonstrate they were not too bright.

THE UNITED STATES PRESIDENCY

A United States President is not directly accountable to the public in the discharge of his duties as chief executive. Unlike European democracies, he has no obligation to render periodically a defense of his acts. The pressure of mass media could conceivably serve as a means of forcing him to defend his performance. However, Presidents prefer using the media to manage the public; the office of the presidency has become an instrument of propaganda. An ever increasing educated class wants the facts, but the White House wants to mold perceptions

8 United States Department of Commerce, "Do You Know Your Economic ABC's?," Washington, D. C., Government Printing Office, 1966.

consistent with not fully disclosed objectives. The presidential office, with a material assist from television, manipulates the public in keeping with the necessity to pursue a quiet exercise of power. Its staff provides the President with their picture of reality and the public with facts designed to prove the soundness of government policy.

Accordingly, a U.S. President is not a democratic office holder in the manner of a British prime minister. He is more like a monarch going out among his subjects in the hustings to stimulate good feeling by theatrical glad handing, so that he may wield power acquired not from the constitution but by a legitimacy equivalent to the divine right of kings. He does not indulge in dialogue with the people, but employs stage craft and advertising technique to control thought so as to promote not fully disclosed purposes. There is no way for a people to summarily remove him from office for not discharging his duties consistent with their will. The people can only wait for the chance to throw him out of office when the next election rolls around, should he run for reelection.

The press of the United States uses the term audience when alluding to a meeting with the President, as is done in England when referring to appointments of the Queen. But relative to its benefits, the cost of American monarchy compares unfavorably with that of the British. The President's wages of $200,000 together with an expense allowance of $50,000 compares with the privy purse of $134,000 for the Queen. Direct expenses in running the American royal residence amount to a million dollars compared to $700,000 for the British royal household. Presidential security costs $28,700,000; a comparison with the costs of security for the royal family is difficult to make since the security there is more ceremonial than actual. On the matter of transportation costs, the President needs 3 Boeing 707 jets as against the Queen's coach and 6 white horses. When the President, moreover, prepares a $230 billion budget containing bounty for every segment of American society but white ethnics, he needs the assistance of some 500 nobles and subalterns costing $55 million annually. Even in the matter of impact on the gross national product, American royalty appears unfavorably. Peepers around the White House produce a lower accelerator effect on the GNP than peepers around Buckingham palace. On balance, the rebellion against King George III appears to have been an extravagance.

In November 1970, President Nixon came to Philadelphia for 84 minutes. He descended from the skies in a helicopter which squatted gently on an empty lot cleaned meticulously by white ethnics of the usual debris to which Philadelphians are accustomed. The President waved from the doorway of his aircraft in a manner suggestive of a papal blessing and thereupon escorted the First Lady along a black carpet unfolded by the working class. His entourage proceeded down streets whose potholes had been hastily filled by the working class. The motorcade, carefully arranged consistent with protocol and battle readiness, included an advance car, 18 motorcycles commanded by Philadelphia's esteemed Police Commissioner Frank Rizzo, a lead car, the President's car, the secret service car, and the mobile communications car. At the Academy of Fine Arts, where the President was scheduled to celebrate America's past heritage, members of the First City Troop, wearing 19th century uniforms with plumed helmets, wrenched themselves into attention. As the President slowly ascended the winding staircase, camera lights playing overhead, the troop presented sabres. A murmur of praise swept through the brilliantly dressed courtiers. Referring to the Academy's director, one gentleman was heard to whisper: "I think this fellow Stevens is on the ball." Twenty-eight minutes later, the President ascended back into the skies.

A U.S. President does not administer the government. He is too busy with ritual and pomp, foreign relations, and legislative proposals to the Congress. His executive departments are run by self-perpetuating bureaucracies as semi-independent duchies. After he discharges his responsibilities in foreign affairs and proposes legislation, his remaining energies are devoted principally to the management of public opinion in a manner that favorably promotes his image.

For these princes of state, the American government writes history purchasable from the university professor disposed to immortalize them. Herbert Feis, the historian, writes:

> In our days, decision makers collect every scrap of paper that enters their office; they command staffs to catalog them and prepare preliminary manuscripts.
>
> They conceive, before retiring, spacious libraries to house the records of their lives and times and bear their names. Admirers or beneficiaries provide the funds; the government pays the expense of their operation and in return retains control of the contents.
>
> Thus, in honorable, even elegant retirement, with ample help, with all their source material in hand or at their call, they can pleasantly pass what used to be called their declining years by composing the interpretive histories of their own decisions.
>
> Incidentally, they can assure the affluence of their descendants.
>
> May I offer advice to the men among you who are planning to make careers as historians about the most promising route to advancement? Train to be President, or if that job eludes you, to be a presidential assistant.
>
> Then, after you have served as President, and either have been worn out by it, or worn it out, retire to a sanctuary which will be named after

you and here in splendor become a great historian—largely at public expense.[9]

Traditionally, a prince of state was shielded from legal action against him on the theory that a king can commit no wrong. While this theory of infallibility is on the wane among civilized nations, it appears on the ascendancy in the United States. The immunity granted to the President shifts at times from his regal person to those of his court. Thus, the federal judge of a district court dismissed an action against two agents who removed an individual from his home on grounds of protecting the President. The judge asserted that the agents are immune from wrong committed in the course of official duties. The Supreme Court refused to grant an appeal of the decision.

A prince of state can assist materially in constructing the official reality by having his nobles and courtiers plant self-serving questions in the press. He can also create law without seeking it from the legislature, and he can thereupon administer and even adjudicate it. In times of stress, his posture, commendably, can be summarized as follows: If you (the subjects) knew what I know, you would agree with my course of action. Therefore, have faith.

The princes attract a young tribe of staff men unencumbered by moral conviction and eager to provide their services in the construction of power strategies. Whether they call themselves Republicans or Democrats is irrelevant. Their party commitment is predicated on which one provides the easier access to power.

In brief, the modern Machiavellian in government is a technician on how to convey an impression calculated to achieve an unrevealed objective; his specialty is duplicity. His impressions are conveyed through staged events on television that generate good feeling in the particular population toward which they are directed. He learns that above all the clarification of problems and the bringing forward of options are to be avoided at all costs. Such candor would be fatal.

This game is bound to command successes because of the considerable resources available in the presidential office. In the long run, however, an army of supporters acquired through duplicity may become a powder keg whose eruption may zero in on the Machiavellians themselves. To minimize the likelihood of such an outcome, it is prudent to change tactics from time to time in the implementation of the overall game plan.

---

[9] *The New York Times*, December 31, 1968. The Lyndon Baines Johnson Library at the University of Texas will house 31 million sheets of paper. The monument will cost a million dollars annually in maintenance charges. Analogous to the history of Roman emperors, the more modest the talent of princes of state, the greater the artifacts they leave of their reign.

American liberalism sired this style of governance. It has fostered a paternalistic elitism. By touching base with power blocs and by obtaining a consensus from them, allegedly the public will emerges. By this tree-top acquiescence, a prince of state feels ready to manage an understanding public. At that point, he only needs to paint a portrait of serenity emitting a glow energized by the meeting of minds with the influential. Regrettably, at times flaws appear in such management. The sub-princes with whom he deals may not represent all segments of the public; some may not actually speak for the constituencies they claim to represent. The press may catch his subordinates in acts of corruption.

The superior wisdom tacitly claimed to exist in the office of the chief executive easily gives birth to a philosophy of benevolent paternalism. The prince of state takes care of the people's welfare, whether the people like it or not. In return, he expects gratitude and fealty. If facts are not fully divulged, it is because such revelation upsets the bestowal of benevolence. Papa knows best.

An astute papa circulates self-fulfilling prophecies to suit his purposes. In this fashion, he can predict the likelihood of an outcome and then proceed to make it come to pass; the populace thereby acquires confidence in his abilities. He can also raise spurious alternatives, such as asking the populace to choose between his policy of international responsibility or selfish isolationism. Thereupon he can choose supporting facts and issue press releases suggesting that only these two alternatives exist. This chore can be performed ably by university scholars. Above all, a prince of power should not burden himself with such naive ideals as adherence to the truth. The valid criterion is not authenticity but impact. A prince can learn much about the rewards of such a guideline from industry.

He never makes the error of spreading his power thin or appearing to be inconsistent. The mistake may be fatal. By trying to do everything, he may accomplish nothing. He must keep his house in order. Thus, if he launches a crusade for a better world, a worthy goal for princes of state, he should do so only if his own society does not appear to be excessively corrupt. While the use of power should be clothed in an image of lofty moral stature, it may often be difficult to do so. For example, while he may be espousing to the world the precept of self-determination of peoples, the public record unfortunately may indicate that his government has a history of toppling foreign governments. In such a case, it would be wiser to go on record as being for peace in the world.

Moreover, to fortify his power, a prince of state should work with the attitudes of his people. For example, vigorous American males at times feel the need to prove their virility. Many such gung-ho types identify this feeling with a call to arms; some women often encourage such an identification. This attitude places the prince of state in the excellent position of being able to heap ridicule on his adversaries in the conduct of his war by hinting that they are sissies.

Lamentably, the populace at times does not behave in a manner that allows the chief executive to use his power effectively. By their actions, elements in the population may create difficulties in reaching goals that are sanctioned by superior reason. In such instances a prince of state can spread the word that these elements are not decent Americans. In their naiveté, the population may seek honesty in communications coming from the palace. This guilelessness, happily, can be successfully discouraged. But it must be worked at. Publicity can assist in obtaining such control. The executive department spends about a half billion dollars informing the public. Most of the money is devoted to informing the public as to how the government is promoting their welfare. The greatest amount of this information comes from the Defense Department.

The handling of inflation by the Nixon Administration is an example of executive rhetoric. In a radio talk delivered in October of 1969, the President, without once using the word inflation, ascribed the spiral of wages and prices to the policies of his predecessor. When his administration took over, he continued, it was determined to stop talking about rising prices and do something about them. He asserted that his cure, dealing with root causes, in contrast to a system of price and wage controls, solved better the problem of rising prices.

> I say to my fellow Americans today: The runaway cost of living is not a cross we are obliged to bear. It can be brought under control. It is being slowed by firm and steady action that deals with its root causes.[10]

A year after the speech, prices were rising at the same rate. The year following, the President imposed wage and price controls, his speech, of course, long since forgotten.

---

[10] The inflation policy of the Nixon Administration was tied to the kite of conservative economists who ascribe price inflation to a sudden surge in the money supply. Institutional economists blame inflation on price administration practices of firms and trade unions. As in most of the controversies between these two camps, both arguments contain merit. The effect of the rise in the money supply is accelerated by institutional practices that can be controlled if the government intervenes early in the inflationary spiral. The organized blocs will not accept such controls as long as they feel capable of transferring the costs of inflation on the unsystem. The speech was delivered October 17, 1969.

The urban worker in the big city has been especially hard hit by the inflation. In New York, the inflation rate of 7.1 percent in 1970 was the highest since after the end of World War II.

The use of guile by the government is not a far step from the employment of surveillance. Computers provide many opportunities for amassing a record of Americans considered suspicious characters. Critics assert that the majority on such lists have no criminal records and that the practice has no basis in law. Under existing criteria employed by the government, it is conceivable that an individual arrested innocently in a protest movement can enter the data bank. Gate crashers and individuals who insist on seeing top officials are prime candidates for these lists of distinction.

GOVERNMENT AND THE ECONOMY

A fundamental economic task assumed by American government is minimizing entrepreneurial risk. This role in the economy is performed through such means as providing research and development services, guaranteeing risk capital directly through soft loans or indirectly through tax loopholes, maintaining profits through tax concessions, and underwriting prices either directly through price controls or indirectly through the maintenance of the gross national product. These devices are frequently inter-locking. In the construction of high-rise dwellings, for example, investors who offer a small fraction of risk capital are guaranteed the remainder by the government. If the investor defaults on his mortgage, the government takes over the mortgage and pays off his bank. The investor thereupon reports his "losses" against his income tax returns. Despite its rhetoric to the contrary, government plays a principal role in the decline of the private enterprise system.

Government's close ties with business have already been noted, an involvement which tends to serve big firms by guaranteeing a rising demand for their products and by underwriting their technological innovation and labor requirements. As the market system fails, the government converts the economy into an operation based on the planning of output, prices, and manpower of big firms. The remaining segment of the economy, exposed to traditional competitive forces, competes with appalling results.

All governments combined in the United States represent approximately 35 percent of the economic activity of the nation, a considerably higher percentage than in "socialist" Sweden. About half of the total expenditure of the national government goes to military defense. The Defense Department spends over two hundred million dollars a day, or more than the total national income of many nations; ten percent of the labor force receives paychecks chargeable directly or indirectly to defense appropriations; huge firms produce only for a military market. In effect, these firms are subsidiaries of the state. Public policy cannot permit them to go out of existence. In addition to these satellite companies of the Defense Department, government exerts a direct influence on output as a prime purchaser of non-military goods and strategic raw materials.

No other organ of government can match the defense establishment in its influence over decisions issuing from the executive and the legislature. No other agency can equal its influence on pivotal decisions. Military appropriations rise precipitously during times of war but do not at war's end fall back to what they were before. The appropriations represent a dramatic example of the decline in the system of countervailing power. They have the support of contractors, the military brass, the patriots in and out of Congress, and organized labor. Senators, Congressmen, the Mayors in whose states, congressional districts, and cities the money goes, lead the clamor whenever a proposal is made to reduce appropriations that surface in their constituency. A United States president who takes their demands lightly may find support of his other programs seriously weakened. A liberal senator lost his campaign for re-election in 1968 because of his attacks on military expenditures. He incurred the particular wrath of organized labor. The electorate reacts favorably to the platitude of a politician that another politician is proposing by his critical look at military appropriations a weakening of America's defenses.

The money and talent needed for a more healthy society requires a cessation of the arms race between the Soviet Union and the United States. Disarmament, however, must run the gamut of powerful contrary interests. Few organizations surpass the arms lobby in power; an organized bloc does not exist that can effectively challenge the advocates of military technology. Long before the phasing out of the Vietnam ground war, the military began its propaganda campaign for the maintenance of a high level of military appropriations after the termination of the conflict. The very individuals who preach the beneficence of private enterprise, through their defense of high military appropriations, foster an economy of managed prices, state-determined output, and restricted markets.

The Pentagon in Washington that houses the military comprises a sterling example of the horrors of giant organization. The place groans with admirals and generals surrounded by huge staffs whose energies focus on catering to the egos of their bosses and pretending they are carrying out orders. The civilian officials who manage the joint often do not know what their subordinate technicians are up to. They come and go too fast to find out. The officials are periodically beset with the nagging feeling that they have to make decisions and then act. The technicians, with the wisdom acquired through time, pretend to abide by the decisions and go their own merry way. The charade eventually requires a sweeping reorganization. It can be upsetting. Organization charts are pulled down from the wall and new ones go up. New job descriptions are written. The buddy you have coffee with has moved to another corridor. The desks are lined up differently. But the inefficiency remains the same.

The defense establishment commands respectability in Academe. Many university professors derive sustenance and prestige from its contracts. The former Secretary of Defense, Robert McNamara, guided the Defense Department to full bloom under management methods developed by university specialists. Mr. Neil Sheehan of *The New York Times* states:

> Some officials even wonder if he (the Secretary of Defense) knows any longer when he is telling the truth. His concept of public information is like selling Fords. You tell 'em all the good things, but none of the bad. The deception is usually practiced by deliberate semantic evasiveness or the deletion of pertinent facts, a technique that has spread to other departments of government.[11]

The former secretary developed an image of a manager delivering the greatest bang per buck. Through his centralization of military command, in the name of better management, he destroyed the countervaillance formerly existing between the military services. The admirals, generals, and airplane drivers joined forces.

Some economists dismiss the impact of defense expenditures on the economy by asserting that they can be shifted readily to private consumption. But it is not that simple. The propaganda machines of the armed services, affected producers, and labor unions would not tolerate a drastic decline in the first place. Secondly, it is doubtful whether the shifting of funds to taxpayers would maintain existing employment. New firms are less likely to evolve as much as existing firms are likely to increase their productivity to take care of the extra volume of sales. Many defense firms lack the competence to enter the private market; few are inclined to do so.

Some defense firms actually discourage offers from private business because of the difficulty in keeping separate accounts. It is problematical in any case whether the national government would give up a major instrument of controlling the level of aggregate demand in the economy.

Some $17 billion annually in public funds goes into research and development in the United States. Thirteen billions of this sum is spent

11 *The New York Times*, October 22, 1967.

by the Department of Defense, the National Aeronautical and Space Agency, and the Atomic Energy Commission. The thrust behind these funds is improvement of the art of warfare and increased status for the particular service using the money. The angel behind the supersonic plane, for example, is the war goddess. The enormity of research and development funds is difficult to grasp. They amount to the entire Defense budget prior to the Korean War. A considerable amount of this money is allocated to specific persons on the basis of private conversations with influential individuals in the roving professor coterie. Some agencies claim in their contracts the right to the facts uncovered and the right to decide if such facts warrant public dissemination. These restrictions are imposed in social science research and in investigations in science and technology. The money spawns professor politicians who learn the art of coming up with the research product desired by the government and who thereby are rewarded by the university managers. Much of the technology that issues from this research goes into the production of goods and services. But the payoff in the progress of man is relatively insignificant.

The Second World War catapulted the government into such research and development. A leveling off occurred in 1955, but the Russian sputnik produced a second spurt. Budgetary difficulties caused by the Vietnam war created another leveling off, the rate of increase falling to two percent annually.

Concomitant with this trend, the government has shifted away from basic research toward research with a particular technical goal in mind. The effect of this involvement is to capture the talents of university researchers and to place them under the influence of shifting government policy. Three quarters of university research is supported by the government. In effect, the government subsidizes a sufficient amount in professor's salaries and graduate student grants to be able to create a crisis by a leveling off of funds. Mere stability of appropriations has the effect of making it difficult to maintain graduate programs initially sponsored by government grants.[12]

These allocations for technological innovation do not derive from public discussion of priorities. They come from shifts in the relative power of members of the establishment underwritten by general public indifference. The voice of the people amounts to a squeak. University

[12] Of the total research outlay of $17 billion, 3 billion goes into science and the remainder into technology. The expenditure in 1970 represented approximately 9 percent of the $195 billion budget. There are urgent needs in science; to cite a few: studies on drug addiction, crime, control of diseases through genetic engineering, biological rather than chemical control of insects. The figures are those of the National Science Foundation.

managers support such policy and reconsider their commitment to government sponsored technological research only when forced to do so by student protest. Professors who bring home a research contract are rewarded and those who do not are encouraged to go elsewhere. The government funnels money into the pockets of professors in the social sciences to perform research on foreign countries, the intent of which is to develop techniques of manipulation and subversion. At times, the person using such funds does not even know where the money comes from.

A considerable amount of basic research government money is funneled through the National Science Foundation, an organization whose stated policy is to exclude political considerations from the awarding of grants. The foundation became involved in the case of a University of California mathematician active in controversial public issues. The mathematics professor roused the ire of a member of an old American institution, the House Un-American Activities Committee. Coincidentally, the foundation discovered flaws in the way the math professor was administering the grant. The lesson seemed clear: professors using government money should rise above playing a countervailing role in their society.

Prudence dictates that those who accept government money for research and consultation refrain from uttering non-conforming ideas and not be seen in the company of controversial characters. For example, the Health, Education, and Welfare Agency has blacklisted psychiatrists for having been seen in the presence of individuals labeled as communists. One scientist was blacklisted by the agency for having served in his youth on a medical committee for the forces of the Republic in the Spanish Civil War three and a half decades ago. A scientist was asked by the same agency not to attend a meeting of the National Institutes of Health because of his political activities in the 1930's.[13]

In addition to the purchasing of output and the subsidizing of technological change, government affects the economy through tax law. In this regard, government provides the greatest services to those with the money to buy them. When it comes to paying taxes, the most exploited are blue-collar workers. The blue collarite who makes a gross of $8500 by dint of hard work finds that $1600 has already been deducted from his pay and given to the national government. The chances of his getting any of it back are remote. By contrast, the individual receiving an income of $40,000 may find that the Congress and an astute tax lawyer have given him the opportunity to declare only half the sum for tax purposes. Thus, the blue-collar worker pays a tax on all his income while

[13] *The New York Times,* October 12, 1969.

the upper middle class suburbanite pays a tax on half of his. The government does not lack imagination in catering to the tax needs of the affluent. Thus, a millionaire owner of a football team reported nonpayment of federal income taxes for two consecutive years. Why? The Internal Revenue Service ruled his football players could be depreciated like physical property. Because the tax benefit could be transferred to his earned income, he paid nothing in personal income taxes.[14]

The tax law allegedly rests on the principle of ability to pay. But the price of taxing the rich is eternal vigilance; for the well-to-do have the resources and legal talent to obtain legislative concessions and to squeeze out of statutes interpretations promoting their interests. The principle of taxation is not one of equity, but the distribution of the tax burden relative to the ability to retaliate. Taxation relative to one's political clout is reflected in a report that the Internal Revenue Service has a unit whose function is to seek tax evasion evidence against political radicals.

In short, economics is now political economy. The government has rendered obsolete the theory of supply and demand of individual buyers and sellers. The allocation of economic and human resources responds to changing configurations of political power.

THE IMPERATIVES OF POLITICAL OFFICE

Political office in the United States is a preserve of the well-to-do. It costs considerably but pays off well. The laws as well as the offices are for sale. Huge sums capture the offices and huge sums control the decisions that issue from them. While Senate offices in the national legislature are more expensive to buy, Congressional seats are less expensive to control. Legislation, accordingly, reflects the array of money and organization working in behalf of the purchase of offices and of their subsequent control.[15]

The two political parties provide the mechanism with which to capture political office. Each contains fluid substructures by which individuals seek to demonstrate their vote capturing abilities and hence their right to run for political office or to select those who can. Each promotes his interests to the extent he can demonstrate his ability to maximize votes.

In a newspaper article written by Richard Nixon, an election for a seat in the House of Representatives costs $100,000 while a Senate race

---

[14] The Philadelphia *Evening Bulletin*, February 20, 1972.

[15] A blatant example of legislation for sale is the attempt in 1971 of a group of millionaires to stipulate the legislative price they would impose on presidential candidates in return for their money. The plan fell through because of adverse publicity.

takes two or three million.[16] Nixon's own presidential campaign in 1968 cost over $20 million. The expense involved in running and the financial rewards of holding office are reflected in the affluence of high level politicians. One out of every five senators is a millionaire. In 1970, 11 of the 15 major candidates for the U.S. Senate from the 7 largest states were millionaires. A preponderant number of governors of the states are wealthy men. In the 1970 campaign, the Governor of California spent $4.2 million to remain in office. The Governor of New York used $7 million for the same purpose. It is estimated that Governor Shapp of Pennsylvania spent $5 million of his own money to capture the governorship. The United States moves toward a rule of monied aristocrats.

The individuals who buy Congressmen and Senators are generally the well-to-do. According to a study released in 1971 by the Citizens' Research Foundation of Princeton, New Jersey, individuals who gave $500 and up to the two parties contributed a total of $17.4 million to the Republicans and $6.1 million to the Democrats. Ambassadorships are for sale also; they go to persons who make big contributions to the two parties. Frequently, contributors play both sides of the street by giving money to both parties.

Corporations make political contributions through their officers and principal stockholders. In the 1968 political campaign, a campaign which cost a total of $300 million, the following firms made contributions in excess of $25,000: Allen and Company; Atlantic Richfield Oil Company; First National Bank; National Industries; Warner Lambert Pharmaceuticals; Olin-Mathieson: Janney Montgomery Scott Investment Brokers; Lehman Brothers Investments; Marshall Field; Ford Motor Company; Peabody and Company; Industrial Container Corporation; National Airlines; Minnesota Manufacturing, Meklon National Bank and Trust Company; General Motors Corporation; Sun Oil Company; Singer Sewing Machine Company; National Homes Corporation; Revlon Company; Chase National Bank; American Distilling Corporation; Monogram Industries; Readers Digest; IBM.[17]

The Indiana Primary campaign of 1968 typifies the importance of money in political elections. Senator Robert F. Kennedy was able to draw on his family fortune. Senator Eugene McCarthy had to rely on contributions from the general public. The money spent in the campaign amounted to over four million dollars. A *New York Times* editorial commented:

16 The Philadelphia *Evening Bulletin*, April 30, 1967.
17 *The New York Times*, June 20, 1971.

His defeat (Senator McCarthy's) will raise once again the deeply trouble-some question—can a poor man win a presidential nomination in today's America?

The question is not simply whether Indiana is for sale but whether the entire American political process is up for sale. It is imperative that Congress and the nation reopen the paths to power for all men of talent, regardless of the size of their checkbook.[18]

The United States stands alone among Western nations in that the amount of money a candidate controls is a principal determinant in his election. In Great Britain, for example, no candidate can buy television time. Each party is allotted time according to its relative strength.

No convictions have ever been made for political contributions under the Corrupt Practices Act of 1925. In 1970, a Congressional attempt to limit television expenditures was vetoed by President Nixon. Speaking for the National Committee on Congress, its director stated:

President Nixon's veto of the first significant reform of campaign finance laws in 50 years is the most flagrant example of partisan interest we have witnessed in the organization's 22-year history.[19]

In early 1972, a court suit brought by the consumer advocate, Ralph Nader, linked acquiescence by the White House to rises in milk price supports to contributions of $322,500 made to dummy finance committees of the Republican Party. The suit alleges that prior to the channeling of this money for Nixon's re-election, dairy interests had placed about $187,000 in the hands of Senators and Congressmen, mostly Democrats. The defense of politicians receiving this money indicates that they will resort to speech making for fees in the event a more stringent law were passed. The prospect is thus continued flow of money and more bull. In the same year, Congress passed a law limiting campaign spending in presidential, senate, and congressional campaigns to sums below those used in 1968. The president signed the bill. Before the law went into effect, he managed to collect a campaign fund of 10 million dollars from wealthy contributors whose names he declined to divulge.[20]

18 *The New York Times*, April 30, 1968.
19 *The New York Times*, October 13, 1970.
20 The Federal Election Campaign Act of 1972 provides more detailed and more timely reporting of political contributions, including those made to dummy committees; sets mandatory spending ceilings in both primary and general elections on mass media publicity based on votes cast, but none on direct mail appeals; sets a limit on the amount of contributions a candidate can make to his own campaign. To suggest the extent of these limitations, a presidential primary candidate can spend about $840,000 in Pennsylvania on the media. In a presidential general election, each candidate can spend $14.3 million.

Two principal factors contribute to the high cost of political office: television time and organizational work. Both can produce high payoffs. TV provides an opportunity to create a favorable image in a relatively short time through sensory appeal. Intensive organization work is necessary to capture an existing organization or to develop an effective rival one. Television has replaced the traditional technology of confrontation between politician and constituents. With the exception of political officers in small communities, the politician is a remote individual in the lives of Americans. This distant quality rises as Americans jam themselves into large metropolitan areas.

Television assists in the obfuscation of issues and in the weakening of party control over politicians. An issue may merit no more time than a commercial. Personality is the thing. In the 1970 campaign, a commercial associated a Vietcong soldier with the foreign trade position of a Democratic candidate. In Pennsylvania, the Republican candidate for governor paraded his wife and many children on the screen and suggested his opponent was against human decency.

The screen makes a politician well known. If he succeeds in conveying an impression of self-assurance, forthrightness in expressing generalities, and trustworthiness, and avoids pitting himself with a rival portraying these qualities in greater degree, he is a shoo-in. He must avoid the fatal error of discussing issues in depth; particularity may be his undoing. He must make responses least offensive to his constituents. Television provides such opportunities. Its portraits are empty of human quality. They are often either harsh stereotypes or favorable images oozing sincerity and greatness, with little basis in reality.

Richard Nixon is the epitome of the Anglo-Saxon protestant middle class image: resolute, fun-loving, but allowing no nonsense. One can best understand his performance in terms of a man constantly merchandising himself for the next campaign. By conservative estimate, he is 20 percent product and 80 percent rhetoric. At times, he overplays his part. Thus, his leading the United States Navy in an assault of the Isle of Capri in 1970 in a display of American power in the Mediterranean vies with the *Pirates of Penzance*. Some facsimile Wasps succeed in duplicating this image. Former Vice President Agnew's is real boss. History has been kind to the Nixons. In their rise to power, they fomented the spurious issue of American communism and ignored the rise of hedonism. Now, after having made a substantial contribution to the collapse of traditional values, they pose as champions of traditionalists.

The capture of a Senate seat by Richard S. Schweiker of Pennsylvania exemplifies the importance of image making in American politics. First, his opponent, a man over 67 years of age, made the error of agreeing to television debates with the much younger Schweiker. A professional consultant advised Schweiker that taking specific stands on issues was less important than conveying the impression of a bold positivism. Be decisive was the prescription. Speak of the elderly Senator more in sorrow than in anger. Make a pitch for the young. Schweiker demonstrated his fertility by parading an ample family on the screen. His backwoods manner conveyed the impression of a man of religious conviction, compared to his recently divorced and quickly remarried opponent. Schweiker won.[21]

Television frequently makes the political process appear to be a drama of aroused passion. The game, rather than the merit of positions, is the thing. The cussedness in presenting indistinguishable positions is contrived for purposes of showmanship. The scenario does not suggest that away from the cameras the differences in views can be easily reconciled. They are more similar than the game makes them appear. Showmanship is the price that television exacts for informing the populace. This price makes difficult a re-structuring of political institutions. Government planning, for example, grew out of necessity. It is difficult to imagine that planning would have come into being as a result of a television debate.

By their own affirmation, politicians believe deeply; feel strongly; are frank and patriotic. These self-portraits provide few clues as to their actual behavior. Politicians do not see issues in terms of a moral code or in terms of an idealistic pursuit of values. On the contrary, most see them in terms of their potential to promote their careers. They view the political process as one of using and manipulating public opinion in the furtherance of this ambition. An issue is recognized or ignored and sides chosen depending on whether these choices promote their interests. They make policy commitments to capture the loyalty of the constituents needed to win an election; and jettison the policy commitments so as to win the next election. Their technology has to do with not the solution of a problem but the winning of the next election. Politicians speak not on the facts but what conveys a self-serving impression; they listen and judge not what is true or false, but what affects their interest; they concern themselves not with educating the public, but with profiting from its ignorance. Thus, like the economic system, the political process requires deception. The system generally abhors authentic relationships.

Politicians are for economies in government provided they do not affect their own pet programs. But the more money they spend to solve problems, the graver the problems become. It is a law of public admin-

21 The Philadelphia *Evening Bulletin*, November 10, 1968.

istration that a public problem becomes more aggravated as expenditures to solve it rise. This outcome is related to the mafia institutions that rise in consequence of the increase in expenditures. As a corollary, the threat of government oppression declines as its inefficiency rises with increased expenditures.

A politician is a manager. He manages the interests of those who control him most effectively. His management reflects the disproportions in power of organized interests. The disproportion shifts with time. Under the presidency of Richard Nixon, the dominating influence served by the politician managers was organized business.

Ideally, politics is the art of communication by which the little guy acquires a sense of importance. By such a standard, many so-called undemocratic societies in the world are more democratic than the United States. The American political process is geared to consensus making between power blocs. Choices in political candidates of the Republican and Democratic parties are usually between tweedle-dee and tweedle-dum. A confirmed Democrat or Republican is either a crank or racketeer. A discernible difference is that the Democrats resolve problems badly while the Republicans seek to evade them, a posture which places Republicans at a short term advantage. Thus, a visitor to the United States during the 1970's would have easily concluded that the Republicans were for decency and the Democrats for indecency. The pleasure of the little guys derives from the joy of throwing an incumbent Republican or Democrat out of office. The decline of the two parties is evidenced by the rise in the number of voters who describe themselves as independents. The pace of this decline is likely to rise as the young enter the ranks of the electorate. Governor George Wallace's national campaigns in 1968 and 1972 manifest indirectly what the little guys think of Republicans and Democrats in particular and the national leadership generally.

The two political parties are not competitive in many jurisdictions. Among national political officeholders, the influence of Southern politicians is most noteworthy. The Southern contingent of the Democratic Party drearily wins one election after another. Only death can dislodge them. They possess the serenity that comes with the guarantee of perpetual political power. The Southern *mafiosi* control much of the output of Congress. Their influence sets a narrow range of legitimate ideas in the political process. In 1968, southern barons had a dominant voice in the selection of all 3 candidates for presidency. In the nation as a whole, moreover, a majority of Congressmen come from constituencies where only a single party is effective. The monopoly produces apathy in the electorate.

The two major parties do not serve the function of formulating a line that the eventual office holders are expected to articulate. Each party provides the opportunity to run for office within its structure. In time, the more successful broaden their base sufficiently so as not to be obligated to those who supported them initially in their rise to influence.

As a general rule of thumb for the typical politician of each party, what is good for his career is good for the country. He pursues his own interest through the management of public money. Unlike managers in private industry, it is difficult to hold him accountable for his lavish use of the taxpayer's money. To give an example, the negotiation of employment terms for civil service employees moves inexorably toward scandalous proportions. With rationale provided by technical elites, politicians give freely from the public treasury. In Philadelphia, the civil service employees enjoy wages and fringes higher than those of industry, including a pension at age 55 almost equal to their regular take-home pay. In the New York City transportation system, a janitor earns $175 weekly and can retire at the age of fifty. His earnings are greater than the average for industrial workers. Compared to industry, the employees of both cities enjoy more pay for less work.

This give-away could be checked through some form of community participation; committing major political decisions to a referendum may serve as a restraint. But politicians are likely to resist any such extension of democracy. Their generosity with other people's money fosters their career. Often, the only recourse a citizen has is to throw the politician out of office. But this is not a measure of control so much as an act of frustration.

The state of the American political process begets a cynical electorate. Day by day events affirm the cynicism. People assume politicians are crooked. The political process obfuscates rather than clarifies issues and seeks to convert the citizen into an object of manipulation. Both parties use the process in this fashion.

THE 1968 PRESIDENTIAL CAMPAIGN

The presidential campaign in 1968, one of the most tumultuous and costly in American political history, is a case study in frustration attending a system of rule by elites. The convulsions produced by the campaign in the Democratic party continue today. The campaign brought to the surface the growing disaffection for political institutions and the growing obsolescence of liberal-conservative alignments. Its denouement, the selection of two organization men, Hubert Humphrey and Richard Nixon, as the Democratic and Republican candidates was assured prior to the beginning of the conventions. An intense game in the Democratic party convention brought forth as preordained the dauphin of President Johnson; the Republican party convention, in a display of wholesomeness and good manners, produced Mr. Nixon according to script. Thus, there emerged from the political process two men, hardly symbols of social crisis, but masters in conversation at the fringe of truth.

The campaign began on November 30, 1967, when Senator Eugene McCarthy entered the New Hampshire primary election. His decision was treated with derision by seasoned newspapermen and politicians. His disinclination to make exaggerated statements and suggestion of honesty gained him adherents. McCarthy convinced a large segment of the public that he was honest, a characteristic in short supply in the political arena. He attracted individuals with no interest in the machine of both parties.

McCarthy's New Hampshire style was a shocking success. His impressive victory changed the decision of Senator Robert Kennedy not to challenge the candidacy of President Johnson. The successful preliminary groundwork for unseating Johnson gave buoyancy to Kennedy's aspirations. Consequently, an exciting figure came into the Democratic campaign, which provided many young whites and blacks with an opportunity to make emotional attachments to a charismatic figure. Kennedy brought with him more money and more support from the urban political machines of the party. He played his role effectively. To many Negroes he was the messiah and to many college youths, particularly women, he gave ecstasy. Like McCarthy, he profited from the grievances against President Johnson. But the hysteria generated by Kennedy's campaign caught a young Arab in its grip. The shooting of Senator Kennedy in a kitchen pantry is an indictment of the political process. The ingredients of political assassination surfaced again 4 years later in the gunning of Governor Wallace.

Johnson's withdrawal, a remarkable triumph for the unsystem, brought in Hubert H. His style reflected an appeal to liberals whose frame of mind was established during the Roosevelt era. He called to witness the beneficence bestowed by Democrats. He sounded hackneyed to adults with no commitment to traditional ideology and out of this world to young persons who had not yet been born during the presidency of Franklin Delano Roosevelt. Soon after the beginning of his campaign, on March 31st, George Meany, the quasi-octogenarian leader of antidiluvian trade unionism, announced his support. So did members of the Southern political aristocracy, who found in Humphrey the most palatable of possibilities, and the urban political bosses in the North. Mr. Robert Kennedy's death on June 5th gained Humphrey more organizational backing. His nomination was a triumph of the Democratic power structure under the baton of Mayor Daley and the remote control button of Johnson from the national capital. In giving the nomination to Humphrey, the party shifted its image to old guard.

George Wallace's candidacy provided the political instrumentality for the appearance of a rising populist force in American society. His querulous voice articulated the frustrations of white middle America. Wallace exploited a fault in liberal leadership in which the lower white middle class was made to feel swindled by the democratic process. His selection of a bombs-away Air Force general for the vice-presidency probably lost him votes. His greater triumphs in 1972 indicated that this populist force was growing larger. The Wallace vote was a vote of no confidence in American leadership.

The Nixon candidacy appeared as a highly rehearsed upper middle class morality play. His television debates were masterpieces of contrivance: the planned spontaneous question from a black face, and the well-rehearsed answer; the suggestion of spontaneity and straight-from-the-heart talk; the well-directed emergence of issues defined so as to allow Nixon to slay the dragon amidst a crescendo of cheers. Richard Nixon was superb in knowing what not to say, what to say, and when to say it. He oozed sincerity; he appeared well-packaged; he presented himself as straight. Nixon demonstrated the lingering profitability of the politics of manipulation. Not one new idea emerged from his campaign. His choice of a vice-presidential candidate was based on the selection of a non-person acceptable to the South, who would neither inspire nor offend.

As the campaign proceeded, Americans chose sides along cultural lines. College educated independents supported McCarthy; workers kept in line by labor leaders went over to Humphrey; a considerable number of the remainder found a standard bearer in Wallace; nostalgic upper class traditionalists found theirs in Nixon; Humphrey lapsed into the rhetoric of the past; Wallace barged headlong into the fears and animosities of the white working class; Nixon convinced gentle Americans of his good intentions on law and order. The campaign did not produce one speech on what ails the system.

On August 26th, shortly prior to the beginning of the Democratic convention, a group of youthful supporters of the late Senator Kennedy announced their backing of Senator George S. McGovern of South Dakota for the presidential nomination. Their support reflected emotional problems preventing them from turning to McCarthy after the death of Kennedy. McGovern had spoken out against the war and had been approached unsuccessfully by anti-Johnson groups in the Fall of

1967 to run for the presidency. His entrance into the contest at the eve of the convention produced a few ripples. In 1972, with more effective organization tactics and mass imagery than had been used by its founder, Senator McGovern succeeded in capturing the McCarthy movement.

The Republican and Democratic conventions were a study in contrasts. The Republicans met in the atmosphere of a Protestant church meeting to solemnize the appointment of the vicar. The Democrats, in scenes parodying at times the Keystone Cops, enacted the initial convulsions produced by the shifting political alignment in the United States. As planned by Humphrey, the script called for his nomination with a middle of the road commitment on Vietnam, one that would appear anti-war in tone but would not repudiate the policy of President Johnson. The President intervened in the drama to write a resolution that defended the view of no halt to the bombing of North Vietnam unless such action would not endanger the lives of American troops. This view had long been the position of General William C. Westmoreland, the former commander in Vietnam. Moreover, the bitterness inside the convention and the melee outside were not according to plan. The role of impresario Daley included deliverance to Humphrey of the 112 votes of the Illinois delegation. He delivered all but six.

The Democratic convention opened in a state of siege. Fifteen thousand soldiers, policemen, and federal agents were mobilized to protect the democratic process. The melee in the streets was described as a police riot. A report of the National Commission on the Causes and Prevention of Violence makes the judgment that provocateurs were present among the demonstrators goading the police with obscene epithets, and that the police over-reacted indiscriminately against bystanders and representatives of the communications media. The report describes the assault as gratuitous, ferocious, and malicious.[22] What emerged from the television screen was a picture of a system blowing its cool and resorting under stress to brutality.

Anti-war demonstrators at the convention sought unsuccessfully to obtain permission for a march to the convention hall and for a ritual outside when they got there. The objective of some yippies and students, predominantly of the Students for a Democratic Society, was to provoke an encounter with the police that would demonstrate the unresponsiveness of the system to the position of youth. The Chicago police, inspired by the mayor's previous call for law and order and shoot to kill in riots, cooperated by giving the yippies and undergraduate revolutionaries what they wanted. In expectation of martyrdom, the agitators played revolution by assault with naughty words. Abbie Hoffman, Yippie

22 *The New York Times,* December 1, 1968.

commander-in-chief, entered the fray with the word FUCK emblazoned on his forehead. The obliging police gave vent to their pent-up grievances against college youth. Many of the police injuries came from hitting individuals too zealously. The performance was witnessed by millions on television.

Commenting on the riot, Tom Wicker of *The New York Times* states:

These were not snipers, looters, or terrorists. No mobs were clashing with one another. No plastic bombs or Molotov cocktails were thrown. The marchers were political dissenters, many of them radical, most of them idealistic, demonstrably brave, concerned for their country and their fellow men, determined to exercise the right of free speech and free assembly.

Contrary to Humphrey's banalties, the lesson of that terrible night was, first, that raw and unchecked police power is not the answer to anything in this country.[23]

The following is a description of a newspaperman beaten by the police:

On the west side of Clark Street, hundreds of police lined the curb after a bottle was thrown. That's when the clubbing began. Night sticks flew so wildly that some policemen came close to hitting one another.

Then law and order was restored. As I passed half the line of policemen one of them who had removed his name tag and badge stepped from the gutter demanding my pad. Give me that goddam notebook, you dirty bastard, he yelled. Then with his left hand he ripped the notebook from my hands, tossed it into the gutter and clubbed me with his night stick.[24]

Hubert Humphrey described the encounter as violence begetting violence. George Meany of the AFL-CIO evoked cheers at a labor convention when he referred to the demonstrators as dirty necked and dirty mouthed. The liberal George McGovern asserted that American youth were beaten as they lay prostrate on the ground for the crime of protesting policies in which they had no voice.[25] Four years later, McGovern took over the role of political darling of college youth.

In the election, Humphrey lost all the Southern states but Texas. He lost also in Illinois, California, Ohio, and New Jersey, all industrial states. He won in eastern states where the votes of large concentrations

23 *The New York Times*, September 1, 1968.
24 The Philadelphia *Evening Bulletin*, August 30, 1968.
25 Chicago has a fine tradition of police violence dating back to 1886. In that year, 6 workers striking against the McCormick Reaper Company were killed by the Chicago police. In a protest meeting the following day in Haymarket Square, violence erupted after the police ordered the demonstrators to disperse. Four men who had addressed the meeting were hanged the following year. In 1937, a line of marching pickets were stopped by the Chicago police in front of the Republic Steel Corporation plant. Without provocation, the police killed 10 of them, most of them shot in the back while fleeing.

of urban liberals and Negroes more than counterbalanced the votes of the suburban corporate and apostate white ethnics. His loss reflected the failure of his party to hold together its diverse elements. Moreover, by way of indicating the felt lack of alternatives, only 60 percent of eligible voters cast ballots, the lowest since 1956. Were it not for the sharp rise in the Southern Negro vote, the percentage of those casting ballots might have been the lowest on record.

Mr. Nixon won the election with 43.5 percent of the popular vote. Opinion polls indicate that only half of this percentage represents supporters of the President, the other half comprising acquiescence to a lesser evil. The victory capped a career of 20 years. Nixon emerged triumphant after two decades as valiant fighter against the Communist conspiracy, to preside over a mini-brain government of Wasps and quasi-Wasps. That mini-brain governments have an affinity for each other without reference to ethnic distinctions is suggested by the way President Nixon and Mayor Rizzo of Philadelphia rushed to each other in a fond embrace. Nixon has shown wisdom in seeing the growing obsolescence of using the ploy of Communist conspiracy and in turning to other more profitable mass imagery. As far as can be determined by the record, his administration marks the first time in history in which the menopause of women exerted a profound influence in the affairs of state.

In summary, the 1968 campaign underlined the instruments of the system: hypocrisy, and its alternative, suppression. The campaign was not an appeal to reason but a masterpiece in evasion of issues and manipulation of the public. In a crisis of purpose, the instrument of accommodation was the club of the policeman. Broad segments expressed their delight in the police behavior. The public was in a nasty mood. If the public could not be mean, it could at least delight vicariously in the nastiness of the cops. To be successful, a system of countervailing power requires its managers to be receptive to new information. The 1968 campaign suggests how managers have fallen behind the available knowledge. Thus, power not only corrupts, but it renders those who have it unperceptive and irrational.

Two years after the 1968 Democratic party convention, 5 demonstrators were convicted in a Chicago conspiracy trial under the 1968 Federal Anti-Riot Act, hastily drawn legislation motivated by the belief of Southern legislators that black agitators had incited the 1967 urban riots. The law defines a riot as 3 or more individuals involved in a public disturbance committing an act of violence that endangers any other person or property. The Attorney General in the Johnson administration testified against the proposed law on grounds it might be employed as a weapon against legitimate political action.

Prior to the indictment of the demonstrators, a federal grand jury indicted 8 policemen for their contribution to the riot. In a show of poetic sensitivity, the Nixon administration thereupon obtained indictments against 8 demonstrators. The policemen were tried and acquitted. Five of the 8 demonstrators were found guilty of inciting a riot. Before the verdict, all were given contempt of court sentences together with their lawyers to a degree without precedent in American justice.

The trial was based on testimony that the defendants had crossed state lines with the intent of inciting a riot. To demonstrate that this illegal thought was in the minds of the defendants, the government prosecutor leaned heavily on interpreting the political beliefs of the defendants. The trial turned out to be a political contest in which the cards were stacked against the defendants. The defendants had only their mouths and they used them in Billingsgate style. Judge and defendants saw each other as devil symbols. Jurors reacted similarly. One stated she simply did not like any of the defendants. The trial emerged as a political contest between second-rate exponents of government power and second-rate buffoon revolutionaries.

The motives of the revolutionaries for their posture in court is puzzling. Their charade may have been the only defense against a biased and hateful judge. They could not have expected their mocking and derision to gain sympathetic reaction. If martyrdom they wanted, they got it. If they were seeking reform through demonstration of the system's injustices, they botched it. History has many examples of unjustly accused men using their plight as the forum for words that place their imprint on society. American history gives this chance to exhibitionists whose words are soon forgotten. They make such unconvincing revolutionaries.

The 1972 presidential campaign, the most costly in American history, brought forward the Democratic Party's difficulties in maintaining the loyalty of its traditional constituencies. In his bid for election to the presidency, Mr. McGovern chose not to placate white middle America frustrations. He banked on commitments to the constituency of blacks, white liberals, and young zealots that gained him the nomination. Relying heavily on the use of surrogates, Mr. Nixon used to advantage the concerns of white middle Americans. He became a symbol of the man who was *against* what they were against and *for* what they were for. His expression of traditional values was nebulous enough so as not to incur disenchantment. Nixon won by a wide margin: a testimonial to his successful management of money, organization, and talent in the use of symbolism.

Paradoxically, the frustrations of white ethnics are underwritten by the very communications media, including prominent newspapers such as *The New York Times,* that have challenged the Nixon administration on the issue of freedom of the press but who give prominence to liberal points of view on social issues while ignoring or often treating in condescending fashion those of white ethnics. By their distortion of what the electorate thinks about social questions, the media contribute to the polarization that produced the Nixon victory. Not one ethnic voice exists in their array of pundit commentators. Accordingly, the election marks a triumph in the isolation of the intellectual class from middle America, a truncation whose foundations were laid by the intellectuals themselves and by their sympathetic communications media. In this respect, the 1972 campaign suggests a new version of an old political slogan: as McGovern goes, so goes Upper Manhattan, New York, and Cambridge, Mass.

CONCLUSIONS

Money corrupts the political process in the election of officials and in the passage of legislation. Players require money for entrance into the game and politicians become beholden to those who furnish it. Removing money as a requisite of entrance and as a means of influencing legislation would assist in returning the process to the individual.

The political realignments taking place in the electorate raise a faint hope that such an objective could be attained. The traditional conservative-liberal confrontation is breaking down. The new groups emerging from this decomposition include white urban ethnics, urban blacks, and an independent suburban class. Should they reconcile their differences an anti-organization bloc would emerge that might make participatory democracy a political issue.

The essence of political strategy is timing, in the discernment of emerging patterns and in the ability to accelerate and profit by the emergence of these patterns. A politician who can successfully articulate the particulars of such a new alliance might ride the crest of a new majority. But he has to take risks. He would have to espouse a negotiation principle for both blacks and whites.

Such a new national force, if it materializes, cannot expect miracles. The huge government bureaucracy impedes both innovation and quick reversals. Government develops policies laboriously through committee efforts that progressively water down original ideas. Once a policy is implemented through allocation of resources, it is difficult to reverse. The committee-planned commitment acquires a life of its own. Each individual in the chain of its management has a stake in its survival and in its evolution in a way that promotes his needs. The momentum continues regardless of the periodic change of personalities, style, and rhetoric. A mistake is eliminated by allowing its forward movement to ebb and transpire slowly.

Moreover, government is caught between unprecedented demands of the mass media for a daily diet of sensational communication and a rising educated class demanding government relationships based on moral principle. These exacting and conflicting demands are unprecedented. As governments find it easier to pursue their activity without daily scrutiny and moral judgment, their reaction to these demands is to develop further the art of propaganda. This response is likely to continue so long as the cost of deceiving the public is less than that of maintaining an open government.

Government has become a partner of organized power. The new source of countervailance must come from the people themselves and be levied at times against the government itself. The legislatures have become generally the hand-maidens of corporate interests. What the people want is not what the legislatures give. The task of restoring participatory democracy is formidable. Politics must be wrested away from those with the money to control it. Politics must be made what it is supposed to be: an act of morality through the reconciliation of inequities felt by people.

A system managed by a rule of power can work only if the power is evenly distributed. For if a hierarchy of power exists, those who feel no part of it will lose their self-respect and become destructive spirits.

Watergate, together with the larger White House style that surrounds it, dramatizes the government deficiencies discussed. This style includes: using burglary, spying, and character assassination in the political process; employing mafia-type bully boys; making secret deals between government officials and corporate managers; politicalizing justice; wiretapping of government officials by other government officials; employing the Counter Intelligence Agency for domestic operations; using lies, conspiracy, and perjury in the administration of the office of the presidency.

Their causes can be likened to a series of concentric circles. At their center is an intraverted President delegating authority to courtiers of small stature who maladroitly practiced the rule that the end justifies the means and who needlessly incurred the wrath of legislative barons fishing for issues. Beyond, the circles include: the accumulative grants of power by the legislature to the President since the end of World War II; the corrupting effect of foreign policy on domestic policy; the pent-up frustrations of conservative elites; the attendant collapse of the system of checks and balances; the failure of the educational system to develop a sense of moral duty to fellow citizens; the high faith in the ability of money to produce desired results; and lastly, the destructive tendencies of hedonism in American society. That the Watergate syndrome was flushed out by a judge whose origins go back to the land of the mafia is a fascinating quirk in history.

Impeaching President Nixon would amount to impeaching the values of the system's managerial class. The nation owes his administration a debt in the opportunity provided to place a bright light on the system's deficiencies. Its conniving power brokers demonstrated the wisdom of organizing a government to maintain constant vigilance over government and the political process.

10

The Very Public Private Sector

*Without some dissimulation, no business
can be carried on at all.*
Earl of Chesterfield

There once was a time the American economy could with validity be described as individual firms producing in private competitive product and labor markets in hot pursuit of profits. Later, economists begrudgingly began to recognize the fact that government and labor unions had something to do with the way a firm behaved. To avoid tainting the purity of the traditional analysis, however, the part played by these institutions was relegated to footnotes. Still later, it was observed that these two institutions encouraged a conflict of competing demands, the resolution of which affected the public interest. The beneficence of this interplay of conflicting demands, a latter day version of Adam Smith's guiding hand principle, was given the elegant label of a system of countervailing power. Today, even this view is outmoded. Big business and big government can now be observed in bed together enjoying each other's company, and the individual must organize to protect himself from the way these blocs supposedly promote his welfare.

This chapter will deal primarily with the large quasi-public corporations as a part of the system, rather than with small firms in competitive markets. Important differences exist between the two. The small firm manager has a more overriding profit maximization motive but is less able to plan his profit margin. Internally he is more authoritarian, more inclined to react favorably or unfavorably to employees as individuals. The manager of the big firm has more diverse motives and must accommodate to more publics. He is more a coordinator of technicians.

219

Moreover, it is erroneous to lump together all managers within the big firm. The lower the level of managers, the less complex are his motives and the less long-range his view of the firm. These distinctions should be kept in mind in reading this chapter.

In official ritual, the American economy comprises private enterprises that compete in labor, capital, and product markets. In reality, big firms free themselves of market restraints by planning, the thrust of which is to contain the uncertainties of competition. The government and trade unions join in the liberation of the firm by their collaboration in imposing restraints on markets. Government policy encourages big corporations to become bigger, eliminates marginal firms, and discourages the emergence of new ones. Trade union policy restricts the number of firms by imposing uniform employment standards which only big producers can afford and by controlling the demand and supply of labor in an industry. Corporations also control the competition of substitute products by buying up firms that produce them. Price competition is considered unsportsmanlike. The decline of competition in major sectors of the economy accentuates the distinction between system and unsystem. Big corporate organizations are no longer in the private sector. Together with government, they form a major part of the mercantilist state.

The realities of bigness thus deserve our attention. We contend that the business firm is evolving as a species of public organization from whose internal and external relations the major economic decisions of the society issue, and that public policy is a macro extension of this decision making process. An overview of the nature of modern organization will introduce this argument.

THE NATURE OF ORGANIZATIONS

We live in a society of multiple organization loyalties. Much of an individual's life is performed as a member of different organizations, including his firm, professional association, church, community association, consumer organization, and political party. To each of these organizations the individual offers his resources and expects a payoff in return. When he considers the payoff insufficient, he disaffiliates if possible. At times, he may belong to an organization simply because he wants to keep it off his back.

Similarly, business has pluralistic affiliations. The firm has to reconcile relations with buyers, vendors, stockholders, government, community, trade and professional associations, labor organizations, and universities. These associations are either voluntarily sought after or forced by pressures on the firm. Even internally, the business manager is faced with different and often conflicting group loyalties. Accordingly, if one persists in the traditional economic thinking that corporations confine their concerns to prices and markets, he blinds himself to the actual imperatives behind business decisions.

Observe what these multiple affiliations imply: A group effort under multiple pressures requires the containment and direction of individual acts. This conflict between organizational thrust and individual inclination necessitates a bargain that determines the extent of control over the individual. Managers have no inherent right to the unilateral determination of such control. Neither law nor conscience provides such a right. Nor do they have the right to manipulate the individual psyche to obtain compliance to partially disclosed objectives.

Thus, one can see how power looms important in the way these external and internal relationships are accommodated. The individual who wants to give weight to his point of view may do so more effectively by channeling his position through organization. In addition, because of the multiple subsystems that act on an organization, each unit cannot possibly have a single overriding goal behind which it channels all of its resources. Correspondingly, an individual cannot possibly expect an organization to address itself solely to *his* interests.

In addition to these multiple claimants, the values of the manager responsible for accommodating them have a bearing on his decisions. A whole human being makes these decisions—an individual with a set of not fully revealed values. Whether he is a WASP, an Italian, or a Japanese has a differential effect, even though all 3 may have on their table the same magazine article on the universal role of management. We should not be misled by the expressed similarities of their perceived role, nor should we expect these cultural differences to vanish because of the pressures of technologies that cross country borders.

The big industrial firm is a species of big organization. As in the case of organization generally, the firm is a complex of interrelated and often warring sub-groups of specialists held together by civility and by managerial definition and control of organizational objective. What distinguishes firms from other organizations is the pursuit of profit as a primary goal.[1] Profits provide a measure of the use of resources relative to output. They are an indispensable measure of performance, even if the techniques of some accountants seem to suggest that theirs is an occult art designed to mislead the public. Profit statements do not fully reveal the human and economic costs of doing business.

The business corporation is a child of the society that grants it legitimacy; it exists as the society wishes. The issue, therefore, is not whether

[1] For a distinguished presentation of this view, see Neil W. Chamberlain, *Enterprise and Environment,* New York: McGraw Hill, 1968.

the corporation is socially involved. Private enterprise was never really private. The term was a cover for the right of the firm to determine unilaterally its relationships with the society. Now, in an unprecedented manner, young people are saying that the relationship of business and society is bargainable, that it should be formally structured, and that government represents only one form of control in the general array of possibilities in the society.

Whereas the corporation in the two decades following the Second World War was effective in selling its point of view to society, the society is today increasingly effective in imposing its view on business. Whereas before it was sufficient for business to use imagery to prove its social responsibility, more concrete evidence of such activity is now being demanded. But the employment of imagery dies hard. The clamor for a clean environment, for example, aroused oil firms into introducing a new gasoline product into the market, and they thereupon, in an extensive advertising campaign, proclaimed themselves champions of an unpolluted environment. Nevertheless an increasing number of discerning individuals is today disputing such imagery.

The firm must determine what aspects of the social, political, and economic environment affect its survival and scan this composite on a continuing basis. This scanning detects trends favorable or threatening to its goals and provides the information for assembling responses that serve the organization's needs. The organization must choose between actively seeking to control environmental trends or responding to those that emerge, in order to protect its planning from unanticipated assaults. These trends may include such factors as technology, manpower, government, university relations, and international affairs. The frame adopted for scanning may become obsolete, in which case the organization may find itself seriously challenged from unexpected quarters. In small towns, the scanning process permits big firms to subtly control the community by membership in committees and by maintaining communication lines with decision making points.

The expectations that the public has of business organization change continually. For example, the public presently expresses concern over the impact of the firm's products and processes on the physical and esthetic environment and the extent to which the firm assists in resolving social problems such as minority employment and housing. Moreover, these expectations vary depending upon particular firm in question. To cope with the public, a business organization may decide that adding a particular social goal to its criteria of performance is indispensable to its long term growth. The organizational structure may have to be changed to accommodate this response. To compete successfully with other demands in the organization, the executive in charge of the new structure may find it necessary to establish communication lines directly to the officer calling the shots. Moreover, the new structure may require internal and external information for the discharge of its function. Mere exhortation is unlikely to achieve the desired results. Nor is the firm likely to make decisions effectively in meeting the social challenge by assigning the role to any of the existing structures.

Whatever particular social goal the business organization adopts reflects the same balancing act the chief executive performs in all his decisions. Inevitably, the choice leaves many outside groups disappointed over the failure of the firm to recognize *their* values, which they consider superior to those recognized by the organization. Their course of action is to demonstrate that the choice was misguided.

The resolution of problems in public policy follows the pattern it does in business organization. The formulation of public policy constitutes an extension of decision making by interacting subsystems in the general system. The same ingredients are present: the conflict of interest; the honest differences as to the techniques available in resolving the problem; the misinformation both honest and deliberate; the imprint of personal ambition and institutional jealousies; the battle of statistics calculated to achieve not fully revealed objectives. The same political and ideological play unfolds that often inhibits the full development of technical options and information relative to the problem.

As the social problem crystallizes, public policy issues from the self-serving position of these subsystems, which include foundations, business, labor organization, government agencies, universities, political groups, and other organizations with an interest in the problem. The information these organizations disgorge triggers a clash of opinion whose end result is commitment to a policy. The weakness of this process lies in its failure to involve the ethnic societies that ultimately bear the brunt of the new policy. There is little public opinion in the process. There is elite opinion with an organization base. Without an organization base, the individual who believes his opinion as a single person is worth anything in such a dynamic process is a crank.

A greater application of science in the analysis of technique and information in public policy would not make these deficiencies disappear. Analysis may clarify problems, but it is not a substitute for the political process, which is an indispensable tool for the accommodation of values and interests. The political game serves as a means of achieving a consensus. The joy of playing politics serves to evaluate the merit of the analysis of technical elites. A partisan attack on analysis serves to sharpen issues; the analysis is often deficient because of the time limits in solving problems and the inevitable shortcomings of available techniques. Nevertheless, the issue is not which is superior, politics or scientific analysis, but what new structures can improve the interplay of both.

Sociologists at times ignore these characteristics of bureaucracy. Bureaucracy is not all bad. Man could not have been lifted from his primordial state without organization. Moreover, as a producer, bureaucracy, modern style, allows the individual an autonomy and independence in judgment not available in the early stages of the industrial revolution. Bureaucracy serves to collect information for complex problems and to generate the political process required for consensus. Intellectual views on policy are only one source of opinion, often based on misinformation. The threat of bureaucracy lies in the way it tends to shut out the citizen from policy formation and, in the business sector, in the manner it converts the individual into a passive consumer.

As organizational bureaucracies age, their innovative spirit declines. In industry, innovators are replaced by wizards in finance, who, with astuteness in undercover dealing and rapaciousness of spirit, succeed in taking over control of the corporate creation of others. These wizards are frequently graduates of universities with reputations as great centers of learning. To survive, the officers of competing organizations cannot devote their energies to corporate statesmanship; they must be equally devious and rapacious. The morality of these corporate plungers is: it's all right if it makes money and if you can get away with it. The extraordinarily aggressive impulses of these men are given respectability under the umbrella of a corporate organization.[2]

The mystique that surrounds corporate managers vanishes as a rising generation topples them from their pedestals. Laid bare, the managers reveal themselves as clever politicians playing their cards close to their chest in order to maintain their position in a class that no longer commands the adulation of the public. The manager of a big organization is no longer boss. The few despots are anachronisms. The manager is more a mediator reconciling the posture of subordinate managers and technicians in his organization. The interest of these subordinates in a business firm is not primarily the maintenance of a good profit record for the organization. Nor do they give much thought to the social consequences of their collective effort. They are not paid to think of social consequences. In managing them, the chief executive has to end the

[2] For an account of how shrewd lawyers, crooked corporate officials, and consultant university professors, with an assist from a sympathetic judicial system, can indulge in chicanery and violence on the public, see Robert L. Heilbroner (and others), *In The Name Of Profit,* New York: Doubleday, 1972.

year in the black, or in the red with the promise of better years to come. He has to achieve this balancing of accounts with specialists interested predominantly in their respective specializations.

Thus, externally as well as internally, the manager must control events in a manner that demonstrates improvement at the end of a planning period. He has to amass data in a way that indicates that his organization has grown. He is judged on his planning ability, his capacity to stipulate realizable objectives. Understatement, therefore, is in his interest. He must be conservative in his projection of goals while generating conviction of his daring. He must dominate forces that pose a threat to the achievement of his plan. He must play a political game that forestalls any threat to his position from subordinates and that persuades his superiors of his indispensability.

In theory, these managers are selected by stockholders in their firms. In practice, they belong to a tight self-perpetuating oligarchy whose members are chosen to a considerable degree by those who control the flow of money into corporations. These money directors include the chief executives of insurance firms, banks, and mutual funds who exert an influence on the choice of managers by their control of voting corporate stock. To a lesser degree, managers are subject to the control of family groups owning blocks of corporate stock. Such is not to say that the union of managers is a closed one. A newcomer can move into the managerial circle if he plays it right and persuades his superiors that he will play it right for them. On the way to the top, the novice must be ready to move freely between plants and corporations and must convince the top dog that he is beholding a self-image.

A manager must make decisions in a way that subordinates department heads to his will. The relative influence of different departments reflects the chief executive's judgment as to the relative contribution of each to the mission of the organization. Unruly subordinates require a delicacy of handling. Thus, the manager can make it difficult for a subordinate by budget allocations, by subtle curtailment of the prerogatives of office, or by assignment of tasks so difficult as to make their accomplishment unlikely. In performing these distasteful but necessary tasks, the managers must at the same time gain the confidence of the subordinate's constituency. He can so curry their favor by lunching with them in a spirit of good fellowship or by announcing an open door policy. In substance, he can be devious but must not be heavy handed. Obstructionists must be eliminated unobtrusively. He must constantly keep in mind that he operates a loosely integrated collection of semi-independent duchies guarding their respective territories and resenting the instrusion of outsiders, be he the chief executive himself.

Tucked away in a corporation's annual report and in messages to employees are propaganda pieces labelled company objectives: The firm exists in performance of a public service and profits are incidental to such a goal. The company is proud to pay taxes and one of its fondest desires is to treat employees as lavishly as resources permit. Wages are not higher in the interest of the life of the company and sometimes the nation. Figures are inserted between the verbiage that sustain the point of view. From a casual reading of their statements one gets a feeling of buoyancy and forward movement. A closer examination indicates, however, that the knowledge they provide is comparable to that given in after-dinner speeches and answers to inquiries from undergraduate students of management.

Accordingly, there is a controversy among economists as to what these firms are really after. Those who manage to weave through the propaganda, who have some experience in the operation of such firms, and who abandon a single-goal explanation come up generally with the following objectives: A firm must make enough profit to give what the industry considers to be a satisfactory return on investment. Sales should also expand. So should assets either from internal growth or outside acquisitions. The firm should innovate and be a leader, a goal that is more "psychological" than "economic." To pursue these goals, a firm must plan so as to control forces affecting its position, including government, labor, financial and supply markets, and even groups in the community itself.

Thus, profits, sales, assets, and personal ambition are principal motivations. These drives shift in relative importance over time, and are reconciled and pursued in strategies that reflect these shifts. To some degree, this shift manifests movement away from a problem for which routine technology has been developed. These movements, together with managerial differences in personality and available strategies and resources, make predictability of firm behavior difficult. However, the overriding imperative of growth (and therefore of control), the shared value orientation of managers, the firm personality derived from the particular product produced, tend to create similar behavior in firms belonging to the same sector.

The cult of becoming bigger should not be underestimated. After each planning period, the manager must demonstrate that his big organization has become even bigger or is on the way of becoming so. To do this, he must sell more products. If his firm already controls a preponderant share of the market, he can either expand vertically or buy firms outside his industry. Bigness emphasizes quantity often to the detriment of quality of product and environment. A "new" product may be one the firm manages to persuade the public is new in order to maintain sales. The cult of bigness, therefore, tends to discourage the employment of a calculus of quality as a measure of progress.

Corporations must plan. Planning consists of stipulating objectives over a time period and forestalling contingencies that may upset the plan.

> As viewed by the industrial firm, planning consists in foreseeing the actions required between the initiation of production and its completion and preparing for the accomplishment of these actions. And it consists also of foreseeing, and having a design for meeting, any unscheduled developments, favorable or otherwise, that may occur along the way. As planning is viewed by the economist, political scientist or pundit, it consists of replacing prices and the market as the mechanism for determining what will be produced, with an authoritative determination of what will be produced and consumed and at what price. It will be thought that the word planning is being used in two different senses.
>
> In practice, however, the two kinds of planning, if such they may be called, are inextricably associated. A firm cannot usefully foresee and schedule future action or prepare for contingencies if it does not know what its prices will be, what its sales will be, what its costs including labor and capital costs will be and what will be available at these costs.[3]

Accordingly, corporations fix desired outcomes by day, by week, by month, and by year. Thereupon, with varying success, they seek to control men, institutions, and events so that these outcomes come to pass. If an organization affecting its calculations produces uncertainty, the organization must be controlled so as to produce a more desirable behavior. Or if the public wavers, it must be persuaded that the firm's innovation is a mark of progress. In this element of planning, success is measurable in terms of the public's acquiescence.

This necessity of control is a mainspring of corporate management. Large-scale production requires investment in expensive equipment and costly specialized labor. These commitments require controlling factors that inhibit their economical use. Price competition fosters uncertainty of income. Therefore, its extent must be limited through such means as the favorable intercession of federal, state, and local governments and through tacit understanding among competitors as to its limits. The cost of funds for equipment cannot be left to the uncertainty of money markets. And the educational system must also be controlled so as to produce labor with the proper training and attitudes. The same requirement of control applies to sources of supply of other needed resources.

The hullabaloo raised in 1961 over the conviction for price rigging of electrical firms including General Electric and Westinghouse ignored

3 J. K. Galbraith, *The New Industrial State,* pp. 25–26.

this imperative of stability. Despite the law, corporations have always maintained prices. The convicted firms merely sought to do so in a more mafia-like style.

Consequently, a dominant motive behind corporate drive lies in the reduction of uncertainty. To minimize uncertainty, institutions must be subordinated to the firm's needs. The firm must shape values in the population that reflect themselves in demand and in political forces favorable to its interests. From the government, the firm requires economic policies that assure stable or rising prices, guarantees of rising demand, the underwriting of technological innovation, a minimum of interference with output and price decisions. From the educational system, the firm expects a supply of needed specialists, and from the consumer, the joy of consumption. The modern corporation prefers living like a secure duchy independent of the life of its management incumbents, whose mission before passing is to increase the assurance of its immortality. For successful accomplishment of their mission, managers acquire the American equivalent of Lenin hero badges in the form of plaques, scrolls, honorary degrees, bonuses and stock certificates.

The internal human relations task of the manager is to develop a labor force of technicians who are amenable to these imperatives of organization. Modern decision making is too diffused a process to operate effectively under a system of compulsion. The better alternative is a system of acquiescence and identification. Technicians who are allowed to employ their technical skills in the solution of corporate problems acquiesce more readily to the purposes of managers. If allowed some liberty to employ these skills, technicians are rarely concerned with the broad implications of what they do. The role of the manager, consequently, is to perform a series of balancing acts. He must give each set of technicians a feeling of influencing decisions within their own functional orbit. He must keep the competition between the different sets of technicians at low levels so as to minimize the sense of loss. As much as possible, he has to eliminate work performed by non-technicians and indirectly the unions that control such work. And he has to fit together the separate sets of technical activities in a way that promotes his overall purposes. The compatibility of the goals of the organization with those of the technicians is often achieved on the basis of an exchange in which technicians are given an opportunity to play with their skills as managers pursue not fully disclosed motives. To effect such an exchange, it often is not prudent to be honest. Indeed, an attempt to reconcile goals in open fashion would serve only to trouble the waters.

Decision making processes in big organizations allow such a live and let live philosophy. The ideas of specialists that are fed into decision-making pipelines underwrite a limited number of options that are difficult to set aside. A manager's choice if challenged by a subordinate can thereby be more easily defended. He can point out that the option he chose came out of the system and not from his own personal predilections. Accordingly, the complexity of the process places him in a position to gain acquiescence from subordinates.

The way in which information fed into the system circumscribes options suggests how managers can acquire some maneuverability. If the decision that seems plausible is not the one desired by the manager, he can try to alter the inputs going into the process. He can initiate studies until he comes up with the answer he wants. A manager, for example, can assure the irrepressible logic of his decision through a fact finding task force whose members are wisely chosen. Facts assembled by technicians acquire cogency in the minds of other technicians. When managers do not like one set of answers, their feasible option is to suggest that changing circumstances make advisable the commissioning of a new task force.

The manager represents a focal point in the reconciliation of a variety of competing norms in the decision making system. He is not a unilateral decision maker so much as a reconciler of diverse positions. Nor does he necessarily confront all role players in the system; mere contemplation of their reactions and assessment of their relative strength often suffices. As an individual who triggers responses by his actions, he behaves in anticipation of these responses and their effects. If the manager can be called a maximizer, he is so by virtue of seeking a maximum salvaging of his values against the internal and external array of claimants that confront him.

He sees his particular coercive orbit of product markets, labor markets, community, and government, as interacting forces. His bargaining position is affected by the amount of productive property, marketable skills, and political influence he commands. He takes a position in anticipation of the cross-currents of pressures he generates. He operates within a system of stress arising from conflicts of interest between groups.

These conflicts are a product of scarcity and differences in perception. A given transaction is likely to be to someone's disadvantage. Decisions bounce about among affected blocs until they find a resting place on the backs of those with the least organized power. If the lambs do not wish to be fleeced by the lions, they have to restyle the decision making process in a manner favorable to their interests. Such a rearrangement is successful when just who is lion and who lamb becomes fuzzy. Conflict decreases as bargaining groups find a widening area of common interest in their transaction as they shift its burden to those not partners to it. But this outcome in turn generates new stresses.

The absence of conflict is not entirely laudable. Little opportunity for justice exists without the ability of all affected parties to enter effectively into a position of conflict. Dissenting positions raise the quality of perception. While the lack of stress may imply a reconciliation, its absence may indicate a distribution of power so lopsided as to make dissent an exercise in futility. Thus, the absence of conflict in organizational behavior may mark a temporary hiatus until such time as effective positions emerge.

Conflict is a tool of both production and distribution justice. Effective conflict obtains agreement or acquiescence on the techniques used in production and the manner in which income is distributed. While production problems can be more easily resolved by appealing to technical grounds of efficiency, distribution questions often rest on emotionally charged moral positions. Therefore, every affected party must have the opportunity to present his view of equity. If the power of those affected is fairly well balanced, these points of view are reconciled on their relative merits. Accordingly, out of effective conflict emerges a sense that justice is triumphant.

Under such circumstances, it can be seen how a manager must behave like a politician. He learns how to be guarded in expressing his views and trades honesty for security. To make his money, he panders to values for which he often has contempt; for so doing he often acquires the disrespect of his children. While the relationships with his subordinates may always be amicable, they are rarely affectionate. But was ever a prince truly loved by his courtiers?

In his ever searching pursuit of control, a manager develops relations with critical points in society. He develops a network of posts in other corporations, public organizations, and institutions of higher learning, with which to promote his interests. The knowledge gained from such affiliation is a valuable resource. But he must pursue these interests in the guise of rendering a public service. If his interests are sensitive to political judgments, he must also mend his political fences. Thus, a university manager may find a politician of modest intellect worthy of an honorary degree if circumstances deem it necessary.

In moments of self-flattery, some role players describe this system as one of pragmatic problem solving. By this they mean a feel for solutions that have proved workable in similar circumstances in the past and a disposition to give them a try. Whatever they are called, decisions often reflect the choice that brings a minimum of backlash and allows the manager to survive. And survival often necessitates a philosophy of mutual back scratching. The state, for example, needs the corporation as the corporation needs the state. The corporation provides the jobs and the consumer products without which the state cannot govern. The relationship between state and corporation is so cordial that the state solicits from the corporation the extent to which it should exercise social responsibility. For example, the government sued the auto industry for conspiring to control the introduction of anti-pollution devices. After intensive lobbying, the government made a deal with the firms in the industry despite the opposition of community organizations seeking to bring the truth out in the open. As a rule, the same effect on society is treated gingerly when caused by a corporation and forcibly when caused by an individual.

It can be observed that economic models of decision making are not especially useful in describing these external and internal relationships. They are geared to explaining decisions on price, output, wages, and employment from the basic assumption that employers seek to maximize profits. In an age of unprecedented consumption, they add up to the conclusion that employers together with their trade unions restrict output. They do not begin to suggest the maze of pipelines that conduct challenges, multiple responses, and accommodation. They ignore the legal structures on the organization and the multiple power centers including government, organized labor, community associations, and other employers that place their imprint on decisions. From over-simplified assumptions, they spin an unimpeachable logic, the facts of decision making notwithstanding.

One gains no sense of movement from economic models. They furnish few clues of where the system came from and where it is headed. *Eppur si muove*. A consumption revolution has taken place unrivaled anywhere, raising income by one third each decade, while research energies focus on how industry imposes a restriction on output.

These factors suggest that a realistic theory of the firm has to be a theory of the balancing of multiple pressures inside and outside organization. But it is easier to formulate a theory of profit maximization than to base one on the vague notion of seeking a reconciliation of conflicting interests.

THE EXTENT OF CORPORATE BIGNESS

The huge multi-face corporation dominates American business. Regardless of the transient managers who work and consume within its structure, the big modern corporation acquires the immortality denied to human beings. The sales of one firm alone, the General Motors Corporation, amounted to $24.3 billion in 1969, or more than the national budget of the world's countries except the United States, the Soviet Union, England, Japan and France.[4] Large corporations are a storehouse of the nation's human and tangible capital. They anoint government, consumer, and education to assure their perpetual life. They dominate the world economy as they become big multinational corporations.

In the year 1946, corporate income was 1.5 times as much as that of unincorporated business. By the end of two decades, the figure rose to three times as much, corporate assets growing from $450 billion to $1,400 billion. At the same time, mergers and acquisitions of corporations began to rise swiftly. In 1949, the number amounted to approximately 175. By 1962, the figure rose to 600 annually. In a 1969 report, the Federal Trade Commission stated that the merger activity had reached the highest on record in the year 1968 and had gone even higher in the first quarter of 1969. The merged assets amounted to $12.6 billion.[5] In the year 1968, the 200 largest industrial corporations owned two thirds of all industrial assets, a proportion held by a thousand corporations in 1941. According to a United States Senate Committee report, in 1929 the one hundred largest manufacturing corporations owned 44 percent of the net capital assets of all corporations. By 1962, the figure had jumped to 58 percent.

Ranked by sales, the 500 biggest industrial corporations in the United States are concentrated in oil refining, motor vehicles, chemicals, basic steel, aerospace, rubber, machinery, steel fabrication, tobacco, food, transportation, soaps and cosmetics industries. They employ approximately 15 million individuals or about 20 percent of the labor force. The 250 largest firms in commercial banking, life insurance, retailing, and utilities employ 4.8 million persons.[6] In other terms, the work experience of 25 percent of the labor force derives from these big corporations of the system.

Bigness is measurable in terms of the percentage of the particular product market controlled by a firm, the size of assets, the degree of vertical integration in a particular industry, and the extent of control in multiple industries. The economic literature and the law concerns itself primarily with the degree of control of a particular product. The data available do not distinguish sufficiently between these different views of

4 *Fortune Magazine*, May 1970.
5 The 1968 data are from *The New York Times*, November 5, 1969, citing an FTC survey. The other data are from the *U.S. Senate, Committee on the Judiciary*, Hearings Before the Subcommittee on Anti-Trust and Monopoly, Economic Concentration, Part 1, U.S. Government Printing Office, Washington, D. C., 1964.
6 *Fortune Magazine*, May 15, 1969.

bigness. This obsolete framework of law and information obscures the issues raised by bigness.

Traditionally, mergers have involved the purchase of competing firms or firms representing part of the sequence of production in a particular industry, from raw materials to the sale of finished goods. The new type of merger, the conglomerate, brings under single management control firms that make non-competing products. For example, one of the three major television networks, whose mandate under the law is to serve the listening and viewing public, owns a major league baseball team, a toy company, 4 musical instrument firms, two film companies, and a major publishing house.

The speed of conglomeration is staggering. In 1948, the 200 largest industrial firms owned half the assets of the nation's corporations. Two decades later, this same percentage was owned by less than 100 firms. Underlying this pace is conglomeration. Despite this pace of concentration the Nixon Administration has elected not to challenge the trend.

A principal impulse behind conglomerating is buying firms in industries toward which the product demand of the initiating firm is shifting. Another is the objective of guaranteeing a steady flow of income through industrial diversification. A third factor is the zest for power of managers liberated by the routinization of operations that modern technology, including the computer, affords. Conglomeration management demonstrates the truth that planning differs with the parts being controlled. For better or worse, the planning of managers of conglomerates is essentially one of playing with money and subordinates.

The Penn Central Railroad, with $7 billion in assets, yet a reputation in the East for equipment and personnel unfit for human beings, was one of the most imaginative of conglomerates. Its managers built an empire that ran from hotels to clothing plants, while purportedly minding the railroad. The firm's investment holding company, Pennco, was reported in early 1971 as having a book value of $650 million. The railroad issued from a merger of the Pennsylvania Railroad and the New York Central, approved by the Interstate Commerce Commission and supported by the business community under the rationale of lower costs and improved service.

Not too long thereafter the empire collapsed. Some of the details border on the romantic. In a deal involving investment in an air carrier the conglomerate was taken in the amount of $4 million by a Bavarian financier disappointed in the losses he sustained in the carrier. His grab was consummated in the following way. Two Washington, D. C. lawyers, brothers Joseph H. and Francis N. Rosenbaum, both with court records but impeccable educational backgrounds and friends in government, arranged a $10 million loan for Penn Central and placed the funds in a Lichtenstein bank. The firm gave Fidel Goetz, sulking over his losses, loan privileges against the bank deposit. Then Goetz appropriated $4 million outright. The movement of the money to the brooding Bavarian was arranged by the creation of a financial trust by the Rosenbaum brothers, unbeknown to Penn Central and the transfer of the $4 million to a firm owned by Goetz. And Goetz is not about to give the money back.

Francis Rosenbaum, in jail for swindling the United States Navy, is permitted leisurely visits to his villa in Virginia. His accomplice in the fraud was allowed to draw interest on the money for two years. The Internal Revenue Service attached the funds after publicity revealed that some $700,000 in interest had been drawn from the stolen government money.[7] These goings-on support our thesis on the genteel treatment accorded upper middle class crooks.

Returning to Penn Central, press reports indicate that 15 of its executives sold their shares of the firm's stock at prices ranging from $40 to $70 before the stock plummeted to six dollars. In addition to key financial executives of the conglomerate, bankers, brokers, and a prominent architect formed part of an investment group known as the Pennphil Corporation. In a typical example of the operations of the investment organization, the group bought shares in a firm on the same day as did Penn Central.[8]

Twenty days before bankruptcy the firm paid out $629,933 in salary raises for its executives.[9] The $132,000-a-year Finance Chairman of the railroad obtained from Lloyds of London a $10 million insurance policy covering himself and other officers against liability for improper conduct.[10] The Finance Chairman comes from a Main Line Wasp family of long lineage.

Mergers have social and economic consequences. They provide fresh opportunities for the management of people's minds. They encourage inflation by enabling firms to maintain prices in a declining market and then raising prices when demand begins to rise. Congress contributes to this inflationary bias by permitting manufacturers to fix the prices charged by retailers. In the case of transportation industries, the regulatory agencies underwrite mismanagement by rubber stamping their demands for price increases.

The securities manipulations these corporate acquisitions entail are

7 *The New York Times*, April 9, 1972.
8 The Philadelphia *Evening Bulletin*, December 20, 1970.
9 The Philadelphia *Inquirer*, July 18, 1971.
10 The Philadelphia *Evening Bulletin*, March 11, 1971.

highly imaginative. Under the impetus of tax law, corporate combinations can be constructed that produce profits that have little to do with service rendered the public. For example, Company "A" with a no earnings record can elect to take over Company "B" with a record of profits. To make the offer tempting, "A" offers the stockholders of "B" attractive unsecured bonds and thereby secures control of the firm. At that point, the earnings of the combined firms rise per share as federal taxes are reduced by virtue of the fact that interest on debt securities is a deductible item for the purpose of estimating taxes.

In August of 1971, the antitrust division of the United States Department of Justice announced the abandonment of its prosecution of three antitrust suits against a giant conglomerate, the International Telephone and Telegraph Company, amid rumors linking the decision to a commitment by the firm to contribute up to $400,000 toward the Republican National Convention. With annual sales in excess of $7 billion, the communications firm is also in the hotel, car rental, insurance and baking business. In the prior decade alone, the ITT had swallowed up about a hundred firms. Four months prior to the announced settlement, the antitrust chief went on record strongly favoring a court suit to determine whether existing law would be applicable in controlling the wave of conglomerate mergers. According to press reports, on June 17th the antitrust chief changed his mind and so informed the Deputy Attorney General. On July 31st, an agreement between the firm and government was reached, settling the suits out of court. Following the settlement, the antitrust chief was appointed a federal judge.

The offer to assist the Republican National Convention was made through the Sheraton Hotel Corporation, a subsidiary of the ITT. An investment management firm hired by the Justice Department to assess the consequences of the antitrust action dealt solely with the securities aspect of the problem. A White House aide placed the study in the hands of a former Wall Street colleague, whose investment firm happened to have an ITT portfolio amounting to close to a quarter million dollars. Several days were devoted to the study.

The Deputy Attorney General denied any knowledge of ITT's contribution until after he had read about it in the newspapers in late November. He conceded later having talked privately several times to a representative of ITT but denied it was linked to any contribution. His role in the negotiations, together with that of his subordinate, the antitrust chief, were kept secret from the staff of the antitrust division.

A memorandum written by a $50,000-a-year ITT lobbyist linked the convention money with the antitrust settlement and contained a plea to keep the action quiet. Together with other files of the lobbyist, the memorandum was destroyed by corporate officials after the incident had exploded in the press. The lobbyist is also alleged to have stated that at a party she had talked about the suits with the Attorney General. The Attorney General denied ever talking to her about the suits, but he conceded having had a philosophical discussion on antitrust policy with the firm's president. The lobbyist denied writing the memorandum. Her denial was issued jointly with Senate Republican Minority Leader Hugh Scott.

In subsequent testimony to the Senate Judiciary Subcommittee, the lobbyist stated her belief that the references in the memorandum to the Attorney General constituted a forgery. She also testified that several weeks before the settlement a White House official had telephoned the ITT Washington office asking for details on the firm's commitment to the convention. Both the Nixon administration and the firm's officials sought to discredit the lobbyist. In hearings before the committee, a maze of contradictory testimony from firm executives and Republican party officials unfolded. The Judiciary subcommittee was asked to excuse the lobbyist because of her heart disease; subsequent examination by physicians at the committee's request revealed no evidence of any such disease.

Following the talks with government officials and shortly prior to the announced settlement, top corporate officials disposed of ITT stock holdings. It was the president's first reported sale since 1967. The stock dropped in value on the first trading day after the settlement and subsequently recovered. There is a law against the trading of stock on the basis of information not available to the public.

Moreover, in 1969 the ITT sold some of its Hartford Insurance Company holdings to an Italian bank, in order to qualify for a favorable tax ruling by the Internal Revenue Service. In late 1970 the bank sold the shares to the Dreyfus Fund. In midyear following, the ITT named the Fund managers of its pension assets of $10 million. The effect of the settlement was government acquiescence to the biggest merger in the United States history.[11]

Two observations can be made by way of postscript. The biggest detractors of government are the government officials themselves. They are the biggest cause of its decline in stature. For example, the same Corrupt Practices Act to which the ITT is liable was used the following year by the government to indict and successfully prosecute several trade union officials for political contributions amounting to $49,250. The count against one of the officials was making a $250 contribution

11 *The New York Times,* March 3, 4, 12, 16, 18, 24, 26, 27, April 1, 2, 1972, and the Philadelphia *Evening Bulletin,* March 5, April 16, 1972.

to a congressman. Second, corporate executives seem to enjoy going to parties, especially to those where high government officials will be present. In such gatherings they can mix a little business with pleasure, secure in their expectation that the government will play ball.

At times, unions assist the process of big firms becoming bigger and less competitive. Through policies that tend to shift production to big employers who can pay more, labor organizations exert an influence on prices and product markets. The separation of product from labor markets is more a matter of convenience in teaching economics than it is a fact of life. Unions generally prefer cozy relations with employers on the principle of mutual back scratching. In the construction industry, contractors have a vested interest in helping their trade union win jurisdictional battles with other unions to avoid a shift in production to other crafts. The union can keep out employers by the device of imposing on interlopers terms of employment difficult to meet. Government and money lenders support this togetherness by underwriting inefficiency, and the costs are transferred to the public in the form of higher rents and prices for new housing. Unions have similar interests in defense industries. We therefore turn next to a discussion of these corporations.

The War Corporations.   The biggest firm in the United States is government, and its board of directors sits in the Department of Defense. The Pentagon controls the operations of some 30 big firms and 3,000 medium and small enterprises. The government cannot allow these firms to go out of business and is committed to underwriting their mismanagement. To say that these firms are in the private sector is pure fiction.

One of these firms, the Lockheed Corporation, does a $2 billion business annually, 90 percent of which derives from government contracts. Many smaller firms feed their products into this corporation. In a government contract calling for 115 aircraft for the U.S. Air Force, at a cost of $2.3 billion, the firm managed to produce 81 planes at a cost of $3.7 billion. In a letter to Deputy Secretary of Defense Packard, the firm's chairman expressed confidence that through litigation against the government, Lockheed would recover the trebling of cost per plane and, who knows, possibly even come up with a profit. The Defense Department has a euphemism for this inefficiency: cost overruns.

The financial mismanagement of Lockheed produces political pressures to assist firms undergoing similar difficulties with government guaranteed loans. Such underwriting is likely to be only the first in a series of steps leading to government management and ownership of private firms, as the history of this kind of financial assistance in Great Britain and Italy indicates. Such an eventuality would further remove the constraints of the market as a catalyst of organization efficiency.

The most feasible way to oust the management of such a firm seems to be to let the organization slide into bankruptcy.

The sheltered corporations are the offspring of war and preparation for war. They form part of an amorphous conglomeration of politicians, military brass, research institutes living on government money, trade unions, and communities supported predominantly by defense spending. Some of these communities depend almost entirely on military installations and defense corporations and would receive a crippling blow if no more government contracts were forthcoming. But the inter-relationships defense production fosters raise a formidable barrier to such an event. The politicians on Congressional Armed Services Committees closely monitor the operations of installations and plants within their political jurisdiction. Defense Department budgets provide funds in the millions of dollars with which to propagandize the Congress and public. Over two thousand high ranking officers are top executives in firms they used to deal with while on active duty. Many university professors provide services for the maintenance of the complex. The arms race attests to its formidable power.

Many of these firms rely increasingly on discharged servicemen, in addition to the top brass, as a source of recruitment of new employees. The junior officers, they assert, are more reliable than are new college graduates. The practice goes beyond defense firms. A personnel agency reports an active file of almost 3,000 junior officers. One recruiter states his delight in talking to applicants with clean-cut hair; corporate executives assert these men have their goals set and have gotten this boyish, kiddish, green thing out of the way.[12]

The major buyer of these corporations, when not the sole one, is a government more concerned with their technical capacities than with their efficiency. The politics of achieving Congressional acceptability of new war technology leans heavily on underestimating costs when making non-competitive bids. The capital and talents of these corporations are geared to the acquisition and fulfillment of such contracts; to expect these resources to be shifted readily to non-war production in a competitive private market is unrealistic. To achieve such a goal requires government planning and subsidy. In addition, a conversion to some other form of public production is more feasible than production for private markets.

Defense production generates a continuous and expanding operational relationship between government and corporation. Defense contracts involve continuous negotiation with firms, and the bargain may be more

12 *The New York Times*, March 17, 1969.

political than economic. Once placed, a contract requires continuous government supervision. Government also provides firms with capital equipment, research and development money, and know-how, which solidifies the relationship even more.

The public does not share in the profits derived from the commercial products that may issue from these forms of assistance. In addition, the initial underestimation of costs serves to preempt a portion of rising government income to technologies that once heavily underwritten are difficult to discard. The research and development money these firms obtain fosters a monopoly in technology and markets. An economist of high reputation, Wassily Leontief, describes this practice as giving a contractor funds with which to build a road and the right to charge tolls thereafter.

This relationship makes it difficult to draw a clear dividing line between government and economy. Corporate and civil service employees in the firm co-mingle. The same person may be a government employee one day and a toiler in the so-called private sector the next. Many such firms use government-owned property whose extent is not known by the government itself. The relationship is analogous to one of a holding company with a subsidiary firm, each with an interest in their mutual survival.

The military-industrial complex is the term used to describe this relationship. Its operation borders on a vicious circle. To cite an example, in cooperation with the military, the war corporation develops a feasible new technological system. The new system gains the support of Congressional sympathizers with the defense establishment, military lobbyists, leaders of veterans' organizations, trade union leaders, and proprietors of military research institutes. Each can gain political, military, economic and organization returns from the new technological development. The system is moved forward to the hardware stage. Foreign adversaries must develop a system that counteracts the counter thrust of the adversary. A similar sequence of events can be generated by the adversary. That this circle borders on lunacy is indicated by the argument in behalf of new military expenditures to the effect that while the system may seem to be outmoded, it may serve the purpose of bankrupting the adversary.

Defense systems are sometimes planned not on the basis of what the adversary is doing *but what it ought to be doing.* For instance, the bulk of Defense Department funds go into 3 major systems, each of which can launch a devastating attack on the Soviet Union: The Polaris submarine system and its successor; the intercontinental ballistics missile system; and bomber planes. The U. S. S. R. has not stressed building new bombers; but the United States Air Force defends bomber expenditures for new planes and defenses on the grounds that the Russians *ought to have bombers*. The logic of the Air Force position is to persuade the Soviet Union to accept an advanced American bomber plane at American expense so that the United States can build a better one.[13]

Financial stakes in the complex are considerable. A study for the Antitrust and Monopoly Subcommittee of the United States Senate reveals that a hundred firms receive two thirds of the military contracts. Between 1962 and 1965, the average profit rate for a random sampling of such firms was 17.5 percent compared to 10.6 percent for a sampling of non-defense firms. In 6 categories of equipment, four corporations perform practically the entire business. One such firm lives entirely by the defense business. For some firms, profits run as much as 22 percent of capital investment.

The career of Roswell Gilpatric, a corporation lawyer, exemplifies the interrelationships of the war industry. From 1951 to 1953, Mr. Gilpatric was Undersecretary of the Air Force. For three years beginning in 1959, he was a partner in a law firm that played a major role in awarding the TFX plane contract to the General Dynamics Corporation. The controversial plane was awarded to the firm in 1962 when the corporation was on the verge of receivership. After some $6 billion in expenditure, the plane proved a failure in the Vietnam War.[14] In a letter to Attorney General Robert Kennedy, Senator Williams of Delaware summarized the involvement of Mr. Gilpatric's law firm as follows:

> From 1958 until January 1961, Secretary Roswell Gilpatric was a member of the law firm of Cravath, Swaine & Moore, counsel for the General Dynamics Corporation and based on testimony he was the member of the law firm who brought the business to that firm and personally handled the account. The General Dynamics Corporation set aside an office for his use and convenience.
>
> The law firm continued to serve General Dynamics and from 1958 through the summer of 1963, was billed for $300,000 for legal fees.
>
> Deputy Secretary of Defense Gilpatric did not disqualify himself in the TFX plane contract competition involving his former client General Dynamics. He took an active role in the contract discussions, wrote letters in connection with the bidding procedures, and recommended that the award be given to General Dynamics. His views in favor of General Dynamics overrode the Pentagon Source Selection Board's recommendation for Boeing on the basis of performance and price.

[13] I. F. Stone, "Nixon and the Arms Race," *The New York Review*, January 2, 1969.

[14] At this writing it appears that the government will obtain some 500 planes of questionable value after some $7.8 billions in public expenditure.

Secretary Gilpatric has indicated that he will leave the government and return to his law firm, a firm that still represents General Dynamics. Mr. Moore of the law firm has become a member of the board of directors of General Dynamics.[15]

THE SOCIAL EFFECTS OF CORPORATIONS

In after dinner speeches and at stockholder meetings, corporate executives often like to talk about the social responsibilities of business. It is not clear whether avowals to do more issue from moral perturbations or from tactical maneuvers calculated to ease pressures generated by social reformers. The managers who indulge in such talk are damned when they do and damned when they don't. The criticism comes from economists, who, starting from premises about the economy that are devoid of reality, conclude with unimpeachable logic that it is not the function of a manager to be socially responsible. At the other extreme are institutional economists who assert the contrary and who are skeptical about the sincerity behind these corporate statements. We must therefore turn to the subject of the corporation and social welfare.

As per capita income rises, an increasing margin of goods is sold on the basis of hoodwinking consumers into believing they need what they did not want before the hoodwinking process began. The margin has reached considerable proportions. If Americans suddenly no longer read billboards, no longer read the newspapers, no longer listened to the radio or watched television, succeeded in keeping salesmen off the telephone and off the property, and no longer yielded to reading their junk mail, the long term effect on the economy would be disastrous. Such disaster is avoided by making certain that the individual remains a tool of the system.

The corporation thus has to generate insecurities that drive individuals to sales counters. It does this through advertising that reaches the brink of falsehood without actually falling in. The few convince the many to do what is good for the system. The control of tastes is motivated neither by the desire to promote the social welfare nor by the intent to sharpen the consumer's perceptions. The advertising pitch is based on the assumption that the consumer is not especially bright. This style of persuasion has been so successful that it is even used profitably in the merchandising of individuals for the office of President of the United States.

A producer who succeeds in developing a substantial demand for a product before publicity on its harmful effects mounts acquires the power to defend himself against subsequent attacks on its use. Thus, cigarette

15 Quoted by I. F. Stone, "Nixon and the Arms Race," *New York Review*, ibid.

smoking, despite its mounting record of lung cancer, heart disease, emphysema, and chronic bronchitis, manages to hold its market, with the assistance of lobbying and advertising in the hundreds of millions of dollars.[16] And the consumption of alcohol, with a record of causing crime in the cities and half the annual deaths on the highways, is treated with respect. By contrast, marijuana smoking, whose effects are not precisely known, is handled as a felony subject to many years of imprisonment. One is drawn to the conclusion that the extent of social responsibility expected of a seller is related to his power to ignore it.

Duplicity is a major tool in business. For example, Metromedia, a New York firm with extensive television and radio interests, sent out forms to 4 million persons with the objective of compiling mailing lists and selling them to firms. The Federal Trade Commission found that the firm got recipients to fill out questionnaires on the fraudulent claim that fabulous gifts would be forthcoming and without advising them that they would end up on a mailing list for direct mail retailers.[17]

Caught in one deception, employers shift to another. According to a report of the Federal Trade Commission, in a study of 43 firms offering prizes to the public, about 6 percent of the prizes were actually paid out. For 3 manufacturers, the percentage was 3 percent. One soap firm was listed as offering four prizes totaling $25,000 each, but nobody won. The Capital Record Club offered $4.5 million in prizes and awarded $14,000. The managers who administer these firms are highly respected citizens.

Power of suggestion is an important element in advertising. The United States of America Standards Institute, formerly the National Standards Association, is an industry-supported body that sets product standards. Its seal of approval is "USA Standard."

In an expression of faith in consumer sovereignty, an ad reads as follows:

A strange change comes over a woman in the store. This soft glow in the eye is replaced by a steely financial glint: the graceful walk becomes a panther's stride among the bargains. A prowling computer jungle trained, her bargain hunger senses razor-sharp for the sound of a dropping price.[18]

---

[16] I have heard that Australian scientists have developed a new cigarette filter that uses the viscera of sheep. But the research, it appears, has hit ?. snag. It seems as though the research subject, after taking a deep drag, keeled over into an unconscious state. Upon medical examination he was found to have a gray lining on his lungs that was diagnosed as sheep dung. The research continues to develop an antidote to this effect of the filter.

[17] The Philadelphia *Evening Bulletin*, April 10, 1970.

[18] Quoted by Ralph Nader in the *New York Review*, November 21, 1968.

Sometimes jungle trained consumers need prodding, as another ad indicates:

> Soup is much more than a food. It is a potent magic that satisfies not only the hunger of the body but the yearning of the soul.[19]

The universal theme of advertising is an optimistic belief that only a small outlay of money will catapult an individual from despair to bliss. A small item such as a deodorant, a pill, a cigarillo, an antiseptic, or a laxative, will convert a mini-person into a conqueror.

It is difficult to state whether advertising reflects American culture or whether the culture is determined by the system. In any case, the manner in which Americans tolerate, if not enjoy, listening to song in praise of gasoline surely must have some profound meaning. The manner in which television commercials radiate happiness and beauty in a people's world of frustration and ugliness surely is also worthy of sociological study. If a visitor from a backward nation were to visit advanced America and try to deduce who its people are solely from commercials, he might conclude the land was populated by buffoons.

Nothing is sacred for advertisers, not even a bowel movement. Irregularity is fair game. The university apologists for advertising state it keeps prices down, reduces the cost of research, and makes the market competitive. All these beneficent effects can even be granted. An equally important question is the social and esthetic effects of advertising: its deception, manipulation, and bad taste.

The cultural orientation of advertising is attested by the following ditty in the London subway:

> Erminrude, my Erminrude
> My softly cooing dove;
> When shall we be joined
> In everlasting love?
>
> Archibald, dear Archibald,
> I've only this to say;
> Take me first to Barrington's
> And you can name the day.

These goings-on disturb economists. Their discipline is based on the assumption that the economic system is ordered by individual preferences expressed by consumer choices. The consumer is king. He expresses his preferences for products at particular prices. And he gets what he wants. It is therefore embarrassing to adhere to a premise that

---

[19] *The New York Times,* January 25, 1970.

brings one to the conclusion that the welfare of the consumer is promoted by his extinction. The position of some economists on consumer welfare is analogous to that of anthropologists who finding the term race difficult to define have concluded it does not exist. Economists have defined their concept and have placed it in such good use analytically that they are disinclined to yield to the facts. If the assumption of consumer preference were discarded, sophomore economics would come tumbling down.

Advertising has been perfected to the point where it can thwart the application of reason to choice and blur the esthetic sense. That is how it has to be; for if advertising were to accept standards of reason and esthetic judgment, it would no longer be advertising.

> To assert aesthetic goals is also to interfere seriously with the management of the consumer. This, in many of its manifestations, requires dissonance—a jarring of the aesthetic sensibilities. This jarring effect then becomes competitive. The same principles of planned dissonance are even more spectacularly in evidence in the radio and on television. They also characterize the design or packaging of numerous industrial products. An effort is made to bring this dissonance within the ambit of social goals. It is defended interestingly by the contention that it "gives the consumer what he wants." If he did not approve, he would not respond. A man who comes to a full stop because he is hit over the head with an ax proves similarly by his response that it was what he was yearning for.[20]

If the purpose of advertising is to fill the public's need for information, the rational course of action would be to support institutions that would better serve such a function. If the purpose of advertising is to deceive, the public, if it were rational, would demand that the deception be stopped. In either case, there would be no necessity for advertising.

Even the most ardent believer in consumer sovereignty must concede that consumers need a little prodding. However, it must be granted that the level of deception reflects a measure of the public's tolerance for it. If television producers can interrupt a movie with 30 misleading commercials in the course of an hour and get away with it, the phenomenon manifests cultural democracy at work. It is difficult to label one factor cause and the other effect. The deception goes on despite government regulation. Being caught in a lie is solved by moving to another. The technology of deception outpaces the technology of control. This provides continuous employment for the Federal Trade Commission.

The argument, therefore, as to whether producer sovereignty or con-

[20] John K. Galbraith, The Industrial State, *op. cit.*, p. 348–49.

sumer sovereignty prevails in the economy raises a false dilemma. Either concept is too neat, reflecting more the politics of academic debate than the demands of reality. The producer does not enjoy sovereign power like that of a Louis XIV. He must manipulate the consumer and work at it within the context of mass values. He must establish an association between his product and the quest for status and pleasant experience of the consumer. Having done so, he must maintain this association by indicating the deprivation that would ensue if the product were not consumed. He must hit the psyche of the consumer hard and repeatedly until he succeeds in obtaining a Pavlovian response. The task is made easier by the constant pressure of the mass media for goods consumption. A forced choice of producer or consumer sovereignty would obscure this interplay.

The consequences of this producer-consumer relationship are unpredictable. Some marketing campaigns succeed and some fail. And their fate is at times determined by a transitory mood. The mini-maxi revolution is a case in point. Who, for example, would have dared to predict that young women would dress to just below their buttocks on the inside and to their ankles on the outside?

Peter Drucker, a man of considerable reputation, suggests that consumer values and expectations are given and that the role of the firm is to develop a marketing strategy that ties its products to these values and expectations.

> As long as one thinks of "our product," one is still thinking in terms of selling rather than in terms of marketing. What matters is the customer's behavior, his values, and his expectations. And under this aspect, one's own business, let alone one's own product, hardly exists at all. In a true marketing point of view no product and no company is assumed to have the slightest importance to the customer or indeed to be even noticed by him. It is axiomatic that the customer is only interested in the satisfaction he seeks and in his needs and expectations. The customer's question is always, What will this product or this business do for me tomorrow?
>
> It is for instance not true that the American automobile industry has not been safety-conscious. On the contrary it pioneered in safe-driving instruction and in the design of safe highways. It did a great deal to reduce the frequency of accidents—and with considerable success. What it is penalized for today, however, is its failure to make an accident itself less dangerous. Yet when the manufacturers tried to introduce safety-engineered cars (as Ford did in the early fifties) the public refused to buy them.[21]

21 Peter F. Drucker, *The Age of Discontinuity*, New York: Harper and Row, 1968.

Mr. Drucker errs in his assumption that consumer values are given. He also seems to miss the point on the so-called safety-engineered cars. After 50 years of brainwashing, the rejection was inevitable. The relative role of producer and consumer in committing the consumer to a choice varies with the product. Consumer sovereignty is essentially accurate in describing the purchase of a bunch of carrots and less adequate in interpreting the sale of an automobile.[22]

A related question has to do with the right of minorities in consumer preferences. In a society of mass markets, votes stated through expression of consumer preferences differ in importance. An overwhelming vote for a particular kind of product means the minority cannot acquire a preferred variation of that product. If a majority of car buyers can be brainwashed into accepting autos without bumpers, a minority cannot effectively demand such protection. Minorities take the consequences arising from majority choice. In a figurative sense, the alternative the minority has is to turn off the television set.

Time is likely to affect the relative importance of producer and consumer sovereignty. Children of the *nouveaux riches* may turn out to be more sophisticated than their parents. Through greater discernment, consumer sovereignty may burst forth triumphant.[23]

But the corporation is not attuned organizationally to the pursuit of fine choices. Departmentalization of functions makes such a possibility difficult. One is reminded of the efforts of oil firms to do something about their hideous gasoline stations. Their architecture departments put up something reasonably tolerable, which can be called oil-gothic. Then the mass marketeers bring in their piles of oil cans, tires, flags, and signs to destroy the original feeble intention. In Europe it is difficult to see a gas station; but its managers somehow make a living.

The question of firm and social worth is not clarified by the levity

[22] The Marshallian concept of demand, on whose foundation economics rests, is carrot-oriented. The automobile offers a complex bundle of satisfactions compared to carrots. Lawrence Abbott has attempted to revise the theory of the firm to allow for this evolution of consumer products. Nevertheless, it is a tribute to the tenacity of the profession that Marshall, and also Hicks, are more revered for the elegance of their analysis than is Abbott for his realism.

[23] The success of the patent medicine industry in the bamboozlement of the public is attested by a Food and Drug Administration report (A Study of Health Practices and Opinions, 1972) indicating a majority of Americans believes a daily diet of vitamins and minerals is indispensable to health, that pain remedies are effective, and that missing a daily bowel movement is courting disaster. This brainwashing suggests a law of health care: the amount of money needed to maintain health is a function of the amount of money available. The phenomenal growth in the past two decades of patent medicines without efficient systems of social control has created a host of new side effects whose toxicity is imprecisely known. The growth has also diverted research away from discovery of cures to relief of symptoms.

with which economics treats values implicit in economic theory. Conservative economists assert that economic generalizations are descriptive rather than normative, describing activities that ensue in response to producers giving what the consumer wants. Radical economists claim that producers do seek to control values. Consequently, by pleading neutrality in values, economists sanction those of the producer. Moreover, state the radicals, concepts in economics are loaded with implications of what *ought to be*, such as the gross national product, income distribution, and monopoly. Accordingly, the levity with which economics plants social values into the society without consciously tipping its hand tends to avoid a serious debate on norms.

Economic institutions develop out of notions of what is socially decent and what is not. The power of producers is circumscribed by what human reason decides to be rights of men not to be violated by the pursuit of economic gain. Society imposes restraints on producers consistent with its ideas as to what constitutes a worthy social objective. But men disagree as to what comprises a worthy social objective, a goal certainly not as precise as the criterion of profit making. In consequence, the restraints imposed on firms appear to be a hodge-podge of improvisation that defies theorization. Regardless of such difficulty, however, the idea that economic activity is supposed to serve man and not just the producer is imbedded in the human conscience. Economic activity does not escape for too long the dictum of what it ought to be. And what ought to be often emerges from the vision of a better man rather than from the dictate of giving power its just due.

Therefore, the question is actually not whether firms should have a social conscience. Society long ago decided that it stands ready to scrutinize economic activity and producers have always sought to mold a social image acceptable to the society and consonant with their interests. Corporations shift the deployment of their resources so as to acquire a more acceptable image when society threatens their profits if they fail to do so. The platitude of service to the community becomes converted into specific acts when a particular program becomes good business. The corporation may have to do something socially worthy to keep the public off its back. A firm may adopt a program with a specific social goal either because the community demands it or because it is so structured as to derive income from the program. Self-interest is continually the motive, its manifestation changing with the expectations of society.

Defense firms, particularly those in big cities, are susceptible to such social pressures. A defense corporation with a wide assortment of skills is susceptible to public prodding to accept a social role such as the up-grading of the hard-core unemployed, particularly if the plant is surrounded by black communities. A firm heavily committed to public markets is a prime source of social production which need not be confined to the making of arms. Thus, General Electric Company heavily supports Negro uplift training and employment programs in its urban communities. Smith, Kline and French adopts a program of housing rehabilitation as the slums move in its direction. RCA has a department of social problems. Insurance firms in city cores commit themselves to urban housing. And firms with a local demand for their products such as supermarkets, oil companies, and banks have active Negro employment programs of enlightened self-interest.

The new urban affairs departments in such firms have stature. Their administrators report to a vice president or the chief executive. Programs are commonly directed toward the community surrounding the corporation, including hard-core unemployment, black entrepreneurship, assistance to public educational systems, institutions of higher learning, and local government. Accordingly, social consciousness is not just a pious expression but becomes structured into the organization and enters into the competition of resources and points of view.

Thus, newly emerging forces tend to convert firms sensitive to public pressures into social corporations. Defense plants faced with declining arms contracts are amenable to such a conversion. The urban revolution forces community-oriented corporations to adopt programs and structures that are likely to have a profound effect on their motivations These two types of firms may be the vanguard of the social corporation of the future. This evolution arises not out of a will by managers and technicians to be more social minded but out of external environmental challenges. The soul food that corporations ingest is a forced feeding.

There are other avenues by which corporations may acquire a greater social conscience. Two merit discussion before concluding this section.

The rising army of corporate technicians, including scientists, social scientists, accountants, and mathematicians, have led some individuals to think that as specialists they will produce a greater corporate social mindedness. These persons will somehow fire their corporations with intellectuality that will make the corporations look to the consumer with an eye toward his redemption. But this benign attitude does not seem to take off. These corporate intellectuals perform specialized activities that do not employ their entire personalities. They pursue their social mindedness outside the firm. After the catharsis, assisted at times by head shrinkers and sundry mind blowers, they go back to their desks and dutifully make their specialist contributions to the corporate machine. If they carried their social awareness into the firm, they would get fired.

Large scale profit making necessitates a manipulation that renders the consumer passive. The outstanding specialists in the art of manipulating the consumer are from the ranks of the most educated. Madison Avenue is loaded with intellectuals. We have not even begun to think what institutions can contain this impact on the individual.

Corporations do not voluntarily assume the redemption of the individual. No auto company came out to stop pollution voluntarily. Firms do not concern themselves with the social diseconomies they create unless required to do so. No firm has ever embarked on a program to raise perceptions. The movie industry cannot make a profit by focusing on the love inducing effects of sexuality. The money is in expressing sex in a context of brutality. So the industry follows suit. The same money-making motive is reducing the performing arts to the uninhibited babbling of neurotics, preferably nude. Firms are constrained to create a mass culture serving their pecuniary interests. And highly educated specialists make it easier to pursue this goal more effectively.[24]

Another avenue to social consciousness on the part of the corporation is more effective control by regulatory agencies of the quality of a product and the claims made for it. But the history of such agencies shows that they are easily subverted by the corporation they are supposed to control. A running battle has taken place for decades between corporations out to weaken initial legislation and its subsequent administration and the new round of legislators out to reinforce the constantly opening dikes. The resources available to protect the consumer are considerably less than the resources of corporations to see that such protection does not damage their interests. An immediate effect of regulatory law is the employment of corporate lawyers to subvert it. Their talents are much greater than those hired by the government to oversee them. Rather quickly, the government lawyers acquire habits of mind of the counterparts they are supposed to control. In some instances, the government agency becomes a training ground for employees of the firm that is being regulated. Hope ever springing eternal, new proposals are constantly brought forth which are designed to protect the consumer. But, in the case of advertising, the art of deception outpaces the ability

24 I am reminded of a large electronics corporation based in Philadelphia with a vice president who established a reputation for the promotion of social causes in the community. He was elected to the boards of many prestigious civic organizations. Subsequently, the firm was bought up by another firm and the person with the power in the parent company to claim his job did so. The corporation sacked the executive with the social conscience.

of control. A more effective means of control would be simply to pass a law making advertising agencies liable to individuals for their lies and injury.

OTHER QUASI-PUBLIC BLOCS

The influence of farm groups and foundations on the economy is of more than passing importance. These two political economic blocs are at different periods of transition in their relationship with the government. The farm blocs, after their rise in power in the 1920's, have become closely tied to the maintenance of old-line government policies. The foundations presently play the part of the reluctant bride. The government is likely to force a closer relationship not only with itself, but between the foundations themselves, as they seek to improve their bargaining position over the terms of a marriage that seems inevitable.

As stated, the farm organizations are no longer important as instruments of structural change in the economy. Their prominence now lies in their ability to require government to serve their interests and to resist in organized fashion any serious onslaught on farm subsidies. This line of defense depends for its strength on the many interest groups maintaining a common front as threats to their position mount. The principal farm groups are The American Farm Bureau Federation, the biggest, with a claimed membership of 800 thousand individuals; and the National Farmers Union, with a claimed affiliation of 300 thousand families.[25] As these farm organizations reap the advantages of a favored position in the mercantilist state, they pronounce their litany on the blessing of private initiative and family farming. The Farm Bureau is, in fact, much more than just an agricultural organization. Its bureaucrats administer an empire of 92 insurance firms with assets of over a billion dollars and a variety of industrial firms. The Bureau describes itself as the agricultural voice of America in public affairs. Many of its affiliates have a rightist political orientation. John Birch Society members are frequent speakers at their meetings. While Farm Bureau bureaucrats lament the centralization of power in the United States, they do not appear to be concerned with the concentration of thier own empire or their favored relationship with the state.

In 1950, when twenty million persons lived on farms, the United States Department of Agriculture had a budget of $2.3 billion in current dollars. Twenty years later, with half the farm population, appropriations increased to $7.4 billion. About half the money represents subsidy

---

[25] Dale E. Hathaway. *Government and Agriculture*, New York: Macmillan, 1963, pp. 221, 227, 230.

payments. Students of agriculture judge that a third of these payments can be employed in rural development without seriously affecting farm output. But the rural poor do not have the political power of well-to-do farmers under the tutelage of Southern legislators; a senator in one year alone drew a nifty $150,000 from the give-away program.[26] The federal agricultural budget accrues to a declining number of persons as large-scale corporations push individual proprietors out of business.

Farm history affords a vivid example of how the state converts the more tractable elements of a particular sector into part of the system and relegates the remainder to sub-castes either left to their own devices or placed on an eleemosynary relationship with the state. The conversion of farming into a state directed economy drove some 95 percent of Negroes in agriculture off the farms and left those who remained in destitution. Doubtlessly, the decay of the cities issues substantially from the rural exodus caused by government farm policy.

Foundations emerged out of philanthropic organizations working quietly in the poverty vineyards. Today, few give money to charity. Rich people do by running Balls. Foundation funds go into support of the social sciences, and education; they are also used to influence foreign policy. Foundation money controls the use of intellectual talent and the manner in which knowledge is developed and used. Some foundations are the creation of imaginative lawyers seeking ways to lower tax payments. Along this line, oil interests show a fertile imagination.[27] It is estimated that these shadow foundations avoid a total of $100 million annually in federal income tax.[28] Foundations afford the rich control, both over the amount of their money that is taxed and the social pur-

26 *The New York Times*, April 5, 1970.
27 The press reports that John B. Connally Jr., former governor of Texas and Secretary of the Treasury in the Nixon administration, received deferred payments in the amount of $750,000 as executor of the Sid W. Richardson Foundation, an organization with large oil and gas holdings. Mr. Connally received $575,000 of the total while governor of the state of Texas. Under the Texas constitution, a governor is prohibited from receiving compensation for services performed in office. Mr. Connally contended, after the newspaper disclosure, that the services were performed before he was governor. The payments were disclosed by *The New York Times* in 1971 when the former governor was nominated for the federal government post. His press secretary during his governorship, because of rumors about the payments, announced that Connally had not performed services or received compensation during his term of office. The newspaper also indicates that Boys Incorporated of America, an organization of which Connally was director, comprised a shell created as part of a tax avoidance scheme for Richardson interests' ownership of a race track in California. The United States Senate confirmed his appointment as Secretary of the Treasury without a dissenting vote. A senator critical of the payments dropped his opposition to the nomination stating no clear legal grounds existed for challenging the nomination. (*The New York Times*, January 31st and February 8th, 1971.)
28 *The New York Times*, November 24, 1969.

poses into which income is directed. They comprise private governments not beholden to a public will.

The number of foundations and their assets have risen considerably
in recent years. The 1967 *Foundation Directory* listed assets of $19.2
billion with annual grants of $1.2 billion. In the 2-year period 1968–69,
the number of foundations according to *The New York Times* rose by
2,000. Much of the increase is attributed to the use of foundations as
tax shelters. The 1971 edition of the same directory reports 26,000
active foundations with 5,454 having assets of $500,000 or more. Total
assets are estimated at $25.2 billion. The three biggest ones are Ford,
Lilly Endowment, and Rockefeller.[29]

To obtain a share of foundation funds, grantsmanship in the universities is an art of no mean proportion. Few institutions of higher
learning would unleash their researchers without first consulting their
public relations experts. Institutions have specialists whose sole function
is to develop research proposals attractive to foundation managers. A
proposal leaving an institution of higher learning becomes a thing of
beauty and a joy forever. Professors are kept tethered close to the foundation grab bag, moving in their careers from one grant to the next.
Administrators judge them by the amount of money they bring into university coffers. The voice of the university is that of those who achieve
the greatest success in grantsmanship.

As government grants have become available for research in medicine
and the physical sciences, foundations have deployed their funds in the
social and behavioral sciences. The foundation sponsored research is
notable for its atomistic blandness. It is difficult to find in the formidable pile of such inquiries pieces on how the system works or proposals
for radical reform. The degree to which inquiries on social innovation
are eschewed is extraordinary. If Santayana's traveler were to come to
the United States in search of a volume on how the American economy
operates, what is there to give him? The foundation output would probably confuse him.

Foundations have relatively less influence in the national legislature
than do industrial firms. They do not supply the same money and skills
needed for the maintenance of the posture of the government. The fact
that many of its directors are also board members of industrial firms
and banks accounts in no small part for the little political influence that
they do have. Their most serious political trial came in 1969. In that
year, the House of Representatives passed a highly restrictive bill se-

[29] *Foundation Directory* (3rd edition), New York: Russel Sage Foundation,
1967; *Foundation Directory* (4th edition), New York: Columbia University Press,
1971; *The New York Times*, April 8, 1969.

verely limiting the life of foundations, defining their purposes, and controlling their public policies. After hastily organizing themselves into a union, the foundations succeeded in easing greatly the restrictions in the final law. The Congress imposed on the foundations a 4 percent tax on annual investment income, annual reports, divestiture of excess holdings in business, and a prohibition on the use of foundation money to influence legislation. To a considerable degree, the impact of these restrictions rests on the capacity of foundation lawyers to make them bland.

This troublesome alignment with the state should not obscure the fact that foundations have many characteristics in common with other elements of the system. Their representatives are a microcosm of the system's power elite. As a segment of the governing elites, foundations are major controllers of talent and funds that shape public policies without the full participation and knowledge of the governed. Like other elements of the system, such as the firm and the university, they resist full accountability and disclosure. The foundations are an integral part of the pussy-in-the-corner games that managers play. John Foster Dulles and Dean Rusk moved from the presidency of the Rockefeller Foundation to the post of Secretary of State. McGeorge Bundy moved from academe to the White House staff, to the Ford Foundation presidency. Shepard Stone shuffled from director of the International Affairs Department of the Ford Foundation to the presidency of the International Association for Cultural Freedom, an organization which under its prior name, the Congress for Cultural Freedom, received funds *sub rosa* from the United States Central Intelligence Agency. As the price for respectability is resolved, the foundations are likely to emerge as one of the authoritarian sub-governments that administer the system.

In their perceptive book, *The New Society,* Joseph Bensman and Arthur J. Vidich comment as follows on the role of foundations in influencing public policy:

Compared with other organizations engaged in the manufacturing of opinion, the economic resources of the foundations are great. When they wish to do so, they invest their money in any area they regard as "fruitful." They understand that their "investments" may produce important ideological and tangible returns. A half-million or million dollar investment in a position paper, a panel report, a "study," or "special report" may have the importance of a policy paper from a major, and certainly a minor, government. The investment not only supports the intellectuals who do the work but may result in a marketable idea. Reports, studies, and monographs resulting from these investments may focus public opinion on a given issue and suggest guidelines for action. Edited, censored, and purified for public consumption, the final report is only a lure to an undetermined constituency which, depending on other factors, may or may not respond. But the point is that the very *process* of developing such studies and reports in itself creates opinions, issues, and policy positions.[30]

In the ranks of the foundations, the Ford Foundation is a barony of no mean proportion. Since its inception in 1936, the Ford give-away of over $3 billion has supported such causes as Negro voter registration, open housing, economic development, reconstruction of city administrations, structural changes in the school system, and the feeding and care of intellectuals forced into unemployment by the sudden death of Senator Robert F. Kennedy. Its $3 billion in investments disgorge an annual effluence of money which its managers bestow on those meeting standards propounded and interpreted by them. In effect, the Ford Foundation operates as a self-perpetuating government unencumbered by an electorate that can throw its managers out of office.

CONCLUSIONS

According to the official truths disseminated by the system, the American economy comprises many enterprises competing in labor, product, and capital markets for resources and producing goods whose demand is expressed in individual preferences in competitive consumer markets. Each year, as the level of consumption rises, so does consumer welfare. This annual progress is measured by the rise in the gross national product.

In reality, however, the competitive economy of consumer preferences no longer exists. A considerable amount of the product results from bilateral relationships between government and industrial firms. Another sizable portion comes out of research and development arrangements made by government with firms and universities. A third hefty segment derives from the allocation of funds by foundations that in effect amount to investment in future production activity. And a formidable quantity derives from the successful manipulation of the consumer's psyche by industrial firms. Even in farming, the amounts and kind of output are established by government policies. The activities of consumers become less those of stating preferences and more those of protecting themselves from the choices planned by others.

By establishing links with other corporations and government, firms have reduced market uncertainties and gained thereby the ability to make plans that terminate on target. Trade unions, through their wage and labor policies assist in concentrating production in large firms and

[30] Joseph Bensman & Arthur J. Vidich. *The New American Society*, Chicago: Quadrangle Books, 1971, p. 194.

in structuring a product that derives from defense expenditures. There has issued thereby a system comprising big firms and government that effectively promote their interests through planning.

Such is not to say that on the criterion of consumption the big firms have not delivered. They have—to the middle class. A rash of books has come into the market suggesting how the wicked corporations restrict consumption through their pricing and market policies. This allegation runs in the face of a consumption explosion unprecedented in the world. It misses the issue by a wide mark. The issue is how to contain private middle-class consumption, how to direct consumption into social production, how to improve the quality of existing products, how to enter all the cost of the product into its price, how to control the firm's cultural power. Bigness cannot be criticized on the basis of consumption. If, instead of the quasi-monopolies, industries comprising many small firms had evolved, their products would not have achieved the level of diffusion existing today.

The managers of corporations are respectable citizens. To be sure, they have ravaged the land, polluted the waters, bulldozed the poor away from their duchies, institutionalized the creation of weapons of mass destruction, and ruined the lives of millions with their products. But they are law abiding. They manage what are in effect public organizations under obsolete laws. Their firms are public organizations in their dependence on government to underwrite their technology and sales and in their impact on society and the environment. But the public is not represented on their boards.

Government bestows its blessing on these managers through the use of old-time rhetoric:

> The American economy has been steadily on the march in the 1960's. It has bestowed great blessings of abundance on the vast majority of Americans in all walks of life.
> Our progress did not just happen. It was created by American labor and business in effective partnership with government.[31]

Consequently, as their physical and social environment disintegrates, Americans make steady progress. And this they do in a partnership of government, business, and labor, as the President of the United States says. The voices that question his assumptions are feeble cries in the wilderness. But this is not new. Much of secular life is based on obsolete faith and not reason. It provides man with verve in an existence that otherwise might degenerate into utter boredom.

[31] From the text of the President's *Economic Report to Congress*, January, 1970.

The GNP is a tool that perpetuates the myth of progress. It is actually a tabulation of activities swollen by efforts of individuals trying to protect themselves from the activities of the system or recuperating from their consumption. It is bloated by failures in the promotion of human welfare. If an accounting system of human welfare were devised, it may indicate that the United States moves backward as the GNP rises. Yet, we have not even begun to think seriously about the problem of allocating resources when the amounts and kind of consumption as stated by so-called consumer preferences are increasingly inconsistent with human welfare. We use concepts that do not fit the time. The distinction, for example, implied in the terms "private sector" and "public sector" is nonexistent. The terms "state economy" and "competitive economy" may be more appropriate. General Motors forms part of the one. Children selling lemonade comprise part of the other. From firm to national tabulations, society should require an accounting that more accurately describes the economy and tabulates all the costs of doing business.

The giant corporations with operations in different countries of the world pose even greater problems of social control. Multinational firms serve as funnels for the fast transmission of the technology and culture of one country to another. They seem destined to dominate the world economy by the end of the century. They are in effect international governments operating under separate national governments with a primary loyalty, if any, to their nation of origin. Here, too, little serious thought has been given to means of their control.

Thus, the traditional economic criteria for judging the performance of firms—output, prices, and efficiency—are deficient. Bigness, *per se,* is bad; social and esthetic criteria must be taken into account. Our laws, including the anti-trust statutes, are outmoded because they rest on criteria that are no longer relevant. Nevertheless, regardless of foreseeable institutional changes, the fundamental problem of exploitation is likely to persist. By placing events within the long sweep of history, we can observe how society constantly generates pressures against the exploitation of men by other men. But the process appears without end. So long as there are differences in intelligence and so long as these differences are used to gain personal advantage, such exploitation will continue.

11

Games Universities Play

*I do not believe that there is a country
in the world where, in proportion to the
population, there are so few ignorant,
and at the same time, so few learned individuals.*

Tocqueville

The university emerged in the United States as a private corporation endowed with legal rights, in which the relationship between trustees and faculties was that of employers and employees. With the passing of time, university administration was taken over by scholars and social reformers and the university became a center of independent intellectual inquiry and dissent. In World War II, university professors were hired by government to develop technology for use in the execution of conflict. With that war's end, industry as well as government sought the services of professors to an ever-increasing degree.

With bulging briefcases, the professors went out to sell efficiency to the managers of the system. They became brokers for university administrators, bringing in grants, contracts, and good will, and were rewarded in money and prestige. Universities were then taken over by managers with a financial outlook, more concerned with keeping the faculty and students in line than with sharing administrative responsibilities. A primary motivation of these managers was to enter the upper middle class elite that controls the disbursement of money in the society. This ambition for status fostered the selection of business types for university boards of trustees. As this shift occurred, undergraduate students were turned over to young teachers of little experience; the professors, the

257

former critics of government and industry, were too busy acting as consultants. In fact, some were preoccupied with setting up their own firms in the pursuit of profits. Thus, the university evolved as the servant of power in society and the focal point of student protest.

These tendencies and their implications are the subject of this chapter. It will demonstrate how, because of the administrator's desire to make it financially successful and the professor's desire for wealth and power, the university has become an adjunct of the governmental and corporate parts of the system. Instead of being neutral havens for the pursuit of truth, universities are the scene of conflict between system and unsystem. As a segment of the knowledge industry, they mirror the needs of business and government and acquire characteristics of the system of which they are a part.[1] They often do not take the purposes of undergraduate education seriously, and treat with levity the problem of how to educate young men and women. They graduate a substantial number of self-seeking, uncivil, and arrogant nincompoops, young people who are of little worth to themselves and to their fellow men. Many reasons exist for this bad product; for much of it, universities are doubtlessly not responsible. But what is significant is that university management treats these bores so gingerly; it is probably impossible to find an affirmation by a university president stating on record what is good about college students and what is bad about them. The best hope for a remedy to this situation lies with a minority of students and professors; for the majority of students are ill-equipped to deal with the problem and many professors are demoralized.

In proposing this thesis, we concede at the outset that toilers in the university, as in institutions generally, cover a wide range of quality. They run the gamut from the ignorant and self-seeking to the brilliant and generous. Indeed, the university, more than other organizations, has a substantial number of men of insight and empathy. Nevertheless, the modern university evidences ruinous tendencies; it is the purpose of this chapter to discuss these propensities. Our observations relate principally to events in the turbulent decade beginning in 1960, a period which witnessed almost a doubling of college enrollments and a change in the ethnic and intellectual composition of students.

THE ADMINISTRATORS

The overriding responsibility of trustees of an institution of higher learning is to maintain the financial viability of the institution. With the

[1] In an advertisement of a book on marijuana (*The New York Review,* June 3, 1971), the Harvard University Press has a full page picture of a young girl over a caption that states that the work presents, in addition to other enlightenment, the constructive use of grass.

encouragement of their executive officer, many boards of trustees have shifted this responsibility onto the professor by making him a salesman of sponsored research. The professor who brings in money is rewarded; the one who does not is not. The role of the university has thus been changed profoundly.

The typical trustee at an institution of higher learning is a business executive making a yearly income exceeding $30,000. Over two-thirds of these executives advocate a screening process for campus speakers. Thirty-eight percent agree that it is reasonable to require loyalty oaths of faculty. Twenty percent disagree that faculty members have the right of free expression of opinions. Most of the trustees from business believe that running a university is like operating a business. A majority take strong exception to the idea that the faculty and student should be given greater decision making powers.[2]

In Philadelphia, the chairman of the board of trustees of a university responded to the idea of shared decision making as follows:

> The trustees constitute the governing board and are entrusted with the conduct and supervision of the affairs of the corporation, having power to make all needful and lawful rules and regulations for the administration of the Institute. The President of the Institute is the chief administrative officer. In his person we have an appropriate head of the faculty since in fact he is also a teaching member of that body. In such context, he represents the faculty in the Board of Trustees. With that exception, we believe in the principle that in an administered institution, as compared to a political organization, those who govern and those who are governed should be separate and not commingled.[3]

These attitudes, of course, vary with the particular university. It is probably fair to say, however, that with the exception of a small number of outstanding universities, these ideas are typical of those held by trustees of most institutions of higher learning. One could also say that university trustees are likely to go down as wise governors by refraining from uttering such myth.

Decisions of college administrators in top echelons reflect a variety of impulses: a desire to create a favorable impression, as witness their concern over the anti-establishment student spoiling their image, an inclination to give power its just due, and a lack of courage under tension. Often, their choices are more the consequence of fear than they are of reason. In short, the motives of many university administrators have little to do with the needs of a scholarly community and the product

2 Morton Kauk. "The College Trustee—Past, Present & Future," Vol. 40, *Journal of Higher Education*, June 1969, pp. 430–442.
3 From a statement to the Philadelphia Commission on Higher Education.

it is supposed to be producing. They mirror the business values of the society. Administrators can be brutal when they think they can get away with it and they rely on the good will and timidity of professors. Even in the case of administrators who encourage the involvement of undergraduate students in governing the university, it is prudent to assume that they are doing so only for purposes of window dressing. Administrators bestow respectability on the behavior of student barbarians when it is good politics to do so. An educator is a man of warmth, of courage, of integrity, and of empathy for the sensitivities of college faculties and students. Few university managers fit this description.

Because of this style of university management, honorable decisions may be foreclosed unless the faculty maintains a constant vigilance. It may be advisable for faculties to borrow an old British military slogan: *Nil Ab Illegitimatis Carborundum*.[4] Acting alone, the administrator often subordinates education to the needs of power. He prefers dissimulation and professors who act as his court jesters. He prefers the adoption of ill-conceived educational schemes to the pursuit of educational ideals; imagery to fact. Thus, it can often happen that a handful of undergraduate blacks, as self-appointed saviors of the black race, can huff and puff and blow the house down. His exalted position contrasts with that of his European counterparts. There the position is often rotated among professors and considered a notch above that of the institution's chief janitor. The rector's modest standing discourages dreams of grandeur.

Prominent university administrators have addressed themselves to the issue of university management. Jacques Barzun, formerly of Columbia University and of liberal arts background, asserts that the university has become a public utility. He states that the tendency of professors to sell their talents to government and industry has had the effect of developing highly specialized courses that have little to do with education.[5]

Clark Kerr, former president of the University of California, criticizes those who, like Barzun, decry the commitment to provide service. As the deposed president of an outstanding university, Mr. Kerr commands serious attention. Writing a year before the beginning of the student movement in 1964 on his own campus, Kerr minimizes factors which were to bring about the disruptions that burst forth shortly thereafter. He only hints at the discontent of undergraduates and does even less on the issue of the community versus the university.

---

4 Roughly translated: Don't let the bastards grind you down.
5 For an analysis of his thesis, see Jacques Barzun, *The American University: How it Runs Where it is Going,* New York: Harper and Row, 1969.

In *The Uses of the University,* Kerr writes as follows: [6]

Federal research aid to universities has greatly assisted the universities themselves. The nation is stronger. The leading universities are stronger.

He indicates his optimism about the wedding of government and industry:

The university has been embraced and led down the garden path by its environmental suitors; it has been so attractive and so accommodating; who could resist it and why would it, in turn, want to resist?

Kerr asserts that the university and segments of industry are becoming more alike as the university becomes tied into the world of work. The two worlds are merging physically and psychologically. He predicts an incipient minor revolt against the faculty. What has happened, however, is a revolt against administrators, with faculty support.

Mr. Kerr states that the educational system of America, good as it is, is in the most trouble, and thus in the greatest need of federal help, at its bottom and at its top. By the bottom he means dropouts, and by the top, research and training in engineering, science, mathematics, teaching, and medicine. He finds Mr. McGeorge Bundy, an architect of the Vietnam war, inimitable and eloquent. In Kerr's concept of the university as a marriage with industry and government, the undergraduate student is a mildly complaining voice.

With the advantage of hindsight, Yale University President Kingman Brewster offers the view that the restlessness comes from students in school because of parental compulsion and a society that requires a college degree for an occupational career. He states:

My elders and betters, my peers and contemporaries are backed to the wall, then driven up the wall, eventually driven over it, by students who are often fundamentally anti-intellectual, who are impatient with learning and research; who think there are social ends other than the advancement of learning which a university should serve; and who see no reason why the majority vote of students should not dictate what those ends are and how they should be pursued.[7]

The prevailing business posture of university administrators generates hostile reaction from a minority of students and faculty who seek to shift the institutions's course. For example, some students and faculty seek to apply social criteria to the institutions's investment portfolio.

[6] Clark Kerr. *The Uses of the University,* New York: Harper and Row, 1963, pp. 22, 68–69, 76, 83, 104, 122.
[7] Quoted by *The New York Times,* News of the Week, December 14, 1969. Mr. Brewster, with his combination of courage, intellectuality, ability to communicate, and competence to negotiate under pressure, is a rare phenomenon among university presidents.

They demand that the corporation in which the university has an investment should fulfill its social obligations. A judgment on an investment, they assert, should be made on the basis of social as well as income-producing criteria. Some go further to say the university should seek to control corporate boards of directors by voting its stock. Since what comprises a corporate discharge of social responsibility is vague, the issue could easily lead to polarization in the academic community.

In placing the university at the disposal of government and industry, the administrators have produced a drastic change in its financial structure, a change that makes it sensitive to the contributions of government and industry and to fluctuations in the economy. The university crisis attending the 1970–1971 recession underscores how such financing rests on a rope of sand. This sensitivity to uncontrollable money flows generates hostile reactions from students and faculty as shifts in income create pressures for retrenchment. Combined with the timidity of professors, the stress taxes the ability of faculty to define its role. Faculty evaluation by administrators often amounts to a unilateral determination of alleged deficiencies produced to a substantial extent by their management and by their lack of candor on policy matters. The faculty's salvation lies in organizing against the administrators, a solution that creates disadvantages to the faculty itself. Replacing the collegiate system of decision making with collective bargaining is likely to differentiate management from labor roles, structure adversary positions, raise to faculty leadership the most insecure, and diminish creativity.

THE PROFESSORS

There are some half million college and university professors in the United States, many of whom represent the top quality brain power in the economy. Their entrepreneurial activity is confined mostly to those teaching business, social and behavioral science, history, law, engineering, and physical science. This group, some 200,000 persons, represents a potential for social innovation; a potential not realized because they are too busy as entrepreneurs, propagandists, lobbyists, efficiency experts, and pursuers of sponsored contracts for their respective institutions. A significant portion of the annual ten billion dollars of revenue going to universities depends on their deft footwork. If they were suddenly to revert to the traditional role of the professor, the effect on the university would be disastrous—or a great service—depending on one's point of view.

For money and prestige, professors hire themselves out to perform secret work in improving the art of warfare and in subverting the aspirations of foreign populations by advising on how to keep tyrannical governments in power. In an indicative incident, history professor Arthur Schlesinger granted that he had lied to the press in the Cuban invasion fiasco and that he did this in the national interest as defined by government officials including himself. Equally indicative of contemporary society is the fact that Schlesinger was offered a chair at the City University of New York, an appointment which caused hardly a ripple in the academic community. In short, the national government uses deception as a *modus operandi* and draws upon excellent university talent to collaborate in its chicanery. And this role is underwritten by university administrators more concerned with problems of finance and image making than with fine points of principle.

Professors cannot possibly serve their role of objective analysis over matters on which they have an outside financial interest. It is difficult, for example, to speak objectively about advertising when one is making money in the advertising business. University of Chicago Professor Yale Brozen in a widely quoted speech attacked actions of the Federal Trade Commission on advertising practices of a subsidiary of ITT. It was later revealed that Professor Brozen was a paid consultant of the firm.[8] It is common practice for attorneys to bar themselves from proceedings in which they have pecuniary interests. If university teaching is to be a profession, the same rule should apply to professors.

With the tacit approval of administrators, the impulse of university professors is no longer truth or creation. Instead, it lies in the application of a specialized body of skills in the service of existing institutions and being rewarded for so doing in money and prestige. Government and industry provide such opportunities. After an enormous effort in teaching and research in the social sciences, these disciplines have developed not social scientists but advocates and technicians. No effort of consequence exists that speculates on what man can be and what social innovation is required to promote such an ideal. Social scientists busily teaching and applying techniques have little time for social creation.

The absentee professor and the stay-at-home professor are distinct breeds. The style of the first is not too different from that of managers generally. Absentees view their confrères who do not market their services as fuzzy-minded and unrealistic. The stay-on-campus set view consultants as violators of academic ideals. Each thus deprecates the attitude of the other. The establishment professor works with the dominant values of the society and annoys his colleagues by so doing. He hires himself out to construct options palatable to the princes, options

8 *The New York Times,* April 14, 1972.

which may not be what the home bodies feel to be decent. Stay-at-homes believe they possess the superior truth but not the power to implement their revelation. Some of the more clever stay-at-homes have lucrative rackets going, including encounter sessions and writing books calculated to gain a wide market. Absentees may have misgivings about the society, but they would rather not talk for the record; non-consultants view their university salary and tenure as guarantees of freedom of thought and expression. Absentees, at a higher university salary because administrators judge them to be more productive, look upon their compensation as a minimum to be supplemented by outside employment. In the outer society beyond the university, absentees acquire the reputation of practical men and non-consultants, of eccentrics and subverters of youth. Administrators are not insensitive to the outside following absentees command.

Radical professors are an extraordinary species of stay-at-homes. Their claim to being radical does not derive from a capacity to get to the root of matters but from their way-out behavior. They fall into 3 general categories: playmates, cop-outs, and revolutionaries. Playmates are disposed to provide students with any service they desire. Cop-outs see their mission as developing a new life style principally by the blowing of the senses. Revolutionaries seek to promote political change by maintaining the morale of students at the firing line. Some radical professors of exceptional talent can legitimately claim to fall into all 3 of the sub-categories.

Actually, radical professors are not teachers. They see the truth in terms of the prevailing student wind. They rarely exert an influence on the student radicals to whom they pander. They reject the rigors of reason as a tool of inquiry. They have a simplistic monolithic view of the system either because they do not give a damn about studying it seriously, because they are rejected by it, or because they are incompetent as observers. Most of them have never analyzed a complex situation and made a decision whose consequences may prove disastrous. If a revolutionary professor were handed a loaded rifle, he would probably faint. Reality eludes the radicals because they are caught in the grip of working out their own neuroticisms. They use students as props for their own not fully disclosed needs. They are precisely the opposite of what the university needs acutely: men who can think. If their numbers increase, they are likely to destroy the university. The playmates would convert the institution into a nursery; the cop-outs, into a ritual of self-destruction; and the revolutionaries, into a political club.

The task of professors with a demonstrated competence in teaching, research, and innovation is clear: they must throw out both absentees and radicals—the one to find employment directly in the system and the other to seek their transfiguration without benefit of tenure. Then they must teach university managers what a university is.

Because they feed and govern the university, businessmen tend to control what professors teach and investigate. The managers use the honorary degree to mosey up to this power. In a story told about such a practice, a college president passed the word he would give one to an alumnus in return for a substantial contribution to the alumni fund. The alumnus got the word back he would prefer his horse getting the degree. Perplexed, but undaunted, the president acquiesced. On commencement day, the alumnus led his nag up the stage and accepted in its behalf, stating it was the first time a whole horse instead of part of one had received an honorary degree.

The absentee professor using his university post as a lucrative base of operations is found everywhere in government: in the Department of Defense playing war games; in the White House cloaking the power decisions of the president with intellectual respectability; in the State Department providing the rationale for the use of the military. He represents the new generation of college professor, the moonlighter *par excellence*. The absentee professor surrenders his integrity for an upper middle class salary. His predecessor was the critic of the system, but the new consulting generation is not inclined to bite the hand that feeds it. The function of its members is to advise and not to criticize the system. Government and industry thus neutralize the university as a source of social innovation; students react by abandoning all three.

As research money in the defense establishment becomes scarce and less respectable, the professor entrepreneurs turn their attention to the city as a source of revenue. They talk of creating a renaissance in the city by transferring technology to urban problems. Thus unfolds the second act of the same play—of professors providing technical elitism to the power structure for solutions designed to perpetuate their joint interests.

The government can always shop around successfully for the absentee professor who would support its point of view. Thus, when the President of the United States required giving South Vietnam elections an aura of respectability, he appointed a Cornell University professor in political science as a member of an inspection team. After a four-day tour of the country, programmed by the government, the professor concluded that the election was as fair as those in the United States. As a postscript, he asserted that irregularities were unlikely since the election law forbade them.[9] In contrast, a professor specialist in Asian affairs not on the official tour concluded that fraud had been committed to the extent of some five hundred thousand votes.[10]

In brief, the university replaces technology for the advancement of human welfare with technology for the promotion of the system. It develops among its professors not social scientists for social inventiveness but technicians for employment in power-wielding institutions. This industrialization of the university places a pall on basic research and education. Research is now needed to determine the meaning of the word research itself. Freewheeling scholars today must yield to individuals whose research is intended to serve the immediate purposes of particular institutions. The gossamer spinners are considered cranks, if indeed they still exist. The pragmatists claim they seek a value-free technology to solve problems of contemporary society. However, their claim to objectivity has little foundation. Their inquiries reflect a disinclination to raise questions critical of the system out of fear of drying up their sources of funds.

When these technician intellectuals become decision makers in national affairs they are a menace to public sanity. Their fundamental skill, making abstractions, leads some of them to the self-sprung trap of the communist conspiracy. They joust with constructs of their intellect and commit someone else's children to death. The detached professor who does not have the stomach to indulge in a hand-to-hand combat with a human being easily commits others to do so from the serenity of his office. A cautious courthouse politician is more assurance of sanity than a professor high in the upper echelons of the system.

Not all professors who live entirely on university salaries can be classified as free intellectuals. In addition to the radical professors, one has to extract those timid individuals who confine their activities to hardly more than putting over a lesson plan. Their inclination to indulge in boot licking with administrators is inversely proportional to the confidence they have in their professional competence. But even those remaining do not automatically merit the title of free intellectual. A professor, for example, adding to the fund of knowledge on the sex life of the human being would certainly earn the title of scientist. Should he also bring forward some outlandish ideas on coupling, then he would join the ranks of free intellectuals.

Accordingly, to describe the faculties of institutions of higher learning as a community of scholars is to yield to self-adulation. Rather, a pre-

9 *The New York Times,* September 5, 1967.
10 *The New York Times,* September 21, 1967.

ponderant number of them comprise a disparate group of self-seeking, insecure individuals within their respective departmental cubicles, who keep their cards close to the chest and who would not give the right time of day if they felt it might benefit someone else at their expense. In such a state of mind, they are easily knocked off one at a time by clever university presidents.

The basic purpose of a university faculty is presumably education. But few of its personnel wish to be bothered with such a taxing pursuit. University managers prefer playing politics; researchers are too busy rewriting the same findings; professor entrepreneurs are preoccupied with pecuniary pursuits outside the institution. The university, in short, has become a bundle of irrelevant purposes. It provides therapy for immature youth in the guise of course work; develops technicians for the system; compiles scholarly knowledge on minutiae. But the professor's role of disciplining minds to think is neglected, and there is no other institution in the society that can adequately perform such a role. The university draws away from this function by serving the interests of government and industry; its timid managers do not employ the power the university actually has over these institutions. In the position to do what the needs of education require and to obtain the funds to do so, they do not elect to take a course of leadership.

Faculty power is a realistic alternative to counteract this occupational disease affecting university managers. However, such power cannot be used in the way it is employed by administrators. The college professor must act as an educator in the hope of setting an example to students and administrators, no matter how asinine and dishonorable he may consider their actions to be. By so doing, he places himself at a disadvantage in the power game with which the university is governed. But this he has to do if he wishes to merit the title of educator.

THE STUDENTS

As the intellectual courage of the university withers and its hypocrises blossom, a minority of undergraduate students have started almost single-handedly a ferment whose consequences have been profound. Accordingly, it is important to describe the who and the why of this student turbulence, the issues it has raised, and the effects of the ferment. To place the unrest in context, student protest has had a long history in Latin America and in some countries of Western Europe. The protest in American universities, with the exception of a few institutions such as the City College of New York, is a recent innovation.

American college students are preponderantly white middle class in origin and moderate in outlook, a conservative orientation obscured by the greater publicity enjoyed by the activist minority within their ranks. Generally, undergraduates are the children of suburbia and have attitudes at variance with those of the children of the city. Even black students, who champion city dwellers of their race, frequently have a similar middle class orientation and are often mistrusted by the blacks they claim to speak for. The people of the black urban community are more pragmatic than black undergraduate militants and look at their position in terms of particular problems and practical solutions. By contrast, the students are more ideologically oriented and tend to be looked upon by the black urban proletariat as long on verbiage and short on follow-through.

Accordingly, the preponderant number of college students have few quarrels with the university and the business values that dominate it. Their sentiments toward the activism of the minority range from indifference to hositility. The majority tends to abide by the traditional rules of the game and focuses its attention on obtaining the degree necessary for entrance into the white-collar employee class. Its members react to minority protest only when their normal routine is disturbed or when university managers, in responding to student disruption, commit what student consensus considers a moral outrage.

The alignment that thereby emerges on a typical college campus is as follows: a quiescent majority, a minority of white critics of the society who come mostly from the middle class, and a small group of blacks who do not identify with either group. Members of the activist white minority run the risk of isolating themselves both from the majority and from the blacks.[11] The majority represents the backlash potential. Its emergence depends on the ability of the minority to keep the majority neutral or to gain its support through reaction to unpopular decisions made by university managers.

For the university as a whole, a typical breakdown would be as follows: graduate students, with few exceptions and these with major interests in sociology and humanities, oriented toward their studies; a majority of white undergraduates, concentrating on courses and undergraduate pleasures; a small closely knit group of blacks; and white critics of the society, ranging from passive loving grass sitters, to a wide band of left wing activists. Among the undergraduates, blacks would be the most cohesive group, sensitive to the social isolation both self-imposed and imposed by students. Each of these groups has a representative view of the faculty. White militants, for example, tend to

---

[11] At Drexel University, the majority was indifferent to the efforts of activitists until the latter used part of the campus reserved for socializing. The majority reacted with an obsolete weapon: water-filled paper bags.

look upon conservative professors as unredeemable lackeys of the establishment and upon liberal professors as possible supporters of their causes. Blacks see in the professor the white middle class insensitive to their perceptions and tend to be suspicious of professors who show an interest in black causes.

No single factor motivates student backlashers. Some react to the neuroticism of activists more than to the issues they raise; some are concerned with the image of the university; generally, they are more patriotic, more submissive to authority. Flag-waving and snappy military bands give backlashers goose pimples. A latent anti-intellectualism may inspire them to bursts of hostile reaction. SPASM—the Society for Prevention of Asinine Student Movements—heralded the birth of these backlashers at Wichita State University by indulging in a milk-in as a reaction against students who wanted the sale of beer on campus. A group of students at the University of Montana organized SCUM—Save the Children from Unfit Materials. Spring does things to backlashers as well as to activists.

A considerable number of undergraduate students are masters in obstructing the intrusion of knowledge into their personalities. This resistance to learning has no respect for ideological boundaries. There are professors disposed to provide these non-students with an experience of pleasure and to replace techniques of language and mathematical symbol with those of light and sound. These professors play games with the youth, performing essentially what amounts to a baby-sitting function.[12] But they fill a need, for the television generation is insensitive to the light and sound nature bountifully provides.

The highest proportion of activists is in the big and prominent institutions, such as the University of California, Stanford, Cornell, Harvard, City University of New York, and Columbia. The size and distinction of these universities make them vulnerable to protest movements and attract an intelligent student elite sensitive to the issue of what a university should be. These activists also serve as models for students in other institutions, who through instant communication become aware of them and feel compelled to keep up with the Joneses. In addition to these universities, smaller institutions such as Swarthmore College, Brandeis University, and San Francisco State College have achieved

---

12 Foreign press reports indicate a possible breakthrough in meeting student demands for instant learning. It seems that a team of scientists have developed a pill that after a few seconds makes the swallower gush forth with all sorts of erudition. There are two snags, however. The erudition triggered by the pill surfaces in dead languages such as Latin, Greek, and Visigoth. The pill also triggers a high that induces destructive tendencies in the swallower. Scientists are reported busily developing another economy pill to convert the erudition into English and to counter the deleterious side effects.

notoriety for disruptive demonstrations. The first two institutions are centers of student intellectualism, while the third has been influenced by political and racial issues in California and by administration-faculty bungling.

The extent of participation in student activism reflects differences in professional orientation. Activists are concentrated in the social sciences and the humanities, supported by young instructors sympathetic to their spirit of rebellion. Students in business, engineering, medicine, and science are more oriented toward achieving a particular professional goal and are more inclined to divide their time between study and leisure activity. They have less social awareness and are prone to view protest as irrational behavior. Both groups come predominantly from a sheltered middle class existence, but with the difference that the social science and humanities students have a greater uncertainty as to their professional future.

Intellectuals who write about student protest tend to generalize in a manner consistent with their ideological bias. Lewis S. Feuer lumps together all student unrest everywhere in all time and explains it on the basis of father hatred and the sense of guilt attending such hatred.[13] Consistent with his own ideological scheme, Daniel Bell of Harvard University describes student unrest as the gasp of humanism against the rise of the age of technology. Psychiatrist Kenneth Keniston points out the difficult transition from a prolonged childhood of food, fun, and middle class futility, devoid of the realities of conflict and death, to a sudden awareness of realities.

The revolutionary romanticists in activist ranks, who would not know what to do with a gun, who never experienced the shock of violent death, who never indulged in a fist fight, fall in love with the game of revolution. The sudden transition from sheltered affluence to hard reality has considerable impact. Activism provides an opportunity for exercises in reaching adulthood. A diet of courses reflecting the specialization of professors ill suits such a goal. These students need group therapy more than they do lessons in iambic pentameter.

The new left romanticists show little knowledge either of American realities or of the strategy of acquring power. Incredibly, they speak of a coalition of workers and themselves. They thereby propose an alliance with persons who would be more disposed to put them against the wall come the revolution. A few new leftists are ambulatory psychiatric cases. They extend their sickness to the larger society in acts of terrorism; some blow themselves up into oblivion with their bombs. A

[13] See Lewis S. Feuer, *The Conflict of Generations,* New York: Basic Books, 1969.

thin element of truth runs through their argument. But fundamentally they are uneducated, the product of absentee fathers and pandering professors. Thus, a society with serious problems produces as its revolutionaries a band of uneducated neurotics.

No evidence exists that the professor sympathizers of the new left collaborate in bomb emplacement or in rendering technical advice in their making. Some seem sick enough or hate American society enough to give the revolutionaries their moral support. They are generally not above setting aside their scientism for the political necessities of the moment. Together with the radical students, they represent the Joe McCarthyites of the left, believing that their distortion of the truth is justifiable because of their superior cause.

Professor W. E. Spicer of Stanford University takes a critical view of the tactics of student revolutionaries. He states in a letter:

> Kenneth Pitzer, who has just resigned as President of Stanford, is a gentle and good man. Above all, he is an idealist. He tried to act as a mediator more than a leader. This spring the Stanford campus exploded about him.
>
> To those who asked for a firmer hand on the campus he said, "I can't believe that people want me arbitrarily to punish a student without giving him a fair hearing to determine whether he is guilty. . ."
>
> But do people want to see $100,000 of windows broken in order to reverse a duly arrived at faculty decision to keep R.O.T.C. on campus? Did people want to see psychological and physical intimidation build on campus to the point where only one side of a question could be heard and where classes could be widely disrupted and faculty and students denied the right to pursue their studies?
>
> Perhaps most tragic is the transformation of a university from a place where all points of view are to be heard to a place where intimidation and force is used to prevent unpopular views from being heard or where attempts are made to gain unanimous agreement for a strongly held viewpoint by intimidation.[14]

Sympathetic professors submit to book burning, window smashing, building burning, personal intimidation, denial of access to their work places, and curtailment of freedom of thought. One academic, spat upon by a child revolutionary, is quoted as saying he would not be provoked. He did not even spit back.

In 1970, a strike at the New School for Social Research in the City of New York against the Vietnam war degenerated into a comic struggle

---

14 From a letter to the *New York Times*, June 30, 1970. One can quarrel with Professor Spicer in the way he constrasts a "mediator" with a "leader." Mediators, of course, differ in technical competence and philosophical premises. Mediators can be competent leaders. Perhaps a Kingman Brewster would be more to Professor Spicer's liking.

among students, administrators, and faculty. Two writers, professors at the New School, describe the students as follows:

> Their language can be direct and shocking but they do not mean it to be obscene. One is reminded of the concrete, pungent, sometimes surrealistic, yet hardly ever pornographic terminology of primitive people. Their music is rhythmic and vital, to be danced to, lived with.
>
> They distrust abstraction: when they occupy the registrar's office they substitute their living selves for the frozen records and filing cabinets. And make no mistake about it, their instinct for our failings is deadly and accurate.[15]

Thus, the romanticists in the ranks of professors poetize on student protest.[16]

Institutions outside the university react to the student protest movement in a manner consistent with their habitual thinking. Mass communications media see opportunities to develop new clientele through the cultivation of the youth's sense of superiority of its values. The judicial system sides with university managers in the preservation of property rights. Some judge can always be found to give college officials an injunction under law; some are disposed to throw the book at students. In California, for example, a dispenser of justice sentenced a student charged with seizure of two campus buildings at San Fernando Valley State College to 25 years in prison.[17]

The national government has reacted to student protest by threatening to withdraw money either from students or from the universities

---

[15] Stanley Diamond and Edward Nell, "The Old School at the New School," *The New York Review*, June 18, 1970.

The authors, I think, raise the students to heroic proportions that they do not merit. I was attending a graduate sociology seminar at the New School at the time of the demonstrations. The majority in the group had neither the capacity nor the inclination to indulge in hard thinking. They were, for example, highly critical of the computer without having the faintest notion of what a computer is. The demonstrations had the aspect of comic opera, of a juvenile game for which the deadly serious players had little competence. The faculty blew its cool. There was no chance of any other outcome but the one into which the farce degenerated.

[16] The counter tactic to the threat of the use of force is to muster one's own forces and wait for the onslaught with cool equanimity. A letter, allegedly written by the rector of a British university, reads as follows: "Dear Gentlemen: We note your threat to take what you call direct action unless your demands are immediately met. We feel that it is only sporting to let you know that our governing body includes three experts in chemical warfare, two ex-commandos skilled with dynamite and torturing prisoners, four qualified marksmen in both small arms and rifles, two artillerymen, one holder of the Victoria Cross, and a chaplain. The governing body has authorized me to tell you that we look forward with confidence to what you call a confrontation and I may say even with anticipation." It is difficult to imagine an American university president writing such a letter.

[17] *The New York Times*, January 31, 1970.

where the disruptions occur. In some states such as Pennsylvania institutions are compelled under law to furnish the names of students involved in campus disorders at the risk of being denied funds. Some
legislation requires the dismissal of faculty members involved in protests.
True to the Anglo Saxon adage, money talks.

> American politicians are not at their best when confronting problems
> which elude a financial solution, and it was only natural that they should
> fall back to other familiar positions. The first consisted of forcing the
> campus problems into legal categories from which, presto, they emerged
> as issues of rule violation and laxity in law enforcement. The obvious
> solution was to withdraw government aid from disaffected students and
> to warn the colleges and universities that they would suffer financial loss
> if they continued to be soft on law and order. The second position was
> equally predictable: trace the problems to an international communist
> conspiracy.[18]

Some local governments go even further. They hire agitators. One
agent provocateur at Hobart College even offered students an informal
course on bomb manufacturing.[19]

Numerous species exist of the genus activist. Super militants consider
themselves revolutionaries in the order of Mao Tse Tung, Ho Chi Minh,
and Che Guevara. Unlike authentic revolutionaries, however, they lack
control and tact, nor do they have any blueprint for action. Their alternative to the university, the so-called Free University, comprises a far-
cical escape from the rigors of education. Some activists are ritualistic
spirits who take pleasure in obstructionism and look forward happily
to martyrdom, which thanks to the timidity of the system often does not
go beyond a trip in the paddy wagon. Their offensive thrusts include
assaults on filing cabinets and charges with toilet-wall words. Their
tantrums convey more the image of theatrical infantilism than that of
revolution. Their posture, when carried to serious proportions, leads
more to repression than to the superior society they allegedly seek.[20]

Black activists do not automatically give white militants a favorable
reception. The blacks either reject the whites or use them to suit their

18 *The New York Review,* Education and Technological Society, October 9,
1969.
19 The Philadelphia *Evening Bulletin,* July 21, 1970.
20 The climate of revolution on campus is exaggerated by young instructors in
the social sciences and humanities who see in every student tantrum an emerging revolution. At Drexel one such instructor has long expected an assault from
the adjoining black community to the point of disappointment over his unfulfilled prophecy. The clinical aspects of the social sciences should be postponed
as late as possible in the career of undergraduate students. Students should
be kept busy with analytical techniques. Instead, they are encouraged to believe
that their judgments are worth more than a tinker's dam. Much of what they
say comprises imprecise summaries of authoritarian minds.

own purposes. They act more out of frustration arising from difficulties in making adjustments to middle class campus life and from a persuasion that the whites managing the property are out of tune with their plight. Blacks tend more to use disruption as a tactic to create something concrete that expresses justice as they see it. Although persuaded that whites cannot grasp the uniqueness of their position, blacks respond more readily than white revolutionaries to patient dialogue and participation. For a minority within the group, the cynicism and mistrust is total and unshakable. Generally, however, they are more angry than neurotic, more humanistic than sadistic. In a confrontation, blacks are more apt to close ranks. University managers perform a disservice to the educational advancement of blacks when they panic under their pressure.

White protesters act from a greater variety of impulses, ranging from goal seeking to enjoyment of disruption. Some are totalitarian spirits; some are as emotionally sick as the instructors who champion them. To allow them participation in the restructuring of the university is like permitting a sick patient to join a surgeon in the performance of a complex operation. In their judgment anyone who disagrees with them has no right to pursue his own individual course of action. Firm believers in their own rectitude, they rebel against the use of arbitrary power by everyone but themselves. In a sense, such students, together with those representing the conservative backlash, have reconcilable objectives: the one group welcomes the opportunity to provoke a suppression and the other entertains the chance to give them an opportunity for martyrdom. The totalitarian leftist student presents non-negotiable demands with a time deadline, often with the expectancy of rejection and with the conviction that he represents absolute virtue and his adversaries, absolute evil. The lack of coherence and follow-through of white protesters, arising from the diversity of their impulses, often makes them ineffectual. Their supreme posture is the unspecified non-negotiable demand.

Because of the fragmentation of their organization, white protesters have a problem building a power base. They need black issues and support. Accordingly, a competition for influence arises, fed by an inclination to direct rather than to work for others. Competition brings about the necessity of provoking issues that may gain popular support. Black issues provide such opportunities, but black activists have their own problem building a power base and often take the position that the pursuit of black causes by white students requires their approval.

The stated objective of the Students for a Democratic Society, a white leftist student organization, is participatory democracy. Yet its members do not seem adverse to violating the participatory rights of students who oppose them. While the style of the SDS is not the same in every institution, generally the organization shifts its tactics from playing it cool to provoking a continual state of confusion fed by demands that are difficult to meet. It is not uncommon for the SDS to stir up racial animosities for allegedly noble purposes.

Student activism is not necessarily actionism. Students who bring forward an issue are often not to be found when it comes to implementing the program that comes out of the issue. Consequently, an administrator may have to operate on the basis of two plans: one under the assumption that students who commit themselves will follow through, and the other based on their subsequent disappearance once the activism shifts elsewhere. The problem often arises from students making commitments for which they have no time or capacity, or from the fact that nihilism and creativity rarely exist in the same person.

Briefly, the dominant issues which concern student activists include: black studies programs, often with concomitant demands that programs be separatist and that special admissions policies be granted to black high school students; the loveless materialism of American Society; the Vietnam war and the draft; the governance of the university; the relationship of the university to the community; the research function in the university; lack of what the student calls relevance in courses and tied to this complaint, criticisms of the rigid compartmentalizing of knowledge into departments and courses and the prescribing of a time sequence that may be in conflict with his rate of development. These comprise the major bill of particulars.[21]

The student unrest these issues trigger is fed by adult behavior. The government which threatens students unless they behave is the same government that creates policies that produce the unrest. The managers of the system strike students as hypocrites. While undergraduates may not see all the nuances in issues, while their actions may be inspired by personal conflict, the issues raised have substance and are not of their own making. Students take courses that do not grapple with what they feel are pressing concerns, that are taught by instructors who are a few pages ahead in the text. Corruption in the society and in the uni-

[21] A report of the United States Bureau of the Census indicates that there were 434,000 black students in institutions of higher learning in the Fall of 1968 compared to 234,000 in 1964. The figure represents 15% of Negroes in the 18–24 year old group or double the percentage of the same group in 1964. The figure compares with an increase of 5 percent to an overall figure of 27% per whites of the same age group. The rise in black enrollment is attributable partly to the waiving of regular entrance requirements and financial assistance and partly to the unprecedented economic growth during the period. (The U.S. Bureau of the Census, *Current Population Reports*, Series P-20, No. 190, School Enrollments: October 1968 and 1967, U.S. Government Printing Office, Washington, D.C., 1969.)

versity in particular is not a student fabrication. Student impulses are
moralistic; that is to say, they see in society a lack of veracity and a
heavy presence of institutions that serve only those who control them.
The manner in which the university preponderantly serves entrepreneur
professors and power minded administrators, and the manner in which
the political economic system uses rather than serves the needs of human
beings, provides students with opportunities for protest. If undergraduates are cynical of authority, valid reason exists for such cynicism. If students receive responses that sound like double talk, it may indeed be the
consequence of evasive professors and university managers. If students
are irritated by hypocrisy, it may be because adults have practiced equivo-
cation for so long that they are no longer aware of their evasiveness. Student objectives—morality in politics and economic affairs, participatory
democracy, and a university less dedicated to serving needs of the power
structure—reflect the immorality of politics and economic affairs, non-
participation in decision making, and conversion of universities into sellers of technique to government and industry.

The students' perception of American life is not the same as that
articulated by influential members of the system. The university president talks to them of the rule of reason, but to assert that the university
is managed according to such a rule does not mean that in fact it is.
A better description of university behavior is business as usual and
change under pressure. Politicians talk of freedom and democracy as
students read about suppression and authoritarianism. Students are
critical of the monstrous bureaucracies that adults take for granted.
Universities have produced two generations of undergraduates at a time
when their most capable professors were out peddling their services to
industry and government under the prodding of university managers.
Students have emerged from 4 years of tutelage by a scrub team teaching
in a philosophical vacuum, harried by administrations to produce some
tangible evidence of scholarship, which often is a euphemism for getting
contracts in applied research. Between plane and train schedules, professors teach a series of irrelevancies and perform outrages upon the
human spirit. From the point of view of the student, it is as if a wall
of silence has been built around matters that trouble them deeply.

Students who seize upon the Vietnam war as an issue are frequently
rebels against the insensitivity of organized institutions generally. A
number of these individuals view their labor as an accusation of immorality. They see society as a bundle of inconsistencies: adults defending the Vietnam war on the basis of expediency; communities demanding
sexual restraint while profit makers market sexual aberration; adults
pontificating on individual rights as the educational system destroys the

individual personality; the forces of law and order going down hard on drug addiction, but treating sparingly tobacco addiction and a serious liquor addiction that accounts for half of the deaths on the highways; the government deploring the violence of students and practicing violence as an instrument of foreign policy.

The Negro students raise issues that come out of experience as a racial minority in a white middle class society. Institutions offer them courses in business, social science and humanities with whose content they cannot identify. The isolation they sometimes choose is a response to the social isolation inadvertently imposed on them. Those who come from all-black schools and communities feel this isolation as a daily experience for the first time. Their reaction is to advocate Negro autonomy in courses, use of funds, admissions, instructors, and organization structure; thereupon they are accused of separatism. To individuals who negotiate with them they sometimes appear perplexing and irrational. Sensitive blacks who perceive this reaction become more intransigent. Some see the immaturity of white militants as a stumbling block to gaining objectives, although a few are not disinclined to exploit the tendency of white militants to look upon black activists as pure gurus.

The tactic of demonstration in pursuing issues is sometimes productive. Administrators often do not have the means or the courage to cope with demonstrations. Participating students can also count on the support of instructors who side with them because of personal needs and ideologies. Two principal weapons against a demonstration are sophistication in the use of counter power and a sense of humor. University managers and professors often have neither.

There are different varieties of demonstration. The silent Quaker type abhors disruption, but can be effective nevertheless. Students who protest silently can obtain results from adults who are troubled by the silence. Some students prefer hoop-la and put together well-timed scenarios, with television cameras in ready position at the moment of crisis. Demonstrations that end in violence commonly have the following ingredients: they take place in a large urban institution not dominated by a conservative division such as an engineering school, but by a heavy enrollment in the liberal arts. A small organized group takes over a building and makes demands reflecting national patterns as well as issues in the particular institution. The administration calls in the police, who after waiting so long for such an opportunity, proceed gleefully with head busting. The action of the police shifts the sympathy of the student body to the demonstrators. Professors utter for the record lofty statements of principle, which generally have little to do with the issue. In some instances, the response of administrators is lightning fast.

Thus, the former president of Rutgers University, responding to a demonstration at a site removed from the University center, dispatched a special messenger to accede to all the demands of protesters, a majority of whom were not even affiliated with the university. The criterion is: make concessions now and pay later. It manifests a style of decision making by university managers that an objective is proper or improper depending upon the power of those pushing it forward.

A timorous administrative response invites inflated demands and backlash from dissenting students and faculty. To maintain the image of a peaceful campus, it may seem prudent to meet all of the demands, to keep the concessions secret from the faculty, and diplomatically to ignore them afterward. Meeting force with force by the police invites raw brutality and shock among the student body and faculty. As in the Columbia Heights battle of 1968 and the Battle of Harvard Common in 1969, entrance of the police increases the likelihood of escalation. The Cox Commission report that came out of the Columbia uprising points to the ingredients that generate this particular variety of disturbance: mistrust and alienation among faculty, students and administration; ill-advised acts by administrators and faculty during periods of tension; student provocateurs who escalate the disturbance; police brutality; and deep emotions generated by such issues as the Vietnam war and the race question. In the Columbia fracas, faculty and students, by resisting the police, gave them an excuse to exercise force. The administration erred in calling the police after the tension reached a peak and in believing that a thousand policemen with a grievance against college students could be controlled according to plan once they were asked to intervene. Peace making by professors, more skilled in presenting a lecture than in negotiating under stress, aggravated the situation.

The academic year 1968–69 might well have been the high water mark in violent student protest had it not been for President Nixon's charge into Cambodia the following year. A study by the Office of Research of the Association Councils of Education in 1970 reveals that disruptive protests took place on 524 campuses or 22.4 percent of the country's institutions of higher learning. Violence occurred on 145 campuses in the same 1968–69 academic year. The form of protest included occupation of buildings, strikes, and furniture wrecking. Eight lives were lost. A good deal of the agitation was for black studies programs and special admissions programs for blacks.[22] The announcement of the Cambodian incursion at a time when the proclivity to dem-

---

[22] From an address by William Thomas Carter, "Black Students, a New Constituency in Higher Education," Bureau of Educational Personnel Development, U.S. Office of Education, October 26, 1970.

onstrate reached a peak, followed soon thereafter by the Kent State University massacre, brought demonstrations to new heights, involving for the first time moderates who formerly had remained aloof. The tactic of the non-coercive strike emerged, in which students and faculty were asked to suspend their normal routine to discuss and take action on issues.[23]

During the same year, student backlash arose on the very campus that kicked off the student protest movement in 1964. A backlash candidate was elected as president of the student body of the University of California. The young man defeated a coalition of blacks and Mexican Americans and a third party of white radicals. The tactics of the left thus seem to produce an organized reaction from moderates.

The Kent affair bore aspects of comedy and tragedy. The combined incompetence of administrators, faculty, part-time soldiers, and the Governor of Ohio, together with student naiveté, led to the death of 4 students almost a hundred yards from the Guard line and the wounding of others in the back and sides. The grand jury's indictment of faculty and students and the white washing of the National Guard falls short of posthumously accusing the dead students of succumbing to the bullets of their executioners. The guilty are those who arouse the powerful into committing violence.

In the autumn of 1970, the U.S. President's Commission on Campus Unrest made its report. In its criticism of far left students, administrators, faculty, the Ohio National Guard, and the Mississippi police, and in its call for national political leadership, the framers of the report appeared to seek a new mood of reconciliation and restraint. The United States Vice President, upset by the Commission's findings that diverse and insulting official rhetoric is dangerous, denounced the report before the President read it.

A sharp curtailment of student unrest has followed, for reasons which are conjectural. Many of the student demands on the university have been met or appear to have been met. The blacks are getting down to

[23] According to a study of a private research group, the first national student strike of 1970 involved some 30 percent of the 2500 colleges and universities in the United States. The level of protest according to the survey stemmed chiefly from the Kent State University killings by the Ohio National Guard rather than President Nixon's announcement of the Cambodian invasion. The greatest amount of protest was in the East, the lowest in the South. The study also notes marked increases in protest by faculty. The principal demand issuing from the protest was termination of university activities in war-related efforts. (From a report in *The New York Times*, June 24, 1970, on a study of the Urban Research Corporation.)

A Carnegie Commission survey issued October 2, 1970 found that the Spring protests were unprecedented in the history of American higher education. According to the survey, the protests were triggered by the Cambodian invasion. *The New York Times*, October 30, 1970.

the business of maintaining their scholastic performance. The ground war in Indochina has terminated for Americans. The decline of student unrest may be evidence of an awareness of the costs of protests.

Throughout the crisis of the 1960's, the initiative rested with student activists, lost by the faculty primarily because its most articulate members were busily compromised as entrepreneurs and secondarily because the stay-at-homes were disposed to timidity or philandering. The student activists have made considerable power gains: They have acquired membership on boards of trustees, curriculum committees, faculty evaluation committees. They have even gained a voice in university maintenance and real estate operations. Their victories have been facilitated by the structural and personality weaknesses of the university. In substance, the students have obtained rights of co-determination and interpretation of policy; in so doing, they have altered power relationships among faculty, administration, and students. The area of co-determination remains in a state of flux. Its containment depends entirely on faculty will, because administrators act as timorous politicians ever disposed to give students a semblance of victory. What the faculty accomplishes will depend on its courage, its acquisition of bargaining skills, and its ability to move from its specialist orientation to an institution-wide frame of reference. Whether the university remains a center of quality undergraduate education thus rests with the faculty.

The rise in student influence resembles the emergence of the industrial labor movement in the 1930's when the Congress of Industrial Organization demanded a redress of power. As was then the case, today's student protest raises the question as to what is bargainable and what the scope of each bargain should be; which raises the point as to whether harassed faculties should thereupon be allowed to choose their students. Students demand bargaining rights without administrative and bargaining skills. They are offering not labor power, but their money as transient customers buying a service whose cost is not entirely covered by them. Once they strike a bargain, few are inclined to assume responsibility for its execution; they vanish. In addition, while the C.I.O. confronted tough executives insisting on a *quid pro quo* in a bargain, students negotiate with easily frightened administrators and faculty. A basic lession in labor management relations experience is that one does not yield power without a commitment to specified future conduct and accountability. If such a strategy of power relinquishment is ignored, the result is infantilism. He who makes unilateral concessions either is a fool or is not acting in good faith.

While undergraduate students succeed in producing these changes within the university, they have less effect upon the outer society. Their protest, when it reaches above nuisance level, triggers suppression. Their success is confined to bringing issues to a crisis stage rather than producing structural change. To a considerable degree, this weakness is caused by the transient nature of their protest and its lack of a philosophy. Moreover, their protest often tends to make them propagandists rather than students; they acquire a habit of thinking that if their point of view or objective is deemed worthy, then obstacles should be placed against the emergence of opposite facts. In short, they cease to be students and thereby diminish their effectiveness.

The life experience of the student disposes him to look for issues. The high school experience tied to middle class community experiences, the emptiness to sensitive young minds of a life devoted to material acquisition, the revolt against the dehumanizing effects of modern technology, the absence of participatory democracy, the discrediting of political institutions including the office of the United States presidency, the bureaucratization of American society, the introduction of blacks into institutions of higher learning in a climate of social protest, the inundation of the humanities and social sciences with students ill-prepared to take on a rigorous curriculum, the frustrations in trying to obtain moral guidance, and the consequent desire to tear down institutions without any clear idea as to what the new institution should be, all these are contributing factors. Moreover, from infancy to college, American middle class males live in a permissive environment shielded from adversity and the consequence of their actions. No accountability is imposed on what they do. It is as if a conspiracy exists to prevent them from becoming men. They go from infancy to adulthood without ever having to make a difficult decision and facing up to its consequences alone. The affluent society fosters a society of child-men swindled of the pleasure of becoming an adult. When confronted with a difficult situation, they fall apart. Pampering administrators and professors underwrite this affliction of prolonged infancy.

Nevertheless, the student activist cannot be ignored because he is often the exceptional student. Unless the professor applies the test of social purpose in his subjects, the better student may abandon his courses. No one has a monopoly on what constitutes worthy social purpose. But if the university is not prepared for its analysis, the bright students will copout and the dullards will set the standards. Colleges of Business are particularly susceptible to this deterioration. When these two sets of students, the job-oriented and those excited by learning basic truths, are in the same class, the professor's task is almost impossible.

Urban institutions surrounded by a black proletariat are especially vulnerable to student activism. If the community is hostile to the institution and students can mount a tactic of disruption, the organization may be forced into an accommodation that may radically change its standards. Tensions are inevitable when different socio-economic groups live near each other in separate oases. As these tensions produce crime directed against the superior group, the polarization rises. To contain these tendencies an initiative is necessary to construct a mechanism of integration that brings together various elements in the community and the university. But there is no guarantee that such a mechanism would work. University administrators are motivated by the necessities of image making. They are not adverse to pitting one community group against another in the promotion of their interests. Students lack the time and inclination to do on a day-by-day basis what has to be done to make institutions work. Those who show an interest seem inclined to move from one ferment to the next. Once matters become routine they disappear.

Moreover, student activists get the message that the United States is ruled not by scientists and humanists, but by oligarchs who see events in terms of challenges to their power. Activists thereby tend to reduce relationships and facts to terms of power. The men they prefer in the faculty body are advocates, propagandists, or buffoons. They become blind to the needs of others, even to the needs of those with whom they identify. They call themselves students, but are often frightfully uneducated and frightened of education. To have an honest educational experience with them is difficult. Rejecting adult competency, they victimize each other with their own immaturity.

The politicalizing of the university strikes a responsive chord with university managers. When political pressure is exerted on college administrators, they behave like timid politicians. The McCarthy era in the 1950's gives early evidence of such behavior, when college presidents were rushing to dismiss professors for exercising rights guaranteed them under the constitution. Administrators do not face up to issues until forced to do so under pressure. Militants sense this tendency and exploit it.

Without the containment of university administrations by men of stature in the faculty ranks, the student of the new left thus has within his means the capacity to convert the university into a political club. He directs his primary revolutionary putsch against the university, which despite its many faults, is the fragile last outpost of civility and honest inquiry. Student pressure can be reduced by accepting undergraduates in university governance. However, experience in Latin America indicates that such a step can lead easily to the further politicalizing of the university. Harvard professor Seymour M. Lipset poses the problem in this way:

> In this era of politicalization of the university, we run the risk that in a desire to accommodate the politicized students the faculty will agree to institutional changes which will increase the political function at the expense of the scholarly, a danger which the faculty itself has introduced by some of its own political activities.
>
> When students judge faculty, particularly in the social sciences, they increasingly are inclined to use political criteria rather than scholarly ones. Harvard, like other American universities, has failed abysmally to provide the needed scholarly concern in the past; it would be a tragedy, for the national and the black community, if as a result of reactions to the current crisis, black studies at Harvard emphasize the political at the expense of the scholarly.[24]

This politicizing tendency extends to admissions polices. The university admits a quota of blacks with financial aid, who are not required to meet high standards of scholastic performance and a bloc of white students whose qualifications are predominantly ability to pay and political connections. Such policy squeezes out the talented sons of low income white ethnics. The price for politicalization, as in Latin America, may be the emergence of small private institutions to take the place of universities as centers for training the intellect and developing knowledge.

CONCLUSIONS

American universities emerged from World War II as major sellers of technical services to government and industry. This commodity fulfilled immediate needs without much thought given to its human impact. As this tide of service mounted, students began to challenge the mission of the university that was prescribed by its managers. In consequence of this challenge, universities are now under pressure from a minority of students and faculty to redefine service as service with a human dimension and to give more power to faculty and students. Consequently, institutions of higher learning are constrained to develop new organizational structures suitable for their shift in role, which would allow for a rebirth of its traditional but neglected function of seeking and describing the truth and imparting such knowledge in instruction.

The university has to find a mechanism that would facilitate the discharge of this role as servant of the society in human terms without weakening its crucial role of critic of the society through scholarly in-

[24] *The New York Times*, April 25, 1969.

quiry. The function of service to mankind and critical evaluation has to emerge from a neglect caused by an overriding zeal to provide technology to government and industry for defense, for profit, and for vested institutional interests.

Education comprises a continuous process of active involvement between teacher and student whose purpose is the human development of both. The process takes place in a context of limited resources and time through planned activity supported by equipment, materials, and administration. The process comprises *creation* of a body of knowledge by the teacher-student interchange, *absorption* of the creation, and *use*. Education must be economical, purposive, and intended not primarily for pleasure but for structuring new capacities that reside permanently in the individual. When education tends to cater to individual needs it tends to become a form of consumption and not investment.

If this premise of education as human development is accepted, the question remains as to what fundamental capacities should be developed. This question relates to the stage of growth of a society. The dual goal of education in an advanced society is the development of self and the relation of self to nature and society. As self, man is purposive and esthetic; therefore, instruction must be provided in philosophy and the humanities, including art, history, language, and literature. For an understanding of self in relation to nature and to an increasingly complex society, instruction is offered in mathematics, verbal precision, laboratory science, management, social sciences, and behavioral sciences. Because, unfortunately, we have neither social science nor behavioral science, we must teach the entire array of their separate disciplines so as to minimize gaps in knowledge. In studying society, we must approach the task in a spirit of critical inquiry. Moreover, for the achievement of these two goals, we provide additional courses for the promotion of physical and mental well being. Since knowledge accumulates at an incredible speed, each individual must be developed not only as a generalist in these subjects but also as a specialist in an area in which he has interest and capacity. Moreover, the exceptional individual should be trained in the skill of contributing to the accumulation of new knowledge.

Because it is necessary to motivate and develop distinct personalities in a working society, opportunities are furnished for the choice of electives to supplement the requisites and to provide greater insight into the array of possible occupational choices. However, experience does not indicate that an exclusive system of free electives promotes the dual goal of education. Today's affluent society permits a delay in the growth of intellectual wisdom. What the young person finds irrelevant today he or she may discover relevant tomorrow when it is too late to pursue such relevance along an economically pursued path. For the purpose of undergraduate instruction, it is too late to discover relevance on commencement day. Unless the student is exceptional, disposed to undergo the labor of learning and to accept the guidance of elders, a diet of free electives produces at the end of an undergraduate career a frustrated individual without purpose.

Therefore, the job of the curriculum is to provide a balance among requisites and between requisites and individual preferences within a specific time period, with the goal of development of the self and of the relation of self to nature and society. A regimen exclusively of requisites frustrates individual perception and motivation; one exclusively of electives does not lead to an economical acquisition of education.

In the pursuit of this educational objective, students, instructors, and administrators raise formidable obstacles. A preponderant number of students are in college primarily because of their ability to pay rather than their ability or desire to learn. With the assistance of philandering instructors and administrators, the level of education tends to be geared to this kind of student. A deliberately designed strategy for the development of exceptional human beings is not employed. Undergraduate instruction is converted into group therapy and group amusement, and the professor is not a symbol of advanced learning but a playmate. The students together with their professor politicians describe with dead seriousness an American socio-economic system that does not exist. They comprise the product of a communications system that appeals not to thought but to the senses.

The student is also a product of the public school system. Its permissive egalitarian philosophy fails to look upon human beings as distinct individuals needing concrete values for the development of positive personalities. American schools, generally, do not systematically develop the child with the exceptional mind and will. The exceptional child is subordinated to the competitive ego needs and values of the group. He is brainwashed. The energies of the system focus on raising the achievement level of the greatest number of pupils as evidenced by standardized tests. Their thrust is to keep the illiteracy at a minimum. But even this achievement often is not so much a mark of ingenuity as it is a manifestation of the family environment of the children. The exceptional child, as is in fact his fellow pupil with learning problems, is sacrificed to the tyranny of the average.

A formidable barrier to the development of competent craftsmen and innovators is the educational establishment itself. The dean of a school of education in a respectable university in the Northeast has done a sweeping job of reform. He has abolished grades and course requirements. Students can take whatever parts of a course they like. His philosophy is that everything is permitted and that no is never the answer. The dean's position is recognition at last of the unassailable fact that what we teach our future public school educators amounts in a word to' crap.

In addition, the university must make a clear distinction between its consultant professors helping in the administration of the system and its scholars developing new knowledge. It should administer the consultants as a separate service garage. In discharging its role as a university of scholars, it must seek to attract the top bright students in the high schools and provide them with a rigorous liberal education. The institution that utters generalities about teacher excellence but rewards the service professor who brings in a contract to defray overhead expense is an institution that operates on the basis of hypocrisy. The university must be honest enough to ask if it fundamentally wishes to develop mechanics or innovators. By its lack of courage, the university performs an inadequate job in either task. In the quiet of its innermost recesses, the institution of higher learning should ask itself: what is our role—developing technicians, innovators, or baby-sitting students?

Many colleges of business and humanities follow the line of least resistance and automatically push their students upward and out. The lowering of standards has reached the graduate level. If a thorough investigation were made of the Masters Degree programs in Business Administration, the results would probably border on a national scandal. A New York State report states that a collusion of mediocrity exists among faculty, administration, and students that disgorges masters degrees required for advancement in employment.[25] Once this mediocrity gains headway, it tends to be fortified by emulation. Thus, when a university in the city of Philadelphia decided to improve the quality of its masters program in Business it rejected innovations on grounds that they were not representative of programs prevailing in the market.

The economy is likely to suffer no critical loss by lessening the educational burden of the mass of undergraduate students. Most of them are bound to enter the bureaucratic class administering the economy in posts that require only a nominal education. While these individuals destined to become middle managers may discourage reform in the system, their timidity will serve to make it less oppressive. Most undergraduate students will become mini-men: individuals continually adjusting to the demands of the system. The university should have programs

25 New York State Education Department, Bureau of College Education, 1972.

for the maxi-men: persons who will lead a life consistent with an idealized vision of what man *can* be. The junior college in some states serves the useful purpose of lowering college standards for the mini-men without being blatantly offensive about it.

The university thus has to strike a balance between meeting the needs of the mini-men and discharging its traditional role of developing intellects of maxi-men through a difficult regimen of inquiry. The university must keep this balance while under siege from professors using the student for their personal salvation, from young idealists with no philosophy and little desire to be students, and from immature boys under the seductive spell of business and government. Moreover, the university's ability to demonstrate the validity of reason to the younger generation has been impaired because of the failure of political leadership to reason with them. The university is ill-equipped to do much with this failure in political management; the faults of the larger society cripple its performance.

Moreover, conflict among students adds to the impairment of university performance. Student addicts needing money badly to support their addiction prey on other students and destroy the camaraderie important to learning. Some students also are uncouth bores who restrict the achievement of other students. The obstruction of these non-students can be reduced partly by delaying entrance of high school graduates into college.

In the pursuit of these objectives, student complaints of course irrelevance should not be dismissed out of hand. A good deal of this criticism derives from professors who are not competent teachers. The process of education cannot be triggered without relating information to the student's experience. Nevertheless, professors write books that ignore this requirement. Moreover, when they go into the classroom, they often do not know how to listen, a failure which borders on an occupational disease.

The student desire for social relevance in education can be served by the organization of university centers in the planning and control of technology for the promotion of social goals. These PACT centers could plan technological change by joining the university and the community in challenging technologies of government and industry that cause auditory, olfactory, ingestive, and esthetic pollution. A nominal tuition tax would provide funds for the hiring of a public interest lawyer to assist in the monitoring of governmental and industrial operations. As a starting lesson in grappling with realities, students would have to seek a favorable response to such a proposal in a student referendum.

On the graduate level, the university has the potential to produce a new style of solving social problems. This style observes a social problem in terms of a total system involving multiple non-linear relationships between men and environment and sees planning as a process of community involvement rather than decision making by elites. It seeks to grasp social change in all its ramifications, including the exercise of bargaining rights by all groups affected by change. It tends to make obsolete much of what is taught in science, social science, and engineering.

The challenge is whether the university can employ this tool of information and technology transfer as a means of shifting its concerns away from industry and government to service for the community. Adequately staffed Colleges of Business are in a strategic position to employ their resources in behavioral science, management, and information systems to assist in making such a shift. Years ago, the university served a need in farming through its organization of an agricultural extension service. Today, the urban university can fill the need of mastering and teaching the difficult systems of thought required by a complex industrial society. The education of an urban citizenry taught to think in these terms provides a basis for reorienting the energies of faculty and filling the needs of idealistic youth.

In furthering this reorientation, the university should cut drastically its output of Ph.D's. The doctoral program should be confined to innovators. To eliminate the commercialization of the doctorate, government and industry should assume responsibility for the development of their own technicians or should confine their demands on the university to a technical degree. For a doctoral program of innovators, no more than a hundred universities would probably be required.

To accelerate these shifts, faculty scholars must wrest the initiative from university managers and entrepreneur professors. The professor salesmen who peddle their wares and score points with the managers should be placed on the defensive. Men of stature in the faculty must take the process of education out of the hands of the triumvirate of students, faculty entrepreneurs, and administrators, who do not understand or care what it comprises.

The so-called reforms of the past decade—black studies, open admissions, relevant courses, student governance, free electives, and courses which despite their names are encounters in group therapy—are likely to be of little educational consequence. They comprise acts of politics to render undergraduate instruction a peaceful base for the pursuit of graduate and outside interests. In addition, these changes are not likely to amount to much because students do not acquire either from their society or from their professors a philosophy of life, without which education has little meaning.

For education has been reduced today to play and to technique whose meaning is not questioned. As rising income and lowering of standards usher into the university larger masses of persons raised on instant culture, persons who are incapable of mastering even technique, the university may be reduced intellectually to an empty shell. If it does not choose to change its course of action, the university will become the nurseryversity.

12

The Untouchables

In modern war there is nothing sweet
nor fitting in your dying. You will die
like a dog for no good reason.
Ernest Hemingway

This chapter examines the defense establishment of the United States and its monumental horror, the Southeast Asia war. It is presented as a case history of failure in the management of public policy; of frustration attending the inability of people to contain government power; of gross deception by managerial elites governing under a philosophy of *L'Etat c'est moi;* of the imposition of sacrifices by the system upon the unsystem in an effort it did not understand and over which it had no control.

The untouchables in the United States comprise a privileged caste of humorless politicians predominantly of Wasp origin, a goodly number of whom reside in the South and the rest, throughout the nation. Some of these patriots bear the party label of Democrat. Many are antediluvian Republicans. With courage, determination, and grim masculine vigor, they discharge the awesome burden of protecting the nation from its enemies, foreign and domestic. In support of this mission, they have given the defense establishment a blank check and have developed the Central Intelligence Agency as a bastion of Americanism. Patriots are untouchables because, while they represent a minority in the population, lesser Americans fail to contain their power. Like the privileged throughout history, they are solid champions of law and order. Their private war in Southeast Asia, a proper exception to their belief in law and

291

order, manifests their influence. Their accumulative error continues end-lessly. If these dour Anglo-Saxons would congregate occasionally and indulge in hearty laughter despite their heavy burden of protecting the nation, who knows if they would not then rule more wisely.

Patriots gain the fealty of a motley assortment of anti-communists, including ethnics who way down deep wish they were Wasps; gung-ho males of more mixed origin and frustration; Hollywood patriots who combine money-making with nationalistic fervor; pious catholics who relinquish their intellects to their president, fire and thunder protestants; and parlor chair warriors in the ranks of university professors who suffer from anti-communism mania. The patriots have led many Americans into believing that since man is inherently aggressive and predatory, the only way to manage international relations is to keep people in line by going around the world either threatening to harm them or actually doing so. That such credence in the devil theory of man has no scientific validity does not deter social scientists from assisting patriots in executing such policy. Time and education may eventually bring such folly to route; but the quicker antidote lies in the patriots losing their war and in not allowing them subsequently through their rhetoric to convert such a loss into a win.

For these supporters of the true faith, communism represents a mono-lithic conspiracy whose international board chairman shifts with the needs for rationalizing anti-communist policy. It used to be Stalin. Then it became Mao. But now the needs of politics force a reevaluation of China and the Soviet Union. Time is necessary to heal the wounds of the Southeast Asia war and to win a presidential election. Many of the supporters of the true faith are thereby thrown into confusion.

Many hyphenated Americans—Italo-Americans, Polish-Americans, Ukranian-Americans—support the untouchables even though they do not mix with them socially. At times these Americans outdo the Daughters of the American Revolution in patriotism. Feeling insecure, they are easily persuaded by the security arguments of the untouchables.

A common bond of these polychromatic crusaders is a belief in demonology. Its political manifestation is the communist conspiracy doctrine. Thus, in a speech by Vice-President Hubert Humphrey to a group of hyphenated Americans, it was stated that the nation was fighting in Southeast Asia because a small country (South Vietnam) was set upon by a powerful communist force (China). But the evil doer (China), thanks to the forces of justice (the United States), had failed. This show of logic brought frequent and thunderous applause.

Patriots control high seats of political power. They are found in higher echelons of legislative and executive departments, especially in the Defense Department where the soft accents of its employees suggest that the South lost the civil war but gained the peace. Untouchables have supporters in the ranks of top management in business and finance, in institutions of higher learning, and, of all places, in the ranks of organized labor. They wish to preserve a traditional society whose disappearance is spurred by the policies they bring forward to preserve it. The disposition of Congress to give them money for past, present, and future wars reflects their influence. Few politicians dare challenge directly these symbols of patriotism; their southern contingent has held the Congress in its grip for decades. Patriots are amply represented on the armed services committees. At crucial moments in the deliberations of these committees, their untouchable chairmen can bring over from the Pentagon colorfully festooned generals and admirals as publicists for the cause. A common strand that runs through their decisions is: Whatever technology with military implications is feasible should not be denied the economy. They confuse military potential for violence with power, and they fail to see that whenever the United States has made use of this potential since the end of the Second World War it has lost power.

Feeling that they act out of a superior love of country, the untouchables do not take kindly to any challenge of their point of view. Actions such as those of the Central Intelligence Agency should not even enter public discussion because of over-riding demands of the national interest. The national interest requires that, if feasible, the arbitrary use of force abroad should be enveloped in a cloak of secrecy. The use of force assures the triumph of virtue in a world full of potential enemies looking greedily at affluent America. Foreigners are either pro-American, hence goodies, or anti-American, therefore baddies. Life comprises an eternal struggle of the goodies versus the baddies, who at times must be removed by CIA hanky-panky.

The American Legion veterans organization makes no mean contribution to the claque of the patriots. The Legion upholds Americanism, defined by one of its functionaries as follows:

> An unfailing love of country; loyalty to its institutions, complete and unqualified loyalty to the ideals of government set forth in the Bill of Rights, the Declaration of Independence, and the Constitution of the United States; respect for and ready obedience to duly constituted authority, and the laws of the land.[1]

With the support of untouchables and their loyal retinue of followers, American foreign policy since World War II has shifted from positive and often successful ideas such as the Marshall Plan for ravaged Europe

---

[1] From a letter to the editor, Philadelphia *Evening Bulletin*, March 25, 1968.

to a negative and not too successful philosophy of military containment. The idea of such a philosophy, roughly, is that if they are not stopped in their own backyard, soon they will be storming the American beaches. Furthermore, to be effective, the implementation of such a view should be kept secret from the American people, even though they should support it. Thus, the substance of the government posture on the American intervention in Indochina was: We are doing what is to be done. We cannot tell you the facts because of the national interest. Have faith. At times, this ascendant military mentality smacks of comic opera, as in the Bay of Pigs Cuban intervention and in the case of the battle-ready marines charging and growling up the coast of Lebanon to be greeted by ice cream vendors and loving bikini-clad damsels.

The period beginning with the Second World War can truly be called the age of cruelty. It has been an age in which barbarisms of unprecedented scale have been exercised by governments throughout the world: in Indonesia, Southeast Asia, Brazil, Greece, Black Africa, the Middle East, the Indian sub-continent. In the interest of foreign policy, the United States has tacitly condoned these barbarisms or, if disapproving, has remained silent.

THE DEFENSE ESTABLISHMENT

The *dame favorie* of the patriots is the military establishment. With a budget that hovers around $80 billion, or more than the national income of a preponderant number of the world's nations, the United States Defense Department comprises the biggest management organization in the economy. Some 2000 firms owe the substantial portion of their business to the defense budget. Another hundred thousand have had at one time or another a significant amount of their business in the form of defense subcontracts. The department operates several thousand major installations in the United States and a similar number in some thirty foreign countries, Alaska, and Hawaii. The total arsenal of nuclear weapons in Europe, the United States, and in foreign bases is more than enough to destroy the world.

Defense appropriations are pushed upward by war ventures but never revert to levels existing prior to the conflict that raised appropriations. The military plans the maintenance of the new level of spending before termination of the conflict. These expenditures are often defended on the ground that they represent a small fraction of the gross national product and that they provide employment. Nevertheless, their real economic effect is assessable in terms of output foregone such as schools and houses, and in the human capacities that may have been created through such alternative outputs.

The disposition of Congress to give the Defense Department even more than it actually wants is demonstrated in a $20.7 billion military procurement authorization bill passed in 1968. The Congress appropriated funds for an anti-ballistic missiles system with a high probability of ineffectiveness. In addition, the military received $4.5 million for Navy vessels not wanted by the Navy and $28 million for a fighter plane which would not be used by the Air Force.[2] This largesse is nurtured by a public that responds emotionally when cynical politicians sound the alarm over curtailment of military budgets, and by a system of propaganda that conveys information to the public in a manner designed to promote military interests. Congressional friends of the military brass are formidable in number. One hundred and twenty-two Congressmen are Reserve Officers in the Armed Forces. Many of these individuals have assignments on defense and foreign policy committees.[3] Their appropriations are not entirely lacking in ingenuity. Thus, the Pentagon has on file a $600,000 contract with the psychology department of the University of Mississippi to train birds to steer missiles.

Theoretically, the American military is subordinated to civilian control. In practice, however, the military brass exercises a significant influence on the top policy makers who are supposed to control them. The establishment exerts considerable influence among executive agencies and operates as a government within a government. It gives foreign countries billions of dollars' worth of surplus weapons without the consent of Congress; it maintains some three hundred offices in the United States with dossiers on political dissenters; it makes secret accords with foreign nations committing American troops under specified conditions and arrogates foreign policy to the military. The untouchables encourage this usurpation of power.

The extent and the ramifications of this military suzerainty boggle the mind. Department of Defense property alone amounts to some $202 billion, or ten percent of the total assets of the economy. Its holdings of nuclear explosives amount to six tons of TNT for every human being on the face of the earth. Its post exchange operations represent the third largest distribution network in the nation, after Sears, Roebuck and the A & P Company.

A linkage between the defense establishment and firms developing military technology takes place through the transfer of top officials in both directions, from industry to government as well as from government to industry, and the payment of their salaries. Thus, General Max-

2 Charles W. Bailey and Frank Wright. "Where Will The Money Go When It Ends?" *Evening Bulletin*, June 8, 1969.
3 *The New York Times*, May 12, 1970.

well D. Taylor, former chairman of the Joint Chiefs of Staff and a principal architect of the Vietnam war, became President of the Institute for Defense Analyses at $60,000 annually under a defense contract paying the Institute $9.8 million for the 1969 fiscal year. Henry S. Rowen, President of the Rand Corporation at $70,000 was a former Assistant Secretary of Defense. His salary is paid through a contract with the Air Force. Similar linkages exist with the Aerospace Corporation and the Mitre Corporation. These salaries in government are second only to that of the United States president.[4]

Simplemindedness characterizes the military mind. For example, the classical purpose of military arms is to destroy enemy forces or to force them to surrender. If a certain dosage of military force does not achieve this goal, the solution is clear: apply a heavier dose. If the political authority finds the amount politically unfeasible, and existing dosages do not produce the traditional objective, the fault lies with the political authority. Thus, a gung-ho Air Force general, alluding to the policy of restraint, so-called, in the bombing of North Vietnam, stated in testimony before an armed services committee that if we had really pounded them in 1965 we would have been better off in 1967. Fed the clincher question by an untouchable, the general also stated that the policy of restraint had resulted in greater American casualties. Most of the exempted targets were bombed subsequent to his testimony. But the general's appetite remained unquenched.

The needs of organization often spur the deployment of new military technology. Deployment, for example, of the anti-ballistics missile system revitalizes the role of the Army after having taken for many years a back seat in military innovation to the Navy and Air Force. Aided by their monopoly on sources of information, the intellectuals in the hire of the Defense Department can muster persuasive technological double talk to defend the new technology as enhancing security.

A conflict exists between the military view of technology and the strategy of disarmament. The one is predicated on the premise that an approach to military parity by the adversary requires new technology to regain the advantage. By so doing, it is alleged, one can negotiate from strength. The disarmament view takes the position that the risk of allowing the adversary to approach parity provides an incentive to negotiate. Under the military premise, the arms race is self-perpetuating since neither side knows fully the technological level attained by the other. Consequently, significant goals in disarmament are more likely

4 *The New York Times,* April 19, 1970.

to be reached when the political authority assumes the risk of overriding military considerations. The vicious circle of more defense borders on madness. In a sense, American security can be enhanced by assisting the Russians to raise the quality of their security. Every new technological superiority by the Soviet Union or the United States that upsets the balance of terror generates a new escalation of arms.[5]

The armament race prepares for wars that either cannot be fought or won. A nuclear war with a major power cannot be fought and a nonnuclear war with a minor power cannot be won. The futility of the use of arms has not prevented the United States from becoming first among nations in committing violence on other nations.

THE CENTRAL INTELLIGENCE AGENCY

Spying in the United States is a $5 billion dollar industry. The snooping is performed principally by 5 government agencies—Defense, Justice, The Atomic Energy Commission, and the Central Intelligence Agency. Created in 1947 when the cold war burst into bloom, the CIA commands the special affection of the untouchables. Its functions divide between research and clandestine activities, including the covert collection of information and covert action such as its private war in Laos. The discrediting of the military as a force in foreign policy management points to the increased use of covert action in such management.

A dramatic enterprise in movies and television, spying is tedious and inefficient in real life. The different government agencies that perform such work often do so at cross purposes. They may have the same agents on their payroll without knowing it and may destroy the effectiveness of the agent of a rival organization out of the desire not to be outdone in fact-gathering. In such circumstances, in the interest of job security, agents are well advised to organize and pool their information while presenting individual reports. In this way, they can create an information bank to be used on a rainy day.

TV spies are handsome, quick-witted, and outstanding lovers. The ones working for us always get their man. Unfairly, the newspapers sometimes paint them as nitwits. Reputedly, spy establishments in dif-

---

[5] In 1969, disarmament talks began between the United States and the Soviet Union which in their potential for a more secure world have no precedent in history. In the following year, Secretary of Defense Melvin R. Laird, in contrast with other data of government officials, stated the Soviet Union was undergoing a broad effort to outdistance the United States in offensive weapons in spite of the arms parley. In 1972, with much fanfare, the talks produced a freeze on defensive and offensive missiles. The immediate reaction of the defense establishment was to propose increased expenditures on other weapons systems.

ferent countries support each other's existence. An effective way for
spies to obtain more appropriations is to indicate that a rival organization's budget has risen. They also keep each other busy by feeding each
other misinformation, a practice which goes under the heading of counter-
espionage.

The tendency of spy information to become tainted establishes the
necessity of organizing delousing units to purge the information received.
Accordingly, it may be actually cheaper to convey to the enemy a semblance of spy activity in order to confuse them and to covertly rely on
information from public communications.

Patriots assign the CIA duties that go beyond traditional spying. The
organization has a network of respectable citizens in law and industry
feeding information. The agency also operates a dirty tricks department. It foments revolutions in foreign countries, subsidizes a foreign
radio network, corrupts student organizations, subsidizes books, magazines, and communications networks, corrupts foundations, labor organizations, and university institutes purportedly pursuing scientific research, infiltrates the staffs of American enterprises abroad, and col-
laborates in deposing anti-American chiefs of state. A conglomeration
of intellectuals in the organization perform their chores steadfast in the
conviction that they protect the nation.

Patriots defend this versatility of the agency on grounds of preserving
the American way of life. But when these functions were publicized by
mistake, they produced public shock. The patriots found that the CIA
had acted properly and praised its efforts. The executive department
conducted an investigation to ease the public conscience and found that
the agency had acted in accordance with government regulations.[6]

Falsehoods are indispensable in the maintenance of power in organization. But lies should not be revealed as such, and furthermore should
be used discreetly and not swallowed by those who perpetrate them.
Lastly, if the facts should unfortunately come out from hiding, public
relations gimickry should succeed in distorting them. The CIA-spon-
sored Bay of Pigs assault against Cuba was inconsistent with these basic
principles of organization. The closed circuit thinking such an operation
as the Bay of Pigs produces, in which patriots are only speaking to other
patriots, encourages delusion. Once the decision was made to invade,
denying an invasion was going on would have been laudable if the denial

---

[6] The pattern emerging from inadvertent publicizing of scandalous acts of
organization is that a system of planned modern technology cannot afford to
indulge in self-analysis and full revelation of facts. The system is thereby
undermined. The system cannot fully reveal its impact on individuals, and its
lack of candor mounts irrational acts against the system.

were successful. Once it began, the CIA started to issue press releases at variance with what was happening. Regrettably, the inconsistency was picked up by the press. As the invasion of hired adventurers was being destroyed, the CIA was announcing the successful uprising of the Cuban people against Castro. On the day of the invasion, Secretary of State Dean Rusk was telling the press that the American people were entitled to know if the United States was planning to intervene in Cuba and that the answer was no. The experience suggests that if fraud is to be competently committed, it has to be inspired not by moral perturbations as it proceeds in course but by complete cynicism and complete control of communications channels. The patriots lacked both.[7]

The CIA performs above constraints imposed by the constitution. When challenged, the courts appear to sustain this view of supra-legality. In a typical case, the CIA was accused of libeling an Esthonian emigré by calling him a Soviet secret agent. The labeling isolated the litigant from his community. The CIA granted before the court that the accusation was a fabrication but stated it was designed to achieve a worthy national goal. The court sided with the agency, stating that the legitimate activities of the government should not be hampered by the application of legal principles.

Patriots supporting the CIA assert that the government has the right to keep secret operational decisions affecting private American institutions so long as the national interest, as interpreted by them, so dictates. The law, state the patriots, supports this view. The secret deployment of funds to organizations without the knowledge of its members is justifiable if designed to achieve a worthy objective. Countervailing power through the exposure of decisions to critical inquiry out in the open is not possible in some operations of government.

As a consequence of the 1967 publicity against the agency, the President established a commission to investigate what in effect amounted to its own operations. The commission found the policy of government worthy. Its chairman stated that a full disclosure as to the nature and extent of the relationships between the CIA and private organizations was inadvisable. Thus the government investigated itself and found itself not wanting. And the Central Intelligence Agency retreated back into the shadows.

[7] The presidential practice of developing and maintaining a war spirit does not lack in strong precedents. American wars have been fought by presidents who manipulated the public by selectivity of information. A long line of presidents have performed in this style, including Wilson, Roosevelt, Truman, Eisenhower, Johnson, and Nixon. The very presidents who plead strict construction of the constitution make no bones about taking away the war power from the Congress, where it belongs under the constitution.

THE INDOCHINA WAR

The war in Indochina is an illegitimate offspring of the untouchables mid-wifed by university intellectuals. The intervention represents decision making in dribbles, calculated use of deception, and technological commitments of no return, whose combined effects was the escalation of a series of errors to disastrous proportions. The war comprises a case history of management based on power calculations devoid of human criteria which civilized men expect in foreign affairs. Presidential credibility as an issue originates from the furtive manner in which President Eisenhower laid the basis for intervention. Those who collaborated in those early decisions, untouchables and professors, established a basis of no return for succeeding presidents. The war came through the back door without support of the public. It was first bothersome, something to get over with as quickly as possible and forgotten. Later, it forged a deep quarrel among Americans, nurtured by the deceptive style in which presidents merchandized the intervention. The untouchables proved a point: they can make errors of small impact with impunity but not mistakes of such proportion as the Vietnam war.

History of the War. The justification to intervene in the early 1950's in support of a client state was that a buffer could be raised against China at little cost. Eisenhower set a course that proved irreversible. He made his decision quietly, in the upper middle class untouchable circles and acquired the wide backing of the system. It gained the support of university professors whose monolithic view of communism sanctioned the president's power play. It acquired the backing of prominent liberals, including that of Robert Kennedy, who years later sought to make capital of his new vision of the war. Of the five hundred-odd· Democrats and Republicans in the national legislature, two spoke out against. Both, Senators Morse of Oregon and Gruening of Alaska, lost their re-election bids. The president of the trade union federation gave the war his blessing and never retreated an inch from his position. President Meany took the position that those in organized labor who opposed the war were communist-tainted. Top management of industrial firms remained silent. When the war took a turn for the worse, some businessmen organized against it. But they turned out to be men in small firms, including enterprises with no defense contracts and managers of real estate, finance, and insurance firms. The public was told that North Vietnam had committed aggression against South Vietnam. But in fact the United States was the aggressor. South Vietnam became a creature of the United States.

Eisenhower fortified the struggle as an ideological conflict by his support of well-to-do rightist elements in Laos and Vietnam. Each of the two successive presidents inherited a deteriorated position. Each president was fed optimistic reports of success by military personnel and by civilians making military judgments, such as Professor Walt W. Rostow. Through the year 1963, until President Diem's assassination in late November, the United States maintained close liaison with the military clique plotting against him. Henry Cabot Lodge, a Wasp of high reputation, managed the liaison. By the following year the die was cast: ever-deepening involvement. By 1970, the feasible option left Nixon narrowed down to extrication in a strategy of minimizing costs and salvaging some returns. The results of his skirmishes in Cambodia and Laos, under an already established precedent of deception, underscored the futility of the intervention.

Those in the establishment supporting the war did not anticipate the moral reaction against it. In early 1968, for example, the former president of Columbia University declared his opposition on the basis the war no longer provided a foreseeable long range benefit to the United States. While students at the university were revolted by the war on moral principles, its president rejected the intervention after applying the managerial technique of cost-benefit analysis.

Former Secretary of Defense Robert McNamara applied a similar management tool. The secretary had acquired in the mass communications media a reputation as a man of extraordinary managerial talents. He became caught in the web of the military mind that responds to failure on the battlefield with ever mounting requests for escalation. In the grip of rising perturbations about the war, the Secretary of Defense left his post and assumed the directorship of the World Bank, to serve, as President Johnson stated, all of mankind.

As frustration mounted, justification for the war by its managers shifted like the pea in a shell game. As the prevailing rationale for the intervention became absurd, the justification was rewritten. Explanations shifted from containing China, to preserving democracy, fulfilling solemn treaty obligations at the request of the Saigon government, stopping North Vietnamese aggression, and thwarting an unprovoked attack upon the United States.[8] The substance of the China containment argument was that national security required a demonstration on the part of the United States that the communist doctrine of world domination could not possibly succeed. The argument was analogous to one sanc-

---

[8] A disclosure by the United States Department of State in 1969 shows no formal written request for assistance was ever made by the Saigon government.

tioning the involvement of the Soviet Union in a Mexican civil war in order to prevent the United States from exerting influence on a border state.

It was soon no longer possible to keep the war under the rug. In 1964 there were some 23,000 American military advisors in Vietnam. In the presidential campaign of that year, President Johnson made the statement that he was not about to send American boys nine or ten thousand miles away to do what Asian boys ought to be doing; soon thereafter, he escalated the intervention to a troop commitment of five hundred thousand. Desperate for a convincing reason, his Secretary of State announced that the purpose of the war was to make North Vietnam stop whatever she was doing. Later, the nub of his argument amounted to: we were there because we were there.

In late 1969 Nixon made his contribution to the word game by stating we were there because withdrawing precipitously would cause future wars. In 1970 the president injected the idea of preventing a blood bath by the North Vietnamese. He brought forward no evidence that any more of a blood bath would occur than that which the continuing presence of the United States produced. As in the case of the assertions of his predecessors, Nixon's assertions appeared to be intended to gain a favorable emotional response from the public. Real purposes had to be sought in oblique references and slips of the tongue.

The war divided university intellectuals between those who assisted in the rationalizations and those who denounced them. Both employed their skill at abstraction to justify the superior merit of their position. Some showed a deftness in being dovish for Vietnam and hawkish for Israel. Pro-Vietnam scholars argued from the premise that the threat of power from an adversary should be met with counter power. If the desired objective is not obtained, the price of not agreeing to one's terms should be raised until the adversary knuckles under.

The armchair warriors showed nimble footwork. Their argument, roughly, goes like this: equilibrium in the world is good and disequilibrium is bad. The United States, as the fighter for freedom, must exercise power so as to maintain international equilibrium by controlling change consistent with the national interest. (Who gives the United States this responsibility and who interprets the national interest are not in the list of propositions.) Therefore, the United States must be ready to use its power in order to maintain equilibrium. Thus, the syllogism, by not questioning its premises, moves to an unassailable conclusion. The pessimism of Cold War warriors over the likelihood of disequilibrium is fulfilled by the way the government moseys around looking for disequilibrium points. The threat of communism becomes thereby a self-fulfilling prophecy. When these university strategists arc asked why the country should become involved this way, their faces light up with incredulity. Three major results accrue from this traditional view of international power: a game plan that keeps bureaucrats busy, euphoria for those who manage it, and a guarantee of perpetual disequilibrium.

A statement of fourteen university scholars reflects the thinking that it sometimes takes a war to stop a war. They state:

> To accept a Communist victory in Vietnam would serve as a major encouragement to those forces in the world opposing peaceful co-existence, to those elements committed to the thesis that violence (that of North Vietnam) is the best means of effecting change. It would gravely jeopardize the possibilities of a political equilibrium in Asia, seriously damage our credibility, deeply affect the morale and the policies of our Asian allies and the neutrals. These are not developments conducive to a long range peace. They are more likely to prove precursors to larger, more costly wars.[9]

As the number of university critics of Vietnam mounted, Secretary of State Rusk was forced to state that he was not afraid of intellectuals. The fact that a man knows everything about enzymes, stated the Secretary, does not mean he knows everything about Vietnam. The intellectual alluded to was a former government policy advisor when government policy was more to his liking. The professor is quoted as saying he knows a damn sight more about Vietnam than the Secretary did about enzymes. There the exchange rested.[10]

In past American wars managed as private affairs, the government often succeeded in giving them a moral wrapping. Mexicans, for example, were killed because they were barbarians; nobody could effectively challenge such a conclusion. The quickness and remoteness of a war made easy the task of providing it with a convincing imagery. The protracted Vietnam intervention and instantaneous information on the part of news media sensationalizing events made such imagery impossible.

In addition, the war lacked a constitutional basis. Its strongest advocates, paradoxically, were those who in other circumstances would insist on a strict construction of the constitution. But a war supported by law and order advocates lacking a constitutional authority would not necessarily be fatal. The flaw of the war lay in its prolongation, which revealed its lack of moral substance. While its managers rose above the nagging moral question, the public did not. As this moral implication spread slowly into the consciousness of people, the war became an obscenity.

9 *The New York Times*, December 20, 1967.
10 *The New York Times*, October 13, 1967.

The war pitted a first rate power against a primitive rural people moved by an ideological conviction absent in the enemy. The military poured on the population a tonnage of bombs in excess of that dropped in Europe during the entire second World War. There was no industrial machine, however, for the bombs to destroy. The bombs failed to force North Vietnam to sue for peace and rallied the people to resist. The bombing alienated a considerable element of world opinion. Yet the military labeled its extraordinary use of firepower a policy of restraint.

The military won each daily battle and lost the war. Its progress reports took the form of body counts reminiscent of a duck shoot. In 1967 the commander in Vietnam in that year of the war, General Westmoreland, announced that the enemy's guerrilla force was declining at a steady rate and morale problems were developing in his ranks. A month before the Vietcong Tet offensive in 1968, the general predicted that many victories would soon be forthcoming. The Tet offensive left some 500,000 civilians homeless and destroyed the pacification program used as propaganda in support of the war. Nevertheless, in an example of official re-think, the United States government announced that the Vietcong had been defeated. How so? The objective of the enemy was a popular uprising and no such event had occurred. General Maxwell D. Taylor concluded the offensive represented a net victory for the allies. Walt W. Rostow, intellectual-in-chief in the Johnson administration, observed that General Westmoreland's assessment could well prove right.

The war's history is replete with one announcement of progress after another. In 1964 the Secretary of Defense promised the troops would be home by Christmas 1965; in 1966, that the war would be over by mid-1967; in 1968 a high ranking admiral stated the Tet offensive was the last convulsive spasm of the enemy. In 1970 President Nixon announced what he called the most successful campaign of the whole war: the invasion of Cambodia. The war was not won but no battle was ever lost.

The biggest impact of American firepower was on the civilian population. More civilians died than American and South Vietnamese soldiers combined. More casualties occurred among civilians than the total combined casualties of all military combatants. The majority of civilian casualties comprised women and children, most of them due to American fire power. At one point in the war the civilian casualty rate reached a hundred thousand annually. In the destruction of the old imperial capital of Hue, some 3,600 civilians were killed. In the extermination of Ben Tre, a thousand civilians died from the use of air bombs, 155mm. artillery, napalm, and rockets to route an enemy force of twice that number.

A considerable number of the civilian casualties were inflicted by anti-personnel weapons whose shot scatters over a wide area and travels through the body in an irregular path. One ingenious weapon contains what are called fish hooks, which perform the job of impaling human beings. The weapons are made by respectable firms including Cessna Aircraft, Honeywell, General Tire and Rubber Company, and the Sperry Rand Corporation.[11]

The policy of military vengeance destroyed the policy of gaining the support of the population. The killing of an American soldier by a nucleus of Vietcong would trigger a decision to destroy an entire village. The military technology destroyed the pacification program itself. A hamlet would be secured. The enemy would infiltrate at night and announce their presence with a spurt of machine gun fire. The Americans would retaliate a thousand fold including air and artillery fire. The enemy would slip away and the civilians of what used to be a village remained to be buried.

The destruction of the innocent is tolerable when performed by remote mechanisms of military technology. An American who kills by pressing a button would find hand-to-hand combat with a knife repugnant; enshrouded in military technology, the task becomes less distasteful, if not pleasant. Modern technology desensitizes him. Air Force pilots approach their bombing chores in a spirit akin to anticipation of the hunting season. It could be sheer excitement up in the wild blue yonder, especially when no rival air force exists of similar fire power. One aviator enrolled in the service after seeing Errol Flynn in "Dawn Patrol" at least eight times. He is quoted as saying he fails to see how the North Vietnamese can take it day in and day out. Air Force killing is a neat sort of killing that protects the killer from seeing the death agony of his victim. It marks a triumph in modern technology.

A soldier who is told he is liberating people expects them to be grateful. But it turned out that the people wanted to be liberated from the Americans. They did not warm up to the idea of gaining their freedom. Accordingly, exasperation soon turns to contempt, to little distinction between the enemy and any "slant-eye," and finally to sadism. In a remark attributed to a Negro combat sergeant, the distinction between a civilian and the enemy was that if the person is running and keeps on running when told to stop with a rifle pointed at him, he then becomes the enemy.

Sixty percent of the civilian casualties in Vietnam were children. The Mylai massacre dramatizes the fact that the intervention was a war

[11] The Council on Economic Priorities, *Economic Priorities Report*, Vol. 1, April 1970, Washington, D.C.

against the civilian population. The press reports witnesses as giving the following accounts:

> A boy, three or four years old, just stood there with big eyes staring around, like he didn't understand; he didn't believe what was happening. Then the captain's radio operator put a burst of M-16 fire into him.[12]
>
> They had them in a group standing over a ditch, just like a Nazi-type thing. One officer ordered a kid to machine gun everybody down, but the kid just couldn't do it. I don't remember seeing any men in the ditch. Mostly women and kids. A lot of guys feel that they (South Vietnamese civilians) aren't human beings. We just treated them like animals.[13]
>
> He just couldn't stop. He thought it was funny, funny, funny. One guy, I heard, shot directly at somebody with an M-79 grenade launcher from 10 or 15 yards. Boom! He blew him all apart.[14]

The military communiqué covering the action of that day stated:

> In an action today American divisional forces have killed 128 enemy near Quangnai City.[15]

The barbarism was unplanned. It evolved slowly from what appeared to be feasible decisions by politicians and military officials, which were subsequently mangled in the machinery that interlaces the State Department, Defense, and the White House. The bureaucratic authority of some one hundred individuals in these establishments limits the control of the President and the two Secretaries and their knowledge as to what the bureaucrats are doing. Consequently, the President may be pursuing a course of action that may be undermined by the acts of subordinates. The inconsistency is aggravated by a President sensitive to security, who keeps his actions and information secret, within the reach of only two or three other individuals.

This delegation of authority and closing of information channels tended to scuttle attempts to terminate the conflict. The war is replete with accounts of top government officials, each not knowing what the others were doing and not remembering commitments made. These styles of management not only frustrated peace efforts but also underwrote a belief in the duplicity of government.

In contrast to the bottom of the military ranks, populated primarily by ethnics, top management rested in the hands of members of old

---

[12] Quoted by Anthony Lewis in *The New York Times*, November 22, 1969.
[13] *The New York Times*, November 16, 1969.
[14] The Philadelphia *Evening Bulletin*, December 16, 1969.
[15] Quoted by James Reston, *The New York Times*, November 26, 1969. According to the reports, some soldiers were revolted by the spectacle. The majority, however, went about their business, laughing, raping, and using Vietnamese for target practice.

American families. Its president managers were Johnson and Nixon; its principal assistant managers Henry Cabot Lodge, Ellsworth Bunker, McGeorge Bundy, General Westmoreland, U. Alexis Johnson, Dean Rusk, Foster Dulles, and Maxwell Taylor.

theory: Unless communist expansion was stopped at its source, it would

The war emerged out of the best of times for Eisenhower's domino spread outward throughout Southeast Asia and across the Pacific, ever closer to the beaches of California. A critical scrutiny of this notion would have been seized upon as being soft on communism. It was the era of McCarthyism and a time when Congress had authorized the setting up of detention facilities for persons suspected of plotting espionage and sabotage.

Each cautious decision to escalate a little more produced only one alternative for the next decision: more escalation. Faced with the criticism of throwing away investment in men and money, the managers found it less risky to try to make a bad decision workable than to reverse it entirely. The series of steps beginning with the covert actions managed by Eisenhower and the Vietnamization policy of Nixon can best be seen in that light.

Gulf of Tonkin. In August of 1964, a United States naval operation in the Gulf of Tonkin off the North Vietnamese coast provided the rationale for the bombing of North Vietnam and a blank check from the Congress to mount a full scale war, which the legislature gave to President Johnson, with only two dissenting votes, in the form of the Tonkin Gulf resolution. The resolution found that without provocation the vessels of North Vietnam had deliberately and repeatedly attacked United States ships lawfully present in the gulf and thereby created a serious threat to international peace.

Facts surfacing after the passage of the Congressional resolution weakened those mustered to produce the vote. It was brought out that the attacks of August 2nd and 4th were preceded by aggressive South Vietnamese naval action in the same area with the intelligence support of American vessels instructed to proceed within eleven miles of the North Vietnamese coast. At the time the resolution was requested, Congress was not told that such an intelligence mission was being conducted. A staff study of the Senate Foreign Relations Committee found that the incident was designed to force the North Vietnamese and Chinese to expose their monitoring systems through provocative American acts. Moreover, it was subsequently determined that a few hours before the bombing of North Vietnam began, the commander of the Pacific fleet was trying to ascertain if the attack had actually occurred. Furthermore, some fifteen hours before the encounter, the two American vessels had warned higher command that the North Vietnamese regarded them as enemy craft. Despite this warning, the destroyers were not ordered to terminate their mission.[16]

The resolution portrayed the actions of the North Vietnamese as a deliberate and systematic campaign of aggression. In testimony of Department of Defense officials before the Senate Foreign Relations Committee, the destroyer patrols were described as having the function of serving as decoys to draw away the North Vietnamese from South Vietnamese coastal bombardment and of gathering intelligence by provoking an electronic response. The Secretary of Defense stated to the Committee that the American Navy had played no part in the coastal bombardment. Technically, he was speaking the truth.

Facts uncovered subsequent to the Senate Committee inquiry also indicate that evidence of an attack on the American destroyers consisted of four crew members saying they saw a wake that presumably was a torpedo coming from a North Vietnamese vessel. In addition, it was revealed that the Johnson administration had prepared contingent drafts of the resolution before the incident had taken place. Press reports of private statements made by White House officials indicate the President had a draft of the resolution in his pocket for some time before the alleged attacks.[17]

Thus, the Tonkin Gulf resolution—what according to Under Secretary of State Katzenbach in the Johnson administration amounted to the legalization of the war—appeared to come out of either a communication failure, self-delusion, or calculated duplicity to provide an excuse for escalation. Under pressure, the Defense Department kept its skirts clean. The Johnson administration conceded that the American destroyers came within eight miles of the North Vietnamese coast, or four miles within the claimed sovereign waters of North Vietnam. But the administration stuck to its claim that the adversary had committed acts of aggression. To explain the decision of the government to seek the resolution in terms of communication failure seems least plausible. Self-delusion is common in difficult circumstances when men often see only those facts that provide the possibility of extricating themselves. On the other hand, the scattered evidence suggests calculated duplicity.

The preamble to the Tonkin resolution reads as follows:

Whereas naval units of the Communist regime in Vietnam, in violation of the principles of the Charter of the United Nations and of international law, have deliberately and repeatedly attacked United States naval vessels

16 *The New York Times,* February 24, 1968.
17 Editorial, *The New York Times,* March 12, 1968.

lawfully present in international waters and have thereby created a serious threat to international peace; and

Whereas these attacks are part of a deliberate and systematic campaign of aggression that the Communist regime in North Vietnam has been waging against its neighbors and the nations joined with them in the collective defense of their freedom; and

Whereas the United States is assisting the peoples of Southeast Asia to protect their freedom and has no territorial, military, or political ambitions in that area, but desires only that these peoples should be left in peace to work out their own destinies in their own way:

Now therefore, be it resolved that . . .

The preamble in effect comprises a series of falsehoods. Aborted fiction requires continuing fictions thereafter.[18]

Beginning the De-escalation.   In late 1966 the Secretary of Defense expressed disillusionment over the war's course and suggested a reduction in bombing as an inducement to negotiate. Other influential voices expressed the view that further escalation would be unproductive. The military chiefs continued to be bullish, proposing more troops, more bombing, and extension of the war into Laos and Cambodia. The cleavage between military and civilian advisors widened perceptibly. A new line emerged from the ranks of presidential advisors that relegated the military to a minority position.

On February 28, 1968, the Joint Chiefs of Staff presented a request for additional troops. Because of their opposition, the President refused to accept the Defense Secretary's plan of a curb on bombing. On March 18th he lashed out against the dove sentiment among his advisors and raised the specter of a Munich style appeasement. But at the same time he invited dovish United Nations Representative Arthur Goldberg to a meeting of policy advisors on March 25th. Each advisor sought to influence the content of a speech planned for delivery by the President in six days. Some argued that halting the bombing would improve the President's domestic and foreign position. The Secretary of Defense urged a termination of the bombing. The President was impressed with the disposition of a hawk such as McGeorge Bundy to defect. Both Arthur Goldberg and Under Secretary of State George W. Ball advocated cessation of the bombing.

On March 28th, the Secretary of Defense, State Department officials, and White House representatives met to polish the impending speech.

18 In an installment of his book, *The Vantage Point*, published in *The New York Times* of October 20, 1971, President Lyndon Johnson presents the first of the two incidents as an attack by North Vietnam approximately 30 miles off its coast and the incident of August 4th as a second provocation.

310 THE INSTITUTIONS

The New Secretary of Defense, Clark Clifford, rejected the hawkish tone of the draft and proposed a revision cutting back the bombing to the 20th parallel. From that moment on each progressive draft became more conciliatory. Three days later the President tied his announcement of a bombing halt with one stating his decision not to seek re-election. Within 36 hours after the announcement, Navy jets struck a target between the 19th and 20th parallel. The Secretary of Defense, against the opposition of Walt W. Rostow, Chairman of the Joint Chiefs of Staff General Wheeler, and General Westmoreland, persuaded the President to push back the line to the 19th parallel.

Soon thereafter, negotiations began with the North Vietnamese for direct talks. Agreement was reached to meet at the conference table in Paris on October 31st. The United States acquiesced to the presence of the Vietcong at the conference. Thus evolved the first step in the withdrawal of the United States through a halt in the air, naval, and artillery bombardment of North Vietnam.[19]

In 1969, the Nixon administration announced the planned withdrawal of American troops. Consistent with the imperative of maintaining an illusion, a strategy was devised to lose the war without appearing to do so by imposing the burden of its loss on the government's South Vietnamese clients. The new policy was labeled Vietnamization.

In the same year, the Green Beret scandal burst forth. A South Vietnamese in the employ of the Army Green Beret Special Forces as an intelligence agent in Cambodia came under suspicion of having moonlighted for the Vietcong. The Green Berets took umbrage at this part time employment. Discussions began with the CIA on what to do with the man. Killing him was one of the suggested options. According to press reports, Saigon advised the Green Berets to return the man to duty. But the instructions arrived too late. The man was murdered gangster-style, dumped into the sea after being weighted down with tire rims. The trigger man is quoted as saying he acted out of patriotic impulse.

Fearing retaliation because of knowing too much, a soldier spilled the beans to the Army brass. The Army, piqued at the deception of the Green Berets, instituted court-martial proceedings. The Secretary of the Army announced he was having success in resisting pressure to dismiss the charges and that such a dismissal would be unfair. Eleven days after the Secretary of the Army announced he was on a virtue course, the Nixon administration advised the Army to drop the courts-martial in the national interest. And so it did.

[19] *The New York Times*, March 7, 1969.

On October 15th of the same year, a group calling themselves the Vietnam Moratorium Committee staged an unprecedented outpouring of several million persons to demonstrate against the war. While most of the demonstrators were college students, they also included professional employees, trade unionists, clergymen, servicemen, and employees in the performing arts and publishing. A White House aide stated that he did not think that the President could be affected by a demonstration of any kind. The Vice President described the moratorium as the creation of an effete corps of impudent snobs who characterize themselves as intellectuals.

The following November 3rd, the day before elections, and prior to the demonstrations of the New Mobilization Committee to End the War in Vietnam scheduled for the week following, President Nixon delivered a speech on the war. The president stated that his prior moves for peace had met intransigeance on the part of the adversary.[20] He summarized in a few sentences the historical antecedents of the conflict as an aggression by North Vietnam. He referred to the withdrawal of American forces and the Vietnamization of the war. A display of sympathetic communications from the public followed the speech. At the time of delivery, the news wires began to print a formidable list of names supporting the President.

On the whole, the November 15th anti-war demonstration was orderly. Its participants appeared more self-assured than the troubled officialdom who had planned their reception. Some intellectuals in the demonstration raised hippy Hoffman to hero status; they proclaimed him the new revolutionary leader. At the protest's climax, the president was reported as watching a football game on television. Referring to the demonstration as akin to the Russian Bolshevik Revolution, the wife of the Attorney General pronounced her displeasure with liberal communists.

Early 1970 produced a dramatic turn in the war's history. On April 30th, the President announced his invasion of Cambodia. Two days later, he referred to college students as bums, adding thereby a cryptic term to the extensive rhetoric of the Vice President. On May 4th, Ohio National Guard troops killed four students on the Kent State University campus. The White House issued a statement which appeared to say that the students got what they deserved. On the following Friday,

20 Actually, Mr. Nixon was involved in the Vietnam intervention long before his talk indicates. In 1953, he was urging the French not to negotiate and President Eisenhower to intervene with American troops. The critical comment by television commentators following the talk provoked the Vice President to denounce the networks. Commentators were critical of the impression the President conveyed. One of the commentors asserted the Ho Chi Minh letter referred to by the President was actually conciliatory.

on the eve of another demonstration, the President announced withdrawal of American troops from Cambodia by June's end. Nevertheless, through his actions, the Vietnam intervention, together with the secret war in Laos, evolved into the Indochina War.

In the year following, *The New York Times* published portions of a Department of Defense secret history of Vietnam pilfered and passed along by an individual who had shifted from a hawk of deep feeling to a dove of equally deep feeling. The papers comprised a mixture of decisions made, assessments of the situation, estimates of future outcomes, recommendations, and contingency plans. The message they conveyed was affected by the researchers who assembled them, the journalists who prepared them for publication, and the absence of related communications of the White House and State Departments. The *Times* held the papers for several months and then published them without alerting the government, arrogating to itself the problem of national security. It presented the papers in a way that highlighted the contrasts between public and private statements on the war.

The following are excerpts from the *Times:*

Public	Private
Mr. President, Representative Laird of Wisconsin declared that the Administration is preparing to move the Vietnam war into the North. Is there any substance to this claim?	The United States policy is to prepare immediately to be in a position on 72 hours notice to initiate the previously recommended retaliatory actions against North Vietnam.
I know of no plans that have been made to that effect.	
Mr. Secretary (of Defense), can you give us the basic reasons for the Gulf of Tonkin patrol?	The destroyer patrols in the Gulf of Tonkin were an element in the covert military pressures against North Vietnam.
It is a routine patrol of the type we carry out in international waters all over the world.	
Two U. S. barracks areas were subjected to deliberate surprise attacks. As in the case of the North Vietnam attacks in the Gulf of Tonkin last August, the response (of an air strike against North Vietnam) is appropriate and fitting. We seek no wider war.	We believe that the best available way of increasing our chance of success in Vietnam is the development and execution of a policy of sustained reprisal against North Vietnam.[21]

[21] *The New York Times,* The Week in Review, June 20, 1971.

Other newspapers followed suit. One reveals McGeorge Bundy, advisor to President Johnson, applying the managerial technique of cost/benefit analysis to the war. In a memorandum to the President, he states:

> While we believe that the risks of such a policy (sustained reprisal against North Vietnam) are acceptable, we emphasize that its costs are real.
>
> It implies significant U. S. air losses even if no full air war is joined. And it seems likely that it would eventually require an extensive and costly effort against the whole air defense system of North Vietnam.
>
> U.S. casualties would be high and more visible to American feelings than those sustained in the struggle in South Vietnam. Yet, measured against the costs of defeat in Vietnam, the program seems cheap.[22]

Court actions against publication of these documents generated newspaper speculation that the issue involved the government's right to protect national security versus freedom of the press. The papers downgraded the security problem and wrote editorials bestowing upon themselves the obligation of serving the right of the public to be informed. Their position was that once having such information they acquired the responsibility of deciding if their duty to inform the public transcended questions of national security. But with more reflection, the issue emerged as one of balancing the interests of government, the press, and the public. Within this framework, some quarters suggested that the conflict comprised a battle between institutions, the government and the news media, on their respective prerogatives in managing the news served to the public.

The published documents are of limited usefulness as a source of new knowledge about the general course of the war. They do not reveal much more than could have been obtained from published information of the prior decade, including government leaks to the press. They are also of limited value as a means of analyzing the government's decision making process. The papers derive from a portion of the total information flow going to and from the President. Even that segment is limited by the documents' management by the researchers and then by the newspapers. They do not reveal the President's basis of choosing among the range of opinions channeled to him. The researchers imputed attitudes and motives to principals from the reading of official documents. By identifying individuals participating in the contest of opinion they provided opportunities for searching out scapegoats. Two principals, the President and his Secretary of State, are shadowy figures.

The New York Times' defense to having published the stolen documents is self-serving. To say that the papers belong to the public is

22 The Philadelphia *Sunday Bulletin*, June 20, 1971.

rhetoric, since no individual member can go down to the national capital to make such a claim. There must be rules, subject to change through democratic debate, that give both the government rights in maintaining its decision making process confidential and give the public rights of access to such information. The newspaper claims to be the agent of the public, interpreting and fulfilling its needs as it sees them. By inference, in a multi-institutional society, accountability and responsibility in the case of newspapers are to be determined by themselves. The government fell for this fallacious reasoning by accepting the issue as one of national security versus freedom of the press.

The newspapers did little to prevent the public from being misled. The reader was not encouraged or helped to distinguish between contingency plans and options chosen and the time references of each. The apparent deception and coldbloodedness of the papers are partly explainable by mitigating factors. The individuals who wrote them were hands hired by the President. Unlike high officials in the British parliamentary system, they do not have their own political base with which to voice the opinion of dissenting constituencies. Moreover, the squeezing of thought into official prose to be sent to the boss may erroneously suggest bloodless individuals of a morality inferior to the indignant one reading the accounts. But this juxtaposition of moral character may be unjustified. Indeed, armed with the advantage of hindsight, the reader can easily conclude that many of the President's pen pals were not especially bright. Third, the apparent deception reflects in part the necessity of informing the public in a way that does not promote the interests of the adversary.

A usefulness of the papers may lie in the drama of their impact on the public and in the subsequent curtailment of a U. S. president's ability to execute a war by manipulating public information. The filching and publication of the documents did not stop the deceptive practices of government nor did the revelations prevent the launching of a massive air attack on North Vietnam in 1972 with the majority support of the public.

CONCLUDING OBSERVATIONS

By their militaristic anti-communist policies since World War II, the untouchables of the United States have made a most significant contribution to the collapse of national unity. In the course of two decades, they changed the image of the United States from the moral voice of the world to the voice of hypocrisy. The result is indeed a paradox. The purveyors of love of country hardly can be accused of wanting such an outcome. Yet their policies have destroyed confidence in the authenticity of national government. Wanting government to be a symbol of unity, they created a symbol of duplicity instead.

At the end of the Second World War, with the approval of the Supreme Court, the United States executed the Japanese General Yamashita for the commission by his troops of crimes of which he had neither knowledge nor control. At that time, in the Nuremberg trial of the Nazi leaders of Germany, the United States developed out of its sense of moral outrage an international law which affirmed that top military and civilian leaders of a nation are responsible for the behavior of their military. Now, some two and a half decades later, the American commander in Vietnam is exonerated by the Secretary of the Army for the behavior of Company C at Mylai on the grounds that he had no knowledge of the incident until months afterward. And the same commander congratulated the company for their body count of 129. Many Americans, civilian as well as military, could be held to account under principles enunciated ex post facto at the Nuremberg trials. The difference lies in the fact that these Americans are highly influential individuals in the system.

The selective service system, a vestige of World War II, became, under the leadership of an outstanding patriot, a focal point in pitting Americans against each other and in employing military service as a tool of vindictiveness against those declining to be patriotic. The system became an instrument of coercing young men into supporting an illegal war and punishing recalcitrants at a rate without precedent in American history. In a moment of candor, a federal judge passing sentence on a draft card burner stated he was concerned with the thousands of soldiers in Vietnam who were just as opposed to the war. The young man, David J. Miller, was convicted not because of the illegitimacy of his opposition, but because finding him innocent would have opened a Pandora's box.[23] In another case, a university professor was assigned to janitorial work by his draft board, the letter stating that for the maintenance of the national safety he had been assigned janitorial work at the University of Kansas Medical Center.

The war was managed according to the following doctrine: when a President finds violence necessary in the pursuit of foreign interests, he can commit the nation to a war that destroys the life and wealth of a foreign people. The President decides what constitutes the national interest while the people are expected to assume the necessary sacrifices in blood and inflation.

23 *The New York Times,* April 7, 1967. In that year, draft convictions reached 750 and penalties averaged 32 months with a substantial number of 5-years or more.

The war was triggered on the premise that the freedom of the United States was challenged by a nationalist insurrection twelve thousand miles from American shores and that the American way of life could only be preserved through corruption, coercion, and killing of foreigners. The war corrupted the minds of moralists. Thus a prominent Catholic arch-bishop, in a masterpiece of abstraction, made the judgment that the war comprised a redressing of morality.

The war forced American presidents to indulge in imagery to obscure the truth. A prince of state caught in a disastrous policy has the option either of keeping the facts hidden or of suggesting that the only alterna-tive is an outrage. The alternative, stated the prince, was abject sur-render or annihilation. And what American would want either? A month prior to the beginning of the escalation, he stated that the enemy of freedom (North Vietnam), had failed to achieve his objective, at a terrible cost to himself. The enemy had failed because thousands of Americans had stated that there would be no retreat from aggression. He hinted that a contrary view to that of these patriotic Americans would constitute betrayal. When we give our word, stated the prince of state, we have given our bond. He reiterated the hope that every American would say in the future: I stood firm with my government to preserve the way of life we hold dear. The President quoted a letter from a university intellectual, Allan Nevins, who exhorted him not to be disturbed by the "croakers." [24] The price for civilization, intoned the Chief, must be paid for in sorrow and blood.

The nobles around a prince of state can promote this re-think in several ways. Opposition to policy can be neutralized by invoking ridi-cule on it as the chief remains aloof and manifests supreme forbearance. Steps can be taken to make opposition leaders appear as fools, above all not martyrs, and perhaps to suggest also they are non-masculine types compared to those fighting bravely for the country. The nobles may cir-culate the belief that demonic forces are at work among the protesters and that the actual facts about them are not being divulged fully for fear of setting off a violent reaction against them. The restraint against the dissidence can also be singled out as proof positive of the strength of the society and the vitality of the people. Subalterns can indicate that the prince insists that the widest latitude be given protesters and that their demonstrations do not diminish his serenity.

This approach in governance is effective when facts are not allowed to emerge out of line with the imagery constructed by the prince of state. A variance creates a rising number of doubters. A rising educational

24 The New York Times, February 28, 1968.

level has the unfortunate consequence of making more difficult such a style of governing.

Another avenue available to a prince of state saddled with unworkable policy is to hint that the policy is not actually his but that of illustrious predecessors and foreign friends. Thus, in his San Antonio speech President Johnson indicated that the aggression of North Vietnam was answered by two prior presidents and by the Tonkin resolution of Congress. The President also listed America's formidable foreign friends with similar points of view: Australia, the Philippines, New Zealand, South Korea, Malaysia, Singapore, Thailand, and Taiwan. The President concluded that the keepers of peace (American armed forces) would prevail, with the full backing of the American people and their allies.

If worse comes to worst, and it sometimes does, the vice president can be mustered into service, and the stock in trade of Machiavellian politics thereby brought into fuller use. Greater poetic license in the use of slogans and invective becomes permissible. Clichés can be used more freely to submerge bothersome facts. The vice president can hint darkly at the treasonable character of the opposition view. A sure-fire tactic in American culture is to suggest that opponents lack masculinity and patriotism.[25] However, the indispensable requirement of such a technique is that the individual using it be of exceptional intelligence. Thus, when a vice president indulges in reverse-think by ascribing to protesting youth a lack of dedication to social goals and to himself honesty and patriotism, it takes impeccable talent to pull off such a reversal.

Each decision in the war comprised an escalation short of what the military demanded and taken under the illusion that the situation would thereby improve. But each decision turned out to be a miscalculation that forced the nation deeper into the quagmire. The abhorrence of each miscalculation caused the managers to seek relief in self-deception. They devised systems analyses to give them the answers they desperately sought. They fed into their systems a premise of invincibility based on an ignorance of the culture with which they were contending.

Under the stress of losing the war, the top military brass resorted to a self-imposed censorship to hide actions in violation of the policies of civilian authority and of the sense of moral decency. And generally,

25 Proving masculinity by warfare, commenced in the Vietnam War by Johnson and picked up later by Nixon and Agnew, is an old tradition in American politics. Theodore Roosevelt, stung by the criticism of Harvard men, accused them of insufficient masculine vigor. To optimize different sets of values and to avoid discharging American virility on foreigners, an equitable solution would be letting the managers shoot at each other to their heart's content. University professors who rationalize the use of violence should be permitted to join the shoot. But there probably would be no takers.

only the conscience of a common soldier uncovered these abuses of power. When the disclosure occurred, two orders of justice were dispensed: one for the top brass and another for the rank and file.

Had the intervention terminated quickly and successfully, the presidential power of starting and conducting a war regardless of constitutional limitations would have gone unchallenged. Success would have given propriety to the use of power. But the intervention failing, the Congress began to assert its war-making prerogative by restricting the options available to the president in the conflict. By so doing, the era of the executive use of arms as an instrument of foreign policy was terminated.

Consequently, with no better manner conceivable, the war corroded the anti-communist policy of over two decades. And the man who was a principal in the development of such policy, Richard Nixon, was assigned by history to oversee its demise. The policy of military intervention having failed in such a grandiose style, the whole policy crumbled. Peace became good politics.

In addition, by using patriotism as a means of gaining support for the war, the intervention generated a critical response against it. The continuing strain on patriotism forced it into an idea of manliness. And manliness meant requiring ethnics to take up a gun in support of the venture of armchair warriors who stay home to plan its execution. The word patriotism was reduced to a self-serving absurdity.

The issue of presidential credibility generated by the war still hovers over the political process. It came into full bloom in the Johnson administration. As a candidate for presidential office, Nixon proclaimed the era of candor with the people; his subsequent style of management indicated no change in the credibility gap. Presidential rhetoric continues to be neither a description of reality nor a statement of intent. The purpose of White House talk is not to reveal the truth but to lay the basis of pursuing a not fully revealed course of action.

The debacle triggered political pressure to contain the military. Rising Congressional sentiment against the military establishment surfaced in a narrow victory for the ABM system of defense in 1969. The forces against the new deployment lost by one vote in the United States Senate. In another action, a group of Senators and Congressmen issued a report stating that the premise behind a defense budget should not be fighting wars abroad but defending American soil. Throughout the analysis runs the theme that defense appropriations are militarizing society, diverting resources from urgent domestic needs, and polarizing the people. These outcomes, it is argued, are encouraged by the creation of a centralized defense department welded together as a single force resisting democratic control. That such a group of Senators and Congressmen could take such a position without damaging their political careers reflected a shift in American sentiment.[26]

Firepower was the only American weapon in an ideological struggle. Firepower gained every particular objective and lost the war. Body counts measured its successes. The government demonstrated a capability in the technology to destroy and an incapability in the technology to win over the underprivileged. The technology supported the corrupt and the privileged, assisting them in suppressing the insurgency of the population; but by so doing the day of reckoning was merely postponed. The war brought the star of the untouchables on a path of decline. The conflict gained nothing for the United States. The greatest profit went to the nation against whom the intervention was initially directed: China.

The government was trapped in a policy of anti-communist ideology supported by the force of arms, formulated by Secretaries of State Dulles and Acheson and brought forward by succeeding administrations. The social scientists assisted by feeding information as to what results could be expected from a new dosage of military destruction. They were consistently wrong in their estimates. By rising up against the intervention, the American public took the government out of the trap. In this sense, the war was a victory for the people over their government.

The war produced a lesson in countervailing power. The traditional power blocs did not prevent its inception and acquiesced to its execution. Against the opposition of traditional power blocs, Americans developed their own organizations to counter the forces of war. These counterforces reached a fullness of intensity in the stunning defeat of the foreign aid program in the United States Senate in 1971. The rise of counter power was slow and laborious. The war also demonstrated that it is easier for a powerful nation to yield to the temptation to exert influence on other nations than to first ascertain clearly the purposes of such exercise. The latter requires restraint, wisdom, and self-effacement, qualities which those who manage influence often lack, which leads eventually to the dissipation of the power they inherit.

EPILOGUE

The United States military venture in Indochina grinds down to a halt. After 4 years of a presidential pledge to end the war, after twenty thousand more American dead, a hundred billion more dollars in resources, and millions more of Indochinese killed, wounded, and

26 *The New York Times,* June 1, 1969. The report was signed by nine Senators and thirty-six Congressmen.

homeless, the American intervention ends. The terms of cease fire are worse than those acquired by the French after their defeat in 1954 at Dienbienphu. The demilitarized zone between the two Vietnams is abolished; the Vietcong are recognized as the legitimate government of territory under its control; the North Vietnamese army remains in the South; the communists become part of a tripartite administrative council in South Vietnam and firmly establish themselves throughout Indochina. The war's objective of a South Vietnamese government under the tutelage of the United States is lost. Thus, in his words, President Nixon finds peace with honor and not peace with surrender.

The war defied rationality. Its significance was the endless slaughter and the endless deception. In terms of its children, agriculture, industry, government, we converted Vietnam into a beggar economy. The American people wanted the war to end much sooner, but no political mechanism existed to force the President to do so. Presidential rhetoric succeeded in blunting opposition to the conflict. The living dead without arms, legs, face, genitalia, were hidden away so as not to arouse the public conscience. Face saving turned out to be more than an oriental custom.

Deception made the war palatable. Vietnamization turned out to be another piece of deception. It emerged not as a call for peace but as a recognition of failure by the United States Army and as a plan for continuing the war by more effective management of the public. It sought terms of settlement not earned on the battlefield. The worthless commando raid on a prisoner of war camp, raised to heroic proportions, was another piece of deception. The doctrine of military action to safeguard American lives was still another deception. The government had lied so much that an additional fabrication produced no outrage. Not telling it like it is had at last become a success.

The conviction of Lieutenant Calley brings to the surface the affliction of abstraction. A liberal clergyman intones we are all guilty. Another laments punishing one individual for the war. Conservatives make the lieutenant a hero. Some find joy in identifying with his brutality. Religious sadists make him an exemplar of Christianity. Everybody, in grief, in pleasure, and in indifference, is to blame; therefore, nobody is to blame. These voices have their fling in a paroxysm of collective guilt, collective pleasure, and collective hatred. They are incapable of envisioning the murder of a child by the cracking of his skull, of weeping, and of condemning one person at a time.

Modern war comprises an organized imposition of cruelty on the innocent for an allegedly worthy purpose. It reaps a harvest of evil. The managers who hold power commit others to die like dogs for no good reason.

INDOCHINA CHRONOLOGY

1943–1945	United States assists Vietminh against the Japanese.
1945	The Vietminh begin operations to expel the French from Indochina. Ho Chi Minh appeals for U.S. assistance.
1950	U.S. Secretary of State Dean Acheson announces military and economic support of the French in Indochina.
1954	U.S. provides Air Force mechanics to French in Indochina. Communist China proposes neutralization of Indochina.
	Geneva accords provide a cease fire between the Vietminh and French, specify that the demarcation line between North and South Vietnam is provisional, stipulate free elections, and prohibit the introduction of the troops of a foreign state. Accord signed by France and Great Britain. U.S. Under-Secretary of State Bedell Smith states that the United States will honor the accords. The American statement expresses the hope that Cambodia, Laos, and Vietnam will join the community of nations.
	Secretary of State Foster Dulles announces the formation of SEATO as a Southeast Asia military alliance under United States initiative.
	Catholic aristocrat Ngo Dinh Diem becomes Premier of the French puppet Bao Dai government.
	President Eisenhower offers Ngo Dinh Diem economic and military assistance in setting up

a South Vietnamese government. The President concedes that 80 percent of the Vietnamese people would vote for Ho Chi Minh in a free election. U.S. begins covert action in Vietnam.

1955   Diem proclaims the Republic of South Vietnam with himself as president after obtaining 98.2 percent of the vote.

1956   U.S. sends additional 350 military personnel to Saigon.

Diem refuses to hold elections as prescribed in Geneva accords.

Vietcong insurgency makes its appearance in South Vietnam as a rebellion against Diem.

1958   Coalition government in Laos falls with U.S. assistance.

1960   The National Liberation Front in South Vietnam is officially recognized by North Vietnam. Hanoi shifts from political to military insurgency.

1961   U.S. breaches the Geneva accords by exceeding limits of military advisors in South Vietnam.

1963   United States participates in plot to overthrow Diem. Premier Diem is overthrown by a military coup and assassinated.

Admiral Harry D. Felt, Commander in Chief of Pacific Forces, predicts a U.S. victory in three years.

President Kennedy in his State of the Union message states that the spearhead of aggression has been blunted in South Vietnam. The President orders covert action in North Vietnam.

The new U.S. President, Lyndon B. Johnson expresses hope the schedule of President Kennedy calling for reduction of U.S. advisors by late 1965 will be kept.

In a period of 18 months after Diem's overthrow, seven military dictatorships come to power in South Vietnam.

1964   Congress passes the Tonkin Gulf Resolution.

United States planes bomb North Vietnam.

1965   United States terms the war in Vietnam a war of foreign aggression and not a civil war.

In a memorandum to President Johnson Secretary of Defense McNamara recommends a troop total of 400,000 by the end of 1966 but warns that the deployment may not bring success.

First of the antiwar demonstrations takes place urging the ending of the bombing of North Vietnam and negotiations.

In a letter to *The New York Times,* Richard Nixon states that a victory for the Vietcong would ultimately mean the destruction of freedom for all men.

President Johnson identifies China as the real enemy behind the North Vietnamese aggression. The President authorizes the use of napalm in North Vietnam.

United States mounts air war against North Vietnam.

National Liberation Front calls for a coalition government in South Vietnam.

In a speech in Baltimore, Maryland, President Johnson announces his readiness to enter discussion provided an independent South Vietnam is guaranteed.

January 1966

In a secret memorandum, Assistant Secretary of Defense John T. McNaughton concludes bombing of North Vietnam would not be successful in the interdiction of men and materiel into South Vietnam.

March 1966

Under pressure from Joint Chiefs of Staff, Secretary of Defense recommends bombing oil facilities in North Vietnam.

August 1966

A secret Institute for Defense Analyses report concludes that the bombing of North Vietnam has had no measurable effect on North Vietnam's ability to support operations in South Vietnam. The scientists making the report recommend an electronic barrier against North Vietnam at a cost of $800 million annually.

1967

The runner-up candidate in the South Vietnam election, Truong Dinh Dzu, is given a jail term of five years.

Under-Secretary of State Nicholas de B. Katzenbach asserts that the Tonkin Gulf Resolution was the statutory equivalent of a declaration of war.

Secretary of Defense Robert McNamara resigns his post.

February 1968

The Tet offensive of the Vietcong causes Allied reverses and a request by the Joint Chiefs of Staff for more troops.

March 1968

President Johnson announces a bombing halt of North Vietnam.

November 3, 1969	President Nixon announces the policy of Vietnamization and phased withdrawal of American troops.
November 15, 1969	Antiwar demonstration by Vietnam Moblization Committee.
November 16, 1969	The Mylai massacre breaks into the news.
November 22, 1969	South Vietnam denies a massacre occurred.
March 19, 1970	Army announces indictment of high ranking officers for covering up the Songmy massacre.
April 1970	First Lieutenant James B. Duffy sentenced to 6 months confinement after revocation of a life sentence for killing a bound civilian. In his defense, Lieutenant Duffy states he believed he was being judged by the number of bodies accredited to his record.
April 1970	A former helicopter pilot states that an Army major killed 33 unarmed men, women, and children as they scattered in an open field.
March 18, 1970	Prince Sihanouk is deposed by a group of Army officers and wealthy landowners and replaced by a rightist government.
April 20, 1970	President Nixon announces the intended withdrawal of an additional 150,000 troops from Vietnam.
April 30, 1970	President Nixon, without the prior knowledge of Congress, announces an incursion into Cambodia, to save American lives and shorten the war. The announcement produces anti-war demonstrations on university campuses.
May 2, 1970	President Nixon refers to anti-war student activists as "bums."

May 4, 1970	National Guard troops at Kent State University, after breaking up a student demonstration with tear gas, fire into the demonstrators killing four students not involved in the violence. The President, through a spokesman, places the blame on the demonstrators.
May 6, 1970	Faculty members of Northeast colleges ask for the impeachment of the President for escalating the war and of the Vice President for crossing state lines and inciting to riot.
May 6, 1970	Secretary of the Interior Walter J. Hickel sends a letter to President Nixon critical of his administration. The letter states: "I believe this Administration finds itself, today, embracing a philosophy which appears to lack appropriate concern for the attitude of a great mass of Americans, our young people.
	I believe the Vice President initially has answered a deep-seated mood of America in his public statements. However, a continued attack on the young—not on their attitudes so much as their motives—can serve little purpose other than to further cement those attitudes to a solidity impossible to penetrate with reason."
May 8, 1970	President Nixon announces in a television press conference the withdrawal of all American troops from Cambodia by the end of June.
May 27, 1970	The South Vietnamese government announces it will assume responsibility for all ground combat operations by the middle of 1971.
June 3, 1970	President Nixon states his decision to invade Cambodia as the most successful operation of the war and that accordingly the Secretary of Defense has resumed the withdrawal of troops from South Vietnam.
June 4, 1970	The United States command in Saigon state that reduction of troops has not yet resumed.

June 15, 1970	The Soviet Union announces increased aid to North Vietnam.
June 19, 1970	A corporal in the United States Marine Corps tells a court-martial he had watched other marines on orders of their patrol leader shoot to death sixteen women and children in a village in Queson valley.
July 1970	Cooper-Church amendment passed in the Senate circumscribing presidential power in Cambodia including hiring of mercenary troops. The amendment represents the first challenge to the war authority of the President.
July 19, 1970	In a series of parliamentary maneuvers without recording of votes and with the support of the Nixon administration, the House of Representatives kills an attempt to vote on the Cooper-Church amendment.
July 14, 1970	A panel of United States House of Representatives finds that the Mylai incident was covered up by the Army division involved and State Department district and provincial advisory teams.
July 17, 1970	An American physician states before the House Subcommittee on Foreign Operations that she had treated the victims of beatings and tortures of a South Vietnamese interrogation center with American advisors.
July 20, 1970	President Thieu states no candidates advocating a coalition government would be permitted to run for office in South Vietnam.
September 1970	Vietcong propose withdrawal of all allied troops from Vietnam by June 1971, subsequent discussion of prisoners of war, an interim government excluding the present South Vietnamese leaders, a permanent government chosen in

elections to be supervised by the interim regime, gradual reunification of the country, and a cease fire after agreement on all points.

September 1970   President Nixon proposes a cease fire under international supervision, an Indochina peace conference, complete withdrawal of all American troops on a negotiated timetable, immediate and unconditional release of prisoners of war, and a political settlement for South Vietnam reflecting existing realities.

September 1970   Russians, North Vietnamese, and Vietcong denounce Nixon proposals.

November 1970   Nixon administration proposes military aid to Cambodia.

November 1970   Hanoi announces the bombing of an American prisoner of war camp in the Hanoi area. The United States reports the announcement is erroneous.

November 1970   United States announces bombing raid in response to the shooting down of a reconaissance plane by the North Vietnamese. United States discloses a commando raid on a prisoner of war camp in the Hanoi area and air bombing of the area.

December 1970   Congress passes $225 million military aid program for Cambodia with restrictions on sending ground combat troops and military advisors.

January 20, 1971   United States tactical air operations reported in Cambodia.

January 22, 1971   Vietcong mounts commando raids on the capital of Cambodia.

January 29, 1971   General Samuel W. Koster cleared of Mylai charges. Army rules that while General Koster had heard of some civilians killed, his failure to investigate did not constitute intentional abrogation of duty.

February 8, 1971	South Vietnamese troops invade Laos with United States air support.
February 21, 1971	Two Vietnamese priests in Saigon jailed for publishing petitions urging end of war.
February 23, 1971	Lieutenant Calley states he was under orders to shoot all civilians at Mylai. He states that he reported a body count of 50 but that his superior reported one of 250 or 300. Calley testifies in his trial that some civilians were kept alive so that they could be walked over mine fields.
February 25, 1971	President Nixon states that roughly 80 percent of the South Vietnamese people live in security.
March 12, 1971	United States Army Colonel brings charges against a General and Colonel for murder and torture of Vietnamese women and children.
March 14, 1971	Senator Edward Kennedy estimates at least 25,000 South Vietnamese were killed in 1970 and some 100,000 wounded.
March 31, 1971	Lieutenant Calley sentenced to life imprisonment for the Mylai atrocity.
April 1, 1971	President Nixon orders Lieutenant Calley released from prison pending appeals of his conviction.
April 4, 1971	Former Army Green Beret Officer states he executed espionage agent and that hundreds of such summary executions took place in Vietnam.
April 7, 1971	Army Court-martial prosecutor of Lieutenant Calley asserts the intervention of the President

in the case weakens respect for the legal process.

April 24, 1971 — 200,000 march in Washington, D.C. against the Vietnam War.

April 26, 1971 — President Nixon states he intends to disengage in Vietnam but that in doing so he rejects the counsel of the new isolationists who increase the prospects of a Communist takeover.

May 11, 1971 — Total arrests in Washington, D.C. demonstrations reported at 12,000. Attorney General compares demonstrators to Hitler's Brown Shirts.

June 15, 1971 — The U.S. government through court action seeks to suppress the publication of Vietnam War history by *The New York Times*.

June 16, 1971 — The U.S. Conference of Mayors votes for a Vietnam withdrawal by the end of 1971. U.S. Senate by 55 to 42 defeats McGovern Hatfield amendment for withdrawal by end of year.

June 22, 1971 — U.S. Senate by 57 to 42 adopts an amendment to the Draft Extension Bill stating as U.S. policy a staged withdrawal from Indochina with return of prisoners over a nine month period.

June 30, 1971 — U.S. Supreme Court 6–3 upholds newspapers publications of Vietnam papers.

July 2, 1971 — National Liberation Front proposes a simultaneous withdrawal of American forces and release of prisoners of war.

Sept 21, 1971 — The Pentagon releases the Vietnam Papers with some deletions including the participation by the Kennedy administration in the coup d'etat against Ngo Dinh Diem and the covert military operations against North Vietnam by the Johnson administration.

Sept 22, 1971

Capt. Ernest L. Medina, the last man to face murder charges in the Mylai incident, cleared of all charges.

December 17, 1971

Col. Oran K. Henderson acquitted of Mylai charges. Of the 25 officers and enlisted men charged with various offenses, one, Lt. William L. Calley, remains convicted.

December 27, 1971

United States planes stage large scale raid on North Vietnam.

March 31, 1972

North Vietnam launches an offensive in South Vietnam.

April 15, 1972

United States planes bomb Haiphong.

May 8, 1972

President Nixon orders mining of North Vietnam ports.

October 4, 1972

A Subcommittee of the U.S. House of Representatives reports American armed forces used torture and threw out of helicopters civilians suspected of being Vietcong agents.

Pentagon reports launching of 7.6 million tons of air ammunition in Indochina in seven and a half years beginning February 1965, or three and a half times the tonnage used by all the Allies during World War II.

October 26, 1972

Henry Kissinger, foreign policy advisor to President Nixon, announces that "peace is at hand."

PART FOUR

THE EMERGENCE OF ETHNIC CONSCIOUSNESS

Successes, Failures, Promises in Negro Protest

Inferiors revolt in order that they may be equal, and equals that they may be superior. Such is the state of mind which creates revolutions.
Aristotle

Blacks have mounted a formidable challenge to the system. The system's accommodation of this insurgence by placing its costs on the backs of white ethnics has produced a mixed bag of returns for blacks and a seething hostility in whites. But the allies of blacks are not the intellectuals who woo them, but the white ethnics whom the system labels racist. They have both been duped by the system. They share the anguish over the loss of cultural values that empties their lives of spirit. They both want a sense of manhood. They both have been used by the liberal as instruments of abstract notions. They do not fully perceive what the system does to them; but an unfolding consciousness makes them aware of their common plight. They will survive as genuine human beings to the extent they acquire respect for each other's rights and form an ethnic coalition.

Black and white ethnics have a common interest in forcing the system to respond to their perceptions. To achieve this response, they must negotiate their differences with the assistance of university technicians in the urban university. Failure to obtain technical assistance in formulating common goals and political strategies may bring disillusionment. Should such a technically assisted coalition come off, the future outcome of American society could be theirs to determine. Paradoxically,

335

the system's failure to negotiate terms by which parity for Negroes would have been sought created the climate of frustration that now provides the rationale for negotiating an ethnic coalition. Such an alliance, however, depends on the emergence of competent white leadership.

The emergence of this ethnic consciousness, then, will be the underlying theme of the next two chapters. The first presents a discussion on the nature of protest and deals with Negro protest and experience in terms of employment, education, welfare, and housing. In the second, these pieces will be brought forward within the context of the city. Occasionally, the point of view will bear down hard on Negro causes. This, however accords with ethnic tradition; to do otherwise could be properly construed as discrimination against blacks. The view expresses the initial posture on the white ethnic side of the negotiating table.

The black poor are an abstraction to the social scientist, a new cause for the liberal, a critical stereotype for white ethnics, an opportunity for a religious exercise for Wasp clergymen, an instrument of politics for the government official. But rarely is there a feeling of anguish for particular persons.

> The penniless boy wandered through the fair with hands in his pockets looking down at the ground. He could not bear to look at the shooting gallery, the ferris wheel, and above all the carousel with the yellow, red, and green horses. He said to himself: what nonsense; it goes round and round and gets nowhere.
>
> One rainy day the boy came upon a round bottle cap on the ground. It was the best cap of the best bottle of beer that ever existed. The cap was so shiny that he grabbed it and ran off to the carousel to buy every possible ride available. But it was raining and the carousel was covered with canvas, silent and motionless. He climbed up on a horse with wings. The carousel began to move and the music began to hurl shouts at the crowd as he had never in his life heard before. The carousel was so great, so great that it never stopped turning and the faces of the crowd retreated. How wonderful it is not to have to go anywhere thought the child, who never was so happy.
>
> And when the air dried up the damp ground and the man removed the canvas, he shrieked. And no child ever wanted to go on that carousel anymore.[1]

In the United States, whites no longer write in this way about the poor. Only blacks write similar literature.

Poverty is not solely a racial problem. If it were, all the poor would be black and all the blacks would be poor. Every reason that would

[1] Ana Maria Matute, "Los Niños Tontos," in *Veinte Cuentos Españoles del Siglo XX*, New York: Appleton-Century-Crofts, 1961.

explain why whites are poor can be used to interpret why blacks are poor. Nevertheless, it is in the interest of many blacks and whites to explain the position of the Negro solely on the basis of his race.

The often-raised question of whether the poor have values different from those of the non-poor compares categories so broad as to render an analysis meaningless. The non-poor range from the rich to a poverty line that varies subjectively with the individual defining poverty. The poor stretch from this ill-defined line to the black urban subproletariat living on casual jobs and public assistance.

In the interest of facing up to the question of whether a culture of poverty exists, if we were to consider the non-poor as individuals with incomes around $15,000 annually and the poor below $6,000, does a culture of poverty exist? The answer is that it does and does not. Both income groups have similar aspirations of improving their living standards and of acquiring a sense of self-esteem. However, the poor are more pessimistic; more fatalistic; more inclined to be leading a harried existence; more short term in outlook; more likely to believe that conspiratorial and institutional oppression cause their situation. But the poor also differ culturally among themselves. In general, attitudes of individuals throughout the range of income groups reflect an appraisal of particular environments and ethnic background.

GENERAL CHARACTERISTICS OF PROTEST MOVEMENTS

Like the lines of an ogive curve, a protest movement undergoes a period of slow accentuation, rapid growth, and decline. In its early stages an increasing number of individuals seek change because of a felt discrepancy between their position and that of the success group in the society. The failure group believes that their inferior situation arises from external factors perpetuated by the success group rather than from their own personal characteristics, whereas the success group on whom the protest falls believes the difference results from failure to emulate their own virtues. The protesters, to the contrary, feeling their situation is due to discrimination, not only seek a reallocation of resources but also a change in the system of rules.

This attitude of persecution is not confined to any one racial or ethnic group. People who feel oppressed generally are persuaded that their position in life is someone else's doing; criticism of their behavior tends to be considered a sign of hostility toward them. Some Jews, for example, often attribute a critical reaction to their policy position as anti-semitism. Moreover their reaction to specific behavior often depends upon who perpetrates the behavior. Thus, Jews reacted strongly against the death sentence of Soviet Jews accused of highjacking a plane, but the same sentence against a Soviet Christian went unnoticed.

Out of this confrontation between oppressors and oppressed, leaders emerge from the failure group who make demands and who threaten disruption if these demands directed against managers in the system are not met. They collect and disseminate self-serving information. They must decide to what extent they can operate within the system without compromising their goals. Concessions forthcoming include jobs, legislation, money, new administrative procedures, new policies, favorable interpretation of the rules, new rules, and sympathy. Or the reaction may be resistance, hostility, and counter-protest.

Consequently, the first stage of protest is a difficult one. The protesters and the managers whom they confront are from different cultural worlds. The protesters may be more talented (though not necessarily more prepared) than the managers, who may be in their positions by virtue of rights of birth. Concessions trigger counter-protest. The actions and reactions create stresses until such time as the protesting group and the reacting groups achieve an accommodation.

The competence of the protest leaders ranges from a capacity to devise and execute strategies to simple rabble-rousing. As in the case of labor movements, protest leaders seek sovereignty and not just a rise out of poverty. Their demands bring returns so long as the costs of concessions by those against whom the demands are made are less than the costs that would obtain for not doing so, and so long as competitors do not take available profits away from them. To minimize this competition, each protest leader seeks to convey to the rank and file the impression that what *he* offers is unobtainable by anyone else. Furthermore, each asserts through his demands and tactics an ideology that interprets what factors in his judgment is producing the inequity. The competition and the ideology together affect decisions as to what individuals and organizations should be pressured, the nature of their demands, and the stability of their organizations. The protest leaders also fulfill their own personality needs. The joy of playing revolutionary, the pleasure that power conveys, are as much a part of the social movement as the quest for profits for the rank and file.

The protest leader seeks change by working through existing rules and organization, by seeking changes in rules and organization, or by shifting between both as strategy and frustration dictate. Their preferences reflect their ideology, reactions to their demands, and the speed with which existing institutions can produce desired changes. The organization of each labor leader may range from a highly structured group whose functions are explicit to loosely structured groups that fall apart with each crisis of the movement. A leader's ability to produce reflects a capacity to gain a following, favorably disposed third parties, technical competence in maintaining momentum, money, publicity, and concessions favorable to his membership. Publicity is considered favorable not in moral terms but in terms of whether it produces concessions. Thus, the exposure of an outrageous act or deception is not a loss if advantages thereby accrue.

Often, a movement has 5 major sets of role players affecting its course: the protest leaders; the managers of the traditional institutions making concessions; sympathetic parties; misbehaving publics (from the point of view of protest leaders), who frequently are also the parties paying the price for concessions; and communication specialists who describe the course of the movement consistent with their own needs, but who also serve the needs of the movement by giving it publicity.

Moreover, movements have a birth, life, and decline. They emerge on an idealistic base at a time favorable for initial successes. As they acquire momentum, they attract opportunists who serve their own needs through jobs, bribery, and theft, but who eventually fall by the wayside, and mentally deranged individuals lured by the excitement of protest. In course, the movement becomes segmented. Hostile reactions emerge from groups not represented at the bargaining table where decisions are made. They become increasingly effective in triggering political reaction against the movement. The movement stirs up conflicting emotions and damages, if not destroys, innocent individuals. The attitude of the managers making concessions shifts from a disposition to share the view that external factors create the inequities to an insistence of personal responsibility in the conduct of the rank and file. A switch in attitude occurs also in the protest leader, who finds that once he acquires power, ascribing the conduct of his supporters to external factors curtails his ability to control them.

As the initial momentum wanes, some of the newly emerged organizations become permanently structured in the society. Others vanish. Older organizations become stronger, weaker, or perish. Thus, the course of a protest movement comprises a ground swell and then a decline in the redressing of environment and institutions. But pressures and counter pressures eventually subside and the system changes in the source of its managers, the rules of the game, and the substantive agreements. And the attitudes of managers and protesters become increasingly indistinguishable.

CONTEMPORARY NEGRO PROTEST

The Negro's inferior status was firmly entrenched as an institution in American society by the time of the nation's founding. Wasp communications kept this fact in obscurity. At the time the founding fathers were uttering their philosophy of freedom and equality, 20 percent of the population were blacks outside the system of law prevailing for whites. This dichotomy did not disturb the Wasp mind.

Since those early days, Negroes have protested their legally sanctioned position of inferiority that at times has been attended by violence. World War II marks the beginnings of the contemporary era of protest in which the law has effectively been challenged as an instrument of maintaining inferiority and has been employed as a tool of Negro uplift. The war triggered in the United States a massive black migration from the rural South to the industrial cities of the North. Its impetus came from the promise of industrial jobs and from government agricultural policies in the South favoring rich farmers at the expense of the poor, most Negroes falling in this latter category. As a result of this migration, the Negro population outside the Southern confederate states rose sharply from 4 to over 10 millions. Much of this rise occurred in an area ranging from Boston as the Northern anchor point, to Los Angeles on the West Coast, to the nation's capital on the Southern tip. The population shift, coupled with the higher birth rate of Negroes and the exodus of the white middle class to the suburbs, produced urban cores with heavy Negro concentrations. In some cities the blacks became a majority. In this fashion, the impoverished Negroes of the South, under the impetus of national government policy, shifted to the North.

It can therefore be seen that to a considerable degree the position of the Negro is one of rural poor forced to leave the land and seek an industrial commitment in the cities outside the South. This historical pattern of industrialization must be kept in mind as well as the difference in race and origin in slavery. The impact of Negro protest on the white working class in the North would otherwise be incomprehensible.

In addition, the urbanization of blacks occurs at a moment in history not favorable to a successful industrial commitment. The Italians, for example, who preceded the Negro entrance into the city by more than two decades, despite similar low levels of education and status, were profitably employed because of their greater compatibility with the less sophisticated technology of that time. Modern technology began to undermine that base as the Negro came on the urban scene in large numbers.

Two other urban characteristics must be remembered to understand the present protest. In its early period of growth, the city was an enclave for ethnic groups with a sense of community and a high esprit de corps that made their poverty tolerable. By the end of the Second World War, however, the city's changing life style triggered a rising sense of alienation and insecurity. Shifting housing patterns produced by the black immigration contributed to the deterioration of this sense of community. The second factor is that the protest movement unfolds at a time when traditional power relations in the city are changing drastically. White liberals have lost the allegiance of white ethnics; they are no longer their spokesmen. Accordingly, the conflict between the two racial groups occurs at a moment when white ethnics lack leadership. This absence of acceptable spokesmen for the whites delays the process of reconciliation.

The United States has had a long history of group violence. Elements outside the system have traditionally used violence as a means of gaining entrance into more respectable levels of society or as a way of simply airing their frustrations. In magnitude of domestic violence, the United States ranks first among 17 western nations.[2] Negro violence is a domestic commodity. Moreover, black aggression in the 1960's was preceded by white assaults. The Negro violence following was generally directed at symbols of authority, was not conspiratorial, did not have a specific goal, and in most instances was not racist in character. It arose from frustration and demoralized family life rather than from calculated design.

Protest comes from moderates, militants, and revolutionaries. Their differences are in objectives, methods, perceptions, programs, and rhetoric. Generally, those long on rhetoric are short on programs. There are separatists such as the Muslims and Nationalists whose solution is divorcement from white society and the Pan Africanists who talk about settling in Black Africa. The moderates include individuals in service organizations performing continuing functions such as lobbying, court suits, and education services. The National Association for the Advancement of Colored People (NAACP) and the Urban League are major examples of service organizations integrated into the system.

Militant actions are generally performed by the young. Militants gain support from spirited adolescents; ideologists; neurotics who find demonstration a palliative. By social group, militancy is concentrated among high school students, college undergraduates, professional employees in tenured positions, and individuals seeking to ideologize the black urban proletariat. Militancy is on the wane.

The tactic of civil disobedience initiated by Martin Luther King is an appeal to civilized lawlessness. In this view, each individual has to decide what laws are unjust, and having done so, he is morally obligated not to abide by them. On the local community level, the exercise of

2 National Commission on the Causes and Prevention of Violence. *Violence in America: Historical and Comparative Perspectives*, June 6, 1969.

civil disobedience often means exerting pressure against one group so as to set up a bargaining relationship with another. For example, pressure would be employed against a community so as to extract a housing law from elected officials. The use of the maneuver eventually produces a backlash from individuals who feel they are not represented in the bargain.

Civil disobedience was employed initially against Southern segregation laws. As the protest movement shifted to the North, it was used to alleviate broader social problems such as housing and unemployment. The exercise of civil disobedience against the draft law provoked indictments against those exercising it.

The ceremonious violation of law declined with King's death. With this decline, disruptive demonstrations assumed a greater role. They became directed against political authority and private groups such as churches. These demonstrations represent a show of power to obtain an exaction. Their potential depends upon the extent to which they can succeed in embarrassing and disrupting the efforts of those against whom they are directed. Their weakness arises from the fact that objectives often necessitate a continuing bargaining relationship with the group against whom the demonstration is directed. A unilateral exaction is useful if the relationship can be terminated forthwith, but such is often not the case. Demonstrators become engulfed either in a bargaining relationship that makes them conservative or in an escalation of polarization.

The urban riots of the mid-1960's hardly merit the term of tactic. They had no design behind them. They did not comprise a racial confrontation. At their forefront were young hoodlums on a rampage whose actions were aggravated by police authorities and exaggerated by liberals. Their lasting effects were an extension of urban rot and white hostility toward blacks.

Shifts in the meaning and use of words suggest the course of the protest movement. The term integration, for instance, used to mean a process of making whole. The word at this juncture in the movement refers to a policy of coercing whites in the interest of blacks as such interest is interpreted by liberals. Equality of opportunity emerges as meaning a quota system for blacks. Sometimes words are sought that have a softer impact on sensibilities. Racial hiring quotas are called goals. The poor used to be called poor before the beginning of the protest movement. In due course, the poor became culturally disadvantaged, suggesting that the non-poor were in their state by virtue of superior advantage. Accordingly, the poor make progress in the manner in which they are described. The upgrading was short lived, however;

the director of the Office of Economic Opportunity in the Nixon administration directed his employees that the poor should once again be called poor. The showdown came when a bureaucrat in the agency stated in a memorandum that the poor were to be referred to as low income individuals. The same behavior, moreover, commands different words depending upon whether it is white or black behavior. For example, the Negro president of a civic association is reported as protesting the construction of a low income housing project near his neighborhood. In so doing, he is being an Uncle Tom, whereas a white civic association president under similar circumstances would be a racist. To cite a last example of the semantic problem, white liberals heap abuse on themselves through the use of verbiage. Thus, they refer to Negroes as oppressed and prisoners of the ghetto and to Caucasians as racist; in this way, they practice self-ablution. Their favorite ploy in discussing social policy is to gang up on undesired alternatives with pejorative words. Thus, two such liberals refer to black community development as ghetto gilding.

Another familiar characteristic of the protest is that those who exert influence on decisions are frequently not those bearing the brunt of them. Government decision-makers are in the happy position of imposing a course of behavior on the misbehaving public without being required to assume responsibility for bringing such change about. Thus, government can order the integration of the races while leaving to someone else the fastidious matter of bringing it off. Liberal newspaper editors are in the happiest position of all: they can pontificate from behind their desks and then go back to their suburban homes.

In fact, the liberal is a major contributor to racial polarization. An incident in Philadelphia is typical: militant protesters persuaded some black high school students to demonstrate in front of the school district building during school hours. Many in the crowd were habitual disciplinary cases. The liberal president of the school board and the superintendent chose to negotiate with them. They thereby violated a fundamental rule of power: never negotiate from a position of weakness. Outside, matters took an escalation course. Some blacks started to stomp on parked automobiles. The police made an arrest. The arrest was resisted. The police used the tools of their trade. The liberals cried: police brutality.

Especially nettled was the liberal president of the board of education who accused the police of causing the violence by using excessive force on what he called the children. The school superintendent referred to the preoccupation of whites as an obsession for law and order. While reporting these judgments, the newspapers came out with accounts of whites assaulted by the children, including one victim who lost his vision by being stomped after the classical karate maneuver and kick in the groin. Within the tranquil atmosphere of his suburban home, a liberal conjures up in his mind a tolerant, gentle police force, with a depth of sociological understanding as to what motivates stomping children. After all, the cop should say to himself, even if it is his automobile that is being stomped, they are the descendants of slaves.

The liberal interpreting the protest movement as a call for integration does not acquire a receptive audience from white ethnics. While the plight of blacks is assumed to be the fault of whites generally, a solution is conceived of alleviating the condition by forcing white ethnics to comingle with blacks. Thereupon, by a reverse Gresham's law, white goodness, what little there is of it, stamps out black badness. In school integration, the rubbing off of white virtue necessitates massive transportation of children. Assuming that the suburban escape valve would not close, the end result of such policy would be massive transhipments of blacks in hot pursuit of the remaining white child in the city. Should the suburbs be annexed to the city, the tricky suburbanites may still escape entrapment. They may move farther out and become country squires. Accordingly, it can be observed that the protest movement assumes at times characteristics of comic opera.

THE POLICY

A basic objective of the protest movement is a rise in the income of blacks. This goal can be obtained through an increase in public services and government transfer payments from high to low income recipients or by developing capacities that command a higher income in the market. Alleviating poverty through public services and transfer payments may have the effect of lowering incentives to raise capacities by undergoing sacrifices for future rewards. White ethnics feel that this is what is. happening.

The development of capacities approach means making oneself economically scarce. That is to say, the Negro has to develop a capacity that is in demand in the labor market in which he lives. A primary difficulty in so becoming scarce, however, is the black's lack of basic educational skills needed to develop marketable talents. In a modern technological economy, a poor background in reading, writing, and arithmetic hounds a man for his entire life.

To raise his capacity, the Negro also has to look not only at his education, but to his environment and employment. These factors—education, environment, and employment—interact. He is often caught in a vicious circle of poor education, adverse environment, and low employment opportunities. The Negro requires the power to control resources contributing to these 3 factors in a manner that maximizes his overall return. To do so, he needs power. He has to rely on government money but cannot expect too much in government creativity. His government's competence lies more in tax collecting than in their allocation and efficient use. He requires an innovative spirit and quality performance in an atmosphere of bureaucratic mediocrity. He must be wary of politicians who are more interested in him as a source of power than as human potential. He has to be circumspect of patronizing white liberals who delegate to themselves the sublime mission of improving the Negro race. In short, to raise his capacities he must dominate his environment. To do so requires the acquisition of power not as an end but as an instrument to attain basic goals. In reviewing the policies generated by Negro protest we should therefore keep these interrelationships in mind.

The battle against poverty ushered in at the beginning of President Johnson's own term of office in 1964 was marketed as an instrument of Negro uplift. The President stated the days of the dole were numbered. Sargent Shriver, his anti-poverty major-domo, added that he did not assume responsibility for the fight simply to direct a hand-out. The battle was on.

Employment. A major problem in employment is how to commit Negroes of low skills not only to jobs, but to jobs with opportunities for upgrading, and how to achieve this goal without incurring the hostility of white ethnics. Jobs must be made available and opportunities provided for movement into positions of higher skill. Educational preparation, to be discussed later, is a crucial factor in the achievement of this objective. Reliance on political pressure such as anti-discrimination laws creates a fool's paradise. Political power may succeed in getting some Negroes promotions; however, it is unlikely that large numbers of blacks will be upgraded on this basis. The use of such tactics invites employers to play manpower politics at the expense of a genuine search for and development of potential; it also incurs the cost of polarization. The long road to Negro upward movement lies in full employment and in preparation to compete with whites on common ground.

A complex variety of government programs emerged in the 1960's to pursue the goal of black employment. They include different training programs, both at the place of employment and in training institutions, assistance in the creation of small enterprise and trade (the so-called black capitalism programs), and anti-discrimination programs. We review them briefly in that order.

Training efforts involves expenditures in excess of $6 billion for some

6 million trainees. A fundamental objective of the manpower training program of the national government is increasing earnings by virtue of the rise in skill produced by the training. This learning effort relies heavily on existing institutions, including the state employment services, an organization that commands no notoriety for competence. In a study of the program, investigators set out to determine the income and employment effect of such training. Their sample included a group of trainees and a group similarly unemployed but not taking part in the training. The inquiry determined that after the termination of the training both groups were obtaining the same wages on their full time jobs. More employment was found among the trainees. However, the difference could be accounted for by the fact that the trainees had more high school diplomas, greater motivation, and more intelligence. The inquiry suggests that government training has little effect either in obtaining better jobs or in more employment.[3]

Black capitalism programs which assist Negroes with money and training to become the managers of new firms offer limited opportunity for occupational advancement. There will probably be few big black industrial corporations. Possibilities are confined primarily to retail shops and specialty manufacturing in black communities. As part of a strategy in comprehensive community development, these opportunities have some usefulness. However, appreciable gains in employment mobility can only come from opportunities in existing big corporations. Black capitalists, moreover, will survive to the degree that firms discriminate in their favor as a source of supply.

Hard-core unemployed black persons create an anomalous situation. They lack marketable skills and the motivation to capitalize themselves. Pressures arise to use anti-discrimination policies to provide these persons with employment. Many of the hard-core unemployed seek jobs for which they have little preparation or find demeaning those for which they qualify. Often, the margin between the wages they command in the market and the income society guarantees them is narrow enough to destroy work incentives. The Negro worker places a higher premium on current income than on the prospects of higher income at some future date if he undergoes sacrifices. This attitude makes him reluctant to take on long periods of apprenticeship training.[4]

Black casual labor is in issue of low quality education, social neglect,

[3] Earl D. Main. "A Nationwide Evaluation of MDTA Institutional Job Training," Vol. 3, *The Journal of Human Resources*, Spring 1968.
[4] Alex Mauriji. "Minority Membership in Apprentice Programs," Vol. 25, *Industrial and Labor Relations Review*, January 1972, p. 200.

and a family life that does not give children a competitive chance. The problem they raise can most effectively be resolved by assuring that the young generation of Negroes does not mount another army of hard-core unemployed. This implies a total attack on black poverty.

Investment in the hard-core unemployed becomes costly when they do not hold on to their jobs. Because of the high separation rates, one program after another is launched to reach the same individuals. To cite an example, in Philadelphia 2262 persons were reached in their homes, restaurants, taverns, and pool rooms. Of this number, 1777 came to the offices of the state employment service. Some 40 percent of the 1355 accepted for training dropped out before its termination. Of the survivors, 318 were placed in government jobs and 153 in training programs of private industry.[5]

The experience of the city's Department of Licenses and Inspections is also representative of the phenomenon of dwindling numbers. In the summer of 1968, 27 young men were hired and classified under the euphemistic title of internees. With some overtime, each of them was able to earn a hundred dollars weekly. Before the year's end, all but 5 had quit.

In the simpler world of the past, discriminating against Negroes in employment meant not hiring them despite their qualifications. Such is no longer the case. Under the current gospel, an employer may subconsciously discriminate against blacks; his psyche disposes him to discriminate without his knowing it. It has reached a point where an employer can be guilty of discriminating against by virtue of not discriminating for. Federal, state, and local laws have created an army of bureaucrats to fish out this disease, and they find it so as to justify their existence. They have converted the concept of equal treatment into preferential treatment. The anti-discrimination laws are but another example of how legislation designed to achieve integration has the effect of creating rigid racial distinctions and animosities in the name of equality.

At times, findings of discrimination border on the romantic. In Philadelphia, the Commission of Human Relations made a study of 23 selected firms under a grant from the national Equal Employment Opportunities Commission. Unsurprisingly, the commission found these firms to be discriminating. Why? Because studies of another selected set of firms showed a greater proportion of minority workers and because the guilty firms had only 9 percent non-whites on their payroll compared to the non-white population of 30 percent. The firms were thereupon

5 The Philadelphia *Evening Bulletin*, January 7, 1969.

asked to sign consent orders pledging to stop discriminating and a brand new program was announced to root out unconscious discrimination.[6]

Some blacks command higher income because the market places a premium on blackness. A black with a graduate degree in mathematics or economics commands a premium because of the color of his skin. Universities receiving national government funds are asked to come up with employment programs that create staffs reflecting minority proportions in the population. The trend affords new opportunities for white ethnics. Poles, Italians, and shanty Irishmen are represented in colleges and universities below their relative number in the population. Sheer logic would compel Wasps, Jews, Indians from India, and Chinese to relinquish some of their posts and would demand that Negro colleges be prosecuted for practicing tokenism with whites.

Serious-minded scholars argue that increasing investment in anti-discrimination laws would produce a greater payoff in reducing the black-white income gap than placing the increment of investment in black education. Orley Ashenfelter of Princeton University asserts that the expected relative occupational position of Negroes could be computed after discounting for unequal educational attainment. The residual percentage difference he calls discrimination. Ashenfelter advocates that the government should go after industries with a high percentage of discrimination as he defines the term.[7]

Starting from a different set of premises, Professor Lester C. Thurow of Massachusetts Institute of Technology comes to a similar conclusion that the income gap can only be eliminated by a more vigorous set of anti-discrimination laws. Furthermore, he states, discrimination against blacks exists throughout the whole range of occupations. As long as this bias exists, no amount of education, training, and mobility programs will eliminate the income gap. Recent improvements in black income can be attributed to the high rate of economic growth and further gains will have to come from structural changes such as those deriving from more stringent anti-discrimination laws. The bias exists, he asserts, not in the initial entry jobs, but in upgrading. Therefore, business must be forced by law to train blacks for higher level jobs regardless of the extra training cost. Discrimination has not diminished and will not diminish in the future unless more coercive law is passed.[8]

Ashenfelter and Thurow have an extraordinary faith in the resolution of conflicts of interest through law. They propose institutionalizing a

6 The Philadelphia *Evening Bulletin*, January 7, 1969.
7 Orley Ashenfelter. *Minority Employment Patterns*, (unpublished paper), 1966.
8 Lester C. Thurow. *Final Report on Research on the Negro Labor Market*, Office of Economic Opportunity, April 22, 1969.

white subsidy to blacks which would be difficult to remove. Its challenge would probably intensify the polarization. If promulgated, their remedy is likely to accelerate the rising insanity in the body politic. In a spirit of avoiding such madness, the government should hire researchers disposed to determine the validity of a contrary view.

The so-called Philadelphia Plan of the national government marks an attempt to raise the proportion of Negroes in the building and construction trades. Union membership is tantamount to employment in these trades. These unions have had a history of impartial discrimination against white and black ethnic groups. They have tended to resist the entrance into the union of individuals outside their group. Under the pressure of government and the trade union federation, craft unions have slowly opened up their apprenticeship programs to blacks, some more than others. The Philadelphia Plan seeks to accelerate this change by requiring contractors with federal contracts of $500,000 or more to hire a percentage of non-whites (meaning blacks), that rises progressively over a time period depending upon the particular craft. The unions claim the plan violates the 1964 Civil Rights Act which prohibits the setting of racial quotas in employment. In defense of the plan, the government states that no inconsistency exists between requiring a qualified individual to be treated equally in employment and requiring an employer to hire a fixed number of blacks.

The plan was contested in court by a group of Philadelphia electricians and the Controller General of the United States. The electricians charged they were denied employment because they were white. The Philadelphia Human Relations Commission turned down the complaint, claiming lack of jurisdiction. After complaining to the national Equal Employment Opportunities Commission, the union was directed to go to the Office of Federal Contract Compliance. The Office of Federal Contract Compliance sent it back to the EEOC. The EEOC turned it down. In the suit raised by the Controller General, a federal court held the plan as not violating the Civil Rights Act by virtue of not fixing a specific percentage of non-whites. These judicial maneuvers apparently favorable to blacks should not suggest they have a significant effect on their employment in the trades. In 1970, according to the U.S. Bureau of Labor Statistics, about 8 percent of the labor force in the skilled trades were minority workers compared to 5.5 percent in 1960. The rise derives not from unilaterally imposed plans such as the Philadelphia Plan, but from full employment and from negotiation between unions, government, and minorities.

In 1970, the EEOC announced that the American Telephone and Telegraph Company was the largest oppressor of women workers in the United States and that its black workers were relegated to the least desirable jobs in the firm. The ATT hires about 13 percent blacks. In New York City, where telephone service is on the verge of collapse, 55 percent of the operators are non-whites. Lest the reader be misled, this percentage the EEOC would prefer to interpret as evidence of discrimination against blacks. Furthermore, believes the EEOC, since most of the operators are women, the firm is discriminating against women. A generation ago, when the daughter of a white ethnic got an operator's job, her family celebrated their rise in status. Today, the same phenomenon is interpreted by the bureaucracy as black enslavement.

To a considerable extent, a short term subsidy for unskilled blacks has validity. Modern technology makes difficult the rise of blacks from proletariat status. In the days of the massive immigration from Italy, a shovel, a strong back, and motivation for work provided the opportunity for an upward movement in the labor force. Today, sophisticated technology poses formidable obstacles in the commitment of unskilled labor. The price maintenance policies of firms, to the extent they curtail demand for goods, and trade union policies, to the degree they push up wages fast enough to make more capitalization economical, impose additional barriers. This handicap supports the case for the government guaranteeing a job to individuals with little or no marketable skills.

Education. Two major events in urban public education mark the decade beginning in 1960: the massive introduction of more money and the equally formidable decline in performance. This decrease occurs as the whites leave and the blacks raise their relative number in the schools. We discuss here the climate in which this transition occurs.

Urban public schools operate in an atmosphere of violence, of faddism, of consumption calculated to amuse students more than investment, of a rigid bureaucratic system that bogs down in its processes. Black children abuse and rob white children. Innovations heralded as the next miracle cure come and go. Teachers give up and try to keep the inmates amused.

A persistent belief in two myths affects the educational system's performance. First is the fantasy that high achievement is associated with what the establishment considers components of a good school: wage expense per student, capital, and what goes under the name of enriched curricula. An educational psychologist of high reputation, Dr. John S. Coleman, indicates that no relationship exists between the amount of money spent on schools and pupil achievement as indicated by standardized tests. Yet, when matters go badly in the schools, the establishment thinks in terms of increasing the use of public funds. Second is the notion promoted by egalitarian minded liberals that black children can be served by a system of equal treatment when they should be treated instead as unique human beings.

Federal judges have used Dr. Coleman's report in defense of the assertion that inequality of educational opportunity exists if school segregation exists. Such a conclusion, however, cannot be deduced from the report's findings. The inquiry found that the scholastic performance of poor black children improved in a school with a majority of youngsters in a higher educational position by virtue of attributes acquired in family upbringing. No educational gains resulted when poor children were in the majority. Nor did the report infer that scholastic gains cannot be more effectively achieved by means other than deliberately balanced integration. Nor would any significant improvement occur in the education of the poor blacks if their introduction into middle class schools were not kept small. The implication of the report seems to be that additional expenditures to raise scholastic performance can be more profitably invested in schemes to improve family life either directly or indirectly through day care centers staffed with competent teachers.[9]

The tenor of findings in investigations since the Coleman report suggests that scholastic performance of children is highly conditioned by their early family life and that forced integration may even produce results opposite of what is intended. Studies suggest that achievement is highly conditioned by experience in the first 3 years of a child's life and that a family environment without the attention coming from expressed affection inhibits achievement. An inquiry by Dr. Thomas Langer of the School of Public Health at Columbia University in New York indicates that poor Negro boys of welfare families find adjustment to school exceedingly difficult. A Harvard University investigator finds no significant improvement in the academic achievement of black children by virtue of busing and that induced integration fails to decrease racial consciousness and actually reduces contacts.[10]

Cynics assert that children coming into public schools with a high achievement potential maintain a high performance regardless of the system. And those who enter with a low potential the system converts into individuals with little desire to learn and with little self-respect. There appears to be merit in such views.

The disruptive child makes group learning difficult. Often black, he

9 John S. Coleman and others, *Equality of Educational Opportunity,* Office of Education, U.S. Government Printing Office, 1966.

10 David J. Armor. "The Evidence on Busing," No. 28, *Public Interest,* Summer 1972. See also the critical response in the Fall 1972 issue of the same periodical, and Christopher Jencks and others, *Inequality: A Reassessment of the Effect of Family and Schooling in America,* New York: Basic Books, 1972.

arouses racial animosities. Where there is not tension and violence, there is often absenteeism and apathy. Writing of the New York City schools, a former principal states:

> Not so long ago, these schools were safe places to learn and grow and have fun in. They aren't safe any more. Danger and fear stalk the halls, the stairwells, the lavatories, the immediate neighborhoods and school buses and trains. The parents and children who can are running from our city schools. They are not deceived by Chancellor Scribner's or the Board of Education's panaceas. They know that the climate of fear that has settled over the schools has nothing whatever to do with the curriculum, the teachers, the principals, the presence or absence of such experiments and innovations as street academies, minischools, and minicourses. They know the score better than the official ostriches at Livingston Street.[11]

The turbulence of protest in the schools generates polarization in the larger community. A circular distributed in a high school reads:

> Black youth have made it clear that they will no longer put up with the miseducation system that the leaders of the white people force on them in order to cripple their black minds.
>
> On Friday, the leaders of the white people turned their paid and armed troops against our black youth who were taking part in a legal and orderly gathering and protest. This outrageous riotous action by the armed forces controlled by the leaders of the white people has greatly increased the tensions and dangers to our black youth.[12]

In such a climate, educational issues are often settled not on the basic facts but on the basic emotions and ideologies. Negroes are sensitive to the suggestion that their children's low educational achievement is associated with racial and family characteristics. This sensitivity surfaces as an inclination to ascribe low achievement to the school establishment and to teachers who they assert do not know how to relate to their children. Administrators who in such circumstances do not speak candidly incur the wrath of teachers caught between the charged posture of parents and the timidity of administrators. Black ideologists using children as instruments of pursuing their philosophies add to the difficult climate. Issues are resolved in a clash of ignorance of facts. The merit of a position depends on what race brings it forward. A politics of education thereby emerges.

In this politics of education different players have different needs. Government and the courts are committed to an ill-defined philosophy of egalitarianism, in which their skills lie more in issuing edicts than in leading strategies of accommodation. Black community leaders fre-

---

11 *The New York Times,* November 20, 1971.
12 The Philadelphia *Evening Bulletin,* November 20, 1967.

quently see in the turmoil an opportunity to acquire prestige. School administrators are moved by the desire to convey an impression of orderly movement toward higher achievement. Teachers are engrossed in the politics of balancing pressures from students, parents, administrators, and other teachers.

The rapid shift in the racial composition of Northern urban schools aggravates the instability, the uncertainty, the deterioration of standards. High schools are particularly sensitive to politicalizing pressures. In Philadelphia, a big high school shifted in two decades from an all-white to an all-black institution. The number of graduates entering college fell sharply. Police surveillance became normal routine. Black ideologues now sell their wares freely, assisted by parlor revolutionaries on the white teaching staff. The school provides the arena in which the conflict of the outer community is enacted. Its top administrators pander to the revolutionaries and by so doing break the spirit of teachers who want to teach. Juvenophiles among the teachers support student power regardless of the merit of its position. The students can do no wrong since they are the standard bearers of the revolution. In one incident, the revolutionaries in their battle against a white teacher accused him of malpractices including distributing mimeographed outlines and taking attendance.

Dedicated teachers are hampered by the administrator's love of form. Administrators trained in the nation's schools become masters in petty detail. Unless the teacher can successfully scuttle the mania for red tape, she bogs down in a quagmire of clerical chores. She checks absentee lists daily; writes out cut slips; checks book slips which do not seem to produce books; checks drop lists and readjusts rolls and seating; fills requisition forms; files weekly reports; sends post cards to the homes of absentees; submits special forms for excessive absences; accounts for monies collected; files parent locator cards and student association cards; pursues discipline cases; executes guard duty known under the euphemism of study period. And she also is supposed to teach.

Police records in Philadelphia indicate numerous school incidents including murder, armed robbery, rape, burglary, aggravated assault and battery, arson, carrying concealed deadly weapons, and vandalism. An air of bedlam prevails in some schools. In one, 6 pupils ganged up on a pretty music teacher caught in a basement classroom. The children showed exceptional achievement in cornering the teacher. In another school, a supposed showcase of quality education, instruction unfolds under the tension of constant fighting and shoving. In referring to these police records, a high-placed school administrator made the perceptive observation that there must be an underlying cause.

The public school central office groans under the weight of 1100 employees administering a system of 290,000 pupils. Its Roman Catholic counterpart, with about three-fourths of this figure, has a central office of 11 individuals. In a public junior high school, a 14-year old black student blew out the brains of a white teacher. The killing was from a distance of 3 feet. Liberals lamented the conditions in society that would produce such an outrage. One black liberal newspaper columnist wrote that the boy was not so much responsible as was the entire nation. But a bullet is propelled by the squeeze of a trigger; a trigger is activated by a finger; and a finger belongs to one individual of a particular family. In a Catholic high school in the same city, after a racial fracas, martial law was declared. The principal announced that so long as the students behaved like criminals they would be treated as criminals. The students were subjected to a shakedown. Anyone caught with weapons or graffiti pens would go out the door faster than he could say Jack Robinson. In the public school system, everyone is responsible and therefore no one is responsible. In the Catholic school system, responsibility is allocated to the specific individual.

In addition to her clerical chores, a dominant role of the teacher in many of the public schools today is to control students under the watchful eyes of the police. In one high school, 33 bell signals in the course of a day's vigilance maintain law and order. Its thousand of students perform the intricate movement demanded by 3 overlapping shifts. Ending the day without a major incident is an outstanding achievement. Seasoned instructors advise young novices to forget teaching and concentrate on maintaining order.

The children of the black urban proletariat have formidable learning problems. They often do not have a habit of sustained concentration. They frequently fail to see the next move in a work sequence, and if they do, they may see no reason to take it. Nor do they readily grasp the consequence of an evolving work situation until a point of crisis is reached. They bring to their learning a different environment, a different vocabulary, a different set of attitudes and motivations from those of white middle class children. Many have a negative image of themselves because of repeated failure at school, home, and in the community. They are suspicious and peer-oriented, and act out their frustrations in aggressive behavior. Despite their outward show of bravado, they are frightened and self-protective in a white middle class environment.

Many of them are unaware of the technical and scientific world in which they live. Through imaginative use of methods, materials, and curricula, behavior must be encouraged that fills these recognized deficits. They must be taught how to formulate and attain step by step a series of inter-connected goals whose effect is a rise in capacity and self-esteem. The computer as a tool of instruction offers considerable possibilities because of its capacity to motivate, diagnose learning difficulties, develop logical thinking, guide the student from the simple to the complex, train in the following of instructions, and test achievement. But the teacher should not abdicate to the machine in directing the learning process. A policy of color blindness hardly assists these children to enter the modern world.

Theories interpreting the low scholastic performance of blacks stress either environment or heredity as an explanatory factor. Some environmentalists contend that the difference in white-black performance manifests superior resources in white schools. As resources are made equal, therefore, the dissimilarity would narrow. A second environmental group ascribes the deficiency to a family environment that does not provide children with a zest for learning. In some instances, the deficiency in the family is extended to the immediate community.

The heredity explanation of Professor Arthur R. Jensen, educational psychologist of the University of California, creates the greatest heat. He observes that while an entire range of human talents exists among races, the Negro tests low in the talent to reason abstractly. I.Q. tests, Professor Jensen continues, measure this ability, which is highly relevant to successful scholastic performance. Other abilities exist, such as associative learning, and their relevance to educational success should be explored. Differences in genetic inheritance create these mental differences as well as physical differences. He concludes that 80 percent of the variance in intelligence as measured by I.Q. is attributable to hereditary differences. He further judges that higher birth rates among the Negro proletariat, compared to the white population, are likely to widen the differences in intelligence between the races. Professor Jensen poses the challenge to his critics that they set up an alternative hypothesis to his explanation of racial differences and test it scientifically.[13]

Responses to Jensen's thesis are vitriolic, some suggesting he is either socially dangerous or simply ignorant. In a popular psychology magazine, two individuals who say they criticize solely on scientific grounds assert that Jensen's accusation of genetic taint is logically erroneous, empirically unproven, and socially dangerous.[14] The authors claim it does not take much reflection to realize that the intelligence test is a

13 Arthur R. Jensen. "How Much Can We Boost I.Q. and Scholastic Achievement?", Vol. 39, *Harvard Educational Review,* Winter 1969.
14 Philip Whitten and Jerome Kagan. "Jensen's Dangerous Half Truth," *Psychology Today,* August 1969.

cultural invention and not a measure of biological characteristics. They assert also it does not necessarily follow that the lower I.Q. scores of black children are due to genetic factors, which is what Jensen states also. Polemics aside, the problem of separating genetic from environmental factors in performance appears insoluble.

Within this emotionally charged atmosphere, huge amounts of public funds go into a variety of programs ranging from pre-kindergarten to college level. They include pre-primary Head Start programs and programs facilitating entrance of blacks into college together with special tutorial education to maintain performance. An alleged effect of the Head Start program is that it kills off the children's interest in school before formal school begins by giving them an early dose of reading, writing, and arithmetic. Thus, Head Start is less Pre-set and more Hate-early. Whatever advantage accrues to such children appears to vanish after several years of primary school. Some $5 billion have been spent alone for Title I grants under the Elementary and Secondary Act of 1965. The intent of the legislation is to improve the education of poor children; facts indicate it has instead improved the living standards of state and local government officials. School districts cannot demonstrate that the scholastic performance of poor children has risen through the expenditure of these funds.

Miracle cures come and go. In early 1972, the much trumpeted contract teaching program to jack up scholastic performance was abandoned by the OEO as a failure. During the same year, a highly touted innovative high school in Philadelphia threw in the towel. The school's coming had been heralded for several years prior by the establishment, including the school district, the chamber of commerce, and the evening newspaper. The arts in public relations reached new heights in a name for the institution: University City High School. Press releases announced a student elite would be attracted who would take only those courses in which they had an interest. The school opened. A few students signed up. Hoodlums took over its informal leadership. Surrounding buildings quickly got the graffiti treatment. The innovative program was quietly junked.

The core of integrated education policy is coercing whites into a course of behavior deemed to be in the interest of blacks. Such a policy can work if only a handful of whites have to be coerced and if whites cannot escape the integration vise by placing their children into a private school or by moving elsewhere. When whites see a threat to their standards as minority enrollments reach significant proportions, they begin to stir. As the percentage continues to rise, the effect of integration policy is a marked rise in the deployment of buses.

White ethnics who are asked to risk a lowering of their standards as the price for integration have only recently made it into middle class society. They persuade themselves that they did so by their own Spartan efforts. They resent the managerial establishment telling them how to behave, coercing them if they do not follow orders, and taxing them for a policy not of their doing. The taxi driver home after a 12-hour day reads about how some university professor says taxing him more would achieve equality. He reads how high minded individuals including liberal politicians, Quakers, judges, administrators, and professors, say that integration makes a fuller white man. The advice is galling; especially when he finds out his neighbor got stomped by some blacks.

Integration serves more the needs of egalitarians than it does black children. The children are not served by a struggle over an abstraction. A conflict exists between egalitarian insistence on integration and the special needs of black children. Moreover, the issue is not integration versus separatism. It is what strategy is most likely to achieve a meeting of minds between the races. Integration as a tactic has failed; it may be gained as an outcome of other policies. It not only has failed as a tactic, but also commands the price of polarization of the community.

Implicit in integration policy is the desirability of emulating the white middle class. However, a valid question can be raised as to what characteristics are worthy of emulation. No matter what new stratagem the integrationist concocts to impose his will in absentia, he is outmaneuvered by Whitey. Even if wily liberals succeed in boxing him in, he uses his rising income as a means of escape. The hot pursuit of Whitey is a waste of scarce resources.

But the courts persist. It is unclear how they intend to implement their newly announced rule of establishing a unitary system of public schools. They define a racially unitary school system as one in which no person is excluded from any school because of race or color. A school system with all-black schools is evidence of the absence of a unitary school system. In the judgment of the courts, eliminating such schools requires either busing or the gerrymandering of school zones whose result is the introduction of blacks into white schools or the reverse. Busing meets white resistance, and gerrymandering has the effect of shifting demographic patterns and thereby accelerating the white exodus. Thus the courts move as though inspired by a death wish. And this they do despite the evidence that integration neither improves scholastic performance nor fosters racial assimilation.

The blacks would be better served by an alternative to the public school system. An option to escape the public schools could be provided in a system of tuition rights redeemable at any public or private institution as a right for both blacks and whites. If a parent selects a public school, the value of the tuition right could be allotted to the applicable school district. Such an option would provide an opportunity for blacks to establish their own schools and see whether they can do better. However such a plan is likely to arouse the opposition of the public school administrators. They prefer captive audiences.[15]

Welfare. The most booming item in the budgets of Northern cities is welfare. In 1968, the last year of an unprecedented sustained period of higher economic growth, some 8 million individuals were receiving assistance. Within two years, the number rose to 13.4 million, or twice the figure at the beginning of the decade, and the payments totaled $12.8 million. In New York City, with one out of every 8 persons on welfare, financing the poor comprises a two billion dollar industry. A family of 4 can qualify for a monthly payment of $231 plus a rental allowance of a hundred dollars.[16] In Philadelphia, one out of every 6 persons is on welfare.[17] A nation-wide movement organizes relief recipients into a labor union to raise their bargaining power with government. The organization calls itself the National Welfare Rights Organization. Its chief executive states that welfare is a right and that he looks forward to the growth of welfare rolls as a healthy thing.[18] Liberal politicians subscribe to such views, but prefer calling welfare guaranteed income.

A major contribution to the welfare explosion derives from the federal government program of aid to families with dependent children. AFDC changed dramatically since its inception in 1935 under the Social Security Act from an assistance program for families with deceased fathers to assistance of families with absent fathers. At the same time, the racial composition of those assisted changed to a Negro majority. In 35 years, AFDC increased tenfold to serve as an income maintenance program for some 5.5 million persons.[19] A rising proportion of the children under the program comprise out-of-wedlock births. In New York City, two-thirds of the children on welfare are born out of wedlock. Every year, unwed welfare mothers produce another 20,000 children. Politi-

---

15 The voucher system has been brought forward by Professors Milton Friedman and Christopher Jencks. The national government began to experiment with such a system in 1971.

16 The Human Resources Administration in New York houses welfare recipients in hotels. It pays $100,000 yearly for guards. *The New York Times,* January 24, 1971.

17 The Philadelphia *Evening Bulletin,* September 8, 1971.

18 *U. S. News & World Report,* October 30, 1967.

19 Leonard J. Hausman. "From Welfare Rolls to Payrolls? The Welfare System as a Manpower and Rehabilitation System," from Weber, Cassell & Ginsburg, *Public-Private Manpower Policies,* Madison, Wis.: Industrial Relations Research Association, 1969.

cians do nothing for fear of accusations of racism. Much of our social ills, including scholastic performance, can be traced to this subsidizing of the deterioration of the Negro family.

Liberals like to assert that the American public has a distorted view of the welfare picture. The thrust of their views is that welfare income is actually inadequate and requires raising taxes in order to eliminate the shortcoming. They enjoy pointing out that most of the welfare recipients are mothers and their children, and where is the man who would openly take a position against motherhood? They thereby maintain the liberal institution of irritating the working class.

The system created the welfare system by encouraging the poor to enter without providing incentives to leave. It finds more prudent institutionalizing the maintenance of the poor than ascertaining and reducing root causes of their poverty. Moreover, the welfare bureaucrats have needs of their own in seeing that solutions preserve their interests. We therefore should expect the permanent maintenance of an army of blacks who do not fit into the system on its terms.

Housing. In the year 1948, the national government announced the goal of a decent home for every American. Since then countless billions of dollars have been spent on low income housing. The situation has gotten worse. But the liberals who sponsor these programs never in their discussions raise the fundamental question of why.

The product market does not provide new houses in urban areas that low income groups can buy. In fact, the majority of American families cannot afford a new $27,000 house, a dwelling in major urban markets of extremely modest dimensions. An unsubsidized rental market for decent housing for low income groups does not exist either. The great mass of the urban black poor lack the money and motivation to maintain their substandard housing and mire down in filth. Much of their housing is acquired by a filtering down process from displaced white middle class groups and by a progressive rise in the population density of these acquisitions. The housing deteriorates as the whites move out and the poor move in, in much greater numbers. Politicians find it expedient to blame these market and social conditions on greedy landlords rather than the entire predatory decision making process.

Government housing policy comprises a cycle that begins as an expression of idealist liberals and terminates with the subversion of the idea by business, local government machines, universities, union craftsmen, and out-and-out crooks. The model cities program provides but one example. Its conception by university elites consisted of a comprehensive development of the community through a series of balanced programs supported by participatory democracy. Through their capacity of sensing an opportunity for a racket, the program became converted into a grab bag for friends of the city machine. Its most dramatic impact was to make black middle class bureaucrats upper middle class bureaucrats. The program was not tied to a source of technical skills and knowledge; as usual it tied instead into business.

It is difficult to find an area of law as complex as federal housing legislation. The legal maze it has created responds to vested interests and conniving politicians. It has little to do with the most feasible way of eradicating slums and preventing the emergence of new ones. The policy of a decent home for everyone is frittered away as the policy runs through a pipeline including land developers, real estate operators, construction contractors, lawyers, landlords, government officials, and banking interests. This society of friends is sometimes joined by middle class black property owners. In the end result, the predatory interests make money, the poor get swindled of theirs, and the neighborhood deteriorates.

I recall living in a poor but highly integrated and stable Italian neighborhood into which high rises were suddenly dumped without our prior knowledge. In jig time, the community took on the aspects of a crowded shooting gallery. The bedlam never subsided. Violence erupted. The Italians began to flee and the community in 10 years became a slum.

So-called urban renewal programs often aggravate these slum conditions. The removal of housing for a new highway accelerates the dilapidation of the housing remaining near its borders. Slum clearance programs become poor clearance programs for the expansion of business, universities, and upper middle class residences. The displaced Negroes who pile up in public housing projects live in the midst of decay, violence, and terror, and pay rentals pushed up by spiraling maintenance costs. The concentration of people and the atmosphere of hopelessness boggle the mind. A thousand individuals, including uncontrollable children, are jammed into space used by several families in the suburbs. Blacks live under tension, pollution, rubble, and rabble. In some cities, such as St. Louis, half the public housing units are abandoned.

Under the law, white ethnics do not have the right to determine how the land in their neighborhood should be used. The system tells them this right is not theirs and that such determination rests with the power establishment promoting social causes. In Philadelphia, the ethnics of Whitman Park protested the use of adjoining land for low income housing. The project was to be subsidized in its initial cost and in its subsequent maintenance and distributed to individuals the establishment deemed worthy of uplifting. People in the neighborhood knew from experience that such housing quickly deteriorates and becomes in turn the basis of spreading blight. They wanted first rights to the housing. The establishment thought differently and used the force of law to maintain its position. The white ethnics concluded that justice is a swindle. Scatter housing is the name given to this policy of placing low income sites into structured ethnic neighborhoods. As a gesture of practicing what they preach, the managing elites who foster such policy should insist that some of this housing be placed in their neighborhoods.

Owner housing for blacks derives from several major sources: equal opportunity legislation designed to provide individuals with legal backing to buy existing housing, legislation to buy new subsidized housing, and rehabilitated existing housing. Equal opportunity law serves the interests of the black white collar class trying to escape the urban black proletariat. A major achievement of such open housing policy lies in the creation of thousands of jobs for bureaucrats in the Housing and Urban Development agency to process complaints. The Negro poor living in dilapidated housing, who can afford some $70 monthly for a dwelling, gain nothing from a guarantee of the right to white middle class housing. New subsidized housing poses two problems: location sites and fixing the burden of the subsidy. The alternative of providing rehabilitated housing attracts marginal employers of low efficiency and ethical standards. The corruption surrounding their efforts borders on a national scandal.

A margin of the poor lack competence in the management of income, whether earned or derived from the state. They lack ability in managing housing. Predatory real estate operators aggravate the mismanagement. As an example, the housing rehabilitation program attracts real estate plungers who buy dilapidated houses and make nominal repairs. They then find a low income black to purchase the house and have it appraised by the government at an inflated value. The real estate operator then walks off with his mortgage money and the black, often a welfare recipient, is unable to maintain the dwelling and defaults. This cycle is repeated until the house becomes an empty shell. Rehabilitation policy is calculated to cost the government close to a billion dollars in losses.

The experience under government housing law is a failure. The squalid conditions in public housing developments and the thousands of abandoned houses in the cities bear testimony to its failure. Solutions brought forward comprise, essentially, spending more money under the same rules of the game. Only a populist movement that wrests the initiative from government and vested interests is likely to provide a genuine alternative.

ASSESSMENT OF GAINS [20]

A precise assessment of gains made in direct consequence of the Negro protest movement is not possible. Acquisitions that would have occurred in the absence of protest are incalculable. In addition, what constitutes a return, whether a job or the joy of disrupting society, is a subjective judgment. In the judgment of some mediators, participation in conflict constitutes a return itself. Even if agreement exists as to what comprises gains, there are differences as to how much change in a particular benchmark would be considered significant. An example can be brought forward in college enrollments. Data indicate appreciable increases for blacks. Nevertheless, some militants assert that the increases have been token. Lastly, information is also lacking on the returns gained relative to investment. While some investment can be measured by aggregate expenditures of uplift legislation, it is not possible to separate expenditures by race (see table below).

Poverty as a whole declined in the United States between 1947 and 1965 despite the absence of special anti-poverty programs. This decline was at a rate of somewhat less than one percent annually. Beginning in 1964, when the anti-poverty and anti-discrimination programs were instituted, poverty continued to decline, but not at any appreciable increase in the rate. Moreover, it is problematical whether any rise occurred beyond that attributable to the level of gross national expenditures beginning in 1964. It is clear that, in any case, the main thrust of an anti-poverty program is full employment.

Some consensus exists that criteria measuring black gains should include political gains, public accommodation rights, education, and housing, as well as income. Another criterion, difficult to assess, would be influence in community affairs. Still another, troublesome because of the lack of information, would be health and nutrition. In political achievements, public accommodations, income, and education, some successes have been scored. More Negroes are voting and winning elections. A rising number of blacks are to be found in the Congress and the state legislatures. Black mayors administer principal cities. These political returns have produced neither the millenium nor the apocalypse. In the colleges and universities, black enrollments have risen considerably, spurred by economic growth as much as by special admissions and remedial programs. Public accommodations are no longer a major issue. In employment, Negroes are rising up the occupational ladder at a

---

[20] For a discussion on evaluation of social action programs, see Glen G. Cain and Robinson G. Hollister, "The Methodology of Evaluating Social Action Programs," in *Public-Private Manpower Policies*, opus cit.

faster rate than whites. Black family income is rising faster than white family income. In the public schools, gains in years of schooling outpace those of scholastic performance. White-black differences have not narrowed by virtue of induced integration and the evidence suggests the wisdom of switching to selective voluntary integration. Lastly, the conquests in housing are small.

AMOUNTS APPROPRIATED BY FISCAL YEAR FOR SELECTED SOCIAL LEGISLATION
(in millions of dollars)

Act	1963	1964	1965	1966	1967	1968	1969	1970
Economic Opportunity			800	1500	1688	1778	1948	1948
Vocational Education			124	202	218	213	210	375
Elementary and Secondary Education				1218	1411	1656	1531	1614
Model Cities					11	312	635	575
Fair Housing Law 1968							2	6
Manpower and Development Training	70	130	397	435	421	429	427	721
Equal Employment Opportunity Title One Civil Rights Act 1964				2	3	5	7	9	16

Source: United States Bureau of the Budget

Major legislative programs as indicated by the table represent a small fraction of total expenditures for the poor as a whole. Conservative estimates place these expenditures at $70 billion annually. The poor would be reduced considerably if these funds were given them directly. But much of the money goes into the pockets of the bureaucracy. This outcome accords with our previously stated law of public administration.

Measured in economic calculus, an improvement in the position of the Negro has taken place. The gap between the median incomes of Negro and Caucasian families has narrowed substantially. In 1969, the ratio of black to white income was 61 percent compared with 51 percent in 1959. Outside the South no real difference exists between the incomes of young black husband-wife families and those of white counterparts. In the North black families with husband and wife under 35 years of age and both present average 91 percent of the income of white counterparts. In less than a decade this figure has risen sharply from 62 percent.[21]

Offsetting these data are those of broken black families in the cities. Little economic gain has materialized for families with no father present. The percentage of black husband-wife families fell from 73 percent to 66 percent compared to a relatively stable 85 percent for white families. Thirty-nine percent of black children live in homes lacking one parent because of death, separation, or divorce. At the same time, teenager Negro unemployment in the cities reached a high of 30 percent in 1972. Accordingly, as the white exodus to the suburbs continues, the cities become the repository of the Negro sub-proletariat class.[22]

Despite these overall gains, pressures mount to give the anti-discrimination bureaucracy more power. The pressure comes from liberals championing minorities, by which they mean blacks rather than all ethnic groups. They have no interest in white minorities. Their simplistic argument is that inequality still exists and therefore we need more laws against racial inequality.

The movement of blacks toward parity with the white working class suggests the wisdom of easing pressures on whites. Much of the thinking of the black power movement accords with how these needs of the black proletariat can be met consistent with the rights of white ethnics. An inter-ethnic agreement lies within the realm of possibility. Should such an agreement be negotiated, resources could be shifted from the low priority goal of converting middle class blacks into upper middle class blacks and could be used in improving the quality of life in ethnic communities. At this juncture in the protest movement, the apocalyptic statement of the Presidential Kerner Commission Report that the United States is moving toward two societies, one black and one white, is not borne out by these data. If any such movement has taken place, it has been generated to a considerable extent by the integration policies espoused by the Commission.

---

[21] U. S. Bureau of the Census. Current Population Reports, Special Studies Series P 23, *Differences Between Incomes of White and Negro Families by Region, 1969 and 1959*, March 10, 1971.

[22] U. S. Bureau of the Census. Current Population Reports, Special Studies Series P 23, No. 27, *Trends in Social and Economic Conditions in Metropolitan Areas*, 1969.

CONCLUSIONS

The Negro protest movement had its origin and initial successes as a Christian movement in the deep South. Its groundswell of protest produced favorable responses from officials in the national government and in the courts disposed to a policy of equal opportunity. However, as the movement spread northward to the cities, the black urban voices of protest spoke of revolutionary change and violence. White reaction was hostile and in some areas commanded the punitive power of the system. The government policy of equal opportunity became favored treatment subsidized by the white working class.

The black wants not only economic returns but status and self-esteem. He needs to develop a sense of self-worth through the development of an identity and through successful negotiation with groups in society. Community influence provides the means of attaining these goals. This appears to be their perception of the problem. The solution of managing elites seems to be to convert him into a quasi-white suburbanite. Thus, Wasps originally made the Negro a one-fifth person and now try to make him disappear into the white mass. But if blacks want self-respect, so do white ethnics. The Negro may acquire these objectives by capturing the city; however, the city may be won at the loss of its viability.

A presumption prevails that once Negroes acquire living standards similar to whites, racial antagonism will disappear. But this outcome may not materialize. The Negro will acquire status in his own group as he becomes a technician and negotiator. However, this prestige will not be automatically honored by whites. So long as the white working class is denied status in American society, it will find it necessary to look at Negroes as inferiors. Thus, Negro uplift policy is a two-edged sword. Concessions to blacks aggravate the psychological difficulties of ethnic whites.

Existing policy fails to come to grips with this problem. To do so, a vision of stages of development is necessary whose particular strategies may even appear to be inconsistent with the long term objective of a negotiating assimilated society. An initial stage requires the acquisition of status by blacks within their own community. At the same time, a policy of white uplift is necessary, a preliminary of which is repairing ruptured communication lines with government and providing opportunities for negotiation. Genuine interracial bargaining should follow, with each side making real gains in negotiation. In subsequent stages, a policy is needed of applying the same competitive standards regardless of race. At the same time, white children will have to be taught that black culture in the United States is part of their own. In short, the road toward the reduction of racial antagonism does not exist under existing policy.

A new morality cannot be imposed by government fiat. It is more likely to come off through staged negotiation. For white managers to impose a burden of guilt on white ethnics and then to punish them for not obtaining the desired behavior is an absurdity in a democracy. Integration policy serves primarily the needs of those who provide its major thrust: guilt-ridden Wasps, Jewish intellectuals, and middle class blacks. The price has been considerable. The reliance has been on coercion from the safety of desks and not on negotiation. Leaders are needed who can talk effectively in both black and white neighborhoods. But rule by government fiat continues relentlessly. The next round appears to be coercion of suburban communities. Despite the manifest costs of coercion, the system continues to rely on mass manipulation. It is presently in the interest of urban blacks, and in that of the society as a whole, not to listen any longer to the obsolete voices of government fiat and to negotiate a consensus directly with authentic spokesmen of white ethnics.

Organized society elected to underwrite by law the entrance of blacks into the industrial market place. This underwriting lacks precedent; blacks should enjoy it in good health. But the non-poor members of the society can legitimately make demands of the poor, as the poor have expectations of other groups. It is absurd to look upon the array of social positions as a clash of goodness and badness. The non-poor, as net contributors to the society's product, can propose conditions as to the amount and use of organized resources going to the poor. To say to low income groups tell us your price and we will honor it is not only an expression of political cowardice but also an obstacle in the path of curing the basic causes of poverty in the United States.

An individual may ask himself: Why should I help the poor? I have no guilt feelings about their condition. I know that what the government does has mixed results. The poor cannot make me respond by threatening to hit me over the head; I will hit right back. If they are willing to negotiate, I will listen. If they want to be left alone, I will honor their desire. But if they want assistance, my point of view should be placed on the table.

If politicians had courage, which they generally do not, they would advise the heads of poor families that they cannot have their cake and eat it too. If they want the full right to breed, they have to incur the responsibility of fully taking care of their brood. If they expect the society to subsidize their children, then the society has the right to control their numbers. Extensive anthropological evidence exists that primitive societies practice family planning. It is when society picks up the tab that individuals become indifferent to the consequences of child bearing.

What we have suggested in this chapter is how the protest movement reflects the dynamic relationships between employment, education, environment, and institutions. Of these relationships we have more to say in the following chapter on the city.

CHRONOLOGY

The Supreme Court decision in *Brown* vs. *Board of Education* in 1954 provides a practical beginning for a chronology of events in the Negro protest movement. The decision unfolded a series of events in which the judicial system became an instrument of formulating and administering public policy in Negro uplift. The court based its decision on the educational knowledge existing in 1954 and concluded that separate schools were by that very fact unequal.

As suggested by the chronology below, the evolution of events from 1954 is as follows: rising black militancy, a shift in public policy from equal treatment to favored treatment, mounting white resistance, and the beginning of a new consensus.

1954	The Supreme Court in *Brown* v. *Board of Education* rules that racial segregation in public schools violates the 14th Amendment guaranteeing equal protection under the laws.
1955	Montgomery, Alabama boycott of city transportation system, with Martin Luther King as a principal leader.
1956	The Supreme Court unaminously upholds a decision of a lower court that bus segregation is unconstitutional.
1957	President Eisenhower orders federal troops in Little Rock, Arkansas to enforce integration in Central High School.
1957	The first Civil Rights Act since 1875 is passed authorizing the Attorney General to seek federal court injunctions against violations of civil rights and providing for a civil rights division in the U.S. Department of Justice.
1960	Civil Rights Act is passed permiting a federal judge to appoint voting referees upon finding a pattern of discrimination against Negroes voting in a certain area and making individuals interfer-

	ing with the right to vote liable to contempt of court.
1960	Lunch counter sit-down demonstrations begin in the South.
1961	The Federal District Court in Macon, Georgia, orders the University of Georgia to admit two black students.
1961	The Georgia legislature approves the repeal of public school segregation laws.
1961	Southern school districts mount a campaign against integration, first under the doctrine of interposition asserting the supremacy of state rights and later under a doctrine of freedom of choice in selection of schools.
1961	President Kennedy creates by executive order a Committee on Equal Employment Opportunity to enforce a policy against racial discrimination by government contractors.
1961	Freedom Riders are attacked in Alabama and Mississippi.
1961	The NAACP approves the tactics of sit-ins, freedom rides, and economic boycott of business.
1961	Anti-segregation demonstrations in Albany, Georgia bring to the fore rivalries between the Congress of Racial Equality, the NAACP, the Southern Christian Leadership Conference and the Student Nonviolent Coordinating Committee.
1962	Two Negro churches near Albany, Georgia, used as headquarters for registration drives, are burned down.
1962	Federal troops force the entrance of a black student into the University of Mississippi at Oxford.
1962	Congress passes the Manpower Development and Training Act.
1962	The NAACP announces it will file charges against unions practicing racial discrimination in housing built with federal aid.
1963	The building trades unions announce the adoption of a program to eliminate racial discrimination in apprenticeship programs, in union membership, and in job assignments.

1963	Violent reaction mounts in the Southern states against black demonstrations.
1963	The Supreme Court announces that segregation of public facilities must end promptly.
1963	Martin Luther King mounts a massive demonstration in Birmingham, Alabama.
1963	Medgar Evers of the NAACP is murdered in Jackson, Mississippi, following weeks of Negro demonstrations.
1963	A Freedom March on Washington is staged by civil rights and religious groups.
1963	Bombs explode inside a Negro church in Birmingham, Alabama, killing 4 girls.
1964	National government passes the Economic Opportunity Act to fight poverty.
1964	The National Labor Relations Board decides that racial discrimination constitutes an unfair labor practice under the National Labor Relations Act.
1964	President Johnson signs the Civil Rights Act. It authorizes the Attorney General to institute court action if he finds a pattern of discrimination preventing citizens from voting; limits the use of literacy tests; forbids discrimination in the use of public accommodations; authorizes the attorney general to file school desegregation suits on written complaint; bars discrimination in employment.
1964	Racial violence erupts in the Harlem section of New York City and in the Bedford-Stuyvesant section of Brooklyn, sparked by meetings protesting police brutality.
1964	Martin Luther King is awarded the Nobel Prize for Peace for dedication to the principle of non-violence.
1964	The Supreme Court refuses to review an Indiana Court's decision which held that school boards were not constitutionally bound to remove racial imbalance in schools resulting from segregated housing patterns.
1964	J. Edgar Hoover, director of the Federal Bureau of Investigation, denounces Martin Luther King as the most notorious liar in the country for claim-

ing FBI agents in Albany, Georgia were taking no action on Negro complaints because the agents were Southerners.

1965   Malcolm X, leader of a militant Black Nationalist group, is shot dead while addressing a meeting in Harlem.

1965   About 500 blacks, setting out on a protest march from Selma, Alabama, are dispersed by state police and sheriffs. Two weeks later, the Alabama Freedom March begins. A white civil rights worker is killed while driving from Selma to Montgomery.

1965   Martin Luther King suggests a national boycott of Alabama products.

1965   The U.S. Office of Education announces complete desegregation of public schools will be required by 1967 for eligibility for federal aid.

1965   President Johnson signs the Voting Rights Act of 1965 which empowers the Attorney General to appoint federal registration examiners in 6 Southern states.

1965   Rioting breaks out in Watts, Los Angeles, after a white policeman arrests a Negro on a drunken driving charge.

1966   CORE accepts the concept of black power. NAACP denounces black power as interpreted by CORE. Martin Luther King warns against a doctrine of black supremacy.

1966   Rioting erupts in Chicago after police turn off a fire hydrant. Race rioting also breaks out in Cleveland. Whites riot against an open housing demonstration organized by Martin Luther King in Chicago.

1967   Stokeley Carmichael announces "we're going to shoot the cops who are shooting our black brothers," and adds that blacks will take up arms for a revolution.

1967   CORE announces the removal of the word multiracial from its constitution, the death of the civil rights movement, and the emergence of the black revolution.

1967   Rioting erupts in major cities including Boston, Newark, Atlanta, Cincinnati, and Detroit.

1967	A Black Power conference in Newark urges a dialogue on partitioning the United States into a white and black nation.
1967	Martin Luther King announces he will shift his demonstrations to the Northern cities.
1967	Negro mayors are elected in Gary, Indiana and Cleveland, Ohio.
1968	Violence erupts in Memphis during a protest march of Martin Luther King.
1968	Martin Luther King is assassinated in Memphis.
1968	President Johnson signs the Civil Rights Act of 1968 for open housing, also makes it a federal crime to travel from one state to another with the intent to incite a riot.
1968	Mayor Daley of Chicago announces his police policy of shoot to kill arsonists and shoot to cripple looters.
1968	Rioting breaks out in Washington, D.C. in the aftermath of the death of Martin Luther King.
1968	The Poor People's campaign begins in Washington, D.C.
1968	The Supreme Court rules the Civil Rights Act of 1866 forbids all racial discrimination in the sale and rental of property.
1968	Supreme Court rules that freedom of choice plans are not acceptable unless they produce desegregation.
1969	The U.S. Department of Labor announces the Philadelphia Plan setting up racial quotas in the building trades.
1969	The Nixon administration announces a slowing down of integration in Mississippi.
1969	The Supreme Court in Beatrice Alexander v. Holmes County Board of Education rules that every school district has to terminate dual school systems at once and operate unitary schools in which no person is excluded from a school because of race.
1969	Police in different cities in the United States kill members of the Black Panther party.
1970	Congress passes legislation forbidding the use of federal funds to force a school district to adopt a busing plan or to deny public school children

attendance in a public school chosen by a parent or guardian.

1970   President Nixon issues a policy statement on the desegregation of elementary and secondary schools, making a plea that constitutional interpretation should be confined to outlawing *de jure* segregation and that the raising of scholastic performance be sought by measures other than racial quotas.

1971   The Supreme Court in a unanimous decision upholds busing, racial quotas, pairing, and gerrymandering as devices to dismantle dual school systems in the South. The Court stipulates that no guideline will be established as to how far the courts can go in achieving this goal. The NAACP hails the decision as one that will achieve integration in the nation.

1971   The Supreme Court upholds the constitutionality of state referendum laws permitting voters in a community to approve subsidized housing for the poor.

1972   President Nixon asks Congress to impose a freeze on new busing orders and to consider alternative means of enforcing the 14th amendment.

1972   U.S. Court of Appeals strikes down ruling of District Court ordering a merger of Richmond, Virginia schools with suburban counties.

14

Management of the City

The American city is dying. It has become an agglomeration of frightened strangers with little sense of community. Man could hardly have planned a better way to kill off the city than what he does by inadvertence. He designs streets inside the metropolis in a way that makes the land unfit for human habitation; formerly serving the movement of animals, these streets now minister to the dispatch of noisy motor vehicles. He constructs highways at the city periphery to accommodate the white middle class flight into the suburbs; and when the highway becomes choked with the traffic of suburbanites moving between abode and workplace, he builds more only to accelerate the movement. By allowing motor vehicles free rein, by developing land on the criterion of profit making, by tolerating the flight of economic resources, and acquiescing to the brain drain from city to suburb, man upsets the balance of city and countryside and destroys the quality of both.

Now man provides the coup de grace: the coercive integration policies of white and black liberals. The middle class at the urban periphery proposes and the working class at the city core disposes. The comedy runs in 3 acts: integration, disintegration, and back to segregation with a residue of polarization. Should man persist in seeking racial assimilation by government fiat, the city will become an enclave of the black proletariat surrounded by a white suburban class paying tribute in government jobs and income guarantees to keep the urban compound quiet.

Fifteen miles from Philadelphia in the county of Delaware lies Chester,

373

a small urban center of some 63,000 population. Chester ranks among the sickest towns in the nation, despite its formidable array of industrial plants of America's biggest corporations. A fraction of their profits would convert the town into a jewel. The city looks brutal. It has a liquor license for every 400 residents, mostly in black neighborhoods where alcoholism is rampant. Twelve percent of the population is on welfare. A majority of the adults are school dropouts. The city has been run for decades by one of the most reactionary Republican party political machines in the country. Policemen must belong to the party organization. Latter day do-nothings known as the War Board control the county machine. The philosophy of this mafia clique is: Do nothing that upsets people. The highly educated whites that live in the county reach automatically for the Republican lever.

The big corporations in Chester make substantial profits, contribute heavily to the town's ugliness, and give generously to the Republican party. One firm, with the assistance of a prominent Republican national committeeman, persuaded the county court, whose judges the party machine controls, not only to prevent the city from raising its assessment but even to lower it. Chester represents a pool of human and environmental decay for which industry and government are responsible. For a renascence to occur, the machine must be thrown out; it is unlikely that this will happen in the foreseeable future.[1]

In the neighboring state of New Jersey, the city of Newark is in a similar state of decay. The city is 60 percent black and has a moderate black mayor. A nucleus of black nationalists, intent on chasing away the remaining white ethnics, use intimidation to do so. The city's unemployment rate is 13 percent for the population as a whole and 30 percent for black males between the ages of 16 and twenty-five. The moderate black middle class is also leaving, which gives the nationalists a good chance of inheriting decaying real estate and unskilled blacks. The Board of Education knuckled under to the demands of noisy black students to fly the black liberation flag on its school buildings when the enrollment reaches a black majority. The mayor acquiesced to the resolution as well.

To the South, in Wilmington, Delaware, this city of 80,000 continues to decay even after national government expenditures on its behalf in excess of a half billion dollars. The rot lies at the center of the Dupont Company empire.

Not all American cities decay. Those that do not, have poverty also. But they are small, culturally at peace, and do not undergo swift changes in economic and human resources. The people of Washington County

[1] Peter Binzen, The Philadelphia *Evening Bulletin*, April 20–23, 1969.

in Maine, for example, are among the poorest in the nation. The obesity of poverty is common among its women. The biggest offense to the eye is the abandoned automobile, junked in a field, the last mile of transportation squeezed out of it. The house trailers are symbolic of poverty; a used one costs $2,000 as compared with $10,000 for a cottage. But the villages have no policemen. It is difficult after leaving Steuben in Washington County to become reacclimated to the noise, the tension, the threat of violence, the rot, the alienation, and the commercialized human relationships of the modern city.

American life in the modern city is a paradox. As Americans become more affluent, the quality of their life deteriorates. The environment becomes ugly, violent, noisy, and polluted. The environment does not make the human spirit soar, but rather places a clamp on the individual's senses. It tells the human being: since I am so ugly I will help you become blind to my ugliness. Men become strangers to each other and to themselves. Human relationships polarize. As individuals jam into metropolitan areas, the deterioration ceases to respect city lines. As the national indicator of progress, the GNP, continues ever to rise, urban dwellers exercise cruelties against each other without any remorse. They devise strategies as to how to protect themselves from the gifts of progress.

People sample justice in these cities. For most, the system's justice is that meted out by traffic courts, juvenile courts, lower civil and criminal courts. It is justice without compassion, dispensed perfunctorily by cynical judges. To observe their behavior is a shocking experience. Justice works on the side of employers by taking away possessions bought by members of the unsystem heeding the lure of manipulative advertising. Justice abides by the rights of criminals and flouts the sense of decency of the innocent. Justice is an expanding university that takes away the home of the poor by the right of power. For the urban white working class, justice means being the most underprivileged group in society. Law and order means somebody else's law and somebody else's interpretation. Justice, either as a sense of empathy for the judged or as a means of retribution for the victimized, can better be gained by individual action outside the system.

Most resources against crime in the city are spent in apprehension of suspects, court proceedings, and penal institutions. An infinitesimal amount is spent in determining and eradicating causes. Most working class crime is committed by the young men who herald their criminal career early in childhood. In Philadelphia, roving gangs of blacks kill each other and abuse the innocent. The system shies away from ascertaining the causes of such madness; to ascribe the rising crime rate to poverty is unconvincing.

As change destroys a sense of community, the city develops a man who feels little responsibility for social norms. He is calloused to the suffering of his fellowman; at times he behaves like a jackal. Science teaches that man is an integral part of nature and that his history, past and future, can be read in the harmony of the cosmos. By undermining man's community with nature, the city defies such teachings.

Despite these drawbacks, the city has something to offer. The city is where the action is. It generates ideas that become a basis for change. There is intellectual activity at its center, in contrast to the cultural void in many suburbs. From the safety of the suburbs, the rich descendants of the city's founders dedicate themselves to support of the urban music hall, the art alliance, and the zoo. Their generosity provides the symbols of urban culture.

The exploitation of human and economic resources for individual profit produced American cities. They became effective instruments of collecting cheap labor, reducing capital costs, obtaining low cost transportation, and accumulating information. They also provided the employer the means to shift other costs to society by granting him uncontrolled use of the environment. This basis for growth no longer exists. Labor protects its interests through organization. New modes of transportation, information flow, and business organization increase the options in plant location. Technology and government labor standards combine to extinguish the demand for unskilled labor. After exploiting the city to the hilt, the employer moves to the not-yet-ruined suburbs, and the city's economic base becomes thereby eroded. The population divides between those who leave and those who wish to do so but cannot. After losing its economic and human resource base, the city survives on defense contracts and transfer payments from the national government.

Billions of dollars pour into the city from the national government in this way. They do not create a dynamic organism, but comprise only a holding action. For decades, an enormous effort has been made to save the city, but few Americans ask whether the rescue is worthwhile. How the land should be used is the vision of only a small elite. Resuscitation efforts come and go. The public relations experts point to an expanding university campus, a cluster of new office buildings, or an upper middle class housing development as evidence of the city's resurgence; they ignore the physical and spiritual rot around the corner from these showcases. In Philadelphia, a model display has been on exhibit for many years depicting the city of the future. After more than two decades, the city of the future remains in the cutouts glued to the plywood board.

A corruptly controlled profit motive has created cities lacking in harmony within and between its neighborhoods and comprising a loose collection of housing by income group, scattered production units, ugly commercial strips, and amenities, each menacing the others' existence. This chapter will present these problems of the city in terms of its population, economy, environment, and institutions and will suggest that these elements should comprise a harmonic whole in each neighborhood of the urban cluster. The city is likely to survive in the degree it brings together these elements into comprehensive communities whose people participate in decisions as to who lives there, their economy, environment, and institutions. This task requires a delicate balancing of elitism and participatory democracy.

THE COMPONENTS OF A CITY

The city can best be grasped through an understanding of its major components: *human resources, economy, environment,* and *institutions. Human resources* comprise the men, women, and children who produce or can produce, their skills, their health, the social network that brackets them, and their attitudes, foremost of which is the degree of their spirit of innovation. Their attitudes and their physical and mental health are important determinants of their efficiency in production. If the education, job experience, and health of these resources could be added and divided by their number, one would have a measure of the quality of human resources in the city. Moreover, these human resources go through a life cycle of *development* in education and training, *utilization* in public and private employment, *maintenance* as their skills become obsolete or as they become unemployed, and *aging* as they approach retirement. A city whose human resources have lost their sense of community and who have deep social animosities one against the other is a city in trouble.

Economy means the production and distribution of goods and services in the private and public sector, financing, and taxation. Direct business taxes and property taxes on dwellings are a major source of revenue for the city and are often a principal factor in its decline. Business taxes provide firms with the incentive to shop for a more favorable city and state jurisdiction. Property taxes on dwellings serve to produce a rise in population density and to reward individuals who cause their property to deteriorate.

A city has two alternatives in the development of its economy: to become self-sufficient or to establish export-import relationships with other cities. The first alternative is unrealistic. The second requires a city to seek new outside markets as the demand for its exports changes through shifts in its production or through losses of trade to other cities.

Stimulating the urban economy through government contracts and transfer payments tends to create a pauper economy that curtails inter-urban trade on the basis of relative efficiency. A viable city is one whose economic performance is comparable to a nation participating in world economy and maintaining a favorable balance of payments.[2]

There are some 10,000 managers in the economy whose decisions have a major impact on the number and location of jobs in the nation. Their decisions serve to increase the already densely populated metropolitan areas. No plan exists to control the location of human resources. Instead, politicians compete for plants on short term favorable offers and indulge in job stealing between cities.

Environment means the physical environment, including design, housing, transportation, air, water, private and community facilities, communications, and open space. Environment is a mirror of the interests and disinterests of organized power—labor officials, politicians, employers, land and housing speculators. The environment takes form consistent with their needs of power and money.

Institutions are the customary ways by which urban processes are discharged. The manner in which a problem is defined and solved depends upon the political and economic institutions of the city. Solutions are no better than the institutions through which they are channeled.

The most significant elements of each of these 4 fundamental urban variables are: the skill composition of human resources, the value and composition of production in the economy, the urban tax structure, the market value of its buildings, and the institution of government.

A dynamic and non-linear relationship exists between the 4 variables that is analogous to the morphology of the human body. Non-linearity implies a lack of simple single cause-effect relationships between parts, a fact which when ignored produces error in observation and resistance to planned objectives. An attempt to produce change in any one part triggers reactions from other parts that may be unwanted and unanticipated. It is like a remedy for a liver ailment which causes the stomach to malfunction and further aggravates thereby the condition of the liver. The same synergistic effect of organization applies to the city: What comes out of the city is more than the sum total of its individual inputs.

Accordingly, the urban system is counter-intuitive. That is to say, wrong judgments may intuitively be made as to what ails the city and policies instituted thereby which are counterproductive in effect. By

[2] For an analysis of this idea, see Jane Jacobs, *The Economy of Cities,* New York: Random House, 1969.

feeding different magnitudes of the various elements of these 4 variables into a computer and calculating the results of their interactions such mistakes may be minimized.

The urban system is activated by decisions whose accumulative effect is equilibrium or mutation. Mutations emerge as a conflict whose outcome produces a revised set of non-linear equations; in turn, however, a rescrambling of inputs creates a new equilibrium. Thus, the contemporary city resembles an ecological system whose balance has been upset and which must be restored to prevent its destruction.

An urban system tends toward workability; that is to say, a system does a reasonable job of maintaining a balance among the 4 variables through accommodating solutions. Most human resources find the solutions emanating from their institutions acceptable or at least they acquiesce to them. But when the balance is upset, as in a sudden change in the composition of human resources, individuals may find solutions intolerable to the point of no longer abiding by the existing rules of the game. Disruption ensues and considerable time may be required to restore the balance. When a new equilibrium of variables emerges the values and power structure will have changed.

A crucial factor in providing this balance is a combination of firms and human resources that makes the city capable of producing an exportable surplus. A departure from equilibrium produces explosive movements that may adversely affect this surplus. For example, firms that decline or move out upset the balance if no offsetting economic growth occurs. And the rise of human resources unqualified to maintain such a favorable balance of firms creates disequilibrium. Once out of phase, these two inputs have a deteriorating effect on environment and institutions. The ambitions of politicians create a short term outlook that tends to aggravate an already deteriorating situation.

These dynamic and non-linear relationships have an important bearing on policy strategy. A decision to ameliorate one aspect of the city may serve only to trigger a more general deterioration. Investment in industrial plants may raise the quality of human resources more effectively than an investment in education. Or the design of structures that grasps the spirit of individuals may motivate them to increase their capacities. Accordingly, investment in these 4 variables must be allocated in a way that obtains the most benefits overall in relation to cost, always keeping in mind that each projected allocation will have the effect of energizing a series of interactions akin to the functioning of the human body. Our analogy of the functioning of the human body and our reference to mathematical relationships should not be overdrawn. A dynamic system functions in the long run to the extent creative ideas are placed into it. Nor can we quantify precisely the magnitude of its variables or determine exactly their relationships.

To expand further on these relationships, we next discuss in greater depth the human resources and institutions of the city. Later in the chapter environment and economy will be discussed as parts of an overall scheme of urban redevelopment.

The Special Problem of Human Resources.   A major problem in the urban system is the low level of human capacities on the one hand and the sophisticated skills needed to make the city a self-sustaining organism on the other. In many cities a change in human resources mix has taken place since 1967 as a result of the white exodus to the suburbs, the black influx, and the higher black birth rate. The poor blacks replacing the middle class whites cost the city more and pay less taxes. This imbalance causes tension and deterioration of the sense of community. A point is reached where opinions do not rest on their merit alone but are assessed according to whether they are brought forward by whites or blacks. The entrenched leadership fails to arrest this trend. Men lose their compassion; extremists head for a collision course; opinions are given moralistic labels that make people indignant and inflexible; the spurious issue is raised of good versus evil.

This evolution provokes a protracted disequilibrium. The time necessary to establish a new equilibrium manifests the incapacity of the political leadership to face up to mistaken policies. When public policy fails, people expect that a shift in policy makers will bring change, but they select a mayor who reflects more their fears than their consciousness of measures necessary to restore equilibrium. The removal of the incumbent changes little because institutions remain the same and because a man elected on the basis of fear often proves to be incompetent.

The rise in the Negro portion of the urban population occurs at a time of rapid flight in economic resources. In Philadelphia, for example, over 500 plants closed down and located elsewhere in the decade beginning in 1956. The exodus continues despite political commitments to stem the tide and further reduces opportunities to upgrade manpower on the job. For cities generally, a decline in the capacities of human resources and in economic opportunities tends to produce a decline of competence in city administrations and in the optimism of the power structure.

A shift from optimism to pessimism by decision makers is aggravated by the lower number of desirable positions. Individuals are in influential posts by virtue of rights of birth or political connections. Talent in the ranks of the blacks emerges slowly. Innovators are considered suspicious characters by members of the power superstructure. The timidity of entrenched white managers contrasts with the energy of the black community. Thus, the city's decline sets up two conflicting forces: an obsolete power superstructure and a new class of inferior status challenging the traditional caste.

As the flight of skilled human resources takes place, the economy of the city shifts from manufacturing to services. The number of mass production industrial jobs that formerly absorbed unskilled workers declines. The proportion of the population receiving welfare rises. So does the number of jobs requiring high school diplomas and college degrees. Small firms with no government contracts and no black customers are indifferent to the resulting idleness. Big corporations whose product has a local demand, such as banks, utilities, supermarkets, transportation firms, and oil refining, maintain their business by hiring blacks. But the shift in the economy toward services tends to make more difficult the upgrading of the black subproletariat.

Concomitant with this change, employers become faced with a biracial labor market with sensitive blacks conscious of their institutional backing and equally sensitive white ethnics viewing change as a threat to their employment and standards. A dual system of personnel administration emerges: one for blacks and another for whites. Equal opportunity is interpreted to mean hiring a percentage quota of blacks. The law does not reward good behavior but encourages among employers a cynical policy designed to keep the government away from the door. They address themselves not to human resource development but to the politics of employment. They are pressured so much by overlapping and conflicting demands that they begin to play politics.

Nevertheless, management rather than organized labor becomes the innovator in the uplift of human resources in the city. Industrial firms devise training programs to fit characteristics of Negro labor; redesign jobs to facilitate entrance into the labor force; experiment with the computer as a tool of instruction; move away from employment tests that have the effect of screening out blacks. Some individual labor officials prod union organizations into performing a role. However, unions function to protect their members, and with the exception of craft unions, do not control jobs. The craft unions employ a strategy of staged withdrawal in meeting the pressures to open up their organizations. Generally, unlike the revolutionary changes in the cities during the 1930's, management and not organized labor is at the forefront of innovation.

Institutions.   Institutions can be depicted as inter-related power centers through whose pipelines the decisions of society flow. There are good and bad institutions. The good ones develop the capacities of those they are supposed to serve. The bad ones promote primarily the interests of those who latch on to them as bureaucrats. As institutions age, they become managed by individuals who obtain their positions through connections. They comprise a coterie of administrators who operate their interrelated bureaucracies on the basis of mutual back scratching. They are not the voice of the people, but to get rid of them is difficult. Thus, the theory of rising bads applies to institutions.

A noteworthy characteristic of urban institutions is the way they proliferate and work at cross purposes. A Ford Foundation official states that some 500 federal programs have to do with some aspect of urban development.[3] Another student of city government estimates there are 30 agencies of the national government that claim a jurisdiction in community development.[4] The significance of these figures lies not only in the problem of coordination between government agencies but also in the conflict of interests among employers with its effect on an ideal urban redesign.

Federal government agencies encourage proliferation by the manner in which they allocate funds. They either do not reveal or do not know the extent of expenditures in the city or the results obtained from such outlays.[5] Different fund recipients perform similar tasks but do not coordinate their efforts. Some work at cross purposes, sensitive to an invasion of what they deem to be their sphere of influence. Programs supported by the national government spew forth from federal regional offices, state agencies, county organizations, city governments, chambers of commerce, community agencies, schools, and universities. No overall plan exists—no meshing of talents, no exchange of information, no public accounting of operations and evaluation of results. It is impossible to determine who is doing what with what results. The public is expected to take seriously the plea for giving these organizations more money without any objective inquiry into the payoff of its investment. The philosophy and management of these organizations are more relevant than the more publicized question of fund shortages.

The antipoverty program of the national government instituted in 1964 produced an eruption of new urban institutions. In the scramble

---

[3] The Philadelphia *Evening Bulletin,* December 15, 1969.

[4] *The New York Times,* December 21, 1969.

[5] An effort to obtain from federal agencies specifics as to the amount of money coming into Philadelphia was unsuccessful. The request was channeled through an organization called the Cooperative Area Manpower Planning system. The Philadelphia Urban Coalition estimates total grants amount to $1.9 billion, including $20.2 million for veterans disability compensation, $26.2 million for aid to dependent children, and $26.2 million for medicare. Most of the federal money goes into building and construction.

created by the deluge of new money, housekeeping habits became shoddy. In New York City, the Human Resources Administration, with 80 percent support by federal funds, became a ghastly mess. The brainchild of an urban expert since departed to the more serene atmosphere of the Ford Foundation, the agency was heralded as a masterpiece of organization. Since his departure, the press has reported mismanagement and fraud in the amount of millions of dollars. The phenomenon typifies the manner in which institutions tend to be converted into a racket serving the interests of those who manage them.

A big city contains many labor market institutions that discharge the function of developing and placing manpower. Numerous organizations perform a variety of functions with varying degree of competence, including diagnostic testing, counselling, recruitment, and referral to employers. Employment brokers range from private and public employment agencies to community organizations and civil rights groups that bring together buyers and sellers of labor. A single organization may perform a variety of duties, including education and training, diagnostic interviewing and counselling, and follow-up after the individual is placed on the job.

These organizations are a blend of competence and ineptness, of rationality and irrationality, of individuals with institutional ambitions inclined to scuttle good ideas if they come from rivals. The very aims of government are often in conflict. Thus, the objective of finding jobs for the hard core unemployed makes difficult the pursuit of another policy of attracting persons into training programs at less pay, which in the long term would be in the interest of the individual and society. Despite the performance of individuals doing their separate pirouettes, the system manages to avoid falling into chaos. The impact of errors is softened by the competitive character of the manpower system, which is opposite to the effect of a blunder committed by some czar calling all the shots.

The rapid change in allocation of funds produces a disequilibrium in the city's institutional relationships. Old line Negro organizations, more acceptable to the traditional urban power structure, assume new functions. New ones acquire acceptability to the degree they contain elements of the traditional establishment. The Urban Coalition is an example of this second category. The Coalition describes its role as developing innovative solutions to urban problems, but it has labor leaders on its board who have not built up their reputations as innovators. In some cities, black rank and file organizations shun these coalitions. Businessmen prefer either operating within their own established organizations or taking over the coalitions entirely. Where racial incidents occur, coalitions tend to disappear. The Urban League, an old organization whose principal thrust is employment and other services for middle class blacks, is accepted by the establishment. OIC (Opportunities Industrialization Center), an innovator in the field of training blacks for blue-collar and low level white-collar jobs, has reached such a point of acceptance that it is difficult to determine which of its accomplishments are fact and which are myth.

The traditional superstructure comprised groups of whites, including managers in banking, industry, and commerce, members of liberal organizations, labor officials, politicians, and members of the religious hierarchy. Each segment of the power establishment derived its influence from the money and votes it could deliver. After a period of aloofness, university managers entered the circle as their interests were menaced by urbanization and the encroachment of black communities. The university, in the weakest position, offered respectibility to managers by nearness to a scientific establishment, technical assistance, and flattery in the form of honorary degrees. The executives, labeled civic and community leaders by the communications media, found that they could promote their economic interests by membership in public organizations.

Events have weakened this power establishment. The power of civic leaders to speak in behalf of a monolithic employer group was broken by the dispersion of firms into the suburbs and by the entrance of new firms not beholden to the old guard. Control of the purse strings in the city shifted toward the federal government. Labor leaders and churchmen lost their ability to control their respective memberships. The rise in education among whites produced a decline in paternalistic attachments to politicians. The changing racial composition of the city brought forth black leaders whose identification with the traditional establishment ran the risk of the disaffection of their rank and file.

With this weakening in the urban power superstructure has come a decline in the influence of white liberals, in whom a city such as Philadelphia abounds. Shake most any Gingko tree and down they come in profusion. The liberals have lost their white working class following, primarily because of the lag in their own perceptions. Moreover, since they have no black working class following, they are not taken seriously by politicians. This failure in intellectual leadership has an important bearing on the introduction of the urban technology necessary for the city's rejuvenation. Complex urban technology requires mass support, but the people who understand it have no mass following. The only leaders with a genuine mass following are blacks.

The political machine controlling the city government seeks to maintain its power within this changing configuration. This overriding concern poses a problem in surban renaissance: The machine must look at development in terms of its own preservation. Federal funds must be employed to fulfill such a purpose. Any emerging institution poses a threat. This subordination of the needs of urban renaissance to the needs of the party machine is pursued in part by upgrading Negroes into strategic posts whose primary asset is not competence but fealty to the boss.

Incompetent city bureaucrats beholden to the machine manage huge development funds transferred from the national government. No comparable situation exists in industry where officials of modest talents control huge sums of money. These top level officials do not plan so much as shift with the swing and sway of daily politics. Neither the talent nor the mechanism exists to place creative ideas into effect. A low income community in the city, for example, can be altered in appearance quickly with a concentrated clean-up campaign, the removal of advertising signs that give it a cheap carnival appearance, and the sprucing up of facades. But the city does not do this and has excuses for not doing so. The city wishes to attract suburbanites to restore its human resources balance but penalizes them upon arrival by raising the tax assessment on the house they purchase. For this, there is an excuse also.

Nor are staffs comparable in efficiency to those of industry, although in some instances, as in Philadelphia, they acquire the right of more pay for less work. The employees of the city government expect their wages to rise at least as fast as those in the private sector. However, these increases are not absorbed by a rise in productivity and the total wage bill mounts annually without the addition of services. Indeed, as the civil service workers develop a distaste for work of quality, the public pays more money for less services. City bosses acquiesce to these demands because of their need to build a loyal party machine.

Whether the city can ever be made livable depends to a considerable degree on the mayor. But his primary concern is not planning but getting reelected. Consequently, the mayor surrounds himself with flunkeys who can assure him that their decisions are based on what enhances the position of the mafia chief. Individuals are always available who in return for status and salaries they cannot get in private markets are amenable to operating in this fashion. Leadership is based not on a vision of a civilized city, but on choices made day by day directed toward the consolidation and maintenance of political power.

In the city of Philadelphia, for example, a corporation pollutes the air to the exasperation of the residents around it. The decision as to which of the two interests would be promoted depended on politics. The firm was investigated for many years and promises were obtained to do something, but little was done. The record indicates that the firm's chief executive contributed heavily to the mayor's election campaign.

But pollution is not entirely an evil to the community. Residents in South Philadelphia who had protested the construction of a prison in their neighborhood were advised by the government of a change in plans because the pollution would upset the convicts. The same city also expresses a sympathetic understanding of the point of view and organized labor, which supports the machine. An apartment house constructed by a labor organization was assessed for tax purposes at $2 million. However, the deputy city solicitor, also a heavy campaign contributor, ruled that the property was a charitable institution.

In the same city, 4 housing agencies share responsibilities for the city's housing. The responsibilities of the executives of these agencies are nebulous; they are more beholden to the mayor than to a vision of decent housing. Either they behave consistent with this allegiance or they get pressured out of their job. Their organizations' structures are so involved and so unwieldy that few dramatic results can be expected from their efforts. Their view of new low income housing is generally in terms of increasing the population density in already crowded communities that are not comprehensively planned. The model cities program of the national government is supposed to move forces away from this traditional thinking. It contemplates converting a Negro proletariat neighborhood into a model community within 5 years. In the initial $25 million recommended by the mayor for the program, $8.7 million represents staff and consultant fees. Goldie Watson, a community figure, was scheduled at a salary of $30,000 as administrator. A community affairs post was created at $35,000. The proposal abounds in vice presidents and executive directors. Forty-six percent of the housing units in the neighborhood are deemed unfit for human habitation. The first target of the plan is either new or rehabilitated units for 50 families.

Many agencies are involved in the city's overall physical development. They include a planning commission, a housing authority, a redevelopment authority, an art commission which controls designs of city-owned buildings and private edifices on major highways. The city charter designed these agencies to be independent of political influence. Through reappointments, forced resignations, and reshuffling of duties, the mayor tends to fill executive positions in these units with loyal followers. Thus, the planning commission was staffed with the president of the Plumber's union, who subsequent to his appointment was indicted by a federal grand jury for stealing union funds. The vice-chairman of the planning commission, a realtor, heads a firm that handles the sale of sites for public housing. By way of gilding the lily, the wife of a banker who was appointed to the planning commission after making a political contribution was in turn placed in charge of consumer complaints at $10,000 annually. Chairmanship of the housing authority was given to a land speculator who contributed heavily to the mayor's campaign. The talents of the former mayor do not go unrecognized; for his efforts he received an honorary degree from a Philadelphia university.

The city establishment is inclined to solve its urban problems by transferring them to the suburbs. Suburbanites are criticized for enjoying the city's advantages while not bearing their share of the burden. The assertion is not entirely correct. If the suburbanite works in the city, his earnings are taxed without the right of political representation. He provides skills needed for the city's survival. He produces tax revenues for the city from the office building in which he works. The city politician who berates the suburbanite may persuade him to stay home altogether, a choice that would be disastrous to the city. If an impenetrable wall were placed around it, the city would perish, not the suburbs. The city should not be allowed to swallow up the suburbs; the suburbs should swallow up the city.

The suburban establishment meets the urban threat by drifting. To pursue their interests rationally, suburban governments would have to join together to divide uniformly among them the burden of social costs the city wants to impose on them and to negotiate concessions. They must ask themselves: How much social costs can we bear? What do we want in return? However, these governments seem more inclined to yield to the pressures of suburban do-gooders and to wait for the courts to tell them how to use their land.

City fathers on occasion have to grapple with internal crises of state. In one instance, the President of Philadelphia City Council called a press conference to announce that a recalcitrant member was demanding a private toilet in his office because the judges had one. The adamant legislator was mollified only after a visit to the Council President's office to prove that even the President did not have one. The Mayor interpreted the toilet crisis as a desire of new councilmen to show their muscle.

City administrations are not adverse to playing a numbers game when it comes to bragging about their successes. Claims of placement of blacks, if added together, reach astronomical proportions. The figures are swollen by individuals who shift from one job program to the next and who drop out soon thereafter through lack of incentive to work. In the spring of 1968, the Mayor of Philadelphia announced at a press conference the institution of a summer program for the disadvantaged that would involve 800,000 persons and that would develop at least

10,000 summer jobs. The 800,000 figure amounts to more than a third of the entire population. The jobs were to come from the National Alliance of Businessmen, who stated at midsummer that they had succeeded in reaching only 20 percent of their original goal.

The record of city government in Philadelphia is replete with failure in achieving a rapport between elites and populace. In negotiating for a bicentennial celebration, an opportunity arose for using the ugly stretch of the Penn Central yards as a major exposition site. This use would have laid the basis for developing an adjoining black community. The opportunity was muffed by spokesmen of the city who have no community base, but who are called community leaders by virtue of the money they manage in organizations. They presided over negotiations that produced only noise and superficiality. The proposal was abandoned and the establishment then went out to the northeast fringe of the city to a white ethnic area. The resulting howl was equivalent in decibels to the roar triggered by a pinch hit home run by a batter on the local team. One evening's hearing reached its climax by a Polack suggesting that the solution to the site crisis was to change the bicentennial into a tricentennial. In desperation, the city fathers moved to the southern fringe of the city to an area noted for its ugliness and stench from the oil refineries. Only the rats rummaging through the junk and debris could object to having an exposition there. But by that time the national government had lost interest and refused to back an exposition.

The administration under former Police Commissioner Frank Rizzo inherits many deficiencies. His good intentions face formidable institutional obstacles. He represents an ethnic backlash without technical knowledge as to what ails the city. Those who supported his election have been amply rewarded with marked increases in income and prestige. But their knowledge of how to elect a mayor does not transfer to insight on the city's ailments. The ability of the mayor to generate an urban renascence depends on his capacity to develop a system that ties together technical elites from universities with community participatory democracy. The right of cultural autonomy, despite its dangers, is the only alternative. The mayor of a culturally heterogeneous city is a mediator and not the keeper of the city's morals.

The most outstanding events in the first year of the Rizzo administration was the flight of two more big firms, the imposition of an airport nuisance tax, the revocation of liquor licenses of establishments on a night club strip, and the collapse of the plan to have a bicentennial exposition. Losing the two firms means a loss of 2600 jobs. The tax levy is for exit and entry from an airport which probably is the ugliest of any major city in the United States; the levy accords with Rizzo's promise not to raise taxes, since 80 percent of the airport's users are non-Philadelphians. Closing the night spots maintains an old Philadelphia tradition of sexual hypocrisy. And the bicentennial proposal to the national government could not satisfactorily answer the cogent question: why encourage anyone to come to Philadelphia?

In the management of the Philadelphia school system, what is not gained in quality education is gained in imaginative executives. An aide of the school superintendent, a man of 28 years of age, wrote a budget memorandum in the following vein: He first suggested that the school budget be made sexy and be prompted by Madison Avenue techniques; it would not hurt to play a little dirty pool. The clever English major, among a group billed as the new look among educators, suggested that the board take a firm position on staff development. If the adult education budget were attacked, he proposed to give teachers material to use in their classes on who was really to blame for cutting the program. The boy wonder from Harvard University slipped from the frying pan into the fire by stating in explanation that the memo was just like hundreds of others circulated every year at the school administration building. For his literary efforts, the man is paid $16,000 annually.

If measured by the number of these bureaucrats relative to pupils, the quality of education in the Philadelphia public schools has increased considerably. In the 10-year period beginning 1960, the number of top level administrators increased 60 percent, to a figure of approximately 300, as the number of pupils rose 20 percent. The payroll for these administrators went up 238 percent to $5.5 million. During the same period, the salary of principals and vice principals tripled. Every year, the school superintendent complains of a budget crisis.[6]

Herein lies the crux of the urban problem. In the power superstructure of the city is a cynical bureaucracy whose overriding concern is not a pursuit of quality but the maintenance of position. The machine rules over a complex of obsolete institutions of government administering decaying communities from the remote distance of a city hall in whose corridors a self-respecting citizen would be disinclined to enter. In microcosm, the city ailment mirrors the national ailment: obsolescence of institutions and rule by politicians who either lack the intellect to see the obsolescence, or seeing it, refrain from indulging in a dialogue about it.

The superstructure has lost the confidence of the community. Since revival of the city is impossible without such a linkage, what is meant by a community should be clearly understood. A community is a geo-

6 The Philadelphia *Sunday Bulletin*, December 27, 1970.

graphical area, such as a neighborhood or even an entire municipality, whose population is drawn together by virtue of its streets, educational facilities, business, churches, public transportation, leisure facilities, and most important, its values. To achieve order, the functions of these units are related in varying degrees. The absence of integrative mechanisms within the community and the presence of different cultural groups in contiguous communities produce warring factions with no commonly accepted rules of the game. The proximity of these diverse groups as separate oases stimulates criminal action on the part of the inferior group against the superior group. Without negotiation to achieve an accommodation, these groups live under an uneasy truce. This absence of leadership prevails so long as the more powerful group finds the returns of an arms-length policy exceeding its costs, and so long as other groups do not upset this favorable balance.

Not all communities are urban communities. By urban is meant a community affected by the urban process, by dynamic forces such as physical environment, population density and mix, economy, institutions, and technology, that produce behavior which is complex, interdependent, conflicting, specialized, and bureaucratized. The terms urban and urbanization are not synonymous, the latter referring to the aggregation of population into dense metropolitan areas.

Healthy, self-governing communities are vital to the viability of the city. An ethnic orientation in these communities serves to foster cultural cohesion. Conflicts at their border require negotiation between them. Shifting demographic and occupational patterns in these communities tend to produce such tensions. For example, a sudden rise in birthrates in one community compared to another may serve to increase tensions, for the rise in birthrate increases the relative number of major sources of friction: children and adolescents. The higher birthrate of blacks together with migration into the city create pressures for housing that cause a breakdown of stable communities. The dislocations, in turn, produce a breakdown in the sense of community. The egalitarian philosophy of the superstructure tends to accentuate this deterioration.

Once the breakdown begins, lack of restraint in expressing views raises deep animosities; communication becomes difficult; whites resent being placed on the side of evil. A meeting of minds between members of different communities is difficult. Resentment is aggravated by politicians who remain silent and do not grant merit to the point of view of those placed on the defensive. To tell such individuals that their fears are unwarranted converts trepidation into exasperation. It is like berating a thermometer for the high temperature it records.

Such polarization adds to the estrangement in the city. One is reminded of a photograph in a local newspaper. A white lies in the gutter, stabbed while picketing a group of members of the Poor People's March on Washington. Blacks look down at him with indifference; two seem to be laughing. Some years ago, a European visiting an American city described seeing a black lying in the gutter. The visitor from a less advanced nation found it difficult to control his emotions in the face of the callousness with which passing individuals gazed down at the man. Disposed to giving the benefit of the doubt, he concluded after seeing the police come to haul off the black that what he had seen was an example of the division of labor. But, in fact, as the society converts human beings into abstractions, individuals become barbarians.

A restoration of the sense of community depends considerably on the rise of community organization such as the Young Great Society in Philadelphia. The organization is operated by young, intelligent blacks who know how to negotiate with the white superstructure. They approach problems on a pragmatic rather than an ideological basis. They look upon black development as a comprehensive goal to be achieved on their own turf, whose interrelated parts are environment, education, jobs, and institution building. The founder of the organization, Herman Wrice, is the prototype of the young black who can lead white and black out of the urban wilderness. If his proletariat community has not blown, the credit goes to Wrice and his associates.

THE POLICY

To present representative styles of organized urban reform, we move next to the Presidential Kerner Commission Report, the Martin Luther King movement, and the community actions program of the national government. Their successes and failures will be discussed in this section and an alternative proposed in the following.

The findings and policy recommendations of the Kerner Commission Report on the pathology of the city blend fact with myth. The report comes up with a simple observation: White Americans are racists and are collectively guilty for the situation of the black. Its findings rank with the indictment of the Germans for Hitler, of the Jews for the killing of Christ, and of the Russians for the paranoia of Stalin. They neither possess scientific worth nor are they good politics. Their sweeping condemnation reflects the sense of guilt of white liberals who suddenly discover the black and begin to beat their breast in a paroxysm of *mea culpa*. To call whites who see their neighborhoods deteriorate and who live in fear racists was a misjudgment of monumental proportions. Little in the report suggests that the policies of white and black liberals contribute to the polarization the commission deplores. Its findings are a hosannah to old time religion. They remind one of Soviet scholars who used to begin their analyses of social events by first making their reverence to Marx and Lenin.

The commission report focuses on the urban riots of 1967. As in the analysis of a conflict generally, the immediate cause of a riot may have roots far back in time and these contributing factors leading to the final end result must be sought and taken into account. Selecting these factors is subjective, reflecting what one consciously or unconsciously is trying to demonstrate. Moreover, the greater the use of abstract terms in explaining the phenomenon—such as racism, oppression, and insurrection—the less meaningful is the explanation.

At the forefront of those participating in the violence and looting were young black males from broken families. Their actions were supported by adults with a grievance against symbols of authority such as the police and symbols of exploitation such as white shopkeepers. Typically, an incident involving police action precipitated the violence, which was escalated by the ineptness of local police, national guardsmen, and state troopers.

The major goal, says the commission report, is a single society. To obtain this worthy objective the policy recommendations appear to say to whites: Bigots, get $10 billion out of your pockets and help the down-trodden black. Feeling guilty, the report's framers thus heap guilt on the nation generally. The accusation, however, is self-defeating; many Americans do not feel guilty. Or some do, but do not find a rational reason for their sense of guilt. These reactions obstruct solutions. Those who feel guilty, like many liberals, confuse self-ablution with black uplift; those who do not, may begin to worry why they do not. Accordingly, the first order of business is not black uplift but white purification. Guilt, like coercion, is a poor basis upon which to restructure urban relations. The report serves the public badly by continuing the fantasy of the good guys versus the bad guys. Its accomplishments lie in the catharsis it provided those who wrote the report.

Many whites are not racists; many Negroes are. White stereotypes of blacks are as confused as black conceptions of whites as greedy shop-keepers, bully cops, rapacious bill collectors, and cruel jailers posing as school teachers. The whites who wept for Martin Luther King and shared their grief with blacks were not all guilt ridden. Some experienced the shock of individuals seeing an extraordinary man abruptly destroyed. The reaction appeared like the eruption of a yearning for brotherhood in a system that places impediments in its path that are not of a racial character.

Considerable good will exists between whites and blacks. Most blacks believe their race has made progress. The report provokes just the action it deplores: polarization. Whites who witness the downgrading of their communities are asked to be statesmanlike. Root causes of poverty are underplayed. The report errs in viewing integration as a policy of coercing whites rather than as an outcome of other policies. Urban blacks have to develop their own political and economic power and they need their neighborhood with which to reach this objective. By constructing their own communities, blacks gain self-respect. Blacks who look deeply into the implications of integration policy are offended. The role of whites in the objective of black community development is to assist unobtrusively with money and talent, and not to expect honors for so doing.

The frustration over not being able to achieve an assimilated society implicit in the Kerner report reflects that felt by Martin Luther King. He practiced non-violence in the cities and this often generated violence. When King himself implemented his principle of disobeying what he deemed to be unjust laws, reason could still prevail, for he could be counted on to make wise choices. But his dictum was workable only to the extent that not too many city dwellers practiced it. His death reflected the city's ambivalence. A white killed him and a white was among the first to come to his aid. Whites wept for him as Stokely Carmichael redeclared his war of the blacks against the whites. Some blacks looted and some reached whites to express their shame at the reaction.

King had an understanding of the urban problem as one curable in legislative halls and public budgets. But he unleashed social forces antithetical to his goal of integration. His biggest enemy was the modern city because the modern city strips individuals of the religious compassion that made King effective. The moral sanctions that would bear down on those not heeding his voice disappeared in the city. His voice came out of a Southern Negro culture. His followers were people with a sense of religious belief. His effectiveness lay more in the South where he articulated the values of many whites. Even Southern whites had to acquiesce or deny themselves.

In the North, King was derided by young members of his race. Migration from the South to the modern city shattered their religious and family life, and King's values seemed obsolete. He spoke of brotherhood and generated scorn. The emotions and oratory unleashed by his death disposed individuals to idealistic courses of action; but the disposition quickly vanished, like the resolution to do good after seeing an emotionally charged film that is forgotten not too far distant from the theater marquee. King had blind spots and some of his policies were ill-advised. He had a saint-like quality, and special dispensations are due saints.

The city's community action program is the final policy to be discussed. The CAP sponsored by the U. S. Office of Economic Opportunity was conceived by intellectuals in the academic community as a comprehensive thrust against poverty with participatory democracy as its mechanism. Once organized, the thought was, the poor would control economic and human resources in a manner that would raise their living standards. But it did not work out that way. The poor are not prepared to deal with the complexities of urban life and need technical assistance to do so. The poor also observe distinctions among themselves and resent the monolithic point of view of liberals. Their proximity to each other is often not based on common consent. Moreover, an assault on poverty comprises more a strategy against economic scarcity than of social togetherness. The titillation caused by fraternizing wears thin quickly; no amount of togetherness resolves the problem of scarcity. Lastly, the urban political machine quickly converted the idea of maximum participation of the poor into maximum dominance by the politicians to serve their interests.

In Philadelphia, the community action program became a play in which the so-called representatives of the poor provided the props for the star players. When a prince finds his power challenged and competence questioned, a show of strength is in order. Such a necessity befell the mayor's antipoverty battler. The appointee, an impresario in the performing arts, and hence prepared for his role, threatened to resign. Thereupon, the workers laboring in the poverty vineyards came in with hundreds of signatures urging him to remain steadfast. Countervailing power being what it is at times, the impresario got caught in a snag. A rival accused him at an open meeting of instructing the antipoverty workers to suspend their battle in order to collect the signatures. The impresario shouted that his rival's point of order was out of order. His critic bellowed: shut up. The impresario responded: don't say shut up to me. The battle against poverty became a game for second rate Machiavellians.

AN ALTERNATIVE

For the city's resurgence, its human resources, economy, environment, and institutions must be redesigned. An interrelated scheme of urban redesign is complex. In multilinear city relationships, the sum of two plus two may be five or three. The problem of redesign is to determine and diminish the particular forces that decrease the quality of urban existence and to generate those forces that would raise its quality. To achieve this goal, a restructuring has to combine the technical assistance of the university with the participation of self-governing communities. Such an approach requires a philosophy that views technology as an instrument of human purpose. It rejects tying man's destiny to the statistical projections of bureaucrats and to physical plans that fit these projections. Moreover, the process by which this vision of human purpose is negotiated is as crucial as its implementation. The negotiation should not be done in an atmosphere of crisis. In addition, the involvement of Negroes is crucial since they represent a major segment of the remaining humanists in the city.

The demoralization attending the destruction of a stable community kills off a humanistic outlook. People who lose control of their lives because of manipulation by the power superstructure lose their generosity. Moreover, realtors who are out to make a fast dollar frustrate the goal of social good will. They encourage blacks to buy into white neighborhoods and then use their initial success to stimulate panic selling. The black manipulated into buying beyond his means holds on by increasing the population density in housing and spending little or no money on maintenance. The greed of realtors thereby adds to community demoralization.

Restoration of the sense of community requires abandonment of forced integration and development of model communities both inside and outside the city. The model community is a coherent community within the old city boundaries or outside, entrance into which by motor vehicle is severely restricted. About 20 percent of the old city comprises streets. What is on these streets is there to make money. If they are not making money, the streets are in a state of deterioration. In the model community, streets are a means of men communicating with each other face to face. The city that permits the motor vehicle easy access, parking, and pass-through soon destroys itself as a civilized place in which to live.

Within the city, the model community emerges from planned change of an existing community. Urban demolition is confined as much as possible to opening up areas and making them green, reducing population density, protecting living areas from the motor vehicle, and providing old communities with more amenities and sources of employment. When open land is available in the existing city or outside, the model community can be developed more effectively and more economically. As the government acquires land, it should be kept in the public domain through leasing arrangements and not sold outright.

Most aspects of life are pursued within the model community. Each such community is a self-sustaining neighborhood of mixed income groups living together on a voluntary basis. The model community has sitting parks; masses of greenery, some of which are owned by particular persons but controlled in the public interest; walk-to plazas which the motor vehicle cannot penetrate; playgrounds; walk-to schools; nurseries with education programs; clinics; work places within walking distance; and park-and-ride lots secluded by evergreens. By using natural buffers, the community is protected from external inroads on the one hand and from the tendency of communities to push outward indiscriminately on the other. Retail shops are concentrated at its fulcrum and small individual food shops placed in living areas. Their advertising signs are flush with the facades to minimize ugliness. Industrial firms are an integral part of the model community and a source of its employment. Clusters of firms in industrial parks are contrary to the idea of a comprehensive community. The overall intent is to give man a full life within his own neighborhood and an opportunity to commune with his fellow-man.

While the scientific evidence is not conclusive, there is reason to think that man has a definite sense of territoriality. This means a community must be developed so that he can identify with a particular plot of land. This association need not be exclusive so long as he identifies with those with whom he shares the attachment.

The community is organized through the device of a public corporation subscribed to by its citizens and subsidized initially by government. The corporation plans and executes the interrelated functions of comprehensive development. It is connected to state and national corporations charged with community planning and funding. A major function of these state and national corporations is the acquisition of land for the development of new communities.

The board of the neighborhood corporation contains different elements of the community, including residents, government officials, specialists in the urban university, and employers. The corporation produces visible returns quickly and continues to provide returns by week, month, year, and by decade. It attracts business so as to export products and encourages internal capital formation. It plans to maintain a high level of skills consistent with full employment. Government assists the corporation by initial capitalization and by tax incentives. As they become profitable, the corporation spins off the businesses it creates.

Accordingly, the model community provides opportunities for change in a climate of voluntarism. White liberals can practice what they preach by moving into them. Suburbanites can remain untainted if they so wish and stay where they are. Blacks can participate in their own development. And the national pastime of Americans—running away from each other—may dwindle.

Outside the city boundary, the initiative for model communities comes from state governments, which have to assemble the land and charter the development corporation. The model community outside the city is entirely new. It commands priority for several principal reasons: to assist in thinning out the urban population with a minimum of disruption, to prevent the city from becoming all-black, and to develop institutions of participatory democracy whose output is not just social discourse. Furthermore, a new model community would be required to negotiate any opposition raised by existing contiguous communities.

Population control in model communities is crucial. Large families inhibit the growth of capital per capita and disperse the allocation of current outlays. Both have an adverse effect on the quality of human resources. A marked decline in the birthrate can produce in the short period of 5 years considerable opportunities for increasing education effort per child. Consumption guarantees to large families frustrate the goal of maintaining a balance between men and environment. Therefore, incentives in the model community are provided for family planning.

This outline of a model community does not imply a universal kind of growth. Each community should express the life style of those who live in it. While basic outlines are universal, the filling in process should be left to the community's members. A development of self-governing comprehensive neighborhoods brings meaningfulness to the goal of a life of quality. But the idea is unlikely to materialize unless an ethnic coalition of blacks and whites exerts pressure on government to implement it.

A city represents diversity. Accordingly, the use of elitism must be reconciled with representation expressing the diversity of people residing in the city. The amenities manifesting diversity must be within easy grasp of those who are partisan to any of their particular aspects. A city expressing only the subjective judgments of elites has little life. A cluster of buildings of elite architecture tucked away on an inaccessible boulevard is suggestive of death, and a neighborhood whose design reflects its people's spirit is suggestive of life. A living city is not what a Mumford, a McHarg, or a Lecorbusier want it to be, but what its different people want its different parts to be.

The modern city, unlike an old town, has little suggestion of history in its facades or of sensitivity in the relationship of people to objects. What one sees can be explained in terms of the profit motive. If objects that please the human spirit exist in a neighborhood, the planner tends to obliterate them with his new design. Either the planner does not see what is in an old neighborhood or he does not care about it.

A university elitist role in the development of model communities faces obstacles created by past mistakes. Its commitment to urban problems began as assistance in high level environmental planning and in government organization. Subsequent involvement in community development schemes, such as that of the Ford Foundation in Philadelphia, produced adverse community reactions. Blacks felt they were being used to promote the interests of elites.

The black's suspicion of university elites is therefore justifiable. As the university expands, it pushes him out of the way. Some university professors have a condescending attitude toward him; they know all the answers. If the black does not accept them, it is the result of his own shortcomings. The professor may view him as an abstraction with a sublime mission to perform or as an object of research. Despite these deficiencies, urban redevelopment requires a non-partisan voice to amass and interpret information, a voice to gain the confidence of the community. By relating the urban university to the self-governing communities, the crucial need of permitting members of the unsystem to interact with those of the system will be achieved. Given the prudent choice of professors, this alternative is better than that of more government. Every day that the national, state, county, and city governments increase the number of their employees by even one should be a day of mourning.

As both servant and critic of the community, the university in the city can perform functions such as: disseminate knowledge in understandable terms; conduct programs to raise the academic achievement of children of working class families; operate a manpower development laboratory experimenting with educational methods; provide a neutral voice to the urban coalition of communities; develop a practical systems approach to urban development; involve students in the monitoring of urban technology. By taxing themselves only a few dollars yearly, students could hire legal talent to monitor technology in the city. In short, the university could provide an urban extension service similar to the agricultural extension services of rural universities.

Discouraging rural migration to urban centers would assist in the rejuvenation of the city. This deterrent requires rural development programs to create self-sustaining rural communities. The costs of both urban and rural programs may run as much as $15 billion annually for a decade. Such expenditures would require a significant change in national priorities.

A strategy of urban growth seeks a rapprochement between the races by consensus, not coercion. Whites are guilt-ridden, hostile, fearful, and indifferent. Blacks in whose ranks exceptional talent exists are not entirely indisposed to bargain out differences with white ethnics. The next stage in race relations should abandon the policy of unilateral concessions by liberals at the expense of white ethnics.

Urban rejuvenation requires honest answers as to what causes decay. The traditional city took its form based on the pursuit of money and power. Neither pursuit creates a civilized environment. Americans are forever running away from each other. They flee from the depredation of a system of elite decision making based on the profit motive. For the city to survive, the criterion of social profit must supercede the criterion of private profit. The power superstructure, together with its servant, the judicial system, is today geared to serve best those with money and power; the unsystem has to amass the money and power to change this thrust. To do so, a black leader may be more productive than a Caucasion. The white mayor of a declining city is a symbol of backlash; a black mayor, without a fawning attitude toward whites and with a sympathy for the position of white ethnics is more likely to achieve a new urban consensus. Whites may thereby discover more humanity in blacks than exists in their own race.

The billions of dollars going into the city serve to prevent the urban organism from becoming a cadaver. The city has to be rebuilt in its entirety consistent with a plan of human purpose. City governments are the weakest link in such a rejuvenation. These governments are not innovators but housekeepers in support of a political machine. Despite the enormous funds given to cities, few have produced a comprehensive concept of development tied to a vision of human quality. Cities think in terms of houses, roads, public facilities, schools, firms, without any concept of their relationship with each other.

A livable city needs social cohesion. Therefore, one must ask what forces create division. A city needs the cooperation of surrounding suburbs, not on the basis of judicial coercion and distortion of facts, but through incentives to cooperate. The technology is available to do what has to be done. What is needed is wisdom, empathy, and new institutions. The course of history gives to corporations the exercise of initiative. If they elect to support model communities and university urban extension services they may be able to remove themselves from their present defensive position. The policy of forced integration produces white fear and black frustration; it is no longer relevant. The policy of self-determination is. If corporate management takes the initiative to encourage this alternative, the city is more likely to reacquire the social cohesion needed for its survival.

A fundamental need of the young black in the city is not paternalism but self-reliance in developing a beautiful idea. He needs to be assisted unobtrusively to the point where he no longer needs such assistance. If his energies were channeled into implementing ideas, the city's rebirth would be more likely. But his involvement must be shared with young whites. If the zeal, flexibility, and honesty of youth can be captured for the city, then the city has a future.

CONCLUSIONS

It has been seen that the city cannot be revived by elites setting up for themselves information and decision making systems. Yet today, technicians cut off from government funds for antipoverty, space, and defense programs are turning to solving urban problems. A massive task does exist, of involving people in self-government, of establishing a populist consensus on goals, of determining who is doing what in bureaucratic structures. But elites cannot be trusted to plan and manage unilaterally; the facts support such a conclusion. They are prone to place decisions in their own hands and to design structures that serve their purposes.

The mayor of a big city faces this difficult problem of elitism versus populism. He may be afraid of how an inventory of the problem may make him appear. He needs quick and visible results politically favorable to him before he can accept the uncertainties of populist involvement. The urban operation may be so vast as to relegate him not to a role of managing but to one of moving from one dampened crisis to the next. Nor may he have any objective standard for determining the effectiveness of particular operations. He must perform the difficult task of reconciling information coming from technicians, managers, civil servants, and public. And these different sets of persons only rarely agree either on what is happening or what should be happening. In the last analysis, his task is resolving a power problem in which every party of interest has to be accommodated. His job, which may well be impossible, demands technical skill, courage, and wisdom.

What the city needs is to be stirred by a sense of creativity among its different ethnic groups. One cannot expect technical elites to provide such an élan. They do not come to the negotiating table with clean hands; they do not demonstrate a notable capacity to lead a process of consensus; they are timid. The initiative seems to rest with blacks whose ascendancy led to the city's polarization and who now have the responsibility to establish a new consensus. The ethnic neighborhood has the right to maintain its identity and to negotiate the changes that the outer superstructure wishes to impose. If outsiders do not respect this right, the ethnic neighborhood is forced to use whatever means at its disposal to protect itself. The neighborhood makes the sense of self flourish. The struggle of black and white ethnics to maintain their neighborhood reflects more sociological insight than that of the educated elites bent on destroying it.[7]

One can speculate on two alternative directions the city may take in the coming years: what is likely to emerge from the continued pursuit of traditional policy and what may transpire by going down the path of populism with the university as an instrument of technical assistance. The first alternative presents a prospect of urban brinkmanship. An additional one hundred million people would jam themselves into already congested urban areas, menaced by each other's production and consumption. The alternative path of cultural autonomy depends to a considerable degree on the initiative of blacks with a mass following seeking a coalition of ethnic forces. If blacks approach such negotiation as the forces of justice against the forces of reaction, they are going to blow it. To minimize the possibility of such an explosion, the university could provide a service of fact gathering, analysis, and neutral chairmanship.

In either contingency, the traditional city will die. The American city emerged as a vehicle of exploitation of human and economic resources. Its proffer of income continues to hold men in its grip. As this nexus is broken, the traditional city has no basis for existence. The city represents the alienation of man from himself and from nature. It must therefore be redesigned in physical and human terms so as to arrest this estrangement.

The legal foundations of American society rest on a fundamental assumption of cultural homogeneity. The very language we use—culturally deprived, culturally disadvantaged—implies the existence of a superior culture, upper class Wasp, and inferior cultures whose life styles are defective. This notion of a universal standard against which the extent of inferiority of ethnic groups can be measured pervades the thinking of liberals. It underlies much of social science research and enters consciously and unconsciously into the thinking of decision making elites.

Liberal elites espouse their notion of equality in a culturally pluralistic world. They use as universal benchmarks of excellence qualities in themselves which give them a sense of self-esteem. Thereupon, differences between the high order of these attributes in themselves and the low order prevailing among other cultural groups are a measure of in-

---

[7] Incredibly, the 1970 census enumeration makes no provision for a count of two major ethnic groups: Puerto Ricans and Mexican Americans. But it does for Japanese, Chinese, Indians, and Filipinos. Thus, the census technicians have by definition erased a portion of the ethnic problem.

equality. They fail to distinguish between their subjective feelings of good intention and feelings of empathy for the way other groups see themselves. They confuse an extension of themselves with the promotion of the interests of other groups. They employ pejorative terms such as ghetto and racism, which have the effect of obfuscating issues and narrowing options. Consistent with these notions, the purpose of public policy becomes the narrowing of differences. And the pursuit of public policy calculated to reduce the so-called inequality is not at their expense, but is imposed on others.

This universal application of cultural norms has caused devastation in the city among ethnic groups and in their relationships with each other. It has deprived many of them of a sense of manhood. It has made people feel inferior when in actuality they are only different. Programs expending huge sums of money have failed because they have been applied without references to these realities.

Such is not to say that this alternative of public policy resting on assumptions of cultural pluralism will be easier to manage. The legitimization of ethnicity is a necessary but risky part of a comprehensive strategy of mutual respect. Cultural groups must be disposed to negotiate conflicts in norms and resources. More options must be provided so that groups can maintain their identity if they choose to do so. The goal of establishing universally applied norms must rest not on manipulation by elites but on the negotiation principle. The task is not easy; but it will certainly provide verve in life.

Elites prefer docility over participation, an attitude which reflects an uneasiness in direct dealings with the public. Elite critics of participation often deride such policy by applying to it the test of efficiency. Thus, for example, they advocate regional governments replacing suburban governments, by asserting that such bigger government would deliver services more cheaply, an economic expectation that runs counter to the history of government. But more importantly, their measure of efficiency ignores other important values that accrue by virtue of participation, values which in the long run are indispensable for the rebirth of the dying city.

PART
FIVE

THE FUTURE

Prospects for Change

For the face was turned toward the loins; and
They had to come backward, for to look before
Them was denied.
Dante Alighieri

Our discussion of what the future holds for American society will be divided into two segments. This chapter will deal with the prospects for changes emerging from the present conflict between system and unsystem, a conflict which we have noted pervades many aspects of American life. The next one will present a proposal based on personal preferences as to what the future should be. By thus placing prediction and personal preference into separate chapters hopefully the difference between the two will be maintained.

Such often is not the case. In his *Divine Comedy,* Dante Alighieri has a special circle for soothsayers. Their hands are tied behind their backs and their heads are twisted around so they can see only the past, a punishment that is especially appropriate for intellectuals who weave predilections into their prognostications. But presenting an unequivocal proposal as to what should happen is even more hazardous than crystal ball gazing; the specifics of a strategy calculated to achieve the desired result must be put forward. Depending upon outcome, one then emerges as a savant or a fool.

Nevertheless, the responsibility of moving from questions of what is likely to be to considerations of what should be is unavoidable. To grant moral sanction to likely future outcomes avoids the issue raised by the young. What they say is: Here is a moral vision; how does one attain it? The young are less interested in technological trends. They

405

are more concerned with using technology so as to achieve a preconceived end. Professors who ignore this preference are ducking their responsibilities.

THE PRESENT SITUATION

American political-economic institutions have changed considerably since the end of World War II. Business and organized labor are no longer private organizations. They are arms of the state apparatus. The system of countervailing power has changed into a system of cooperating oligarchs mistrusted by white-collar and blue-collar groups in the population. The people have become servants of the oligarchs' technology. Forms of control to contain this dominance do not emerge in a planned manner, but appear here and there through the back door in piecemeal fashion. Even the system's managers do not see any necessity for a radical transformation of institutions, or they do but are disinclined to talk about it openly.

The system expects individuals to behave consistent with its needs. It imposes commands on the individual for its own orderly survival. It manipulates the individual into buying goods and services for which he feels no prior need. As industry propagandizes him for the maintenance of profits, the government assists with manipulatory monetary and fiscal policies. The work which the system provides can be performed by a decreasing number of toilers, and relief is sought in the promulgation of rules prescribing forced idleness and income guarantees to consume a rising surplus of middle class goods. To consume in idleness, accepting passively the goals of planned authority, is to be patriotic. Accordingly, the system controls social change consistent with the demands of a production machine geared to profit making.

A timorous management elite responds with palliatives rather than with candid expressions of the imperatives of a life of quality. The accepted measure of success, the gross national product, shows that more and more goods are produced annually but reflects neither the actual costs paid for these goods nor the extent to which they represent social goals foregone. The profits system as an instrument of promoting human welfare is dead; but the timorous elite dare not declare the wake.

The university servants of the system provide techniques in support of the production machine. Econometricians have worked out a series of interrelated mathematical equations describing the economy as it is. With these equations, they seek to solve the problem of the impact on output and employment of a particular public policy. For the equations to work, however, individuals have to act in a predictable fashion. Accordingly, the success of public policy could be enhanced if individuals were so trained to behave.

Thus, the system molds behavior in its interest. To work effectively, it requires passive minions; the steady improvement in mass manipulation techniques developed by university professors makes it progressively easier to fill this need. Moreover, the rules of the game are promulgated in the interest of the system's managers. Since the managers select successors in their own image, the rules have a life independent of the system's transient players. Each succeeding round of aspirants is inclined to accept the rules of incumbents in return for taking over their posts. The institutions that could channel the unprecedented surplus of the economy into men and environments of quality do not command similar resources. The society, after laboring under the tutelage of eminent Wasps to develop a philosophy of a Great Society, can only promise another scoop of ice cream.

As a society develops a routine to meet day-by-day exigencies, it curtails its competence in meeting newly emerging challenges. A bureaucratic system of routinized interrelated actions is the offspring of past challenges. Its orientation discourages an exploration of new methods and goals. A modern society has an increasing stake in the maintenance of a systematic and uniform procedure and therefore abhors a radical departure from existing commitments. But a rising number in the population resists being forced into the system's mold. A conflict thereby emerges between forces that seek to protect the investment in the modern technology operating the system and individuals seeking life styles inconsistent with the demands of mass technology.

This demand for uniformity is being further undercut by the contemporary decline in reverence for authority. As modern man relinquishes his belief in immortality, he seeks an individual identity on earth; the measure of this individual identity is scorn for organizational power. The decline in deference to organization elites converges from many directions. The permissiveness in modern educational philosophy weakens acquiescence to authority. Ineffective public policy diminishes the unquestioning reverence formerly held by the independent college educated class and the state. In addition, white ethnics in increasing numbers are mistrustful of big organization generally. As these forces against the system appear, subsocieties arise in opposition to positions of the system. The forces of reaction against this irreverence are at times demonic. The system's managers cling to old forms of rule until forced to retreat by the havoc their positions create.

The managers are committed to traditional dogma. They claim a

monopoly on acceptable thinking and they are supported by traditionalists in the population who feel insecure when their beliefs are challenged. Mired down in inbred opinion, the managers are wary of critics.
Creativeness from their own ranks is unlikely, and from the ranks of
their critics it is intolerable. These dispensers of traditional faith espouse
freedom, private enterprise, respect for authority, law and order; the
opposition is frustrated by their materialism, hypocrisy, and brain washing and improvises methods with which to protect itself from the official
virtues. The traditionalists describe a world that no longer exists, to the
frustration of critics who suspect that the traditionalists deliberately
avoid expressing what troubles the spirit of dissenters. The one speaks
platitudes; the other cannot talk back for the record. A clash of loyalties
emerges. Those of dissenters transcend national boundaries and offend
the sensibilities of traditionalists. The language expressing these loyalties
offends. Until this clash of ideology can be reconciled by a relative shift
in power, the best that can be expected is a truce.

As a system of countervailing power matures, a new institutional
problem unfolds: how to control power blocs without relying on a government that is supposed to control them in the public interest but which
in fact has mercantilist sympathies for them; where to obtain leadership
for the legitimizing of emerging values when government can no longer
be trusted to perform such a role. As the system of countervailing power
changes into the system of cooperating elites, the conflict is not between
organized blocs, but between system and unsystem. As big government
and big business seek to maintain their dominance of society, communication between managers and population deteriorates. The traditional
decision making process of a clash of liberal and conservative opinion
obsolesces. The liberal clings to his belief of promulgating goodness by
government fiat. The conservative errs not in his espousal of humanistic
values but in his blindness as to the factors that cause their breakdown.
As the conservative draws income from investments in corporations
that destroy traditional values, he sees the solution of preventing their
destruction in oppression.

Accordingly, the absurdity arises of organized power as a criterion of
value governance: Might does not make right, but rather acquiescence
because of lack of an alternative. In foreign as well as domestic affairs,
the national government is a symbol of the futility of power as such a
criterion of governance. In a world of instant communication, the decisions of elites immediately generate a critical reaction that serves to
thwart their goals. Those in the seats of the mighty can only use power
covertly, an alternative that eventually corrupts them. They contravene
the very principles they allege to promote. They assume that men of

virtue such as they can operate outside a morality of honesty, without damaging the institutions they claim to defend. The major corruptors of the nation are those who protect it most zealously from corruption. The managers are trapped. They can only exercise their power under cover. But the elitist exercise of power becomes publicized, often in distorted fashion, and generates a critical reaction that frustrates its goals.

War and the preparation for war have stimulated the rise of this irrationality. The war system has taught the population the legitimacy of violence and the wisdom of mistrusting organization. Historically, some great powers have emerged from long periods of warfare into an era of a highly civilized existence; presently, it is difficult to defend the thesis that American society is more civilized now than it was 3 decades ago. The task is to contain the decision making of the princes of power so as to achieve a more civilized life. To accomplish this goal, the conditioned population would have to become conscious of what the system does to human beings; but the system encourages the frustration rather than the emergence of this consciousness. Accordingly, change is trapped in a vicious circle.

THE SOURCES OF CHANGE AND THEIR CHANCES FOR SUCCESS

Structural changes may be generated by an initiative effectively seized by one or more of the following sources: the system itself; the social sciences; the education system; college youth; foundations; churches; mass media; the legal profession; and a humanist power bloc. The issue is which of these groups, if indeed any of them, can effectively bring forward an analysis of the society's needs and use the information to bring about a modification of the system's decision making processes. It is to a discussion of this issue that we now turn.

The System. The possibility of the system reforming the system is unlikely. That the managers knowingly nurture institutions that would bring about a decline in their influence is too much to ask. The system can hardly be expected to foster practices to subvert itself. As in the case of corporations, its impulse is to make whatever strategic withdrawals are necessary to maintain its interests. Modern man makes little progress because the forces that keep him chained—fear, insecurity, imagery— are vital to the system's smooth operation. The system abhors basic cures and prefers to legislate against the sickness it generates. The system demonstrates a continuing capacity to lull individuals into a sense of going places. It easily creates a man who neither laughs, cries, nor feels pain, who commands symbols of affluence, and who is disposed to take the gaff. For those who reject the system, the acceptable remedy is commanding sufficient income to withdraw as much as possible from the game. The dual objective may conflict, but more the system cannot guarantee.

The Social Sciences. That the social sciences in their present state will initiate social innovation is doubtful. Compared to natural science, social science suffers from a deficiency in human and economic resources and in methods of development; from a lack of genuine scientists or a lack of interest in developing them; and from a dearth of organizations in which social scientists can flourish. The bulk of funds going into research for social innovation is managed by cautious government bureaucrats disinclined to give an investigator free rein in the development of new ideas.

In the universities, the social sciences are geared to the development of practitioners for the system. The technician professors who teach them load their courses with technique and produce another generation of technicians rather than innovators. The social science research they perform provides tools for managers or options designed to promote the immediate interests of government and industry. Practitioners who manage organizations do not buy research for the purpose of innovation the way producers in goods production do. Their interest focuses on information that promotes their position in organization and their policy commitments. They have little inclination to expose their routine to scientific analysis.

Unlike natural science, the social sciences have failed to develop a system of creation, prototype development, use, and evaluation of social ideas. They have much to say about the average man and little about a particular man in a particular context. Social ideas are left to literary intellectuals who pour forth millions of words not subject to scientific verification and who have neither the ability nor the resources to translate them into effective institutions. No systematized analysis exists, for example, of the social evolution of American society since World War II. If we do not know precisely the social condition of the nation, it is because the system has little interest in finding out.

The system generates a systematic flow of the most talented not into social innovation, but into the production and sale of goods. Education prepares individuals for such service rather than for social inventiveness. Organizations do not provide employment opportunities for social innovators to the same degree as for innovators in good production, for such employment does not lead to a product that can successfully be marketed. A social scientist is typically employed as a subordinate to a practitioner who expects him to supply strategies that promote his interests. Moreover, the monetary rewards for the physical innovator exceed those awaiting the social innovator. This suggests that public financing is in order; but political power in its behalf is difficult to acquire.

In the economics branch of the social sciences, men of learning such as Kenneth Boulding tower over a field comprising primarily technicians in applied mathematics. Most of the literature in the area of industrial relations bears little upon an understanding of the evolutions of industrial ideas and institutions. Of the many hundreds of investigators, a small fraction have succeeded in providing a sense of historical development to social ideas, and fewer still concern themselves with the manner in which social inventiveness emerges. The great mass of published industrial relations research in the 1960's deals with the structure and functions of the National Labor Relations Board of the federal government. Other major subjects of inquiry include collective bargaining in the public sector and manpower policy. Most of the studies in these 3 areas deal with issues of interest to managers and most of the supporting funds come first from government and secondly from foundations.

A manpower specialist, Garth L. Mangum, states:

> The sixties were a period of experimentation in manpower policy. The surface was hardly scratched in manpower research. A cadre of manpower researchers has been developed and their appetites have been whetted by intriguing problems, and available, though limited, funding. But researchers are fickle. They tend to go where the headlines and the money are. Hopefully, the interest in manpower policy research can be maintained in a period of stability, at least until a few of the major issues are resolved.
>
> But research is only the first step. Research for research sake is a good way of life for researchers, but that hardly justifies the expenditure. The payoff for manpower policy research must be more effective policies.[1]

In a list of the outstanding achievements made by the social sciences since emergence of Keynesian economics a periodical includes: opinion poll technique, information theory, game theory, and budgeting. Clearly, the trouble with the social sciences is that they are not social science. They comprise either techniques calculated to serve particular organizational interests and developed along these lines or the mishmash of a rhetoric of bores. The profession is dominated not by men of science but by technical consultants feeding at the trough of government and industry or by egoists using social science as a put-on, with the dominant

1 Garth L. Mangum. "Manpower Research and Manpower Policy," in *A Review of Industrial Relations Research,* Madison, Wisconsin: Industrial Relations Research Association, p. 111.

motive not of adding to the truth but of discrediting someone else's work in the hope of acquiring status and notoriety.

The division of the sciences in the universities into unrelated disciplines tends to confine the development of knowledge to one in keeping with these organizational interests. The natural sciences have taken over man's body while the social sciences claim his mind. While the separation serves the purposes of specialists, it discourages the evolution of a unified body of knowledge on the nature of man. By concentrating on techniques for specialized disciplines, social science misses the big issues.

Organized knowledge comprises a flow that originates from scientific observation and proceeds through different pipelines into specialized compilations. The flow of the social and behavioral sciences is less clearly structured than that of the natural sciences. It starts with loosely related individual efforts by scientists formulating new findings into language. Their findings flow through several conduits. One goes to social engineers who seek to apply the scientific knowledge toward devising new social structures that achieve a specified social objective and toward formulating strategies to acquire acceptability of the new structures. But there is little of this kind of inquiry. The major accomplishments in social engineering issue by improvisation in the political process and by mediation designed to reach an accommodation among parties of interest. Moreover, the engineering required to resolve social problems is painfully slow and laborious. To cite an example, the cost of medical care in the United States has reached astronomical levels. There is on record a case of a blue-collar worker with heart disease spending 29 hours in a hospital and amassing a bill in excess of seven thousand dollars. The problem has gotten progressively worse in two decades and the end is not in sight. Generally, the translation of scientific knowledge for profit is much faster than the translation of scientific knowledge for social welfare.

The different flows of information that go to public policy managers are used to make decisions involving conflicts of interests and rights in large groups, decisions which at times restructure the relationships of individuals in such groups. From the point of view of the public interest, the information channeled and managed by these managers is grossly inadequate. A small amount of their information derives from the findings of social and behavioral science. More frequently, it accumulates from intuition and trial and error, or derives second hand from their technicians who employ their general knowledge as a source of advice to managers. Moreover, the conditions necessary for valid research do not materialize until long after the policy is implemented. Policy is often based on imprecise information and wishful thinking. For example, integration policy was developed from piecemeal findings ranging from pure speculation to particular isolated incidents from which conclusions were drawn that the induced bringing together of blacks and whites would reduce inferiority feelings of blacks and raise mutual confidence. But these findings were not based on dynamic analyses of different social groups under the heel of public policy management. In addition, research funds are often controlled by the policy manager with a vested interest in research findings that support his policy commitment. Findings inconsistent with this commitment tend to be ignored. Thus, the U. S. Civil Rights Commission, using selectively the Coleman report, concluded that the inferior educational achievement of Negro children was due to their being denied attendance in white schools.

An urgent need exists for a more intensive development of basic scientific knowledge and applied research on social problems. Organization and decision making theory provide the greatest opportunities for such growth; economics and sociology have not reached a stage that would make them useful for such a purpose. One must conclude that breakthroughs in social innovation from the social sciences in their present state are unlikely to materialize.

The Education System.   Can an initiative for social innovation come from the education system? The university intellectuals are generally more capable of talking and writing about power than they are of developing or managing it. Those having a talent for understanding power management hire themselves out to the system. Those who stay on campus deploring such a commitment are frequently insecure and undiscerning. Common to members of the academic profession, an incapacity to work collectively toward the social goals they espouse exists among the university intellectuals. Faculty meetings are testimonials of this incapacity. The influence of university intellectuals is more likely to be felt, if at all, in the slow and incalculable effects of teaching.

The practitioners at the university convert their institutions into a service garage for peace and friendship with the system. Losing government money generates the same alarm as does the loss of a military installation. It is not necessary to wait for some remote future to see what may happen when these technicians have greater control over the decisions of the system, for they have considerable influence now by the way they structure problems. The individuals who control decisions today are engineers, accountants, management specialists, economists, and specialists in finance, either teaching in universities or trained in institutions of higher learning. It is as unlikely that these university technicians will lead modern society out of the wilderness as it is unlikely that the army will be led by university intellectuals. As standards fall in the colleges and universities, their efforts create either more technicians or more consumption fops. The education they provide is geared either to the maintenance of the system or to its passive acceptance. College education is designed primarily for income or consumption, not for greater wisdom. It can hardly be said that the wisdom of Americans has risen as the amount of their college education has increased.

In the primary and secondary schools, the likelihood of teachers inculcating reformist values in the new generation may be fostered by the demeaning view the public has of their profession; the person who feels no sense of status in society is apt to be critical of its values. However, public school teachers are timid. With some exceptions, a clash of issues moves them toward a politics of survival. Moreover, they are too weighted down by duties that reflect the needs of the educational establishment to be able to give innovation serious attention. If teachers with imagination manage to enter the school system, the boards of education, superintendents, and their subalterns soon relieve them of it.

Here and there a university professor or grade school teacher may fire the young into being critical of the system without letting the power structure know what they are up to. Members of boards of trustees and boards of education are often sufficiently undiscerning to allow the deception to come off. When these subversives graduate they may in turn be able to bank on the similar traits of managers. Despite these possibilities, however, to expect the charge for change to be led by individuals representative of the universities and grade schools is totally unrealistic.

College Youth.   The task of social change is so complex that it is comforting to yield to romanticism and assume that it will be resolved as youth assumes the management of society. Inevitably, one would like to think, a young army of college toilers increasing in relative number. is going to change the system for the better. The fall in the age level of the labor force and the rise in the proportion of professional and technical workers should make this challenge successful. The system will be vanquished by loving youth.

But this may not come to pass. The preponderant majority of college youths are a younger copy of the organization men that manage the white-collar structure in the larger society. Moreover, the relative rise of youth in the labor force may in fact be in the system's favor; for there is no group more disposed to dance to the tune of the system than the young of little education.

In the Catholic Church there is a group of young persons together with a smaller number of sympathetic elders, of priests who are parishioners and parishioners who are priests, who seek to inject honesty and affection into life. Their attitude is contagious; it disarms cynics. They do not mire down in the old controversies of the Church. They do not believe that the conflict is between the old and young, but between the honest and dishonest. But the potential force of this kind of youth is obscured, partly because we live in an age of moral bankruptcy that renders us insensitive and partly because we do not know whether such youth will meet the challenge of maturity.

They sing songs of expectation:

We've only just begun to live
White lace and promises
A kiss for luck and we're on our way.

Before the rising sun we fly
So many roads to choose
We start up walkin' and learn to run
And yes, we've just begun.

And when the evenin' comes we smile
So much of life ahead
We'll find a place where there's room to grow
And yes, we've just begun.[2]

Like many college youths in non-catholic institutions, they are men and women of good will. But they are overshadowed by the poseurs and the sick in their ranks. Moreover, like the young of the first television generation, they seem disinclined to undergo the toil necessary to acquire social wisdom. They rarely seek that sense of well-being that comes from the formation of a new idea. They acquire a greater high in a romp of the senses. They will make the same old mistakes, commit the same foolishness, be victimized by the same manipulators. They are inclined to listen to an instructor only when his ideology meshes with theirs. But this is not education. This disposition commands patience. We cannot ask them to understand readily institutions that after emerging slowly for two centuries have bolted into the future. The college youth has to be encouraged to think that in the choice of goals he need not be a machine. He must be given the experience of face-to-face encounters with the different communities. And if he gains wisdom, he must be forewarned that the days with which to use it diminish fast and he should not delay in making honest commitments.

Youthful openheartedness and optimism, *per se,* provide no magic

2 In a song book of a Roman Catholic Folk mass.

solutions; romanticism is a disposition more than a cure. The greater optimism of the young has always existed. Parents nurture and subsidize this optimism, and rightly so. The young are more inclined to be idealistic because they can afford to be so and because they are unencumbered by a habit of disciplined discernment. As the young switch roles from subsidized consumers to responsible producers, many abandon their ideals and the generation gap narrows. The indiscriminate veneration of youth is a measure of the escapism in our society.

Can institution building derive from the left wing elements of college youth? An even greater unlikelihood. Their radicalism ranges from a variety of forms of anarchism to a variety of forms of dictatorship. Each sect along the continuum is highly volatile and intolerant of every other sect. A common thread runs through the entire range: lunacy. Their analysis is on the level of the talk issuing from undergraduates sprawled out on the grass mouthing inanities to the lyric accompaniment of sympathetic professors. The communist party, in which some find interest, persecuted by the national government, ignored by the working class, and held in contempt by most liberals, does not even have nuisance value. The Socialist parties continue to interpret events as though the world has not changed since the 1930's; their explanation of the Indochina war boggles the mind. Three decades ago left wing college students were Stalinists, Lovestoneites, Norman Thomas socialists, and plain ROTC baiters. Today they are Maoists, Che Guevarists, plain dropouts, and ego trippers. They dislike each other more than they do the establishment. Their left-wingism is a prop for the painful transition from childhood and adulthood. Many don't make it.

Foundations.   Can foundations provide the initiative for social innovation? Unfortunately, their underwriting of research in social science produces little science, and the little social engineering they do produce, when effective, incurs the hostility of government. Resentment arises in part from the posture of foundation officials who convey the impression that they rise above the constrictions reserved for the populace. In prestigious organizations such as the Rockefeller Foundation, the relationship between official and applicant is akin to that of baron and peasant. Entering the offices of such a foundation is like going through the gates of a city state. One stands patiently on the outer side of the moat, with hat in hand, waiting with proper demeanor for a signal to enter. The baron presumes to know more about science than the peasant and expects this superiority to be acknowledged in the supplication. While these foundations have bundles of money, they lack a political base on the outer side of the moat.

Churches. The prospects of the church initiating change are small. The white protestant churches accept the operating ideologies of the society. They are generally instruments of status and middle class consumption. The few clergymen with social perturbations preach love and practice relief for the poor and thereby perpetuate the system. Negro churches also fall into line as their parishioners become middle class. Some Negro ministers do manage to use their church as a base for institutional change, but those who do so with money from the power structure become conformist in short order. The Roman Catholic church is in crisis, disarmed by cleavages among its clergy and parishioners. Some Catholic clergymen try to organize white ethnics, but with what success and for what purpose remains obscure. American rabbis remain in the shadows with the exception of one who sounds like an ethnic. In all, little can be expected from the churches.

The Media. The compulsion of the media is not institutional reform, but manipulation of particular publics to build a loyal army for their advertisers. Television networks are indisposed to portray in depth those aspects of American life that may curtail their sources of income. The new non-commercial network shows such a potential, but has not brought it to fruition. It is similarly constrained by the necessity of communicating through pictures. The muckraking magazines are written by intellectuals for their kinfolk. Their voice is rarely heard by the establishment and even less by the general public. They need a scandal to obtain wide currency of their views and when they find one, broad dissemination depends on whether the big media pick them up. Generally, the media are servants of the economic system, not its reformers.

The Legal Profession. Members of the legal profession obtain their greatest income via maintenance of the system. Their major sustenance derives from promoting the interests of corporations and from the administration of the predatory effects of the motor vehicle. Attorneys are not trained to serve humanistic purposes or to promote good will. Someone wins and someone loses in the interpretation of law and the losers often seek to subvert the law or amend it in their favor. Legal advocacy is hardly a strategy of obtaining consensus. The investigations in the legislatures preceding the passage of more law create a mirage of what constitutes reality by the choices those who control the inquiry make. As advocates, lawyers are masters in delay and obfuscation; confusion more than clarification serves their purposes. Their proclivity to rely on more laws in moments of crisis causes the system to shift with the ebb and flow of transient turns of events. The passage of such law has a pump priming effect. A new set of lawyers is needed to interpret the new law and another set to devise counter-interpretations all the way to full employment.

The law is applied to promote short term interests. Whatever the law is, it is not what the statute says but rather a statement of the philosophy of its changing interpreters and the prevailing configurations of power. The law today by one set of judges and administrators may not be the same law tomorrow under a different set. The passage of new law is often a ceremonious acknowledgment of a new winner and triumph of injustice.

It must be conceded that there are Lancelot lawyers who have promoted the public welfare. One of the most extraordinary events of these times was the way in which a young lawyer, an ethnic, countervailed against the most powerful firm in the United States. Single handedly, Ralph Nader extracted a public apology from the chief executive of the corporation for a piece of corporate deception that backfired and moved the government reluctantly into the field of auto safety. To be sure, the circumstances were fortuitous. The crusader was first of all riding astride political forces in his favor. Secondly, the General Motors Corporation committed an error of monumental proportion by being caught in character assassination; it lacked the fine hand of the ITT Corporation in its days of adversity. Nevertheless, the strategic accomplishments of this social minded lawyer must be granted. The weakness of such efforts, however, lies in their lack of a broad political base.

Humanist Power Bloc. The experience of such men as Ralph Nader provides a lesson on how a humanist bloc against the system's excesses can emerge. A competent public interest defender must exploit favorable ground swells of power. He cannot become involved in the traditional clash of liberals versus conservatives. He must be aware of the fact that a dramatic exposure of inequities that stir indignation against a big organization will find favorable reception among many Congressmen. He must know that a strategy adept in fact finding and gaining the sympathy of the press as well as of politicians makes structural change possible. The experience suggests that a public fourth bloc can effectively exert a leverage against government, business, and labor organization.

An organization in defense of the public interest at all government levels, structured to process complaints, disseminate information to the public, and generate change, would require considerable funds. Government may not be inclined to support a public organization that would become its severest critic, but to place talented young persons into business as public interest defenders would require such assistance as well as enabling legislation. Without statutory support, their initiative is likely to wane.

Such individuals would require a combination of talents: the zealousness of youth; an understanding of the processes of power; an ability for honest inquiry; a sense of timing; a capacity to suggest well thought out alternatives. It may be possible to recruit them from among young graduate students in economics, law, political science, communications, and sociology. They would have to be zealots, but they would also have to be competent planners and managers. They would have to attract wide community support and attach themselves to urban universities as a source of information and as a neutral ground for the accommodation of interests. And they would also have to be leery of attracting do-gooders. An incursion of intellectuals would probably be fatal.

The frustration resulting from the inability to proceed effectively against power could be diminished by such an institution defending the people's interest. The Achilles' heel of the establishment is public exposure, disruption of routine, and its inability to use the tactics that can be employed against it.

What would be the government's role in such a fourth bloc society? It would continue to perform its traditional function of accommodation; but it would do so more effectively with a fourth bloc presenting initial analyses and solutions. By having them brought forward by a fourth bloc, government is not placed in the position of having to back away from initial proposals. It would make government less a symbol of collusion and more an instrument of unity. Its prerogatives of legislating and administering would remain the same.

A fourth bloc does not automatically bring a superior wisdom to issues. Its usefulness arises from preparation and participation. It represents more diffused loyalties. However, if its staff is motivated by insecurity and felt lack of status, its usefulness may diminish. Fourth bloc representatives have to see business from the point of view of its players. If they deal with images and do not see the society as it is, they cease to be idealists and become eccentrics. They can serve a useful watchdog function because the solution of problems is dependent upon the manner in which the solution is made. Groups faced with the reality of bargaining away part of their interests cannot be expected to describe reality in terms that weaken their bargaining position. A fourth bloc fills this communications gap and comes forward with proposals that advocates cannot espouse because of institutional constrictions. Organized interests prefer being pressured into accepting a solution that off the record they would grant as equitable but difficult to adopt on their own initiative.

A fourth bloc must understand these tactics of bargaining. If structurally tied to a broad people's base, a competent fourth bloc could serve a useful purpose. Its emergence lies within the realm of possibility.

Thus viewed, the problems of the system are forever countervailing ones: how to counter the effects of organization grown fat by promoting new organization; how to curtail respect for the powerful in favor of compassion for the impotent; how to protect the government official from the pressure of group interests and at the same time make him more accountable for his actions; how to expose the behavior of decision centers to public scrutiny without inhibiting their day-by-day operations; how to reconcile the sum total of group preferences with preconceived social objectives; how to ward off the manipulations of business that infiltrate via the telephone, the television set, the radio, the mail box, and the front door; how to create an effective buffer against the self-styled modern decisions of technologists without severely curtailing productivity; how to shift from a democracy of oligarchic power to one of participation; how to find a genuine national ideal out of the self-serving sermons of the power establishment; how to grapple with the problem of justice; how to develop an effective organization at the disposal of an individual against organized power. These goals are contradictory; but society itself is a contradiction.

By these conservative estimates of the future we do not wish to convey the impression that the public is reasonably satisfied with the accomplishments of the system's political and economic managers. The facts are to the contrary. Disillusionment over American leadership pervades the ranks of both white-collar and blue-collar forces and directs itself against all big organization generally. The assault against corporate organization is part of the general attack against institutions. Furthermore, the greater relative disenchantment among youth, if it survives the effects of time, may strengthen this hostility as the young enter the mainstream of the society. But whether this disaffection will produce structural changes or simply engender greater frustration is another question. No assurance exists that either the Republican or the Democratic party will bring forth an individual who will articulate this disillusionment, rise into national political power, and pursue an effective strategy of making the system more responsive to the people. The system's management is out of phase with individual and environment. Whether the political process will respond to this challenge is an open question.

Nor do we want to convey the impression that the challenge to the corporation has reached its zenith. A marked rise is likely to occur in the product liability of firms with reference to the risks a product imposes on the consumer. The doctrine of *caveat emptor,* orginated by the courts in the interest of producers, will probably continue to fall into discard. Moreover, the imposition of more stringent controls can be expected on the plants and sales outlets of firms in order to raise esthetic standards in the community. Despite its shaky legal ground, the right of the individual to a decent environment is apt to evolve in a way that relates not only to plant design but also to the impact of a firm's processes on the community. Lastly, the consumer will probably be increasingly protected from unconscionable contractual terms offered by corporations, even though he may voluntarily enter into such an agreement. The corporation will remain on the defensive for a long time to come.

But revolution there will not be. The system defuses persisting new movements by eventually giving them prestige and profit, and blending them into the legitimate mafia economy. The system prefers routine and orderliness, and manages to acquire both.

CONCLUDING OBSERVATIONS

Americans respond more readily to physical than to social innovation. They conceive progress more in terms of machines, consumer goods, and services than in the quality of environment and human beings. They are more disposed to find different ways of producing goods than to understand the social consequences of these goods. Progress tends to be measured in terms of more production of particular groups rather than in terms of an overall idea. Progress obtains when the managers of defense have more arms; when lawyers win more cases; when car manufacturers sell more cars; when educators grant more diplomas. Accordingly, the best brains in the society serve the production machine, locked inside organizations of government and industry and employing their talents to serve the institutions that feed them.

This orientation toward production spawns excesses controllable not by self-policing methods but by counter-organization. Even if individuals within producer organizations were to bring forward proposals of restraint, little would come from such an initiative. They may be considered cranks and ignored or sacked. Or their proposals would be weakened as they moved through the administrative pipelines of their organizations; decisions would preserve the interests of the different layers of administration through which they passed. Compromise would produce blandness. Initial expressions would have little semblance to the end product.

Successful counter-organization requires huge outlays in economic and human resources. But the society is not geared to produce such funds, and the individuals of heroic stature needed for such a venture are fast disappearing. Few are yet to be found among social scientists, educators, college youth, foundation officials, churchmen, and lawyers.

Moreover, the relief from the power of production groups through counter organization is transient. To a considerable degree, freedom derives from qualities that exist in the individual himself, qualities which liberate him from the necessity of subservience to organization. Nevertheless, these qualities need underwriting by the dispersion of producer power and by the ability of choosing among a wider array of options issuing from producer organizations. Freedom implies self-sufficiency. But it also implies full knowledge, more options, participation in the control of choices, and the power to require that the choices of others enter into negotiation.

The ideal life would be a life of prudent anarchy. But such freedom is not within the reach of many. An individual may have to struggle in order to attain economic independence and in so doing may have to compromise himself. He may have to be cautious in order to acquire a good income; by so doing he may become a creature subservient to organization. He may be himself if he ignores as much as possible the demands of society, but few can do so with impunity. He has to organize if he wants protection or retribution; but if he wishes emancipation, he has to develop attributes that afford within reason the means to ignore the system. If he cannot beat the machine, he can at least try as much as possible to live without it, and occasionally, as an act of patriotism, to subvert it.

It would also help to indulge in fantasy. The individual could try to grasp the enormity of space by going on imaginary journeys. If he could succeed in attaining the speed of light, it would take him 5 years to reach the nearest star. And if he decided once there to send a message back to earth seeking an affirmation of love, it would take 10 years to determine if his love were requited. But if the message came from more distant Vega, a star visible to the naked eye, he may not live long enough to find out the truth. Or he could try to move the sun from the center of the solar system and replace it with another star, Betelgeuse, and crowd out all space in the solar system as far out as Mars. Or he could imagine "peering" into ever bigger radio telescopes until at last he would observe the beginning of the universe.

With such counter-organization, self-sufficiency, and fantasy, modern American man may find an exquisite combination of solitude, human rapport, and transcendence of self.

16

The Decades Ahead

*The future is a convenient place
for dreams.*
Anatole France

In this final chapter, the problem of system and unsystem will be summarized, a preferred solution proposed, and the effects of the solution, both good and bad, explored. With this exposition of what should be, our picture of the future of modern American society will be completed.

This work has suggested what amounts to a strategy of retribution more than a plan of liberation. It proposes a politics of counter power more than the abolition of organization. Accordingly, the price of such a new order may indeed, once again, be fraud and cruelty. Human needs may again be manipulated, this time by the new Goths. One's intellect suggests we require a system to maintain surveillance of the system. But one's spirit likes to believe that the system will fall with the emergence of a new era of honesty and empathy.

A fundamental solution will require such a change of heart. Men must feel each other's anguish. One man must begin to talk honestly to another in his own subculture, then to a second in a different subculture, thence to another, and thereby create a basis for institutional change. We must talk to each other not as adversaries but as individuals sharing the same plight. Such is the road to redemption. At best, counter power can facilitate its attainment.

This evolution is thwarted because we live much of our life within the grip of the self-serving ideology of big organization. In a society of modern technology, our worth is commensurate with our value to big organization; separated from its fold, we stand naked and worthless. Big organization induces a flight from reason that proceeds down alternative paths of romanticism, infantilism, and cruelty, yet most of us acquiesce to the scheme it imposes of individual worth commensurate with organizational value. A few sabotage the system or seek to change it. However, to change it organization must be understood, and few are disposed to undergo the sacrifice needed to gain such understanding. We lack any consciousness as to what purpose big organization is supposed to serve. We do things because they seem to work and discard them when they do not. But we do not ask ourselves in a moment of reflection why we do what we do.

A principal tool of organization is dishonesty in human relationships. Within an organizational frame, the individual is indifferent to the moral implications of his acts. The organization solves the problem of efficiency and creates a problem of morality. Moreover, and even more horrifying, the bigger the organization, the more its decision making process becomes analogous to a nuclear reactor with its damping rods removed. Once the process begins, even its managers find it difficult to shift its course away from a path prescribed by the ingredients that brought the process into being. As individuals in organization become more specialized, the system increasingly acquires a momentum such that once it is generated it cannot be stopped. The Indochina war can be better understood if approached in this way. Once the process was initiated, the only change possible was to redefine objectives consistent with an anticipated outcome. Nevertheless, although the temptation to do so is sharp, we must not conclude that the issue is man versus organization. The issue is rather what kind of man in what kind of organization.

A conflict exists between the technology of modern organization and the expectations of individuals. The decisions forthcoming from big organization irritate because its managers seek to control them so as to pursue not fully disclosed interests and because the solutions are mass solutions that do not address themselves to the plight of any one person. Pressures thereby arise to reorder decision making so that the individual has enough power to force the organization to grapple with his particular need, even at the loss of efficiency. In addition, a conflict exists between the yearning for social goodwill and the frustration of this yearning by organization.

Nevertheless, to assert the inexorability of this technology is pure and simple defeatism. Despite the obstacles, humanistic values surface against technological trends as the initiative is seized not by intellectual critics and creators of abstract verbiage, but by those who through action exert an influence on institutions. These individuals reduce the influence of exploiters and educate men to be less exploitable. Moreover, the issue of technological values versus human values is again phoney. The issue is rather technology for what purpose. The alleged issue of institutional change versus values is phoney too. Changes in institutions and values occur simultaneously. Concededly, technology remains a powerful force in behalf of those who have money and power and who seek more of the same. Their technology moves the economy toward the day when government emerges as a principal source of income for consumers. Their technology creates a mass of individuals unwanted or unprepared for production, whose consumption is underwritten by government. To concede this, however, is not to admit defeat.

The system's major elements—the government, the two-party political process, the universities, the corporations—come up with decisions that weaken the fabric of community. These elements are unlikely to reform themselves. They failed when the persons who took them over lost their honesty and magnanimity. They became petty, greedy, and self-serving; and, in the main, so have their intellectual critics. The single nation is dead, destroyed by the trusteeship of government and corporations, with an assist from the universities and an inept intellectual class.

Never in the history of the nation have people viewed their institutional leadership with such mistrust. The failure is there to be seen in the people's relationship with government, in race relations, in collective bargaining, in the university, and in the destruction of the sense of community. Elitist power does not achieve a meeting of minds. It rather forces the weaker party to knuckle under and to resent his defeat. It becomes intolerable in a society in which the level of education is rising. The manipulation of lives by United States presidents, judges, bureaucrats, corporate managers, anti-discrimination commissions, organized interests, is a demonstrable failure. Compounding the problem is the tendency to patch up this failure with more elitist coercion.

A new social force must either wrest from these elements the power to make decisions or control factors that enter into their decisions. But this force must be prepared in craftsmanship and philosophy. The outstanding accomplishments of organization in both public and private sectors obtain when its members bring together craftsmanship, honesty, magnaminity of spirit, and sense of community. When they assemble these qualities, Americans are unsurpassed. Decision making processes such as those of NASA should be studied to see how they worked and how they can be transferred to the system generally. If the people mount a political movement without such technical and spiritual preparation, they may bring the nation to its final chaos.

This search and commitment is necessary because our institutions suffer from general obsolescence. The two parties are obsolete. A process of change initiated by liberals flitting from one cause to another is obsolete. Manipulation by politicians and managers is obsolete. And social change by the management of the courts is obsolete also. The time has come to produce along modern lines the substance of the hinterland. Man urgently needs a sense of collaboration in the promotion of ideas; his other problems pale into insignificance. He needs this more than neo-Freudian intellectualizing and self-analysis. We pay in alienation and hatred for the lack of collaboration. We continue to allow elites in corporations, government departments, legislatures, and courts to usurp the right of community self-determination as though we were possessed by a death wish.

How can we move toward this collaboration? College educators can generate a movement toward honest human relationships by articulating issues and through their relations with the new generation. But the university—its administration and teaching staff—is dominated by specialists who sanctify its wedding to big organization and who are disinclined to advise how to break it up; who are more disposed to play games with students seeking escape from boredom and a college degree with which to enter white-collar society. Under existing structures, the indiscriminate use of college educators as a means of changing the system would be unproductive.

Structural change may be possible by a massive involvement of individuals examining their institutions and posing practical alternatives. However, most of the college educated class acquiesce to the demands of organization. Its members may grumble, but they do little. They want to be liked. The intellectuals who want reform cannot establish a consensus among themselves let alone with the working class. A change in either case is unforeseeable.

Ideally, politics is an act of morality through the reconciliation of felt inequities. But American politicians pose solutions expressing configurations of power and not felt inequities. No significant change of their style is foreseeable. The possibility of change in human relationships would be enhanced by a United States president who raises fundamental questions honestly before the public. No such president from the ranks of either of the two parties is foreseeable.

Moreover, to create a new countervailing institution within the fold of government would be folly. A solution that enhances the power of government is no solution. The relief lies not in more government but in self-government. Much of our evil derives from the management of life as a national abstraction under the aegis of government. Our managing elites generally suffer from an uncontrollable diarrhea of abstraction. The intellectuals who yearn for a society managed by technocrats suffer from the same malady. Government solutions spawn elites and bureaucracies that take power away from the people. Government should be a bargaining partner. Indeed, the routine operation of government should be resisted at every opportunity. Such resistance should be considered an act of patriotism. The solution lies not in more government but in civilized anti-government.

The task of reconstruction is difficult. New political structures must be devised for a society of cultural coalitions. As the nation feels its way toward such a society, groups cop out and seek to impose the cost of their keep on toilers. A United States president who urges the return of power to the people by the transmission of national funds to state and local governments offers the wrong remedy for the right goal and thereby delays this emergence.

An individual acquires a vital psychological need—self-esteem—as a producer participating in decisions. But the system deceives him into thinking he can fulfill this need as a consumer or as a worshipper of mass images of success. At best, consumption and adoration serve the greater need to produce. A person acquires self-esteem as he stretches his potential by reaching out in his life experience for successes in creation. He risks failure, because the rewards for creativity are sweeter. Successes develop a capacity to treat casually critical judgments of his accomplishments. With self-esteem, he also acquires a sense of freedom. Moreover, if he is a creative person, he seeks to change his environment so that probing for his potential brings even greater successes. The society that provides externalities that reduce the sense of failure and increase the rate of successes is the humane society. The society that sells consumption and adoration of mass images as the road to self-esteem is the exploitive society.

To serve this individual need for success, we must discard the nonsense that in social relations any one cultural group commands a superior moral position. The upper class Wasps are certainly entitled to their values. But they lack the inherent right to impose them on other subsocieties. The only social morality the state can apply uniformly is that we be civil with each other.

Thus, the task comprises structuring a society of minimum cultural coercion. This movement toward a higher order of individuality must be sought in the framework of a federated larger society. The intellectual's dream of living free like birds is sheer fantasy. Civilization cannot be maintained without a system of social restraints. The road to more individuality lies in the acquisition of culture power through political power in a federated society.

But ethnicity would not mean a regimen of sameness. The appellations Irish, Italian, Pole, Puerto Rican, Mexican, represent symbols of cultural diversity. Distinctions exist within each group. Nor does ethnicity imply the hardening of differences. Our plea is for the organization of cultural enclaves so as to place power behind cultural self-determination through bargaining arrangements that promote a life of live and let live. Liberals have achieved such culture power, but they are alarmed by the possibility that other groups may acquire it. All enclaves, including youth enclaves, have a right of self-determination, provided they do not inflict harm on other cultural communities and are ready to bargain out conflicts between groups.

To foster this new order, new sources of information must be developed. The extent of reform in society depends heavily on the ability of reformers to take control of mass communications media. So long as the system monopolizes the media, the system cannot be reformed. Fundamental changes can be achieved only by reaching people directly with an alternative message. We must assume that government and corporation will continue to deceive the population and that mass media will continue to distort information. We can look to the university as a source if the university formulates information in a way that is understandable to the community. But we must also—as with government, corporation, and mass media—be wary of the university.

Consequently, to develop sources of honest information is a staggering task. In modern society, the truth is whatever promotes the needs of the organization from which the information comes. The same individuals utter diametrically opposite views as they move from one organization to the next. The intellectuals who claim a monopoly on precise information arrange data to support their own ideologies. We need institutions capable of observing particularities and describing them accurately and understandably. We require commentators who can discern patterns in such information and suggest how social forces can move communities toward a new consensus. Fortunes are spent to improve information flows that serve government and industry. Little is available for improving information to the public. The public evidently merits propaganda, not information.

We require also a reorientation of power toward the people. We need this realignment so as to produce a decline in the influence of big organization and a rise in cultural pluralism. The good guys and bad guys theory of social relations is an absurdity. In the ethnic bargaining society, no group represents virtue or evil. The distinctions are those of values and perceptions, and these must be reconciled.

To achieve these goals, each individual has to identify with the technical community of the university or with a university affiliated ethnic community. Through such affiliation, he seeks his genuine self and reconciles this revealed identity with his social obligation to assist in the formulation of a community consensus. An understanding of self and society comprises an act of reconciliation. An excess of introspection leads to inaction and self-pity; but social action without introspection leads to self-deception and cruelty.

The alternative to manipulating organization is an accommodation of values through ethnic participatory democracy supported by a continuous flow of information and by men skilled in the arts of mediation. Elitism must be anchored to ethnicity as its servant and the decision making process pushed back in the direction of the neighborhood and family, for the family is the only remaining institution in modern society where a human is loved because he exists. But if this informed search for a value consensus ends in power play little will have been gained.

In an ethnic participatory democracy, the roles of technical elites and community advocates would intertwine. One provides analysis and the other improves the analysis by criticizing it; the partisans can even offer counter-analysis. No presumption exists that the analysis of elites is the final word. The role of elites embraces recommending changes in process including changes in institutions. The role of community advocates is to attack the recommendations. Elites are partisans themselves: partisans of efficiency. The final resolution comprises an accommodation of positions brought forward.

Citizen participation based on the neighborhood brings together a variety of the needs of individuality. Cultural differences surface as a basis of reconciliation. The consumer movement is but a part of the broader problem of containing corporate power, which in turn constitutes a facet of the general need of returning power to people. An ethnic bargaining society meets head-on the two issues of people involvement and democratic resource allocations.

We propose, in summary, a techno-ethnic bargaining society as a tool of cultural pluralism. Its instrument would be the university urban extension service subsidized by the national government on condition that it attract the advocates of different cultural communities to a continuing seminar of community development; that the urban extension service provide technical assistance to the community alliance; and that state and local governments recognize these neighborhood alliances as having self-governing functions. The people should participate in decision making not because they will necessarily make more satisfactory decisions, but in order that they realize the limits of resources and collaborate in creative action.

It may be argued that seeking unity by organizing diversity would foster deeper polarization, but this result need not occur. When asked to make sacrifices face-to-face by competent mediators, ethnics respond by doing what is decent. The little conscience that prevails in American society is to be found mostly among ethnics.

By relating a government financed university community extension service to self-governing communities in metropolitan areas, the unsystem will interact with the system. The university would perform major roles of technical assistance and mediation. The functions of the community alliances would include: planning under the university umbrella the comprehensive development of communities; proposing technological innovation and monitoring technology within their geographical jurisdiction; processing complaints of their members; initiating complaints on their own initiative; prodding public authorities; negotiating priorities among its affiliated neighborhoods and recommending these priorities to a national planning board; selecting representatives to the national planning board.

The community alliances should be guided by these criteria: an alliance must be affiliated with a university and must operate within a context of specific goals; resources must be made available to these alliances through the urban university extension service; the alliance must have a neutral chairman of professional competence in mediation and arbitration; the chairman must use mediation to reconcile differences and must have the power to invoke arbitration in the event of a deadlock; each university affiliated alliance must be related to a national planning board; community members of the planning board will be elected from a congress of representatives of the different community alliances; each neighborhood will be affiliated with the university-based community alliance through a community advocate; affiliations will be determined in such a way as to avoid domination of the alliance by particular ethnic groups; the boundaries of an affiliated neighborhood will be subject to negotiation; after initial seed funding, money for research and operation of the community-university pacts will be related to the number of individuals represented by the community advocates; funding for particular projects will be based on technical analysis and consensus by the community alliance; proposals will be submitted to the national body for determination of priorities.

The community alliances would serve the need of face-to-face communication between government officials, corporate managers, and community representatives. Their policy stages—information gathering, analysis, consensus, and control—should be open to the public, with the exception of critical stages in negotiation.

Doubtlessly, such a system could bog down in ego tripping. A competent neutral chairman and staff would minimize such a possibility. The successful experience of the War Labor Board during World War II in bringing together university professors as neutrals with hard-nosed labor leaders and corporate executives indicates that such a multi-partite system can work. The citizen feedback we propose could serve to reduce tensions between system and unsystem by bringing its members face-to-face in an environment of objective inquiry. If such community alliances were to be converted into an all-black show, it would be a disaster against the interests of blacks themselves. It is in the long term interests of blacks to assist in the development of white ethnic leadership.

Cultural consensus expresses the ideal that man should have the freedom to propose choices and to join with those who are affected by such choices in reaching an accommodation. For man, this is the essence of his being. Man becomes a man by creating structures that give him the power to make choices and that dispose him to join others in the ultimate decisions. In this way man creates, becomes loving, and in turn again creates. What fuller life can one have than to work for social structures to facilitate these tied-together purposes of loving and creating?

We foster loving human relationships to the degree that we succeed in breaking away from the vicious circle of the indifference we generate toward us in others by a felt sense of inadequacy in ourselves. If we relate to another person through feelings of inadequacy, we inhibit our ability to understand him—or her—and to respond to his or her needs. Because we do and say things that reflect our inadequacies rather than the other person's being, his interest in us wanes. And this indifference fortifies our sense of inadequacy.

How does one break out of such a vicious circle? By an effort of will to see the other person the way *he* is and to react sympathetically to *his* needs. By so doing, we generate a love toward us that undermines our sense of inadequacy. We perceive better as we tear away the veil created by the sense of inadequacy and achieve redemption as we, with this understanding, serve others.

The first stage of this breaking out is stormy. A confrontation denies, confirms, elucidates, obscures, validates, invalidates, constricts, confirms, encourages, discourages. Led by a competent mediator, conflict ends in an act of creation; man creates by revealing himself through such conflict. Every day can be an act of creation. But man must be disposed to stand naked.

This emancipation requires new institutional structures to facilitate its emergence, and literary intellectuals propose no feasible alternative to an ethnic dialogue. Their position rests on the notion their elitism would produce a better society, but they offer no proof of their allegation. Nor do they respond to the blunt question of ethnics as to who in hell gave intellectuals the right to determine man's destiny. In a consensus of values, an intellectual has no more votes than the trash collector.

More freedom derives not from wallowing in constricting self-pity over the oppressiveness of society or from fishing for the oppressed to champion but from understanding power and playing with a piece of it and then cutting it down. Intellectuals are too immersed in their own life and their own thought to be able to grasp with precision the dynamism of interacting human beings, let alone the mediation of such interaction. If they show some competence in describing social conflict, they are next to hopeless in dealing with it. They try to graft on to the society a social analysis that derives from their own troubled spirit; but the graft is rejected. Their social heroes are the incompetent who become sick trying to grapple with the society's oppressiveness.

Man moves forward by using his brain to grasp patterns in the social and physical environment and then using these relationships to promote his vision of a better life. By this tough process of discernment and control he obtains order and productivity. We need, therefore, innovators who can see these patterns and who can assist in planning. We require men who can talk to ethnics and who can help create a new political structure of upward communication. To do this, they must look at events in historical perspective, for to be ignorant of history is to be ignorant of one's life. It is crucially important to know what men have done in the past and why they have succeeded or failed. We must, then, patiently develop in our youth a sense of history.

We have in the course of history used men and nature as tools for conquest. But the day will come when we no longer will have the power to employ men in such a way. The day will come when the warrior class managing corporations and government no longer can use inferior ethnics as tools for their aggression. That day will arrive because no power can prevent intelligence from mustering the organization to arrest this exploitation. Conscience and truth are the only inexorable forces. Man is responsible for the choices that lead to his destiny.

This change is likely to destroy the linear dimensions of a society dominated by big organization and produce a dimension of interrelated cultural subsocieties brought together by mediators rather than princes of power, with the assistance of technical consultants rather than authoritarian elites, whose vehicle of communication would be the bargaining communes. Ethnicity will be a tool of reacquiring honorability and not a grab for top dog at some other group's expense. The blacks have shown their ethnic clout for a decade. They can now serve the nation by working for a policy of cultural pluralism.

We must recognize our differences in order to reestablish a viable society. Each cultural enclave has a voice that should be heard. To foster this communication, new political structures must be built that express these differences. Each neighborhood must have its own government, if only in the form of one individual who would be its immediate public servant. To facilitate the emergence of these structures, we require social innovators skilled in the art of accommodating points of view. And to assure the success of this process, we must appropriate funds to produce what people feel are returns for their participation.

Our policies today, foreign as well as domestic, are blind to this cultural pluralism. They are imposed by one group upon others through the use of public resources, under the cloak of patriotic and egalitarian principles. But they do not command consenus. Americans are constantly running away from decisions not of their own making. Accordingly, in the modern sector of the nation away from the hinterland, the sense of community is defunct.

The ethnic voice comprises a particular orientation that should be allowed to bargain its point of view, and competent mediators should accommodate these views. University technicians must come up with options to facilitate the mediator role of reconciling goals and transferring them to appropriate political and planning bodies. But the analytical work of the university technicians is of little use unless brought to a stage of commitment. This process of participation should tie together the rural area, where the neighborhood may be the entire community, with the metropolitan area. The new order should be cultural democracy.

The era of behavior in conformity with a national ethic fades relentlessly. In the area of consumption, this disappearance portends a future decline in the demand for goods for conspicuous consumption and a rise in the demand for those that reflect cultural autonomy. Thus, the emergence of cultural pluralism provokes a decline in the effective management of mass tastes. Today, the man ensconced in two tons of shiny motor vehicle is a hero. Tomorrow, he will be a fool.

The homogenization of the American is losing the battle on the political front as well. With time and vision, the right of cultural autonomy will enter the political process. The present cop-out of ethnics marks but a stage on the road to a new political order. America's greening will come not from upper class youth but from a system of cultural autonomy. American society is likely to evolve into self-governing federations emerging out of a series of truces and agreements between cultural groups. The present divisiveness represents the start of a transition to the new federated society.

The debate as to who will manage this future society divides into two major camps. Business-oriented scholars believe it will be businessmen, and intellectually oriented scholars believe it will be university technicians. A third, smaller group, believes it will be a combination of the two. But it is unlikely that a combination of militant blacks, white ethnics, and a young college educated class grieving over elite management of the system would tolerate a reshuffling along any of these lines.

If the scientist wants to serve this future society, he must break away from his servant-master relationship with government. No scientist merits the name if he has to cater to the political needs of a government agency in order to acquire money; furthermore, he should not even be trusted if he indulges in such peddling. If the scientist wants to serve society, he will thus terminate his meretricious relations with government; he will see through the hypocrisies of university managers and make them his servants; he will organize and demand that government either place funds at the disposal of universities in the interest of improving the quality of life or accept his refusal to perform research; he will assist in the design of a mechanism that effectively links cultural viewpoints with public and business policy formation. Social and behavioral scientists recognize the need human beings have for cultural identity. They can assist in devising the social engineering necessary to allow this identity to enter the decision making process.

It is irrational to expect individuals to accept policies that run counter to their values. It is presumptuous to hold that the values of those who presently manage these policies are superior. The ethnic should participate in decision making not because *his* values are superior, but because by such participation his shattered sense of manhood may be reconstructed.

As this participation unfolds, those who sit at their desks writing words of complaint and violence and those who romp at the fringe of society will be left behind. American man will move forward again to the degree he succeeds in wresting away the initiative from government and business. The new radicals will be the toilers for cultural autonomy. The opportunity to join in a revolution will be theirs. Because the United States is a country in which oppression cannot survive for too long, it is the only nation in the world where a revolution not only can take place through the democratic process but actually is taking place. Its momentum is indomitable as a growing number of persons renounce their loyalty to the system and join those who never had such an allegiance.

The day will come when, conscious of each other's viewpoint, these two groups will go forward together.

The new consciousness will be individual will through ethnic pluralism. As we become a nation of many nations we will develop greater individuality. People yearn for leaders to generate movement toward reconciliation. The use of abstractions as bludgeons with which to manage people has failed. We will rejoice in randomness. The mass culture for profit will collapse from its own excesses.

We will move forward toward this goal to the degree that we show competence to go ahead bit by bit wherever and whenever the opportunity arises. Solutions will come not from the generalizations of intellectuals, but from a search for opportunities that emerge from the daily living of the nation. But greater cultural autonomy is meaningless without greater access to power. This must be worked at seriously; for the biggest affliction of the population is the frustration that attends a sense of powerlessness.

There is little doubt that man's behavior is highly determined. But it is also demonstrable that man has an insatiable thirst for the new knowledge that would explain his condition and that this knowledge gives him more freedom to make choices. We do not have a science of human behavior; therefore, we cannot claim to have a technology of human behavior. In the absence of a systematic body of fundamental truths, we can only expect a human behavior technology improvised out of a contest of persuasion in which all cultural groups have the resources to assert their views effectively. Therefore, man is likely to proceed in a system of reinforcing through rewards what a pluralistic consensus determines to be desirable while continuing simultaneously ever to gain new knowledge and to modify purposes.

The secularization of society makes man responsible. He can no longer surrender his fate either to the Deity or to the semi-gods of the system. He must, and will, create a new morally based social order out of personal acts of will.

Sources of Information

References

Business Periodical Index
Library of Congress Book of Subject Headings
Poverty and Human Resources Abstracts
Public Affairs Information Service
Social Sciences and Humanities Index
The New York Times Index
United States Government Monthly Catalog of Publications

Journals

Academy of Management Journal
Administrative Science Quarterly
Advanced Management
American Journal of Sociology
American Sociological Review
California Management Review
Harvard Business Review
Industrial and Labor Relations Review
Industrial Relations
Journal Human Resources
Journal Management Studies
Management Review
Management Science
Michigan Business Review
Social Forces

Suggested Additional Reading

CHAPTER TWO

Bensman, Joseph and Arthur J. Vidich. *The New American Society*. Chicago: Quadrangle Books, 1971.

Boulding, Kenneth E. "Environmental Quality." *The American Economic Review*. Papers and proceedings, 83rd Annual Meeting, American Economic Association, 1970.

Churchman, C. West. *Challenge to Reason*. New York: McGraw-Hill, 1968.

Galbraith, John Kenneth. *American Capitalism: The Concept of Countervailing Power*. Boston: Houghton Mifflin, 1952.

———. *The New Industrial State*. Rev. Ed. Boston: Hought Mifflin, 1971.

Gintis, Herbert. "Consumer Behavior and the Concept of Sovereignty." *The American Economic Review*. Papers and Proceedings, 84th Annual Meeting of the American Economic Association, 1971.

Johnson, Harold L. *Business in Contemporary Society: Framework and Issues*. Belmont, Cal.: Wadsworth, 1971.

Marris, Robin. "Is the Corporate Economy A Corporate State?" *The American Economic Review,* Papers and Proceedings, 84th Annual Meeting, American Economic Association, 1971.

Weisskopf, Walter A. *Alienation and Economics*. New York: Dutton, 1971.

CHAPTER THREE

Aguilar, Francis J. *Scanning the Business Environment*. New York: Macmillan, 1967.

Albrook, Robert C. "Business Wrestles with Its Social Conscience." Fortune 78 (August 1968).

Argyris, Chris. *Management and Organizational Development*. New York: Macmillan, 1967.

———. "The Individual and Organization: Some Problems of Mutual Adjustment." *Administrative Science Quarterly* 2 (June, 1957).

Bowen, Howard R. *Social Responsibilities of the Businessman*. New York: Harper, 1953.

Chamberlain, Neil W. *Enterprise and Environment*. New York: McGraw-Hill, 1968.

Cheit, Earl F. "Why Managers Cultivate Social Responsibility." *California Management Review* 7 (1964).

Child, John J. *The Business Enterprise in Modern Industrial Society*. Toronto: Macmillan, 1969.

Clapp, Norton. "Corporate Responsibility to the Community." *University of Washington Business Review* 27 (Spring, 1968).

Corson, John J. *Business in the Humane Society*. New York: McGraw-Hill, 1971.

Davis, Keith. "Can Business Afford To Ignore Social Responsibilities?" *California Management Review* 2 (Spring, 1960).

————, and Blomstrom, Robert L. *Business, Society, and Environment: Social Power and Social Response*. New York: McGraw-Hill, 1971. (Chapters 1, 2, and 3).

Feldman, Arnold S. "The Interpretation of Firm and Society." *Dynamics of Modern Society*. Edited by William J. Goode. New York: Atherton, 1967.

Frederick, William C. "The Growing Concern Over Business Responsibilities." *California Management Review* 2 (Summer, 1960).

Hayes, Douglas A. "Management Goals in a Crisis Society." *Michigan Business Review* 22 (November, 1970).

Henderson, Hazel. "Should Business Tackle Society's Problems?" *Harvard Business Review* 48 (July-August, 1968).

Katz, Daniel, and Kahn, Robert. "Open-System Theory." *Readings in Organization Theory*. Edited by John G. Maurer. New York: Random House, 1971.

Levinson, Harry. "Reciprocation: The Relationship Between Man and Organization." *Administrative Science Quarterly* 9 (March, 1965):

Levitt, Theodore. "The Dangers of Social Responsibility." *Harvard Business Review* 36 (September-October, 1958).

Loasby, Brian J. "The Decision Maker in the Organization." *Journal of Management* 4 (October, 1968).

CHAPTER FIVE

Friedman, Murray. *Overcoming Middle Class Rage*. Philadelphia: Westminster, 1971.

Howe, Louise Kapp. *The White Majority: Between Poverty and Affluence*. New York: Random House, 1971.

Gooding, Judson. "Blue Collar Blues on the Assembly Line." *Fortune*, December 1970.

Levitan, Sar A., ed. *Blue Collar Workers: A Symposium on Middle America.* New York: McGraw-Hill, 1971.

McDonagh, Edward C. and Eugene S. Richards. *Ethnic Relations in the United States.* New York: Appleton-Century-Crofts, 1953.

Rogin, Michael. "Wallace and the Middle Class: The White Backlash." *Public Opinion Quarterly,* 30 (1966).

Sheppard, Harold L. "Who are the Workers with the Blues?" *W. E. Upjohn Institute for Employment Research,* Washington, D. C.: September 1970.

"The World of the Blue Collar Worker." *Dissent* 19 (Winter, 1972).

Tomasi, S. M. and M. H. Engel, eds., *The Italian Experience in the United States.* Staten Island, New York: Center for Migration Studies, 1971.

CHAPTER SIX

Domhoff, G. William. *Who Rules America?* Englewood Cliffs, N. J.: Prentice-Hall, 1967.

Goulden, Joseph C. *The Superlawyers: The Small and Powerful World of the Great Washington Law Firms.* New York: Weybright and Talley, 1972.

Heilbroner, Robert L., et al. *In the Name of Profit.* New York: Doubleday, 1972.

CHAPTER SEVEN

American Economic Association. "Population and Environment in the United States." *The American Economic Review,* Papers and Proceedings, 83rd Annual Meeting, 1970.

Barnouw, Erik. *A History of Broadcasting in the United States.* 3 vols. New York: Oxford University Press, 1970.

Boulding, Kenneth E. *The Meaning of the Twentieth Century.* New York: Harper & Row, 1964.

Brown, Les. *Television: The Business Behind the Box.* New York: Harcourt Brace Jovanovich, 1970.

Burke, John G., ed. *The New Technology and Human Values.* Belmont, Calif.: Wadsworth, 1967.

Commoner, Barry. *The Closing Circle: Nature, Man, and Technology.* New York: Knopf, 1971.

Emshoff, James R. *Analysis of Behavioral Systems.* New York: Macmillan, 1971.

Faunce, William A. "Automation and the Division of Labor." *Social Problems* 13 (Fall, 1965).

Harvard University Program on Technology and Society. Reviews of Literature. Cambridge, Mass.: Harvard University Press, (eight reviews of the literature on technology in various fields.)

Harvey, Edward. "Technology and the Structure of Organizations," *American Sociological Review* 33 (April, 1968).

Hodges, Wayne L. and Matthew A. Kelly, eds. *Technological Change and Human Development, An International Conference.* Ithaca, New York: New York State School of Industrial and Labor Relations, Cornell University, 1969.

Mesthene, Emmanuel G. *Technological Change: Its Impact on Man and Society.* Cambridge, Mass.: Harvard University Press, 1970.

Mishan, Ezra J. *Technology and Growth.* New York: Praeger, 1969.

Mumford, Lewis. *The Myth of the Machine: Technics and Human Development.* New York: Harcourt Brace, 1967.

Perrucci, Robert and Joel E. Gerstl. *The Engineer and the Social System.* New York: John Wiley & Sons, 1969.

Roszak, Theodore. "Technocracy's Children." *The Making of a Counter Culture.* Chap. 1. New York: Doubleday, 1969.

Schoen, Donald R. "Managing Technological Innovation." *Harvard Business Review* 47 (May-June, 1969).

Scott, Ellis L. and Roger W. Bolz, eds. *Automation and Society.* The Georgia Reliance Symposium, Athens, Ga.: The Center for the Study of Automation and Society, 1969.

Silberman, Charles E. "Technology and the Labor Market." *Fortune* (January, February, April, 1965).

Silverman, William. "The Economic and Social Effects of Automation in an Organization." *The American Behavioral Scientist* 9 (June, 1966).

Spengler, J. J. "Economic Growth in a Stationary Population." *Annual Meeting Population Association of America,* Washington, D. C. April 23, 1971.

Taviss, Irene. "Are Computers Dehumanizing?," *Computer and Society* 1 (November, 1970).

Thompson, James D. and Frederick L. Bates. "Technology, Organization, and Administration," *Administrative Science Quarterly* 2 (December, 1957).

United States Department of Labor. "Technological Trends in American Industries," U. S. Government Printing Office, 1966.

Vickers, Geoffrey. *Value Systems & Social Process.* New York: Basic Books, 1968.

CHAPTER EIGHT

Bernstein, Irving. "Labor's Power in American Society." *California Management Review* 4 (Spring, 1962).

Dunlop, John T. *Industrial Relations Systems.* New York: Holt, 1958.

Indik, Bernard P. and Georgina M. Smith. "Resolution of Social Conflict Through Collective Bargaining." *The George Washington Law Review* 37 (May, 1969).

Kennedy, Thomas. "Freedom to Strike is in the Public Interest." *Harvard Business Review* 48 (July, 1970).

Lekachman, Robert. "Academic Wisdom and Union Reality." *The American Economic Review,* Papers and Proceedings, 84th Annual Meeting, American Economic Association, 1971.

Perry, G. L. "Inflation versus Unemployment: The Worsening Trade-Off," *U.S. Monthly Labor Review* 94 (February, 1971).

CHAPTER NINE

Aron, Raymond. *Democracy and Totalitarianism.* New York: Praeger, 1969.

Commager, Henry S. *America in Perspective.* New York: Random House, 1947.

de Tocqueville, Alexis. *Democracy in America.* New York: Mentor Books, 1956.

Green, Mark J., James M. Fallows, and David R. Zwick. "Who Runs Congress?," New York: Bantam Books, 1972.

Kohlmier, L. M., Jr. *The Regulators.* New York: Harper & Row, 1969.

Phillips, Charles F., Jr. *The Economics of Regulation.* Homewood, Ill.: Irwin, 1965.

Schultze, C. L. *Setting National Priorities: The 1971 Budget.* New York: Brookings Institution, 1970.

Staats, Elmer B. "Industry-Government Relationships." *California Management Review* 12 (Fall, 1969).

Van Cise, J. "Regulation By Business or Government." *Harvard Business Review* 44 (March-April, 1966).

CHAPTER TEN

Adelman, M. A. "The Two Faces of Concentration." *The Public Interest* 21 (Fall, 1970).

Berle, Adolf A. and Gardiner C. Means. *The Modern Corporation and Private Property.* New York: Harcourt, Brace & World, 1967.

Blair, John M. *Economic Concentration,* New York: Harcourt Brace Jovanovich, 1972.

Black, David H., ed. The Multinational Corporation, Philadelphia: American Academy of Political and Social Science, September 1972.

Chamberlain, Neil W. *Enterprise and Environment.* New York: McGraw-Hill, 1969.

Child, John. *The Business Enterprise in Modern Industrial Society.* Toronto: Macmillan, 1969.

Drucker, Peter F. *The Concept of the Corporation.* New York: New American Library, 1964.

Friedman, Milton. *Capitalism and Freedom.* Chicago: University of Chicago Press, 1962.

————. "The Social Responsibility of Business is to Increase Profits." *The New York Times Magazine* (September 13, 1970).

Granger, Charles H. "The Hierarchy of Objectives." *Harvard Business Review* 42 (June, 1964).

Hill, Walter. "The Goal Formation Process in Complex Organization." *The Journal of Management Studies* 5 (May, 1969).

Jacoby, Neil H. "The Conglomerate Corporation." *The Center Magazine* 2 (July, 1969).

Kuhn, James W. and Ivar Berg. *Values in a Business Society: Issues and Analyses.* New York: Harcourt, Brace & World, 1968.

Mason, Edward S., ed. *The Corporation in Modern Society.* New York: Atheneum, 1969.

Mockler, Robert J. "Theory and Practice of Planning (Keeping Informed)." *Harvard Business Review* 48 (March-April, 1970).

Silk, Leonard S. "Business Power, Today and Tomorrow." *Daedalus* 98 (Winter, 1969).

The Annals. "The Government As Regulator." *The American Academy of Political and Social Science* 400 (March, 1972).

Vazsonyi, Andrew. "Free For All: The History of the Rise and Fall of PERT." *Management Science* 16 (April, 1970).

Veblen, Thorstein. *The Theory of Business Enterprise.* New York: New American Library, 1932.

Vernon, Raymond. *Sovereignty at bay. The Multinational Spread of U. S. Enterprises.* New York: Basic Books, 1971.

CHAPTER ELEVEN

Bensman, Joseph and Arthur J. Vidich. *The New American Society.* Chicago: Quadrangle Books, 1971, (chapter 11 "The Intellectual and

Public Policy" and chapter 14 "Rejection of the New Society by Radical Youth").

Bowan, Howard Rothmann and Gordon K. Douglass. *Efficiency in Liberal Education*. New York: McGraw-Hill, 1971.

Dietze, Gottfried. *Youth, University and Democracy*. Baltimore: The Johns Hopkins Press, 1970.

Eckert, Ruth E. "Participation in University Policy-Making: A Second Look." *AAUP Bulletin* 56 (September, 1970).

Hansen, W. Lee and Burton A. Weisbrod. "A New Approach To Higher Education Finance." Madison, Wisconsin: Institute for Research on Poverty, Reprint 79, 1972.

Harbison, Frederick H. "The Campus Revolt from an Industrial Relations Perspective." Madison, Wisconsin: *Industrial Relations Research Association,* Twenty-Second Annual Winter Meeting, 1969.

Henderson, Algo D. *The Innovative Spirit*. San Francisco: Jossey-Bass, 1970.

Keniston, Kenneth. *The Young Radicals*. New York: Harcourt Brace and World, 1968.

————. *Youth and Dissent*. New York: Harcourt Brace Jovanovich, 1971.

Lewy, Guenter and Stanley Rodhman. "On Student Power." *AAUP Bulletin* 56 (September, 1970).

Lipset, Seymour Martin and Gerald M. Schaflander. *Passion and Politics: Student Activism in America*. Boston: Little, Brown, 1971.

Mayhem, Lewis B. *Arrogance on Campus*. San Francisco: Jossey-Bass, 1970.

Simon, John J., Charles W. Powers, and Jon P. Gunneman. *The Ethical Investor*. New Haven, Conn.: Yale University Press, 1972.

CHAPTER TWELVE

Adams, Walter. "The Military Industrial Complex and the New Industrial State." *The American Economic Review,* Papers and Proceedings of the 80th Annual Meeting, American Economic Association, 1967.

Anderson, Richard M. "Anguish in the Defense Industry." *Harvard Business Review* 47 (November-December, 1969).

Austin, Anthony. *The President's War*. Philadelphia: Lippincott, 1971.

Domhoff, G. William. *The Higher Circle: The Governing Class in America*. New York: Random House, 1970. (See his chapter "How the Power Elite Makes Foreign Policy.")

Gaddis, John Lewis. The United States and the Origins of the Cold War 1941–1947, New York: Columbia University Press, 1972.

Lieberman, A. E., "Updating Impressions of the Military-Industrial Complex." *California Management Review* 6 (Summer, 1969).

Melman, Seymour, ed. *War Economy of the United States.* New York: St. Martin's Press, 1971.

Raymond, Jack. "Growing Threat of Our Military-Industrial Complex." *Harvard Business Review* 46 (May-June, 1968).

Reich, Michael, Walter Adams, Richard F. Kaufman, et al. "The Economics of the Military-Industrial Complex." *The American Economic Review.* Papers and Proceedings, 84th Annual Meeting, American Economic Association, 1971.

United States House of Representatives, Committee on Armed Services. *United States-Vietnam Relations 1945–1967.* 12 vols. Washington, D. C.: U. S. Government Printing Office, 1971.

Yarmolinsky, Adam. *The Military Establishment: Its Impact on American Society.* New York: Harper & Row, 1971.

CHAPTER THIRTEEN

Banfield, Edward C, *The Unheavenly City.* Boston: Little, Brown, 1968.

Campbell, Angus. *White Attitudes Toward Black People.* Ann Arbor, Mich.: Institute for Social Research, 1971.

Chamberlain, Neil W. *Contemporary Economic Issues.* Homewood, Ill.: Irwin, 1969.

Committee for Economic Development. *Education for the Urban Disadvantaged: From Pre-school to Employment.* New York, 1971.

Crossland, Fred. *Minority Access to College.* New York: Schocken Books, 1971.

Downs, Anthony. *Who are the Urban Poor.* New York: Committee for Economic Development, 1970.

Farmer, Richard N. "The Pros of Black Capitalism." *Business Horizons* 13 (1970).

Gilman, Harry J. "Economic Discrimination and Unemployment." *The American Economic Review* (December, 1965).

Jakubauskas, Edward B. *Human Resources Development.* Ames, Iowa: Iowa State University Press, 1967.

Jordan, Winthrop D. *White over Black: American Attitudes Toward the Negro 1550–1812.* Chapel Hill: University of North Carolina Press, 1968.

Lebov, Myrna. "Racial Strife in the United States." *On Record* Vol. 4 (October 1968): New York: McGraw-Hill.

Mangum, Garth L. *The Emergence of Manpower Policy.* New York: Holt, Rinehart and Winston, 1969.

Mauriji, Alex. "Minority Membership in Apprentice Programs." *Industrial and Labor Relations Review* 25 (January, 1972).

Nelkin, Dorothy. *The Politics of Housing Innovation: The Fate of the Civilian Industrial Technology Program.* Ithaca, N. Y.: Cornell University Press, 1971.

Northrup, Herbert R. "Will Greater EEOC Powers Expand Minority Employment?" *Labor Law Journal* 22 (August, 1971).

Sanday, Peggy R. "The Application of the Concept of Cultural Pluralism to U.S. Domestic Social Policy." Sixty-Ninth Annual Meeting *American Anthropological Association,* 1970.

Sheehy, Gail. *Panthermania: The Clash of Black Against Black in One American City.* New York: Harper & Row, 1970.

Sheppard, Harold L. *Effects of Family Planning on Poverty in the United States.* Kalamazoo, Mich.: E. E. Upjohn Institute for Employment Research, 1967.

United States Bureau of Labor Statistics. *The Social Economic Status of Negroes in the United States.* Washington, D. C.: U. S. Government Printing Office, 1971.

Weiss, Leonard and Jeffrey G. Williamson. "Black Education, Earnings, and Interregional Migration: Some New Evidence." *The American Economic Review,* LXII, (June, 1972).

CHAPTER FOURTEEN

American Institute of Architects. *A Strategy for Building A Better America.* Washington, D. C. 1972.

Bourne, Larry S., ed. *Internal Structure of the City.* New York: Oxford University Press, 1971.

Branch, Melville C. *Comprehensive Urban Planning.* Beverly Hills, Cal.: Sage Publications, 1970.

Campbell, Alan K. *The States and the Urban Crisis.* Englewood Cliffs, N. J.: Prentice-Hall, 1970.

Chamberlain, Neil W., ed. *Business and the Cities: A Book of Relevant Readings.* New York: Basic Books, 1969.

Cohn, Jules. "Is Business Meeting the Challenge of Urban Affairs?" *Harvard Business Review* 48 (March, 1970).

———. *The Conscience of the Corporations: Business and Urban Affairs, 1967–1970.* Baltimore, Md.: The Johns Hopkins University Press, 1970.

Duncan, Beverly and Stanley Lieberson. *Metropolis and Region in Transition*. Beverly Hills, Cal.: Sage Publications, 1970.

Elazar, Daniel J. "Are We a Nation of Cities?" *The Public Interest* 4 (Summer, 1966).

Edgar, Richard E. *Urban Power and Social Welfare*. Beverly Hills, Cal.: Sage Publications, 1970.

Forrester, Jay W. *Urban Dynamics*. Cambridge, Mass.: M.I.T. Press, 1969.

Friend, J. K. and W. N. Jessop. *Local Government and Strategic Choice*. Beverly Hills, Cal.: Sage Publications, 1969.

Green, Constance McLaughlin. *The Rise of Urban America*. New York: Harper & Row, 1965.

Haakenson, Robert. "The Urban Crisis: What One Company is Doing." *Management Review* 57 (July, 1969).

Henry, Edward L., ed. *Micropolis in Transition*. Collegeville, Minn.: St. Johns University, 1971.

Isika, Daniel. *Urban Growth Policy in the United States: A Bibliographic Guide*. Los Angeles: University of California, School of Architecture, 1972.

Jacobs, Jane. "Strategies for Helping Cities." *The American Economic Review* 59 (September, 1969).

————. *The Economy of Cities*. New York: Random House, 1969.

Kain, John. *Race and Poverty*. Englewood Cliffs, N. J.: Prentice-Hall, 1969. (See especially the chapter on "The Negro American Family," the so-called Moynihan Report.)

Kain, John and Joseph J. Persky, "Alternatives to the Gilded Ghetto," *The Public Interest* 14 (Winter, 1969).

Keating, Stephen F. "Management's Role in the Urban Crisis." *Advanced Management* 34 (January, 1969).

Loewenstein, Louis K., ed. *Urban Studies: An Introductory Reader*. New York: The Free Press, 1971.

Moynihan, Daniel P., ed. *Toward a National Urban Policy*. New York: Basic Books, 1970.

Pascal, Anthony H., ed. *Thinking About Cities: New Perspectives on Urban Problems*. Belmont, Cal.: Dickenson Publishing Company, 1970.

Porambo, Ron. *No Cause for Indictment: An Autopsy of Newark*. New York: Holt, Rinehart and Winston, 1971.

Rigby, Gerald. *State and Local Government and Politics*. Belmont, Cal.: Dickenson, 1969.

Rogers, David. *The Management of Cities*. Beverly Hills, Sage Publications, 1971.

Romnes, H. J. "Role of Business in Community Development." *Advanced Management* 34 (April, 1969).

Schmandt, Henry J. and Warner Bloomberg, Jr. *The Quality of Urban Life.* Beverly Hills, Cal.: Sage Publications, 1969.

Seashore, Stanley E. and Robert J. McNeill, eds. *Management of the Urban Crisis.* New York: Free Press, 1970.

Spergel, Irving A. *Community Organization: Studies in Constraint.* Beverly Hills, Cal.: Sage Publications, 1972.

Tabb, William K. "Viewing Minority Economic Development as a Problem in the Political Economy" and references. *The American Economic Review,* Papers and Proceedings, 84th Annual Meeting, American Economic Association, 1971.

Thompson, Wilbur R. "The Economic Base of Urban Problems," in Neil W. Chamberlain, (ed.), *Contemporary Economic Issues,* Homewood, Ill.: Irwin, 1969.

Williams, Eddie N. *Delivery Systems for Model Cities: New Concepts in Serving The Urban Community.* Center for Urban Studies, Chicago: University of Chicago Press, 1969.

Wilson, Q. James, ed. *The Metropolitan Enigma.* New York: Doubleday, 1970.

CHAPTER FIFTEEN

Boulding, Kenneth E. "General Systems Theory—The Skeleton of Science." *Management Science* 2 (April, 1956).

Buckley, Walter, ed. *Modern Systems Research for the Behavioral Scientist.* Chicago: Aldine, 1968.

Caws, Peter. "The Structure of Discovery," *Science,* 166, (12 December· 1969).

Haire, Mason. "The Social Sciences and Management Practices." *California Management Review* 53 (Summer, 1964).

Huff, David L. and Joseph W. McGuire. "The Interdisciplinary Approach to the Study of Business." *University of Washington Business Review* 19 (June, 1960).

Meij, J. L. "Management: A Common Province of Different Sciences." *Management International* 52 (1962).

Marris, Peter and Martin Rein. *Dilemmas of Social Reform.* New York: Atherton, 1967.

Wadia, Maneck S. "Management and the Behavioral Sciences." *California Management Review* 54 (Fall, 1965).

CHAPTER SIXTEEN

Altshuler, Alan A. *Community Control.* New York: Pegasus, 1970.

Blau, Peter M. *Exchange and Power in Social Life.* New York: John Wiley & Sons, 1964.

Bohm, P. "An Approach to the Problem of Estimating The Demand for Public Goods." *Swedish Journal of Economics* 73 (March, 1971).

Clark, Dennis. "Toward Assimilation or Ethnic Identity?" *The Urban and Social Change Review* 4 (Fall, 1970).

Colm, Gerhard and Luther Gulick. "Program Planning for National Goals." *National Planning Association,* Washington, D. C., 1968.

Cummings, Larry. "Organizational Climates for Creativity." *Journal of Personality* 33 (June, 1965).

Habermas, Jurgen. *Toward A Rational Society.* Boston: Beacon Press, 1970.

Hall, Edward T., Jr. "The Anthropology of Manners." *Scientific American* 192 (April, 1955).

Hawley, Willis D. and Frederick M. Wirt. *The search for Community Power.* Englewood Cliffs, N. J.: Prentice-Hall, 1968.

Maddi, Salvatore R. "Motivational Aspects of Creativity." *Journal of Personality* 33 (June, 1965).

May, Rollo. *Love and Will.* New York: Norton, 1969.

Mee, John F. "The Creative Thinking Process." *Indiana Business Review* 31 (February, 1956).

Reissman, Frank and Alan Gartner. "Community Control and Radical Social Change." *Social Policy,* (May-June, 1970).

Spiegel, Hans B. C. *Citizen Participation in Urban Development.* Vol. I. Washington, D. C.: NTL Institute for Applied Behavioral Sciences, 1968.

Ziller, Robert C. "Individual and Socialization: A Theory of Assimilation in Large Organizations." *Human Relations* 17 (November, 1964).

Appendix

The 300 Largest Industrial Firms in the United States *

1. General Motors
2. Standard Oil (N.J.)
3. Ford Motor Company
4. General Electric
5. International Business Machines
6. Mobil Oil
7. Chrysler
8. Texaco
9. International Tel. & Tel.
10. Western Electric
11. Gulf Oil
12. Standard Oil (California)
13. U. S. Steel
14. Westinghouse Electric
15. Standard Oil (Ind.)
16. Shell Oil
17. E. I. du Pont
18. RCA
19. Goodyear Tire & Rubber
20. Ling-Temco-Vought
21. Procter & Gamble
22. Atlantic Richfield
23. Continental Oil
24. Boeing
25. Union Carbide
26. International Harvester
27. Swift
28. Eastman Kodak
29. Bethlehem Steel
30. Kraftco
31. Lockheed Aircraft
32. Tenneco
33. Greyhound
34. Firestone Tire
35. Litton Industries
36. Occidental Petroleum
37. Phillips Petroleum
38. General Foods
39. North American Rockwell
40. Caterpillar Tractor
41. Singer
42. Monsanto
43. Continental Can
44. Borden
45. McDonnell Douglas
46. Dow Chemical
47. W. R. Grace
48. United Aircraft
49. Rapid-American
50. Union Oil California
51. International Paper
52. Xerox
53. Honeywell
54. Sun Oil
55. American Can
56. General Dynamics
57. Minnesota Mining

* *Fortune* Magazine, May 1972. (ranked by sales)

58. Beatrice Foods
59. R. J. Reynolds
60. Cities Service
61. Boise Cascade
62. Ralston Purina
63. Sperry Rand
64. Coca-Cola
65. Burlington Industries
66. Armco Steel
67. Consolidated Foods
68. Uniroyal
69. American Brands
70. Ashland Oil
71. Bendix
72. Textron
73. U.S. Plywood
74. Gulf & Western
75. TRW
76. National Steel
77. Owens-Illinois
78. CPC International
79. National Cash Register
80. United Brands
81. Georgia-Pacific
82. Alcoa
83. American Home Products
84. American Standard
85. U.S. Industries
86. Standard Oil (Ohio)
87. Republic Steel
88. FMC
89. Amerada Hess
90. Warner-Lambert
91. Getty Oil
92. Allied Chemical
93. Colgate-Palmolive
94. Raytheon
95. Genesco
96. B.F. Goodrich
97. Weyerhaeuser
98. American Cyanamid
99. Signal Companies
100. Whirlpool
101. Inland Steel
102. Columbia Broadcasting
103. PPG Industries
104. Celanese
105. American Motors
106. Pepsi
107. Philip Morris
108. Deere
109. Marathon Oil
110. Borg-Warner
111. Carnation
112. Olin
113. Johnson & Johnson
114. General Mills
115. Teledyne
116. Reynolds Metals
117. Nabisco
118. Bristol-Myers
119. Combustion Engineering
120. Standard Brands
121. Mead
122. Kennecott Copper
123. Norton Simon
124. Ogden
125. Eaton
126. Campbell Soup
127. Iowa Beef Processors
128. General Tire
129. H. J. Heinz
130. Crown Zellerbach
131. Babcock & Wilcox
132. Martin Marietta
133. Pfizer
134. Anaconda
135. Kimberly-Clark
136. Burroughs
137. Motorola
138. NL Industries
139. St. Regis Paper
140. Kaiser Aluminum
141. Anheuser-Busch

142. Lykes-Youngstown
143. SCM
144. Avon Products
145. J. P. Stevens
146. Allis-Chalmers
147. Associated Milk Producers
148. Interco
149. White Motor
150. Squibb
151. Merck
152. Hercules
153. Dart Industries
154. Studebaker-Worthington
155. Dresser Industries
156. Ingersoll-Rand
157. Grumman
158. Crane
159. Otis Elevator
160. Illinois Central Industries
161. Texas Instruments
162. American Metal Climax
163. American Broadcasting
164. Del Monte
165. Central Soya
166. Scott Paper
167. Whittaker
168. Clark Equipment
169. AMF
170. United Merchants
171. Gillette
172. Eli Lilly
173. Land O'Lakes
174. Evans Products
175. Pet
176. National Distillers
177. Phelps Dodge
178. Jim Walter
179. Walter Kidde
180. GAF
181. Pillsbury
182. White Consolidated Ind.
183. Pullman

184. Avco
185. Geo. A. Hormel
186. Johns-Manville
187. Quaker Oats
188. Kellogg
189. Agway
190. Farmland Industries
191. McGraw-Edison
192. Archer Daniels Midland
193. American Smelting & Refining
194. Emerson Electric
195. Sterling Drug
196. Oscar Mayer
197. Colt Industries
198. Carrier
199. Dana
200. Magnavox
201. Amstar
202. Anderson, Clayton
203. Zenith Radio
204. Time Inc.
205. Northrop
206. Corning Glass
207. Kerr-McGee
208. Alco Standard
209. North American Philips
210. Koppers
211. Essex International
212. Liggett & Myers
213. Ethyl
214. Diamond Shamrock
215. Control Data
216. Diamond International
217. Northwest Industries
218. Armstrong Cork
219. Sherwin-Williams
220. U.S. Gypsum
221. Budd
222. Loews
223. City Investing
224. Owens-Corning Fiberglas

225. Libbey-Owens-Ford
226. Wheeling-Pittsburgh Steel
227. Container Corp. of America
228. Joseph E. Seagram & Sons
229. Polaroid
230. Jos. Schlitz Brewing
231. Lever Brothers
232. Times Mirror
233. Union Camp
234. International Minerals & Chemical
235. Paccar
236. Brunswick
237. Lear Siegler
238. Rohm & Haas
239. Foster Wheeler
240. Brown Group
241. Akzona
242. Castle & Cooke
243. Cluett, Peabody
244. Staugger Chemical
245. Cummins Engine
246. Allegheny Ludlum Industries
247. Freuhauf
248. Kayser-Roth
249. Scovill Manufacturing
250. Kaiser Steel
251. Universal Leaf Tobacco
252. Abbott Laboratories
253. National Gypsum
254. A. O. Smith
255. Chromalloy American
256. Crown Cork & Seal
257. USM
258. Indian Head
259. Eltra
260. M. Lowenstein & Sons
261. Universal Oil Products
262. Airco
263. Ward Foods
264. Upjohn
265. Schering-Plough
266. National Can
267. Sunbeam
268. International Multifoods
269. Westvaco
270. Di Giorgio
271. National Industries
272. Cerro
273. Flintkote
274. Addressograph
275. Timken
276. Richardson-Merrell
277. Admiral
278. Pennwalt
279. Levi Strauss
280. McGraw-Hill
281. Hoover
282. Coastal States Gas Producing
283. Hershey Foods
284. Revlon
285. Tecumseh Products
286. Crowell Collier & Macmillan
287. Heublein
288. Kelsey-Hayes
289. Gold Kist
290. Bemis
291. Libby
292. Hewlett-Packard
293. Lone Star Industries
294. Warner Communications
295. Hart Schaffner & Marx
296. Hammermill Paper
297. American Beef Packers
298. Allied Mills
299. Mattel
300. A-T-O